Little Minnesota

100 Towns POPULATION **AROUND 100**

A NOSTALGIC LOOK AT MINNESOTA'S SMALLEST TOWNS

by Jill A. Johnson, photography by Deane L. Johnson

Adventure Publications, Inc.
Cambridge, MN

Dedication

For my mother,

Who washed uniforms for the Strandquist basketball team

And for my father,

Who made small towns bigger than life.

Photo Credits

All photos by Deane L. Johnson unless noted.

Page 70 inset 4, James S. Jacobson **Page 84** insets 2 and 4, James S. Jacobson

The following photos provided courtesy of: **page 6** inset 4, Wadena County Historical Museum **Page 12**, inset 2, Joanie Kramer **Page 14** inset 4, US Post Office-Beltrami **Page 54** inset 3, Jan Louwagie **Page 56** inset 4, Camp Ripley Military Museum **Page 58** inset 1, Beltrami County Historical Society; inset 2, Chelsey Johnson **Page 60** inset 4, Gordon Slabaugh **Page 64** inset 3, Jill Johnson **Page 66** inset 4, Sheila Crowley, *Murray County News* **Page 70** insets 1 and 3, Janet Vanderplaats **Page 98** inset 2, Gwen Sletta Branstad **Page 104** main photo, Jill Johnson **Page 106** inset 1, Kathleen Bergan **Page 108** inset 3, Lac Qui Parle County Museum **Page 110** insets 3 and 4, Paul Jensen **Page 112** inset 1, Manhattan Beach Lodge **Page 116** inset 2, Kathleen Bergan **Page 120** inset 2, Chelsey Johnson; inset 3, Beltrami Co Historical Society; inset 4, Jill Johnson **Page 126** inset 1 and 4, Lac Qui Parle County Museum **Page 164** inset 4, Strandquist Community Center/Jim Musburger **Page 168** main photo, Jill Johnson **Page 174** inset 4, Heidi Haagenson **Page 180** main photo, Brita Sailer; inset 1, Beltrami County Historical Society; inset 2, Brita Sailer; insets 3 and 4, Jill Johnson **Page 194** inset 1, Tracy Fischer **Page 200** main photo, Brita Sailer

Cover and book design by Jonathan Norberg

Edited by Brett Ortler

10 9 8 7 6 5 4 3 2

Copyright 2011 by Jill A. Johnson and Deane L. Johnson
Published by Adventure Publications, Inc.
820 Cleveland Street South
Cambridge, MN 55008
800-678-7006
www.adventurepublications.net
Printed in China
ISBN: 978-1-59193-319-9

Table of Contents

Thank you to all the contributors to *Little Minnesota*:

Sandi Pratt, Lyle Waldahl, Marie Henriksen, Frank Guenther, Nelia Gary, Nathan Temple, Joanie Kramer, Elaine Swiers, Albertha Bendickson, Gary Gulleckson, Bruce Mosher, Matthew Wooley, Carol Myers, Rob Myers, Mark Fogle, Douglas and Betty Melin, Sam Flom, Verlyce French, Linda Kurth, David Markworth, Jim Heiling, Anne Ibberson, Peggy Butenhoff, Jill Steichen, Pamela Guest, Diane Koepp, John Connolly, Vince Connolly, Chuck O'Malley, Marlys Gallagher, Brenda Werner, Lee and Karen Anderson, Bob Ketchmark, Gordon Jacobson, Doretta Olson, Annetta Martin, Sylvia Peterson, Helen Iverson, Robin Shaw, Brenda Kruger, Mary Shipper, Kathy Powell, Mark Anderson, Dan Brinker, Dan Alt, Darlene Hansen, Pam Lundquist, Cecelia McKeig, Shirley Pagel, Gerald Tschida, Sandra Alcott Erickson, Dolores Preimesberger, Norma Hanson, Dale Hanson, Marjorie Iverson, John Lovly, Cindy Kolling, Ed and Barb Sellers, Nancy Lee, Dale Pavlis, Shane Olson, Janet Vanderplaats, Deanna Smith, Chad Magnuson, Doris Martin, Karen Odden Roske, Melvin and Theresa Hinderscheit, Millie Odenthal, Laura Odenthal, Janice Koenig, Melvin Thorson, Ron Rinkel, Andrew Filer, Emilie Peterson, Mary Ann Swan, Trish Lewis, Brad Hemmes, Marshal Hemmes, Jim Vatne, Joyce Rodman, Don and Elaine Johnsrud, Dave Groen, Sue Tweet, Kristy Vander Ziel, Christine Carlson, Deb Stadin, Shirley Keyport, Sheila Bos, Tony Stalboerger, Gwen Barstad, Archie Pearson, Steve Gross, Amy Stafford, Beatrice Hilliard, Elaine Kildal, Diana Gerlot, Bev Lundmark, Kelli Reichert, Donn Reichert, Frank Klabechek, Terry Johnson, Paul Dove, Barb Redpenning, Joyce Letrud, Paul Jensen, Marguerite Ylilsaker, Wilda Solberg, Angie Hannegrufs, Kista Brunkhorst, Doreen Galaway, Dawn Clark, Gregory Glavan, Kathleen Bergan, David Pries, Harvey Langseth, Lucille Schue, Rose Heim, Sharon Rittenour, Sally Wood, Trish Schuelke, Bruce Larson, Nancy Nettum, Jack Graba, Sue Lerud, Lorraine Loween, Deanna Satter, Duane Koehntopp, Virgil and LeVon Gerber, Ann Manley, Denise Wuertz, Kristi Butler, Warren and Ollie Parker, Gil Ebner, Sheila Widness, Wendy Sparks, Pam Sheeran, Eunice Hawn Holz, Shawn Freiler, John and Dorine Schwagel, Bruce and Sandy Leino, Jan Bryan, Danielle Greiger, Judi Hart, John Wenning, Shannon Bican, Carol Antony, Paulette Jelen, Linda Bauer, Trish Lewis, Gula Stromgren, Shirley Ryden, DeWayne Rudningen, Nancy Feldman, Kathy Haugse, Amber Wyttenback, Lynne Black, James Kiefer, Heidi Haagenson, Kirsten Schwab, Marcia Petermann, Jeanne Putnam, Muriel Keaveny, Sylvia and the late Howard Flateland, Tony and Virginia Weber, Gary and Cindy Burger, Ladora Siems. Margaret Carlson, Ardelle Anderson, Jerome Peters, Adeline Thompson, Michael Kirchmeier, Joanne Manniko, Cindy Adams, Vickie Anderson, Rick and Carol Jenniges, Mary Olson, Don and Donna Schumacher, Janet Macy, Barb Bentfield, Micki Friedrich, Pam Gierke, Ernie and Joan Johnson, Harvey Jokela, Clarence Paurus, Marlys Gallagher, Jan Louwagie, Brigid Shields, Brita Sailer, Joel Maxwell, Steve Hoffbeck, Jan Fredell, Joan Krey, Cathy Reich, Joayne Judson, Janine Weideman, Terri Young, Jim Musburger, the Park Rapids Library staff, Chelsey Johnson, Nate Johnson, Daniel Johnson, Ann Grace, and Deane, always Deane. Thank you to the kind people omitted unintentionally—you know who you are.

Introduction

When my father returned from a 50th class reunion in 2008 for the first graduating class that he taught in Strandquist, he remarked, "You know, the little towns aren't going to be around much longer. Everything that I remember is gone." Could this be true? Would the little towns that so many of us lived out our childhood in be wiped off the map? His comment sent me on a quest to discover exactly what was happening in Minnesota's smallest cities. Choosing little communities for inclusion in this project was not an easy task. Each one has an amazing story to tell, but for the sake of brevity, I chose cities that are incorporated (mayor and council) with close to one hundred residents, according to the 2010 census. Since a 1973 Act by the Minnesota legislature, all incorporated former towns are now officially cities, although the familiar descriptions "town" and "village" appear throughout the book. The most important legal advantages of incorporation are the provision of police services, fire protection, sewer and water. Also, an incorporated city has the power to regulate buildings, sidewalks, and municipal businesses like the liquor store. Most importantly, incorporation gives the power to levy taxes and share in state revenues. The 2010 census results arrived too late to include a few cities that recently dropped below one hundred.

I chose to focus on the beginning of European settlement in each city, with the understanding that American Indians were the first landholders in Minnesota. Mary Lethert Wingerd writes an unflinching account of American Indian life in her book, *North Country: The Making of Minnesota*, a history that influenced me deeply. The author charts the mutual cooperation between Europeans and Natives for two centuries, before western expansion and violation of treaties by the U.S. government in the 1850s led to The Dakota War, which Wingerd refers to as "Minnesota's Civil War."

What I discovered in Minnesota's smallest cities surprised and delighted me. Each one of the cities shared many common threads, such as the arrival of the railroad, a rich agricultural heritage, incredible perseverance, and a will to survive against all odds. Early immigrants traveled across the sea to homestead in a country that promised a better life, and most of them stayed. They developed incredible farms, built business districts, erected the prettiest churches in the state, and sent their men and women to war. Along the way, the amazing settlers found time for music, art, dancing, and baseball teams that were second to none in the state. Many residents of these small cities went on to national fame and recognition in politics and government. Today, little Minnesotans continue to celebrate centennials, holidays and their indomitable community spirit. Richard Lingeman, author of *Small Town America*, maintains that the history of America is the history of its small towns and "for better or worse, small town values, convictions and attitudes have shaped the psyche of this nation." Our smallest cities embody all that is best in Minnesota.

One of many challenges that Minnesota's smallest cites face is the ongoing loss of hometown post offices, at one time the backbone of each community. The United States Post Office has plans to close most of little Minnesota's post offices within the coming years. It is not too late to visit our state's smallest post offices for a collectible cancellation stamp, and to pay homage to Minnesota history.

I owe my deepest thanks to all the people who shared their lives with me through interviews, letters, phone calls and of course, email. The people of Little Minnesota are the most generous, fun loving and hardest-working people that I know. Special thanks to the mayors and city clerks who are incredible historians and detectives. County historical societies, museums and libraries throughout the state worked hard to help me find treasured information about each city. Friends and family researched and offered editorial comments. My father, Jim Musburger, offered historical commentary and incidents on our travels that helped define the character of the area. The Park Rapids Library staff worked with MnLink, a state library service that evens the playing field for those of us in greater Minnesota. Gordon and Gerri Slabaugh, owners of Adventure Publications, took a chance on little Minnesota and a new author. My editor, Brett Ortler, shaped the stories to perfection. My husband, best friend and photographer proved once again to be the best road companion ever. This book would not be possible without you, Deane. Along the way, I fell in love with little Minnesota and the people who keep history alive in our state's last frontier. You are my heroes.

—Jill

TOP: BNSF train speeds through Aldrich

One Christmas, General Jack Vessey, Chairman of the Joint Chiefs of Staff for President Reagan, stopped in at Aldrich's cheese shop. He ordered 32 pounds of cheese as gifts to the military chiefs of 15 NATO countries.

Aldrich

Shots Fired: Extortion and Tragedy on the Prairie

THE OLDEST CITY IN WADENA COUNTY, Aldrich is home to the first railroad, the first post office and the first Catholic Church in the county. The city also witnessed the only recorded conflict between the Ojibwe and white settlers in Wadena County, known as the "Red Eye War of 1874." A more local conflict with the natives happened in Aldrich as well. Bob Costello, a part-time employee for the railroad company store, lived in a log house in Aldrich with his wife and his daughter, Agnes. Costello pilfered flour, meat and other groceries from the store, trading these goods with the Ojibwe. Their village band of 500 men, women and children camped three miles south of Aldrich on the Partridge River. One of the natives, Kaby Won-A-Skunk, lived near

the depot and worked for Mr. Kelly, the station pumpmaster. As told in Ann Kelly's journal, Mr. Costello agreed to trade 50 pounds of flour for six beaver skins from Kaby. However, when Kaby delivered the skins, Costello demanded the skins plus two dollars. The Indian explained that he had no money, so Costello accepted the skins and insisted that Kaby pay him later. During a second confrontation, Costello hit Kaby, giving him two black eyes, humiliating him. Costello had cheated other Indians, and this incident provoked two dozen braves to seek revenge. Late one evening, his friends followed Kaby to Costello's home where Kaby shot through the door to frighten Costello. At that instant, Costello's daughter Agnes turned toward the door; the bullet hit Agnes in the temple, killing her instantly. Costello and two other men in the house

6

shot Kaby in the shoulder, and Indians hiding in the woods carried Kaby back to camp. The next day, the frightened settlers sent depot agent Kelly on the locomotive to Fort Ripley to seek help for an expected Indian reprisal. Within three days, three hundred soldiers and their drummer stepped off the train in full uniform and carrying loaded rifles. Two Ojibwe chiefs, dispatched by the tribe, met the soldiers to explain how Costello had cheated them. The commander of the soldiers thoughtfully listened to their story, and requested that the Indians surrender Won-A-Skunk for a trial by white man's law. If he was found guilty, he would be punished. The Chiefs replied that they would surrender Won-A-Skunk only if Costello were turned over to them for trial under tribal law. After further discussion, both sides decided to drop the matter, and the soldiers returned to Fort Ripley.

Nestled on both sides of Highway 10 near the banks of the Partridge River, Aldrich was named by officers of the Northern Pacific railroad in honor of Cyrus Aldrich, a popular and respected politician who represented Minnesota in the U.S. Congress from 1859 to 1863, and won a seat in the state legislature in 1865. When he died October 5, 1871, the railroad had just laid track through Aldrich. As the town lacked a telegraph for some time, messages were delivered from village to village via a wood-burning locomotive. Business boomed in the 1880s when a general store opened, as did the Aldrich Hotel, a meat market and a blacksmith shop. Two sawmills also went up on the banks of the Partridge River, and fearless river drivers guided logs downriver.

The oldest church in Wadena County, the Mother of Sorrows Catholic Church, was founded as a mission in 1870. Eighteen charter members erected a building in 1885 on land purchased from the Puget Sound Railroad Company. A walk through the Catholic Cemetery north of Aldrich reveals tombstones dating back to the early 1860s. The historic church closed in 1970. Another church, the Aldrich Congregational Church, opened in 1915. Lacking the funds to purchase a bell for the church, local actors performed the play *Poor Married Man* to

successfully raise money for one in 1917. Across the road from the Congregational Church, School Districts 19 and 79 began in 1883 with teacher Addie Gill and 29 students. In 1916, the district erected a beautiful two-story building. This local landmark educated students until 1958, when a new school replaced the aging structure. By 1970, only 7 students were enrolled, and the school consolidated with Staples and Verndale.

V.I.P.s visit the Aldrich Cheese Shop

In 1947, the John Fredli family put Aldrich on the map when they purchased the empty Equity Creamery building and opened the Aldrich Cheese Factory. Later, new owners Burton and Doris Fredli Peterson renamed the business the Aldrich Cheese Mart, and continued to draw attention. Until the factory closed in 1973, employees churned out 5,000 pounds of cheese daily. General Jack Vessey, the future Chairman of the Joint Chiefs of Staff for President Reagan, also stopped in frequently. One Christmas, Vessey stopped in and ordered 32 pounds of cheese as gifts to the military chiefs of 15 NATO countries. The owners received a letter from the general: *Dear Petersons, Thanks for the prompt service. The cheese arrived in time to take it to the December NATO meeting. Consequently, there is Aldrich cheese in the capitals of 15 of the 16 NATO nations this Christmas (Ireland has no military forces; hence no military chief). I have already received good reports on the cheese from a couple of cheese-making countries—Netherlands and Denmark. Merry Christmas, Jack Vessey.*

Aldrich Today

Today Aldrich is home to the post office, Adams Electric, Aldrich Tractor, Homestead Veterinary Clinic and PAWS, a pet adoption service, Ted & Gen's Bar-BQ, and Aldrich Repair. City Hall resides in the old school, and is used for council meetings and reunions. A replica of the Aldrich depot, constructed from lumber from the razed depot, resides in the Wadena historical society.

One sunny day in 1951, employees at the Aldrich Cheese Shop were surprised by a visit from movie actor Tex Ritter, with his beautiful horse, White Flash, as well as Ritter's white dog. Ritter ordered cheese for his wife in Hollywood.

Arco is home to a sensational gas station and
scenic garden noted for its stonework, which
once drew busloads of tourists. The stone station
eventually included stone sculptures and statues,
including a Viking ship and Statue of Liberty.

TOP: Former Texaco station built by H. P. Pederson

Arco

A Gas Station Festooned with Fieldstone

SMACK DAB in the middle of Lincoln County rests the prairie city, Arco, home to a sensational former rock-covered gas station and garden that once drew busloads of tourists. When H.P. Pedersen bought the Texaco Station in 1936, he began to cover the entire exterior with stone. For years he had used the rocks that turned up in plowing the farm fields to build lamps, ashtrays and bookends. The stone station progressed to an amazing stone garden and sculptures, including a Viking ship and Statue of Liberty. Now a private home, most of the sculptures are gone, but several remain in Anderson Park on Lake Stay.

Settled by citizens of German descent, the railroad officials strangely chose to name the city Arcola in 1900, after an ancient village in Italy. Later the last syllable was dropped to avoid confusion with another rail station named Arcola in Washington County. European settlement began when five families from Nebraska took the "emigrant train" to Arco with all their earthly possessions, including livestock and machinery, loaded together in boxcars. After three days of train travel, the Westphal, Wendorff, Ertle and Nottleman families arrived to find eight feet of snow and temps of twenty below. Breaking trail through the snow and cold (with livestock) must have seemed insurmountable, but they prevailed and made Arco home.

Within four years of incorporation in 1903, Arco hosted a full main street including an opera house, a school, two churches, a bank, a creamery, a hotel and four grain elevators. Unfortunately, mice chewed on matches in the hotel on Halloween night 1908, and the resulting fire destroyed everything on the north side of the street, including the bank and several businesses, which were all rebuilt on the same spot, except for the bank, which moved across the street. The post office in Chris Larsen's general merchandise store was spared from the inferno, and citizens enjoyed rural mail delivery beginning in 1903.

A new brick school built in 1920 housed students until the late sixties, when the district consolidated with Ivanhoe. When the school was demolished, two engraved cement slabs from the high school, "GIRLS ENTRANCE" and "BOYS ENTRANCE," were saved and now grace the entrance to the new Arco Community Center.

In 1927, Chris Simonsen, principal of the Little Blue Schoolhouse (named because of its color), helped organize Bethany Lutheran Church. Built in 1940 by church members, Bethany Lutheran used much of the lumber from the recently disbanded Congregational Church to save money. The church initially organized in 1927 and celebrated its 75th anniversary in 2002.

Arco is well known for a chapel as well. Percy Pearson, a recovering alcoholic, erected the New Life Chapel in 1983 on the west side of Arco in gratitude for his renewal. A 10 x 16 church replica with three pews and a pulpit, the two-acre site is designed for rest and meditation. The Bible on the pulpit is open to Psalm 23.

See Some of Arco's Famous Sculptures

Located one mile east of Arco is Anderson Park, named for Manfred Anderson, who donated land for the park. The park is the brainchild of the Arco Sportsmen's Club, a group organized in 1948 to develop a recreation area on Lake Stay. Today, campsites, a swimming beach, picnic shelters, a playground and a boat launch surround some of the original stonework that made H.P. Pederson's Scenic Rock Garden and Gas Station famous. (It attracted 4,000 visitors in 1949.) Pederson created the work by incorporating stone and mortar around a metal framework. In all, he and his son, Vernon, sculpted thirty-five pieces, including a school, a miniature village with castle, a miniature farm and a complete railroad scene with a depot, a grain elevator and a stone locomotive. Most of the pieces are gone but Anderson Park includes sculptures of the Liberty Bell, Hugo the Ram, a 30-foot-long Scenic Rock Garden sign, and a re-creation of the Statue of Liberty, which weighs one thousand pounds.

Bethany Lutheran Church is also a sight to see. Built completely by volunteers and recently renovated, Bethany Lutheran Church showcases a beautiful stained glass window over the altar and an arched ceiling with woodwork. One hundred twenty-three members keep the church doors wide open for community events and celebration.

Arco Today

Today Arco boasts the post office, Bethany Lutheran Church, Brick Manor Supper Club, Community Center, Clahow's Repair, and the former stone Texaco Gas Station. A used clothing exchange, the Clothing Center, is staffed by local volunteers one day a week. Arco celebrated its centennial in 2003 with a parade, free root beer floats, a dance, and a program in the good-sized city park.

Arco is also great for an outdoor getaway, as its location near twin lakes Lake Stay and West Lake Stay provides easy access to fishing and boating. Water depth varies wildly depending on the amount of rainfall. Extremely high water due to recent flooding contrasts with a drought in the 1930s, when you could walk across the lake.

Leola Westphal writes about her father, Adolph Johnson, a rural mail carrier in Arco for forty years, who used horses and a cutter to deliver mail through blizzards and deep snow. Determined to get mail and other much needed provisions to his customers, he would shovel the horses out when they got stuck in the drifts.

Fire has been cruel to Barry. The first two schoolhouses burned to the ground. Over the years, fire
also destroyed several elevators, main street stores,
the lumberyard, and many homes.

TOP: City view, Parnell Street

Barry

A Resilient City Plagued by Fire

TRAVELING FROM LOWELL, MASSACHUSETTS, IN 1879,
Irishmen Edmond and William Barry settled on land they named
Lowell, after their hometown. The brothers hired a locator to find the
land claim their brother James had filed the previous year, and Edmond immediately filed a claim on land that became the city of Barry.
Later that year, their parents and sisters moved to adjoining land, and
started the post office in their farmhouse, with younger sister Maria
Barry as postmistress. The strong-willed Maria exerted her influence
and changed the name of the town to Barry. When the Great Northern
Railway arrived in 1880, Maria picked up the mail from the train rather
than the stagecoach. Along with the mail, the Great Northern brought

settlers, and settlement of the city began in earnest. James Barry opened
the general store and lumberyard, the Clark brothers erected a general
store, the Clearys opened a restaurant, and later, in 1891, the Barry
brothers built a bowling alley and a grain elevator. John McRae and his
sons shipped in six carloads of lumber to create the McRae Hardware
Store, and later, in 1910, the McRae brothers opened the First State
Bank. On May 22, 1900, William Barry successfully petitioned the
county commissioners for incorporation.

Fire has been cruel to Barry. The first two schoolhouses, built in
1901 and 1908, burned to the ground. A new WPA school opened in
1938 with two classrooms: one room housed grades one through four,
and the other held grades five through eight. In 1970, the school

consolidated with Graceville and Beardsley, and although not destroyed by fire, the building has since been demolished. Over the years, fire also destroyed several elevators, main street stores, the lumberyard, and many homes. Three times seems to be the magic number in Barry. After the first two churches were destroyed by fire, a new Catholic Church, St. Barnabas, was constructed out of brick and opened in 1931 under the leadership of Father Byrne. The church served the community well for many years before the congregation dissolved and the building was demolished in 1991. When St. Barnabas closed, the parish packed up the cemetery and moved all the graves to Graceville. One of the church highlights was a trip led by Father LeMay, who took thirty-six parishioners on a centennial pilgrimage to Rome and other European cities in 1959.

Small towns have a great love for baseball and Barry has fielded some excellent teams over the years. Horseracing and car racing were also popular. (John Mullin typically led the pack in auto racing.)

In *The History of Big Stone County*, Patrick Hanratty, lifelong resident of Barry and County Commissioner from 1933 to 1952, explains the decline of small towns, "In its prime, our village was a thriving farm trade center for grain, livestock and farm produce. As has been the experience of most small towns, Barry lost much of its trade to larger trade centers because of the automobile and good roads."

A Pair of Well Known Priests

Father Barron, born in Ireland and educated in England, served St. Barnabas Church for many years. He is remembered by many for wearing a tall beaver hat while walking through the fields to visit his parishioners. His hat graced the heads of many actors in plays performed in Barry throughout the years, and the hat now resides at Big Stone County Museum in Ortonville.

The Father Henry F. LeMay Award was created in 1984 to honor the memory of the late Reverend Henry F. LeMay, who co-founded Dignity/Twin Cities, and was a national leader in the creation of ministry to gay and lesbian people. He served St. Barnabas Church in the fifties and led the centennial pilgrimage to Europe.

Barry Today

The only place to get a cup of coffee in Barry, other than your neighbor's house, would be the Beardsley Farmers Co-op Elevator, where manager Nathan Temple staffs the elevator six days a week, except during harvest, when he works Sundays, too. Farmers bring their wheat, oats, corn and soybeans to the Co-op, formerly the Barry Farmers Elevator, which is the last stronghold in one of Minnesota's smallest towns. Local farmers also stop in daily to share coffee and talk about crops. Nathan gladly drives the fifteen miles to his home in South Dakota each day, happy to have a job in Barry, home to the best farmland in the world. According to Nathan, they haven't loaded grain on a train for over a year, as trucks do most of the hauling today. If you are lucky, you may hear the seldom-seen train, which runs to nearby Beardsley, picking up a load of corn, soybeans or grain. And while Barry is small, don't count it out: a brand new grain storage bunker on the west end and a new dryer signals the growth of progressive farms in the area. A local farmer is also remodeling the old bank into the Double Barrel Brewery.

A pair of houses in Barry also provide a window to the past; built in 1889, the original residence of Edmond J. Barry, one of the town's founders, is now owned by Nelia Gary, the town clerk of Barry. The original house owned by John Barry, another of Barry's first residents and once home to Patrick Hanratty, now belongs to Patrick's granddaughter. Although updated with a new kitchen and bathroom, the house maintains the integrity and furniture of the original structure. An old granary sits next to the house, and is now used for storage.

Frank Guenther, who grew up in Barry, recalled that the entire village was Catholic, except for postmaster Fred Carlson and his wife, Annie. Guenther had this to say about the Irish Catholics, "The Irish Catholics were the best people in the world until they drank too much and beat the hell out of everyone around. If no one was around, they beat the hell out of each other."

Following a beautiful Fourth of July, 1978,
celebration attended by 1,000 people, a
devastating tornado caught the city by surprise.

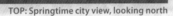

TOP: Springtime city view, looking north

Bejou

Life on the White Earth Reservation

JUST NORTH OF MAHNOMEN on Highway 59 lies Bejou, one of
six communities on the White Earth Indian Reservation. Encompassing
an area of 837,120 acres, the reservation was established by a treaty
between the Chippewa Tribe and the United States in 1879. In 1904,
the Soo Line created the railroad village, Bejou. The town was named
for an Ojibwe salutation that means "How do you do?"; this phrase
originated from the French *bonjour* (good day) of the old fur traders
and voyageurs.

The town was originally established on land donated by Russ and
Annie Bethel; however, white settlers brought in by train had no legal
rights to the land, as Indian reservation land was held in trust by the
United States government. It was not until 1905—when the Indian
Bureau permitted Indians to sell land of deceased family members—
that land could be legally purchased by the settlers. This had an impact
on the Indian population, and they lost significant acreage. By 1909,
90% of the land allotted to full-blood Indians had been sold, lost to tax
forfeit or mortgaged. The Ojibwe now own less than 10% of the land
on their reservation.

From a population of 85 in 1910 to an all-time high of 332 in
1920 when the city incorporated, Bejou experienced rapid growth. The
Farmer's Co-op Elevator, Folstrom's Livery Barn, Hallstrom's Store
and Dancehall, Shasky's Store, and the German-American State Bank
opened their doors to serve the citizenry. Located on a deep slough,

the bank personnel could shoot ducks out the back door of the bank. A two-story brick school opened in 1915, educating about 700 students before consolidating with Mahnomen in 1971. Back in the early years, the home economics teacher cooked for the students, and the principal taught botany and agriculture. A Holstein cow housed in one corner of the school garage provided students with milk and first-hand experience milking a cow. In 1978 a tornado completely demolished the school building. Fortunately an all-school reunion four years earlier had made it possible for former students to celebrate one last time in the old building. When the fun-loving citizens finished work and school, they danced to the music of the Gregoire Brothers and other local fiddlers, played baseball with Mrs. Shasky's clothesline as the backstop, and hosted parties and basket socials in their homes.

A Tornado Just After the Fourth of July

Following a beautiful Fourth of July, 1978, celebration attended by 1,000 people, a devastating tornado caught the city by surprise the next morning at 3:09 a.m. The north and south walls of the school blew away, the education unit of Immanuel Lutheran church was flattened, and several homes were destroyed. Near the elevator, eleven boxcars on the railroad tracks were lifted off the track and set down east of the tracks. Oddly, the boxcars' wheels remained on the track. Steel from grain bins littered the highways and streets, rendering only County Road 1 passable. But the greatest loss was the hundreds of trees and entire shelterbelts uprooted by the storm. Within ten days, over 1,000 truckloads of branches and debris were removed from the city. With help from the Red Cross, the DNR, Governor Rudy Perpich, and a Mennonite Relief Team from Canada, the city rebuilt and planted many trees. Despite the storm in 1978, the celebration was held the next year, albeit with a few additions. In addition to the crowning of a Fourth of July Queen, Albertha Bendickson, Bejou also crowned Diane Osenga, naming her the Tornado Queen.

Bejou Today

Today travelers pass through Bejou on their way to the casino in Mahnomen, but not before stopping at the well-tended baseball field and quaint Main Street. A Community Center, with a portion leased to the Lean To Tavern, lines Main Street as well as the post office (now painted lime green), which was established in 1906. On the opposite side of the street, Stump's Bar & Grill, the D & G Lounge, and VFW Wild Rice Post #1226 form a trio of businesses. Along the highway Bejou Fuel and Grocery, Dave Kalzer Welding, Larson Repair, and West Central AG support the community. Immanuel Lutheran Church, founded in 1935 and the only remaining church, is tucked quietly behind the baseball field. The original church building served as the Bejou Community Co-op Store for many years, and was well known for homemade pies and good food. The train still rolls through town alongside the Bejou Elevator.

On September 12, 2010, Joanie Kramer, director of the Mahnomen County Historical Society, sponsored a "Triumph and Tragedy Cemetery Walk" through Bejou Cemetery and Immaculate Conception Catholic Cemetery, both one mile north of Bejou. Local citizens dressed in period costumes and re-enacted the lives of Bejou pioneers. Tim Anderson's restored 1951 hearse and Scott McConkey's 1938 Packard car stood watch over the gathering.

A former Standard Gas Station owned by Herb and Lillian Bendickson from 1955 to 1972, sat empty until 2006 when Dean and Peggy Gunderson renovated the building. The Station Gift Shop, located on Highway 59, awaits a new owner to carry on the Gunderson tradition.

Bejou is located on the White Earth Indian Reservation, which is home to the White Earth Land Recovery Project, led by Winona LaDuke. It works to recover the land base of the reservation, promote responsible land stewardship and preserve the Ojibwe's cultural heritage. You can support this project by ordering Native wild rice, organic coffee, Ojibwe arts, and other items at their online store at *nativeharvest.com*.

INSETS L to R: Beltrami Mall • Farmers Elevator •
Today's Tackle • old USPO

One year, during Beltrami's annual parade, only
one resident actually watched the parade; everyone
else participated.

TOP: Beltrami Café, morning coffee

Beltrami

The Sounds of the Prairie

IN HIS MEMOIR, *GROWING UP IN BELTRAMI*, Jerome Boyer
writes about the sights and sounds he experienced growing up in small
town Minnesota in the 1920s and 1930s. On the vast prairie, sound
traveled far, and every sound had meaning. The hissing sound of the
steam engine letting off steam, the engineer blowing the whistle at every
mile intersection, and the rhythm of a long freight train as it crossed the
divisions between rails are vivid memories. The steam whistle on the
grain threshing machines signaled the beginning of the day, the noon
meal and quitting time. When the bell on the fire station rang, everyone
in town dropped whatever they were doing and ran to help. Depending
on the time of day, the church bell called you to worship or called you to
the funeral of a friend or neighbor you knew well.

When the St. Paul, Minneapolis and Manitoba Railway, later
James J. Hill's Great Northern Railway, first blew the whistle through
Beltrami in the early 1870s, the site was named Edna after postmistress
Edna Webb. Later in 1900, the fledgling village was renamed Beltrami
after the Italian exile, Giacoma Constantino Beltrami, who explored
the Red River Valley and the upper Mississippi River in 1823. On July
22, 1901, 42 citizens gathered at Iver Johnson's Store to cast their vote
for incorporation with 35 ayes and 7 nays. President K. O. Flakne and
Recorder Iver Johnson were elected to run the new city of 183 citizens.

At the turn of the century, Beltrami boasted three hotels, two department stores, three grain elevators, three banks, and the Scenic Theatre. William Bond, the meat market owner, sold lean beef for 10 cents a pound and operated a large icehouse behind the market. In 1918, fire swept through Main Street, destroying E. W. Johnson's store, the Lekve elevator, a bank, the barber shop, the shoemaker shop, warehouses, and Boyer's Store. Over the years, fire destroyed most of the businesses, and only the original blacksmith shop remains intact.

On December 20, 1883, the Norwegians gathered at the Flakne and Onstad Store to organize the Norwegian Lutheran Church. Pastor John Krogstad from Ada, Minnesota, hopped the train once a month to conduct a worship service in the schoolhouse. In 1915, Scandia Lutheran Church voted to build a church on Tom Standem's land in Scandia Township. After a lightning strike destroyed the church in 1937, carpenter Julius Swenson led the members in the construction of another church. After building two earlier churches, the Norwegians once again picked up their hammers in 1979, and erected a third church, now called Trinity Lutheran Church, on land donated by Miss Gladys Johnson.

Perhaps alarmed at the large number of Lutherans in the community, nine women in Beltrami organized the Alpha Sewing Society, and decided to pursue building a Methodist church. Charles Welter, a transplant from New York, offered considerable financial support, and the determined women scraped together one hundred dollars to purchase a lot from Jim Hill. At a cost of $835.60, the Union Church was dedicated on May 21, 1899. On the 50th anniversary of the church in 1949, plans were hatched for a new United Methodist Church, which opened on May 8, 1955, across from Trinity Lutheran.

In 1900, the Beltrami Village School was replaced with a three-room school. One early teacher, Miss Truesdell, faced a room of children who were unable to speak any English. Despite many challenges, she taught all her pupils to read and write fluently. In 1918, the children of Beltrami proudly moved into a new $25,000 brick school with a four-year high school. A total of three graduated in the first class of 1919. A school crisis arose during World War II, when qualified teachers were hard to find due to the war effort. On June 21, 1943, the board voted 4–2 to consolidate the high school with Fertile. Only the school janitor, Alvin "Smokey" Richards, who shoveled tons of coal over the years, remained with the school for all twenty-six years.

A United States Senator from Beltrami

Senator Joseph Hurst Ball, the son of one of Beltrami's first teachers, became a U.S. Senator when Senator Ernest Lunden died in a plane crash on August 31, 1940. A newspaper reporter for the *Pioneer Press and Dispatch*, the 35-year-old Ball was unexpectedly appointed to fill the remainder of the term. The youngest member of the Senate, Joseph Ball went on to win a six-year-term of office in the 1942 election, and in 1943, he co-sponsored the bill which established the United Nations. In 1948, the Republican Senator soundly lost his reelection bid to an upstart Democrat, 37-year-old Hubert H. Humphrey.

Beltrami Today

For the last five years, the city has hosted a hometown parade the weekend after July 4th, at the end of the Polk County Fair. Past entrants have driven antique cars, tractors, bicycles, fire engines, even a rickshaw. One year, during Beltrami's annual parade, only one resident actually watched the parade; everyone else participated. He moved his lawn chair from one block to the next. That same year, one of the tractors in the parade overheated, and the driver headed for a garden hose. Assuming it was part of the parade route, the vehicles behind followed, and the entire parade ended up at the garden hose.

Today's Tackle, owned by Bruce and Patty Mosher, manufactures the *Ice Buster Bobber* and other tackle. An old highway sign that resides in the shop reads "**BELTRAMI POPULATION 137 +1 +1.**" When Bruce and Patty adopted their son Max, they added a +1 to the sign, and when son Carter joined the family, Grandma raced down to the population sign on the edge of town, and added another +1 to greet them on their return.

TOP: Big Fish restaurant, west of Bena

During World War II, Bena was home to a prisoner
of war camp housing German prisoners.

Bena

The Escape from Bena: Nazi POWs Attempt a Breakout

DURING WORLD WAR II, some prisoners of war captured by the
Allies were held in camps in the U.S. Many of these camps were in
Minnesota. Bena was home to a camp housing German prisoners;
escape attempts were rare, but Bena's POW Camp #4 experienced just
such an attempt. The *Escape from Bena* began on October 28, 1944, when
German prisoners Walter Mai, 21, and Heinz Schymalla, 22, slipped out
of the barracks in the middle of the night and climbed aboard a flimsy
boat, *Lili Marlene #10*, made from scrap lumber. Using small maps in an
English dictionary for navigation, the two believed they could follow
the Mississippi River to the Gulf of Mexico and jump a ship for home.
Packing blankets, pillows, food donations from fellow prisoners, and

essentials like shoe polish, a chess set, and a cigarette rolling machine,
the Afrika Corps soldiers dipped their paddles into Lake Winnibigoshish. Camp officials did not have an accurate count of the number
of boats, and did not notice that one was gone. Unfortunately for the
escapees, a snowstorm arose within five days of their departure, and
they stalled at Jay Gould Lake in Grand Rapids. A resort owner spotted
the thwarted Huck Finn and Tom, and thought it highly unusual to find
two men who barely spoke English roasting sausages on the banks of the
river. They meekly surrendered and were punished with thirty days of
isolation and two weeks of bread and water.

The POW camp was preceded by a Civilian Conservation Corps
camp, which was built in 1933 and was the first in Cass County. Located

16

300 yards behind a tourist camp on the lakeshore, the CCC boys of Company 702, up to 212 men, stayed at the camp until it closed in 1942. From 1943 to 1945, the POW camp operated on the site. The 219 POWs worked on reforestation in the summer, and spent the winter slicing tie bolts, skidding and cutting logs. When the men weren't logging, they played in an orchestra, took music lessons and classes in French, English, chemistry, history and math. After World War II, visitors to Germany who wore a Bena shirt were often approached by former POWs and thanked for the excellent care they received. One German prisoner even returned to live in Bena after the war.

Nestled in the heart of the Chippewa National Forest and on the southernmost bay of Lake Winnibigoshish, Bena is part of the Leech Lake Indian Reservation. The Ojibwe word *Bena* means "partridge," a term Henry Longfellow used in his literary classic, *Song of Hiawatha.* Before the city incorporated in 1906, the Great Northern Railway laid track through Bena. Recognized as the founding father of Bena, entrepreneur Ernest Flemming opened a general store near the tracks and invested heavily in the logging industry. When a keg of powder exploded and burned down the store in 1906, Mr. Flemming recovered from his injuries in time to build a larger store. Two years later, the post office was robbed under his watch. The thieves carried off $300 worth of stamps, $500 in cash and $100 worth of store goods in mail sacks. More distressing to the owner, the robbers took his private papers, notes and mortgages. Once again, fire reared its ugly head, destroying the store for a second time in 1913. Building yet a third store, the determined Mr. Flemming lost half the store merchandise in 1925, when a band of thieves loaded up a truckload and made their getaway. He survived another robbery the next year losing $7.50 in cash, a Marlin repeating rifle and 21 jackknives. His business closed in 1937.

Early pioneers capitalized on the future tourism industry. George Perry opened "The Pines," a summer resort on Lake Winnie in 1902, and Tom Sheehy opened the Commercial Hotel in 1905. Following her husband's death in 1930, Mrs. Sheehy continued the business for another 30 years by offering "special plate dinners, better food, and best beer."

The city of Bena barely escaped destruction in 1931, when a fire heading straight for the city shifted direction at the last minute, jumped the railroad tracks, and burned to the shore of Lake Winnibigoshish. Over 9,000 acres were scorched. Bena was home to one of the three Indian Boarding Schools built within the reservation. Situated on a small knoll overlooking Lake Winnibigoshish, the two-story school opened January 1, 1901, with 28 girls and 28 boys, and closed in 1910.

A Restaurant That Looks Like a Giant Muskellunge and a Real Muskie Record

Built in the '50s out of bent one-by-fours and sheets of tar paper, the famous Big Fish Supper Club has appeared in the *National Lampoon's Vacation* movies with Chevy Chase, and also in Charles Kuralt's television series. The restaurant resembles a giant muskellunge, and to enter, patrons walk into its wide-open jaws and dine in the belly of the beast. The eyes are made out of round Coca-Cola signs, and the sign on the door reads, "Please don't steal the teeth!"

Bena Today

Bena continues to draw tourists and fishermen to beautiful lakes and first-class resorts, including: Becker's Resort, Cherney's Resort, Denny's Resort, Four Seasons Resort, Iowana Beach Resort, Nodak Lodge, Sunset Beach Resort, McArdle's Resort, Northstar Resort, and the New Leech Lake Campground. Bena also supports the Big Winnie Bar & Café, the world-famous Big Fish Supper Club, and Winnibigoshish General Store and Resort. Named after a famous Ojibwe chief, the Bug-O-Na-Ge-Shig School opened in 1975 and enrolls students from the Leech Lake Reservation.

Bena is also known for a coveted fishing record. Bena resident Art Lyons caught the state's largest muskie in Lake Winnibigoshish in August, 1957. It weighed 54 pounds.

Population: 110   **Incorporated:** 1951

INSETS L to R: Winchester Lutheran • Old school •
A. J.'s Bar & Grill • Fire Dept.

During World War I, the Red Cross sent out an appeal for money to support the troops overseas, and Borup responded with an event that is still remembered almost a century later.

TOP: Original elevator buildings

Borup

The Pioneer Life: Dedication Amid Hardship

A TYPICAL PIONEER WOMAN from Borup, Mrs. Oline Mattison raised a large family without any modern conveniences. She baked bread every other day, sewed the family's clothing late into the night, raised and plucked the chickens, made butter, and in her spare time carded wool, spun it into yarn, and knit stockings. Following a church service at Olines's home on July 4, 1883, eleven women decided to help organize a Ladies Aid Society to raise funds to build a Lutheran Church. Members walked several miles carrying babies and with small children hanging on their skirts in order to meet in homes and plan fundraising events. When the church was built in 1903, the Ladies Aid Society proudly presented $100.00 in hard-earned cash. The only

midwife in the area, Mrs. Mattison delivered over three hundred fifty babies, the last delivery when she was seventy-five years old. When a family had no help following the birth, she stayed to do the housework until the mother was strong enough to leave her bed.

By 1880, Borup consisted of a Great Northern Railway station, a grain storehouse and a post office, all of which were just two miles south of a small settlement dubbed Goose Island by railroad construction crews, who noted the large flocks of geese in the area. Grain buyer Louis Bowman from Ada drove his horse and buggy to purchase grain from the area's farmers, and then loaded their grain into the warehouse with large baskets.

Borup's citizens soon became legendary for their determined spirit and work ethic. Clara Midthune recalls the great lengths her father, Ole Mattison, went to build his store. He hauled lumber from Ada to the Wild Rice River and manually floated the lumber down the river by pulling it with a rope as he walked alongside railroad tracks that paralleled the river. While the settlement at Goose Island grew, the Borup railroad siding began sinking in mud and was plagued by water and mosquitoes, all characteristics of the swampy terrain. Finally, in 1892, the farmers joined forces to move the siding and buildings in Borup to Goose Island and renamed it Borup. Shortly after Ole and Oline Mattison platted the village in 1899, Ole opened a hardware store next to Peter Melberg's General Store and two others, but fire completely destroyed all four buildings a year later. Once again, the settlers walked to Ada, Glyndon or Moorhead for their supplies. Undaunted, Ole and his son, Oscar, built another hardware store, and a depot was built in the early 1900s. Depot agent J. J. Bowen was soon busy loading the wagons of grain into the boxcars. The business district continued to expand to include the Palace Hotel, the Playhouse Cafe, Stenerson Brothers Lumber Company, Herman Kreier's meat market, three elevators, and Torske Brothers Store. No child left the Torske store without a five-cent sock of candy, and all the customers received a Christmas gift.

Railroad magnate James J. Hill named the city in honor of his good friend Charles William Borup, who founded Borup & Oakes in 1854, the first bank in Minnesota. Borup's namesake acted as a good luck charm for the Bank of Borup, which opened in 1898 and survived the Great Depression, an unusual victory for rural banks.

In 1909, Pierre Schranz organized the Borup Cornet Band with twenty-four musicians, half from town and half from the farm. All of Borup turned out to hear the well-rehearsed band, which dressed in dark trousers and white jackets with gold buttons and braid. The musicians performed concerts and often played before baseball games, a real balancing act for the band members who also played on the team.

A Town Dedicated to Service and Giving

Borup's citizens are revered for their generosity and community spirit. During World War I, the Red Cross sent out an appeal for money to support the troops overseas, and Borup responded with an event that is still remembered almost a century later. Auctioneers Brantner, Volland and Writer auctioned off an egg, laid that day, for $103. A calf sold for $87, a goose egg brought $75, and a cake baked by Storberg's in Ada sold for $505. On a cold day in March, 1918, tiny Borup raised $2,300 for the Red Cross, an incredible sum for the times.

Typical of the can-do spirit of Borup, in 1972, citizens volunteered their labor and materials to build the combination Borup Community Hall, Fire Hall, and Town Hall. Over fifty people turned out just to shingle the roof. Today, the building houses two fire trucks, the Borup City Council, and the Town Board.

Borup Today

Today Borup is home to AJ's Bar & Grill, Randy's Body Shop, the post office, and Borup Community Hall and Fire Hall. After fire destroyed Ed Arnbert's grocery store and locker plant in 1947, the fire department organized under Fire Chief Carlott Mattison, and remains a vital force in the community. When the elementary school closed in 2010, local men bought the building to manufacture a ground grid system to prevent erosion. Winchester Lutheran Church and Jevnaker Lutheran Church, just east of town, complete the proud little city.

The former site of the Torske Brothers Store, AJ's Bar & Grill hosts bar bingo, karaoke night, and makes the best homemade soup you'll find in a bar. The bar displays the original Borup depot sign on the roof. Borup celebrates hometown living with their annual Borup Days the second weekend in July. It features a pedal tractor pull for kids, a car show, a parade, a horseshoe tournament, watermelon bowling, and ends with karaoke.

In addition to raising a family, Mrs. Oline Mattison was also the only midwife in the area. One stormy night, a man arrived at her home, obviously full of whiskey, and asked for help with his wife, who was about to give birth. During the birth, the door kept blowing open, but the husband was too incapacitated to help. Before delivering the baby, she had to hold the door until it could be nailed shut.

Since 1953, Boy River Hobo Day is held annually over Labor Day weekend. What used to be a vegetable-judging contest has given way to games, a trap shoot, a canoe derby, a pig roast, and "Hobo Stew," a local concoction.

TOP: Main Street, looking south

Boy River

Yes, That's the Mayor Paving the Streets

FROM HIS VANTAGE POINT on the corner of Main Street and First Avenue, Mayor Mark Fogle can keep his eye on the whole town. Being small has its advantages. "When we wanted to pave the streets, we just got out there and did it." This hardworking mayor and his council of six take care of the streets, paint the community center, write grants, and do what needs to be done to keep Boy River a community. Rooted on a hill of rock and surrounded by dense forests and swamps, this active city sits on the Boy River a mile and a half east of Leech Lake.

Prior to European settlement, the area was inhabited by the Dakota and Ojibwe. When the Ojibwe expelled the Dakota from Mille Lacs following the Battle of Kathio in 1744, they forced the Dakota from the Leech Lake area as well. The first European residents, like trapper Aaron Collier, learned the art of canoeing from the Ojibwe and used the rivers to trade furs with the Indians. As permanent settlers arrived in the 1800s, logging and hunting were the primary sources of income. When 40,000 acres of land in the national forest reserve opened for settlement on September 14, 1908, August Toffle stood in line for six weeks to file for land at the Cass County Land Office. One of the first European families to move into Boy River, the Toffle family from Cass Lake rode on trails wide enough to get a team and wagon through the heavily wooded area. Mrs. Toffle did not see another white woman for a year, until the Frank Foote family arrived to start a general store and barge service.

The Soo Line laid track on the river's edge in 1910, and large logs from the river were placed on loading cars and shipped to Duluth. From the train depot, people walked two blocks to the Foote Hotel and Store, which doubled as the post office, for refreshments and supplies. By the time Boy River incorporated as a city on April 7, 1922, several businesses lined Main Street: the First State Bank of Boy River, Johnson's Store, Raines Boy River Garage, Boy River Hotel, Pete Spatgen's Barber Shop, Boy River Lumber Company, Bonick's Hotel, Farmer's Produce Association, and Camp's Hotel and Meat Market. Ahead of their time, the city council elected Mary Aldrich as the first female city council president in 1926.

A new four-room, solid brick school building went up in 1926. The WPA provided funds in 1930 for a school addition using salvaged materials; even an old barber chair found a home in the school basement where the janitor gave the boys haircuts.

The Last Chapter of the Indian Wars: The Battle of Sugar Point

The last Indian conflict in the United States, the Battle of Sugar Point, took place on Leech Lake near Boy River. Upset over years of exploitation from the lumber companies, who underpaid them for their timber and flooded their wild rice beds, the Ojibwe were reluctant to cooperate any further with federal authorities. On September 15, 1898, Bug-O-Nay-Ge-Shig, a member of the Bear Island Pillager Band of the Ojibwe, was arrested in Onigum for refusing to appear in Duluth as a witness to a stabbing incident. While waiting on the dock for the steamboat to carry him and another prisoner to Walker, he pleaded with his nephew to let him escape. Bug-O-Nay-Ge-Shig retreated safely to his cabin on Sugar Point. Unwilling to concede defeat, the War Department in Washington sent eighty soldiers, led by Brigadier General Bacon and Major Wilkinson, to arrest the Indian. On October 5, 1898, boats carrying the soldiers left Walker for Sugar Point, only to find Bug-O-Nay-Ge-Shig had slipped into the woods. Instead, they arrested two

men with outstanding warrants and brought them to a boat. One of the guards on the boat shot at a canoe containing two Indian women. He was then shot by someone on shore and later died. At about this same time, the soldiers on shore began to stack their guns when one rifle slipped and accidentally discharged. Hiding in the forest, Ojibwe men fired back. Six soldiers, including Major Wilkinson, were killed in the ensuing battle, which continued throughout the following day, and nine more were wounded. One Indian policeman was killed, but no other Ojibwe were harmed. Father Aloysius, a priest from White Earth, arrived to mediate the dispute and the surrender of those wanted by the federal government. They were sentenced to prison terms but were later pardoned by President McKinley. Bug-O-Nay-Ge-Shig refused to surrender and was never captured.

Boy River Today

Since 1953, Boy River Hobo Day is held annually over Labor Day weekend. What used to be a vegetable-judging contest has given way to games, a trap shoot, a canoe derby, a pig roast, and "Hobo Stew," a local concoction. Residents of the area bring vegetables and meat to throw into a large pot, which is then stirred with a canoe paddle.

The Soo Line ATV trail from Boy River to Cass Lake is lined by several large bogs with great wildlife viewing, including herons, wood ducks, mergansers, teal, otter and bald eagles. The trail has an all-weather gravel surface.

Today Boy River is home to Boy River Propane, Dave's Garage, American Legion William H. Robbins Post 458, Zion Lutheran Church, Boy River Log Chapel, and the Boy River Community Hall. Jerry's Bar and Cafe provides senior meals and hosts the Cass County Public Health clinic before the cafe opens at 5:00 p.m. Boy River is also home to the Boy River Log Chapel, which has an unusual pulpit made from the burl of a large birch tree.

Boy River has a literary connection. The *Northland* steamer, used for transportation between Walker and Boy River, was owned by Mr. Thomas Welch. His daughter Mary eventually was a war correspondent during World War II, and married Ernest Hemingway in 1946.

Population: 141   Incorporated: 1907

INSETS L to R: Immanuel Church • Fond du Lac Headstart •
USPO • 2nd Ave.

On October 12, at 4:30 in the afternoon, a fire was discovered along the Great Northern tracks at Milepost 62, four miles west of Brookston. It eventually destroyed Brookston and blackened 500 square miles of land.

TOP: City view, 2nd Avenue

Brookston

The Fire That Burned 500 Square Miles

BRUSH FIRES, CLEARING FIRES, AND RAILROAD FIRES were smoldering all along the Great Northern Railway line from Floodwood to Cloquet during the fall of 1918. But on October 12, at 4:30 in the afternoon, a fire discovered along the Great Northern tracks at Milepost 62, four miles west of Brookston, eventually destroyed Brookston and blackened 500 square miles of land. The name Milepost 62 means little in this century, but it haunted an entire generation.

On Thursday, October 10th, a passenger train from Duluth called the *Wooden Shoe*, after the conductor's wooden leg, stopped at Milepost 62 near a siding used for loading wood products. Ten thousand cords of pulpwood, railroad ties and cordwood, surrounded by wood chips and

bark, lay in piles on both sides of the tracks, a tinderbox for train sparks. Farmers Steve Koskela and John Sundstrom, culling ties at the siding for Koskela's barn, noticed a column of smoke after the train pulled away. Dropping everything, they dashed over to the smoke to find a grass fire near the piles of wood, which quickly spread under the piles of cordwood. Unable to trample the fire, they rushed home for pails and shovels, and called for help to make a firebreak. By the time the section crew arrived at 6:00 p.m., businessmen and neighbors joined in the effort to contain the fire. When a strong northwest wind hit on the 12th, Koskela prepared his farm for a fire. He was able to save his family and house, but lost his stock and outbuildings. Two miles south of Brookston, John Iwasko and his wife moved their valuables to the root cellar. As the sun turned red from the smoke and burning leaves fell around the farm, Mrs. Iwasko hid in the root cellar while her husband went to release a team of horses from the burning barn. The fire hit in an instant, and blew the roof off while John ran to the creek, where he watched the fire destroy his horses. Meanwhile, his wife, suffocating in the cellar like so many in the fire, attempted a daring escape by wrapping herself in a blanket and running one hundred feet to the creek. Unable to see and badly burned, she made it to the creek, saving her life. Mr. Iwasko carried her to Brookston for help, but by the time he got there, Brookston was gone.

Back in Brookston, a town of 500 people, city Mayor Charles DeWitt was awakened by his wife at 2:00 p.m. He had just spent all night working for the railroad and woke to a rising wind, smoky air and a red sun. Soon, houses along the streets burst into flames from the intense heat, even before the fire emerged from the woods. By 4:10 p.m. a relief train carrying two hundred people left Brookston, only to encounter intense flames that scorched many of the refugees in the open gondola cars, including DeWitt, his wife, and their three small children. The blackened car and injured, hysterical refugees eventually made it to safety in Superior. Many people were killed attempting to flee by automobile, including sixteen-year-old Earl Miettunen's mother, who was thrown out of their car after hitting a tree in the road. She was never seen again.

After reducing Brookston to ashes, the fire jumped the St. Louis River and spread rapidly inland across the Fond du Lac Ojibwe Indian reservation, where the Ojibwe people had no railroad access for safety. Grace Sheehy lived on a farm with her five children, aged eleven months to twelve years, while her husband, Paul, worked in the shipyards in Duluth. At 3:30, Mike Beargrease arrived to help carry the children to the neighbor's home. On the way, the fire crossed the road and they were forced to detour toward Cress Lakes. Luckily, a boat was moored on the lake, and Beargrease paddled them into the center of the lake, where they watched the fire burn all around them. Fifty-seven Ojibwe homes were destroyed, along with their livestock and feed crop.

Prior to the fire, business in Brookston had boomed when the railroad arrived. Mr. C. A. Tester, a widower with six children, arrived from St. Paul to assume his role as the new depot agent. Along with a jail and depot, the J.F. Ryan Store, Epperson's General Store & post office, the Shurman Hotel, Mrs. Brittany's Restaurant, and the Edlund & Olson Mercantile Company drew customers into town. In August 1905, land on the Fond du Lac Indian Reservation opened for homestead settlement, and the Northern Lumber Company built a warehouse in Brookston, with plans to begin logging on the reservation. One year later, Rowe McCamus and his father, Samuel, commenced the publication of the *Brookston Herald*, which ended the day of the fire in 1918.

The Most Infamous Fire in Minnesota History

Named the worst fire in Minnesota history, the Milepost 62 Fire cut a swath of destruction forty miles long and twenty miles wide. By comparison, the Moose Lake-Kettle River fires scorched a piece of earth thirty-one miles long by fourteen miles wide. Four hundred and fifty-three people died in the area, and the financial loss topped $30,000,000.

Brookston Today

Although completely destroyed by fire in 1918, Brookston rebuilt. Located on the Fond du Lac Indian Reservation, the city is now home to the Brookston Community Center, the post office, Stony Brook Saloon, Colonial Homes, and Immanuel Lutheran Church, as well as The Doug Melin Ballpark. On the Fourth of July, the Community Club puts on a parade and fireworks extravaganza that draws up to 2,000 spectators. Brookston also features some good fishing; a boat landing on the St. Louis River provides access walleye, crappie, northern pike and catfish.

Remarkably, only one Ojibwe person died in Brookston during the Mile 62 Fire, a little girl who fell from the wagon in which she and her family were fleeing the flames. The Ojibwe's knowledge of woodland living included coping with forest fires.

TOP: Petersen Service Center

Population: 45 **Incorporated:** 1950

INSETS L to R: City Hall • Lions Park •
Edge Bar & Grill • St. John's Lutheran

The history of Cedar Mills goes all the way back to settler Daniel Cross, who moved to Cedar Mills in 1856 with his wife and three children. By 1862, he was dead, killed during the Dakota War.

Cedar Mills

A Mill Town Amid the Dakota War of 1862

ONE OF THE LAST of Minnesota's smallest cities to incorporate, Cedar Mills waited until February 28, 1950, to officially elect Mayor Stan Ridgeway and a city council. But its history goes way back to settler Daniel Cross, who moved to Cedar Mills in 1856 with his wife and three children. By 1862, he was dead, killed during the Dakota War while looking for a friend with a search party. Cross and his family had fled Cedar Mills to seek safety in a recently constructed Hutchinson stockade, and would have survived if his friend, Caleb Sanborn, hadn't left the stockade to return to his farm in Cedar Mills. When Sanborn failed to return, Cross and two other men left the stockade September 23 to look for him. Before they found Sanborn's body, a volley of shots killed

Cross. His companions fled, leaving the bodies until both were recovered the next day. No one knows where Sanborn is buried, but Cross's grave is in the Oakland Cemetery, in Hutchinson, Minnesota, next to Stewart B. Garvie, another casualty of the conflict.

The city name has its origin from events in 1838, when Joseph Nicollet, assisted by John Fremont, led an expedition of the U.S. Army Corps of Topographical Engineers to map the region between the upper Mississippi and Missouri rivers. Stopping at a lake near Cedar Mills, they christened the lake Cedar Lake, after an island in the lake covered with red cedar. Their map designated the lake as *Rantesha Wita*, the Dakota words for Red Cedar Island Lake. Following the arrival of Daniel Gross, settlers R. J. Brodwell, O. S. Merriam, Philander Ball and George Jewett settled in Cedar Mills, along with Mr. Nichols, who erected a flour mill in 1858. The mill was capable of processing 60 bushels of flour per day. Dr. V. P. Kennedy, a Civil War veteran, operated the Cedar Mills flour mill from 1867 to 1869. A skilled physician and also a state legislator in 1860, Dr. Kennedy opened a medical practice in Litchfield, Minnesota.

In 1860, Miss Sophie Pratt taught classes at a school located in the Daniel Cross home; she received $25 a month, and taught there until the first schoolhouse opened in 1869 under the strict hand of teacher E. B. Comstock. Later a new school was constructed on the south end of Cedar Mills. During the Dakota Conflict, Postmaster and Reverend Henry Lasher buried all official records of the post office, and the office closed until 1870. When the Electric Short Line Railroad Company arrived in 1920, the village moved one-half mile south away from the trees and flour mill for easy access to the railroad. In 1923, the City Investment Company platted the village, and a large crew of men rushed to move the Cromwell Elevator, renamed the Victoria Elevator, from Litchfield to Cedar Mills in time for the fall harvest. George Haggenmiller opened a hardware store, Harry Ahlstedt managed the new Victoria Elevator, and the Montifard family opened the first grocery store. In 1925, Henry Barfknecht sold groceries and beer out of a new brick grocery, a building that still stands today. That same year, Frank Runke opened another grocery store, and the store is now a private home. A large dance pavilion soon opened and later sold in 1947 to Stan and Berney Ridgeway, who started a hatchery. The hatchery evolved into "The Three Gabled Pub," until 1996, when the building was demolished.

In 1892, Henry Schulte and Christof Schultz donated nine acres to begin building St. Johns' Evangelical Lutheran Church, and St. John's Lutheran School, a 12-by-28-foot building with 12 benches. Both the church and school have been replaced with new buildings—the church in 1950, and the school in 1930. A beautiful house for the school Principal, now a private home, overlooks the school, playground and church cemetery. The church is 400 members strong.

A Washington Power Broker from Cedar Mills

Born in Cedar Mills on October 20, 1870, Colonel Charles Hoyt March managed President Coolidge's Minnesota campaign in 1924, and was appointed by the President to the powerful Federal Trade Commission in 1929. Although a staunch Republican, his commitment to protect investors against security fraud won the respect of President Franklin D. Roosevelt, who reappointed Colonel March for another seven-year term. Colonel March co-authored the Securities Act of 1933, a law that forced full disclosure from companies selling securities to protect investors from fraud and deceit.

Cedar Mills Today

Today, Cedar Mills is home to City Hall, Cedar Edge Ballroom & Edge Bar, and Peterson Service Center, a full-service grain, feed and seed business. Arvid Luthens purchased the District #34 school building and opened Cedar's Edge, a food and liquor establishment that lives on as Edge Bar & Grill. A city park is located next to the bar. The Cedar Mills Lions Club offers an annual pork chop dinner, hosts Santa Day, and coordinates the Lighting of the Remembrance Tree. During the summer on Saturdays, the Cedar Mills Carting Club rev up their go-carts for a run on the grounds of the Gun Club. The Gun Club serves a pancake breakfast every month, and sponsors an annual fish fry at Cedar Mills Ballroom to raise money for community projects. The Luce Line State Trail, a former railroad grade, travels through Cedar Mills on a 63-mile jaunt from Plymouth to Cosmos. Surrounded by tallgrass prairie, the trail resembles a stroll down a quiet country road.

For a window into history, visit St. John's School, which still retains an inner room of the original schoolhouse. The tin walls and ceiling from 1892 reflect a simpler era of school benches and slates. The school remains in use for youth activities.

In 1996, the city of Cobden hosted two busloads of tourists from Cobden, Australia. Known as the "Cobden Connection Tour Group", the group visited all five cities named Cobden in the world, with Cobden, Minnesota the smallest city, and the last stop.

TOP: Cobden Community Park

Cobden

The progress of freedom depends more upon the maintenance of peace, the spread of commerce, and the diffusion of education, than the labors of cabinets and foreign offices.—Richard Cobden

A Town Named in Honor of a Pacifist Finds Time for Fun

PLATTED IN 1901 and incorporated in 1905, Cobden was named in honor of British politician Richard Cobden, who advocated peace, non-intervention, and international free trade. He also opposed British foreign policy, denouncing both the Crimean War and the Second Opium War in 1857. A fierce advocate of freedom for all men, he supported the North in the Civil War. His final speech before his death in London in 1865 laid the groundwork for the argument against government production competing with private enterprise.

Initially named North Branch due to its location near Sleepy Eye Creek, the principal north branch of the Cottonwood River, the Chicago and Northwestern Railway renamed the village Cobden in 1886. Located on Highway 14, six miles west of Sleepy Eye, Cobden's population peaked in 1910 at 150 citizens. Main Street bustled with the Cobden State Bank, the Cobden Creamery, Zeiske General Store and post office, two schools, a Lutheran church and Baptist church, Blackburg Grain and Feed, Davis Garage and Blacksmith, a fire department, and Steinke-Seidl Lumber and Hardware store. A flour mill opened in 1904 for one year, and later burned to the ground. The city incorporated April 7, 1905, with Thomas Peterson, president; J. F. Brodish, recorder; and councilmen, Herman Altermatt, A. C. Klein and A. Newdall.

Cobden made time for fun, too. During the forties, the Cobden City Hall hosted a dance every weekend, and until the hall burned in 1980, the local children used the building as a playhouse and basketball court. The town band marched, Cobden baseball and softball teams were top-notch contenders, and, of course, pranks were an everyday occurrence. One well-remembered story is the night that two gentlemen tried to get Don Utz's horse into the back seat of a Ford Falcon. They managed to get the horse in, but she stepped through the floor.

A Cobden World Tour

In 1996, the city of Cobden hosted two busloads of tourists from Cobden, Australia. Known as the "Cobden Connection Tour Group," the group visited all five cities named Cobden in the world, with Cobden, Minnesota, the smallest city, and the last stop. Mayor Don Utz, City Clerk Rhonda Groebner, Councilman Butch Krebs, and community member JoAnn Treml presented the Aussies with their Main Street sign in exchange for the Australian flag and a commemorative plaque from their new friends down under. All five Cobdens are named after Englishman Richard Cobden.

Anne Ibberson owns the Ridin' High Saloon, a biker-friendly bar purchased from previous owner Joe Sterns, who died unexpectedly. A former employee who worked eight years for Joe, Anne continues the tradition of a community-centered business. A popular stop for bikers on their way to the motorcycle rally in Sturgis, South Dakota, offers more than ice-cold beer and good bar food. A large 3,000-square-foot addition hosts dances and community celebrations. Formerly called the Iron Horse Saloon, Ann changed the name to Ridin' High Saloon in memory of Joe, an avid biker who also owned a Harley-Davidson golf cart. The new name conjures up an image of Joe riding his cycle in heaven.

In 2001, Cobden citizens celebrated their centennial over Labor Day with a grand party. An antique tractor pull drew 144 competitors, and was followed by a pork chop and homemade sauerkraut dinner and street dance. A new historical marker placed in the city park commemorates the 100th anniversary of Cobden.

Cobden Today

Now the Canadian Pacific Railway barrels through town, "half a dozen times a day on a brand new track, at a pretty good clip," according to former mayor Jim Heiling. Two new storage bins along the tracks hold 330,000 bushels of corn and soybeans. Downtown Cobden is home to the Ridin' High Saloon, the Red River Co-operative Elevator, and the Sports Page Bar & Grill, located in the original 1915 State Bank building. The Cobden Community Club hosts raffles and sauerkraut feeds to maintain a lovely community park with a picnic shelter in memory of Vic Stage, a children's playground, and new bathrooms. A concession displays a sign with a line from a Ray Charles tune, *"You got the right place baby, Cobden, Minnesota."* Riding around town on his golf cart or riding lawn mower, Jim Heiling happily does the volunteer mowing and city clean-up when spring arrives. This proud and tidy city keeps city hall open thanks to their hardworking citizens.

Cobden Days is an annual tradition held the day before Labor Day. The party begins with a tractor pull followed by a motorcycle stunt show, and ends with a dance at the Ridin' High Saloon.

Cobden's former jail is a sight to see. Built around 1900, the Cobden Jail was recently removed from the National Register of Historic Places, as it was remodeled and now serves as City Hall. Although the fire hall burned down and the new fire truck was sold, one of the oldest fire trucks in the area, with a 1907 manual pump, remains in Cobden.

Cobden was also home to a major league pitcher. Born in 1909, Roman "Lefty" Bertrand, who batted right and threw left handed, pitched for the Philadelphia Phillies in 1936. His parents, Mr. and Mrs. J. P. Ed Bertrand, owned the town phone company.

TOP: CW Valley Co-op

One day a group of Indians, armed with bows and arrows, stopped at the Roen cabin to boast of their superb marksmanship. Narve decided to test their skill by placing a 25-cent coin on the granary wall, with the promise that the Indian could keep the coin if he hit it dead on.

Comstock

A Determined Group of Immigrants

NEVER UNDERESTIMATE THE POWER of a Norwegian Lutheran woman. In 1872, Norwegian immigrants David C. and Mina Askegaard arrived with ten children at their 160-acre homestead in Cass County, Dakota Territory. Before long, David grew disenchanted with the difficulties of pioneer life, and decided they should return to Norway. However, his wife Mina was determined to make a new life in America, and refused to leave. David, certain that Mina would relent in the end, made preparations to leave, while his wise wife insisted that he sign the farm over to her, which he did before he left for Norway. After two years in Norway, David returned to America, where Mina refused to sign the farm back to her husband.

The Askegaards were one of many determined and stubborn families who settled near Comstock. In 1870, Swedish immigrants Bernhard and Kerstin Bernhardson and three children arrived on their claim with a covered wagon and 17 cents cash. They lived in their wagon until they completed a one-room log cabin with hay stuffed in the windows. By morning, the horse had eaten all the hay out of the windows, and the family scrambled to keep warm. As new Swedish settlers, including Hoken Hicks, his wife and ten children, arrived in the area, Bernhardsons provided shelter until they established their own homes. At one time four families lived with Bernhard and Kerstin, a hospitable woman who ruled with a simple decree. "There is room for all of us, but if there is any trouble, someone is going to move, and it will be the one that caused the trouble."

Norwegian immigrant Narve Roen took advantage of land given to Civil War veterans, and settled near Comstock after grasshoppers destroyed his crops in Audubon in 1872. One day a group of Indians, armed with bows and arrows, stopped at the Roen cabin to boast of their superb marksmanship. Narve decided to test their skill by placing a 25-cent coin on the granary wall, with the promise that the Indian could keep the coin if he hit it dead on. The Indian stepped a good distance from the wall, and hit the coin on the first try. A nickel and a dime yielded the same results.

When the Great Northern Railway laid track in 1890, settlement in Comstock began in earnest as farmers, who shipped their grain by boat on the Red River, could now transport by rail. In anticipation of the arrival of James Hill's railroad, David C. Askegaard's son, David Martin, moved his grain warehouse from the river to the Comstock siding, and secured his place in history as the founder and builder of Comstock. He built a large brick home and opened the Halland & Askegaard Store along with several other businesses. By 1918, David Martin increased his land holdings to 5,800 acres, well over the 3,000 acres needed to qualify as a bonanza farm. One example of his astute business acumen occurred when Mr. Askegaard bought 320 acres of land from August Hicks, seeded the entire acreage with flax, and paid for the property within a year thanks to a high yield and a high selling price.

Customers traveled from other towns to shop at the large and well-stocked Halland & Askegaard General Store. An experienced merchant, Sam Halland offered everything from dry goods to farm implements, and kept the doors open until 11:00 at night. The store also housed the post office, processed real estate loans, and provided passage for the White Star and American transportation lines. When the building was dismantled in 1969, the store went the way of the bonanza farm era.

Candy Ole

One of many colorful men who worked on the farm was Ole Uphaug, known as "Candy Ole," a boastful farmer who bought candy for the farm girls, and loved to stroll around town in fancy duds. One Fourth of July, while stepping off the train in his new suit and white vest, Ole slipped and fell in the ditch filled with silt mud to the delight of all. Another day while in a Comstock store, Ole boasted of his strength to Axel Rustad, a fellow farmer. Axel apparently had heard enough, picked Candy Ole up, and hung him on the harness pegs on the store wall until someone rescued him.

Comstock Today

The city's rich agricultural heritage continues today in Agriliance LLC, CW Valley Co-op, Comstock Farmers Co-op Elevator, and Dakota Ag Cooperative, all lined up around an active railroad terminal surrounded by massive storage bins. Other businesses include Askegaard Brothers Irrigation, Dean's Bulk Service, the post office, Community Center, Red River Repair, Comstock Lutheran Church, and Comstock and Holy Cross Farmers Mutual Fire Insurance Company. A park and baseball diamond surround the original Comstock School, now used for storage.

The first consolidated school in Clay County, Comstock School District #69 retains the grandeur and dignity of 1909, when Minnesota Governor Adolph Olson Eberhart gave the dedication address. A new high school addition in 1929 produced the first graduating class on May 28, 1930.

When Black Friday in 1929 closed the Comstock State Bank, the Comstock and Holy Cross Farmer's Mutual Fire Insurance Company moved into the bank until 1989, when they erected a new structure. Organized in 1896 to provide low cost insurance to area farmers, the oldest firm in Comstock remains a vital service.

People living in Comstock have a great sense of humor. In 1986, several families put together a parade for Syttende Mai, the Norwegian Independence Day. They built their own Hjemkomst Ship, created a Nor-Ski Team with Gerry Ishaug, Merle Kirkhorn and Karen Hendrickson all on the same skis, and placed King Myron and Queen Janice Taasaas in a manure spreader.

A band of robbers hitched a night train to Correll
in 1908. They proceeded to break into the Correll
bank, blowing the safe apart and sending the safe
door hurtling through the front of the building and
into the street.

TOP: BNSF train passing through Correll

Correll

Sports Shenanigans, Wild Weather, and a Train Robbery

THE CORRELL HIGH SCHOOL BASKETBALL TEAM made
history by defeating Appleton 26–23 for the 1936 District Championship, and still ended up losing the game. During half time, identical
twin forwards, Dale (No. 4) and Dean (No. 1) Knoll switched jerseys to
confuse the already confused Appleton guards. During the second half,
one of the Appleton players noticed that Dale Knoll's eyes watered. He
knew that Dean's eyes watered, not Dale's. Also, No. 4 scored most of
the points in the first half, while No. 1 scored the majority in the second
half. The Appleton team protested and the officials ruled that the game
would be replayed behind closed doors. Correll lost the title 29–11, but
remain hometown heroes. Correll never returned the original District 11

Championship trophy. Seventy-five years after the losing game, the loss
still stings. One of the surviving players, Donovan Doring, commented,
"This was a great disappointment to the team and the whole Correll
area. There was bad blood between Correll and Appleton for many
years. Each of the players on that team has an engraved souvenir trophy
to show to his children and grandchildren to prove that there was such a
game and that he indeed was a member of that team."

In 1879, public surveyor David N. Correll of St. Paul platted a new
village for the Hastings and Dakota Railroad Company. Named in his
honor and incorporated as a city in 1881, bad weather and isolation led
to a slow and shaky beginning for this railroad town. For a number of
years, the only residents of Correll were the employees of the railroad,

who lived in the depot. The older residents tell incredible stories, like the night that the wife of a railroad employee died while living in the depot. Her body was left in the freight house for a week until help arrived to remove the remains. Another story is that during the winter of 1881, the snow was so deep that while crossing the tracks through town, a horse and wagon drove right over a boxcar. One extremely long winter left the citizens of Correll with no communication with the outside world for five months. Apparently, the horrible weather forced the Thomas F. Koch Land Company to sell the townsite to Charles Woods, who saw a future in grain, and developed the Farmer's Elevator in 1893.

As a railroad town, Correll has seen its share of train accidents. Over the years, there have been three recorded train accidents in Correll since 1902, when two trains collided, killing the engineer and brakeman. In 1950, several feet of track were demolished when a train left the tracks, but luckily, no one was hurt. And in 1959, derailed rail cars went right through the depot and demolished the entire building. Some trains hauled more than grain; a band of robbers hitched a night train to Correll in 1908. They proceeded to break into the Correll bank, blowing the safe apart and sending the safe door hurtling through the front of the building and into the street. The thieves were never found, and, following the crime, a burglar alarm and fireproof safe were installed.

When a new brick school opened in 1914, students were transported by five horse-drawn vehicles complete with foot warmers and wool blankets. The high school continued to serve area students until consolidation with Appleton in 1943, and the grade school remained open until 1977.

A Centennial Celebration with a Beard-judging Contest

Correll celebrated the state centennial June 14, 1958, with a home parade and a program in the school auditorium. Once again, in 1981, Correll pulled out all the stops and celebrated their city centennial July 17–19 with a Kittenball (softball) Tournament, a beard-judging contest,

a tug-of-war and a talent show. Correll's oldest resident, 93-year-old John Grutzmaker, led the parade as Grand Marshall. Mayor George Korstjens presented the key to the city to Eugene L. Correll, grandson of David Correll, the founder of the city.

Built with money borrowed from the Congregational Church Building Society in New York City, the 8-member United Methodist Church maintains the original structure from 1897.

About twelve miles north of Correll, Artichoke Baptist Church is one of the oldest churches organized in Big Stone County and the second Norwegian Baptist church in Minnesota. The first pastor, Hans Hanson (he changed his last name to Gaard), sailed from Tromsø, Norway, in 1864 directly to Quebec, Canada, one of only two ships to ever sail this direct route. Passengers brought their own food, but ran out of provisions as terrific storms and winds stretched the journey to over nine weeks. When the immigrants weren't longing for food from the wealthier passengers, they argued religion with the Mormons. After boarding a steamer in Lacrosse, Wisconsin, they ran aground on a sand bar on the Mississippi River. While the crew attempted to dislodge the boat, Gaard's brother Jens decided to swim, was caught in a treacherous current, and was swept away. He was never seen again. Built in 1889, the church celebrated its centennial in 1989.

Correll Today

Once a boom town on the western plains of Minnesota, Correll now maintains the Stock Service Station, a miniature fleet store, which sells and delivers bagged animal feed for cows, horses and dogs. The hub of Correll, local farmers pack the place on Saturday morning to shop, drink coffee and swap stories. The town is also home to the fire and town hall, and Dick Wiese Building and Ronglien Excavating.

The Correll post office is one of the smallest in Minnesota and has only one active mailbox in town. The lobby hours are 9:00–11:18 each morning.

Early in its history, the flooded streets in Danvers were impassable. A picture from the turn of the century shows Main Street in Danvers covered with water, and a boat tied to the sidewalk.

TOP: Catholic Church of the Visitation

Danvers

With Main Street Underwater, A Boat is Better than a Horse

IN 1876, BISHOP JOHN IRELAND OF ST. PAUL secured 117,000 acres of land in Swift County from the St. Paul & Pacific Railroad to establish the Catholic Bureau of Colonization, an organization for Catholic settlement in western Minnesota. The Bureau assisted Catholics from Canada, the British Isles and Europe to escape famine and persecution by providing homesteading land in railroad towns in Swift County. The first resident priest, Father Anatole Oster, served the surrounding communities, including Danvers, platted in 1892 after the construction of the Great Northern Railway from Benson to Appleton. An influx of German and Irish settlers to Danvers opened their own church, Catholic Church of the Visitation, until a grass fire on April 7,

1931, completely destroyed the wood-frame structure. Undaunted, on Christmas Eve of that year, the first mass was celebrated in a beautiful new brick and stone church, built for a cost of $30,000.

Perhaps named by a homesick railroad worker, Danvers bears the name of villages in Massachusetts and Illinois. The railroad quickly established a depot, the Central House Hotel, and a post office in 1892 with Edmund Juvet, postmaster. Four elevators, including the Northwestern Elevator Company, lined the railroad tracks to ship wheat crops to St. Paul. Meanwhile, the flooded streets in Danvers were impassable due to a lack of trees, which were needed to absorb water from the black prairie soil. A picture from the turn of the century shows Main Street in Danvers covered with water, and a boat tied to the sidewalk. The railroad stepped up to offer free transportation from St. Paul for saplings, and empty "deadhead" freight cars loaded with sand and gravel dropped the loads free of charge at depots along the line.

The first businessman in Danvers, Andrew H. Mattheisen, opened a 12-by-16-foot general store, and by 1900 Danvers boasted twenty business interests, including Joe Halvorsen's blacksmith shop, the Rykken and Tiegen general store, and Edmund Juvet's general and furniture store. Charles Dolan, the town butcher and hotel operator, ran the West Hotel for the Irish Catholics, while the East Hotel housed the Lutherans. The city voted to incorporate January 19, 1900, and had a population of 122. Fire reduced an entire city block of wooden buildings to ashes in October 1931, and only the State Bank of Danvers, which was made of brick, survived. Largely because of the Depression of the 1930s, merchants who had lost their businesses were unable to recover.

A remodeled village hall served as a one-room school until 1920, when a new brick building went up on 12 lots purchased from Thomas H. Connelly for $1,200. Danvers School District 84 celebrated its Centennial on May 6, 1949, with a program of speeches by the pupils, early teachers Mrs. Morris Coy and Mrs. C. E. Carruth, and school board member C. J. Ryken. Seventy pupils attended District 84 in 1948–1949. The school consolidated with Benson in 1970, and the building was razed in 1983.

The first names may change but the last name stays the same at the State Bank of Danvers, which has been run by the Connelly family since 1904. Initially owned by the DePue brothers of Olivia, Minnesota, farmer Thomas H. Connelly sold his wheat farm in 1902 and assumed management of the bank on January 1, 1904. Bank President Connelly created a multi-generational family business that thrives today. By 1908, total bank deposits topped $40,000, and a new two-story building replaced the former structure. The second floor of the bank housed the Danvers Rural Telephone Company until 1957, when the company dissolved. An avid automobile enthusiast and owner of one of the first cars in Swift County, Thomas Connelly and his wife traveled with friends to both coasts by car. After Mr. Connelly's death while cleaning city hall following a tornado in 1928, his son, Daniel, successfully guided the bank through the "bank holiday" and the Great Depression in the early 30s. By 1957, the bank exceeded $1,500,000 in deposits, and erected a one-story brick building. After Daniel Connelly's death in 1960, his son, Thomas C. Connelly, assumed the role of CEO until his son John Connelly took over leadership of the facility. The bank built an impressive building in 1979, which dominates Main Street.

A Taste of Continental Architecture

The Catholic Church of the Visitation, a gem set on eight lush acres, was erected in 1931 to replace the former wood church, destroyed in a fire. Designed by architect Glynne Shifflet, who studied in France and admired country churches, it was built of stone in French Normandy style, with a clay tile roof and a copper steeple. The architect found an ally in Father Joseph O'Neil, the priest at Danvers who had also traveled in France. Twenty years ago, the parishioners could not afford to replace the tile roof, and had to settle for a shingle roof. The church now holds mass one weekday and is used for weddings and funerals.

Danvers Today

Today, the bank anchors this well-kept community along with the post office, Ted & Bob's Locker Plant, the municipal liquor store, and Ascheman Oil, Gas & Groceries. Cummerford Construction & Gravel, Syngenta Seeds, and State Bank of Danvers employ most of the residents. A city park, built with donations from the community, sits across from City Hall.

Tucked at the end of Main Street, Ted and Bob's Locker sells freshly cut meat. At my request, employee Chuck O'Malley sliced up a pound of the best bacon and summer sausage in the state.

TOP: Former First Presbyterian Church

Population: 70   **Incorporated:** 1902

INSETS L to R: Former Delhi State Bank • Meadowland Farmers
Co-op • remaining insets from former Lutheran church

In early Delhi, folks made their home wherever they could. Residents C. O. Borg and A. H. Anderson lived above their store, H. J. Heath, the grain buyer, lived in a farmhouse, depot agent and postmaster Rodman Hurlbut lived in the depot.

Delhi

A Hardy Group Surviving However (and Wherever) They Could

IN SEPTEMBER, 1892, DELHI CITIZEN Mrs. S. M. Atkinson hopped on her John Deere Moline Special bicycle and pedaled six miles to Redwood Falls. Four years later, the fearless woman pedaled eighty-eight miles to visit the closing of the Great Cycle Show in Minneapolis. No one in Delhi, much less the county, could have predicted the rapid rise of the automobile at the beginning of the twentieth century. When Fred J. Starr exchanged his E-M-F Studebaker for a four-door Everitt, he boasted that no one could catch him in his 30-horsepower auto on a road trip to Minneapolis. By 1913, 5 out of the 491 cars registered in the county were in Delhi.

Long before Mrs. Atkinson's bicycle trip, the first settler in Delhi, Carl Anton Simondet, fled the Dakota War in New Ulm in 1862, and joined the Mounted Rangers to take part in various Dakota Territory battles. Just north of Pettibone, North Dakota, Simondet's name is etched on a historical marker on the Sibley Trail. Three years later, the immigrant from Wurtemburg, Germany, settled permanently in Delhi to raise his two sons and three daughters. Only the toughest pioneers stayed to weather the impossible climate in Redwood County. By the time he died in 1879, Mr. Simondet had experienced prairie fires, the grasshopper plague of 1873–1877, and the horrific blizzard of 1873. A hardy group of Scots also toughed it out on their farms, pushing the population to 186 by 1880.

The arrival of the Pacific Railroad in 1884 led to the creation of a depot, a grain elevator, a general store, Ole Knutson's blacksmith shop, and a post office to serve the thirty adventuresome souls clustered around the railroad in a town with limited housing options. Residents C. O. Borg and A. H. Anderson lived above their store, H. J. Heath, the grain buyer, lived in a farmhouse, depot agent and postmaster Rodman Hurlbut lived in the depot, and John McGuire, the section boss, hung his hat in the section house. A native of Delhi, Ohio, Alfred M. Cook opened the Delhi Roller Mills in 1870 and named the city after his hometown. When the mill was destroyed by arson in 1896, the uninsured building was not replaced. A brick school opened in 1891 with 97 pupils, burned down in 1916, and was rebuilt the following year. Severely damaged by a tornado in 1948, the school was completely destroyed by another tornado in 1992. The elementary school closed in 1971 with 35 students.

A talented group of musicians, the Delhi Coronet Band played at events all over the county, including the Republican Rally in Redwood Falls in 1892, and the Fourth of July celebration in Renville. Led by band president Henry Engeman, the band initiated a drive to build a village hall for performances. Community support for the project solidified when the musicians arrived in a new bandwagon drawn by six horses to play for the school picnic in Anton Merten's grove. On June 11, 1886, the band played to a full house in the new Cornet Band Hall, a 25-by-64-foot building with a stone foundation. In 1902, the city voted to incorporate in the historic hall.

On April 24, 1902, the Delhi Creamery opened, at a cost of $2,900, with great pomp and ceremony. The Redwood County Dairy Association officials welcomed creamery No. 18 by holding a dairy meeting in the Coronet Band Hall. Area farmers delivering milk that day (over 6,000 pounds) were awarded with an outstanding dinner, served by the women of Delhi. Only three months later, the creamery shipped 2,400 pounds of butter to New York, and the value of the creamery was assessed at $42,657. When the United States government developed the Liberty Bond campaign in 1917 to raise money for the war effort, Delhi ranked first in the county by purchasing $800 more than their $12,000 bond quota. Locals also collected nut shells to use for carbon in gas masks, knit hats for the soldiers, and supported the Fatherless Children of France Fund.

The 1910 Delhi State Bank served as the post office until 1977, and is now a religious icon, with a painting of Our Lady of Guadalupe and a lighted cross adorning the building.

A Centennial Celebration

Delhi hosted a centennial party June 23 & 24, 1984, with over 1,000 visitors. Celebrants were treated to cabaret players, a pork chop supper, street dance, and a muzzleloader shooting exhibition. The festivities ended with an ice cream social.

Delhi Today

Delhi is now home to the Meadowlands Farmer's Co-op and the Town Hall, which replaced the Cornet Band Hall. On an early October afternoon, a continuous stream of grain trucks rolls through Delhi, all delivering the fall harvest to the Meadowlands Farmer's Co-op.

The First Presbyterian Church was erected in 1886 by twenty-five Scottish immigrants. In 1957, the last original member, Annie Cummings, died at 99 years old. The church broke with tradition in 1981, when Mrs. Harold Sundquist became the first female elder. Although closed, the church and grounds are lovingly cared for with freshly mown grass and new lilac bushes.

The First Evangelical Lutheran Church closed January 1975 after serving the community for 75 years. A confirmation service on June 8, 1975, was the last event held at the church.

Delhi had both a Presbyterian Church for the Scottish inhabitants and a Norwegian Lutheran Church for the Scandinavian population. In the early Norwegian church, it was traditional for the men to sit on one side of the church and the women on the other. The story is told of a couple who attended the church and sat together, unaware that this was forbidden. A bolt of lightning did not descend to strike the church, and from then on parishioners sat together.

TOP: Faith Lutheran Church, northwest of Denham

Population: 35 **Incorporated:** 1939

INSETS L to R: Denham Run Bar • Old creamery • Denham Bar • City Park

On June 24, 1912, Denham celebrated its 25th anniversary with a picnic and parade down Main Street. Bernard Johnson's father carried a one-hundred pound sack of flour, an impressive sight for the spectators who didn't know the sack contained sawdust.

Denham

Halley's Comet, Mark Twain and Denham

THE APPEARANCE OF HALLEY'S COMET in 1910 created great excitement in Denham and all over the country. Many people were led to believe that the comet signaled the end of the world, and they were pleasantly surprised when life continued as before. Only one famous American predicted his demise. Author Mark Twain, born in 1835 during the appearance of Halley's Comet, stated that he would die when the comet appeared again in 1910. On April 20, 1910, the comet reached the point closest to the sun. Twain died the next day.

Alas, the world didn't end, and a couple years later, on June 24, 1912, Denham celebrated its 25th anniversary with a picnic and parade down Main Street. The parade highlighted pioneer life: there was a lumber

wagon driven by oxen, and O. Bernard Johnson's father carried a one-hundred pound sack of flour, an impressive sight for the spectators who didn't know the sack contained sawdust. Other marchers carried guns, tools and utensils used by the early homesteaders. Ironically, the highlight of the parade and crown jewel of progress, a new roadster owned by banker Fred Olson, wouldn't start that day and missed the parade.

When farmer Frank Lind sold his land to the Soo Line in 1908, the railroad platted the townsite, and sold lots for the city of Denham. Soon after the founding of the city, George Cunningham opened a general store with the post office located in the store. F. Egnar Anderson assumed the position of Postmaster and later purchased the store from Cunningham. Joseph Suk moved Suk's Store and Butcher Shop from

Sturgeon Lake to Denham, and reportedly made "sausage to die for." He added a saloon next door, with the top floor hosting many community gatherings and dances. Across from the Suk store, The Denham Farmers Cooperative constructed a building, and the Herberg Brothers opened a second saloon for the growing community. Adolph Shoberg put up a hotel, and the Farmers State Bank organized with Fred Olson as cashier. Nearly all the buildings were destroyed by fire, a typical occurrence in rural cities lacking a fire department.

Although the passenger traffic from trains was never substantial, the freight traffic was—vast quantities of wheat were hauled from the Dakotas and western Minnesota to Duluth. Delighted to have transportation for their cream, dairy farmers used the railroad to ship cream to Moose Lake or Duluth at a cost of fifteen cents for a five-gallon can of cream. But wood was by far the main commodity shipped from Denham, where stacked piles of cordwood covered forty acres.

Relying on customs from the old country, Denham School District 19 moved in 1903 to a lot between the Swede Park and Swedish Methodist Churches, in order to be in the center of the community. This arrangement was typical in Scandinavian countries, where outlying farms surrounded the school and churches. When the school was leveled by fire in 1958, the little two-room building was not replaced. Following incorporation on February 28, 1939, the city expanded with a modern creamery built by Land O' Lakes. The Farmer's Co-operative Telephone Company had a single wire strand, with up to twenty members on one party line. Located in Adolph and Annette Shoberg's home, the switchboard allowed each member a designated ring. One long ring signaled the operator, and six successive rings meant an emergency.

A Town That Loved to Build Churches

Denham loved to build churches. Built in 1894, the Swedish Methodist Episcopal Church was destroyed by lightning in 1957. One month after the Methodists opened their doors, another group of Swedes founded Swede Park Lutheran Church, a building of hand-hewn logs. Not to be outdone, the Norwegians completed the Nordlund Evangelical Lutheran Church in 1903. But the Swedish immigrants were unstoppable, and erected the Oak Hill Lutheran Church in 1910, the building financed primarily by the Ladies Aid. A typical Sunday afternoon found the neighbors gathered around the piano with an accordion and harmonica player, harmonizing on favorite songs. The Indian songs "Hiawatha" and "Red Wing" were frequent requests, as well as the old standbys "Silver Bell," "Let Me Call You Sweetheart," "In the Shadow of the Pines," and "Arrah Wanna." By the 1940s Oak Hill, Swede Park, and Nordlund Church had consolidated into a new church, Faith Lutheran, which remains in the township today.

Denham Today

Once an important railroad town and agricultural center, today Denham is home to the Denham Town Hall, Birch Creek Township Hall, Mike's Diesel, and two bars: Denham Run Bar & Grill, and Denham Bar, which is painted bright orange. The old creamery co-op building, with its original asphalt siding, serves as the Town Hall, where the council meets every other month. Mayor Lee Anderson and his wife, city clerk Karen Anderson, also host city council meetings in their home.

Denham is close to some exciting outdoors activities; the Soo Line Trail, a state trail for snowmobiles and ATVs, runs through Denham on the way from Genola to Lake Superior. On a typical March Day, a line of snowmobiles can be seen outside the Denham Bar & Grill.

Denham is also home to something of an oddity: the smallest city park in the state. It features one picnic table, a flagpole, and a city announcements sign.

Denham was home to a livestock loading yard, which held cattle for shipping, and at one time, a carload of broncos for sale at auction. However, the horses proved to be wild and difficult to break for farm use, so that ended bronco sales.

TOP: Highway 75 north

Built in 1899, the Nordic Korner, located on the corner of Highways 75 and 11, served as a restaurant and bar. Originally Martin Hennum's general store, Martin sold everything from furniture to coffins.

Donaldson

Bonanza Farming, A Civil War Captain and a Company Town

WHEN THE GREAT NORTHERN RAILWAY arrived in 1878, Captain Hugh W. Donaldson followed the tracks from the East Coast to Donaldson. Donaldson had served as an officer in the Civil War, and he continued to exude power after the war, as he was the manager of the Kennedy Land Company, an adjoining farm of several thousand acres. He also had connections with James Hill's farming interests in Northcote. If you wanted to buy a farm or yoke of oxen, needed a job, or wished to marry, you were told to "see the Captain." One year later, Edward Davis and family arrived, opened the first general store with a post office, and named the new settlement Davis. The railroad took three years to build a depot in 1881, and during this interval, Postmaster Davis unhappily stood outside in the cold waiting for the mail to arrive by rail.

Donaldson was known as a "company town," a town founded to serve as a trading center for the bonanza farms, large-scale farms that stretched over many acres. When Martin Hennum arrived in 1890, the Ryan Company owned all the land on the north side of the village, and Ed Davis held most of the lots on the south side. Mr. Hennum tried without success to purchase a lot from both, but did manage to buy a lot from a Minneapolis man, J. A. Phillips, on which to build his blacksmith shop. On November 20, 1903, the city voted to incorporate. After a heated discussion, the voters deferred to Captain Donaldson's commanding personality and gave the village his name. Edward Davis

38

had to settle for Davis Township, and the section line between the Donaldson and Davis land became the main street of Donaldson. Later, as the large bonanza farms divided, farmers had the opportunity to purchase small tracts of land, and the village began to prosper.

Following incorporation, the city boasted a full main street. In addition to his blacksmith business, Martin Hennum established a general store in 1899, which remained in business as a restaurant until 2001. A large hotel built by Martin Borgeson served as a well known stopping place for travelers heading to northeastern Minnesota. In 1904, the State Bank of Donaldson opened to serve the growing population, just two years before pioneer Andrew Blomsness founded Blomsness Telephone Company. On August 16, 1907, a weekly newspaper, *the Donaldson Record*, advertised for the Stockholm Saloon, F.C. Taft Company, Martin Lund General Store, Donaldson Elevator, and the St. Hilaire Lumber Company. Surrounding farms, offered for sale by Johnson Land & Loan Company, sold for $32 to $50 per acre including all buildings on the land. A four-room brick schoolhouse, a church, two restaurants, and four grain elevators symbolized the booming economy. Farmers made a tidy profit on bountiful grain harvests, and were pleased to find they could also raise 65 bushels of yellow dent corn per acre. The construction of new homes, including one farmer's $4,500 modern home, marked the increasing wealth in the area.

A General Store, Then a Roller Rink

Built in 1899, the Nordic Korner, located on the corner of Highways 75 and 11, served as a restaurant and bar before its demolition in October, 2005. Originally Martin Hennum's general store, Martin sold everything from furniture to coffins. In later years, Leonard Diamond opened a rollerskating rink and dance hall, where Lawrence Welk and Whoopee John played to standing-room-only crowds. Shortly after purchasing the business in 1969, the final owners of the business, Arlo and

Ann Davis, discovered that the coolers were not working. They tore off the insulation, and found that the coolers were made from shower stalls, a nod to earlier days when folks came to town to pay 25 cents for a shower and shave. When Arlo died in 1997, and Ann in 1999, their children could not afford the expense of updating the building to modern standards, and sold the building to MnDOT, who demolished the structure for safety reasons.

In the 1960s, the city elected Mrs. Elphie Bogestad as mayor, the first female mayor in Kittson County. She served four terms (eight years) in office.

Donaldson Today

Today, Donaldson is still surrounded by rich Red River Valley farmland. Multiple storage bins filled with wheat, soybeans and corn line the tracks as the Burlington Northern-Santa Fe train follows Highway 75 through Donaldson to Winnipeg, Manitoba. The former Minn-Dak Growers Elevator is now privately owned by Harrison Peterson, and a city park is nestled in a large grove of trees next to St. Olaf Lutheran Church. Donaldson is also home to one of Minnesota's smallest post offices, where Postmaster Doretta Olson shares a building with Kittson-Marshall Rural Water, the social hub of the community, which offers coffee and doughnuts. The steady sound of the trains signals the survival of Donaldson, once the stronghold of bonanza farming in northern Minnesota.

Highway 75 has also been designated as King of Trails Scenic Byway, the newest of Minnesota's 22 State Scenic Byways. The name is derived from a trail that passes through Donaldson that was previously used by Native Americans and early settlers. In its entirety, Highway 75 stretches from Winnipeg to Galveston, Texas.

Only the sound of mourning doves, prairie chickens, and the train passing through the tiny city breaks the peaceful prairie quiet. Doretta Olson commented on the busy train schedule through Donaldson, "The train runs through all hours of the day and night. One night the train came through early in the morning and the engineer blew the horn, and scared the hey out of me."

TOP: Springtime city view

Doran resident John Oksness pioneered the use of a one-man self-propelled combine, and helped organize the "Massey-Harris Self-Propelled Harvest Brigade," which harvested 25 million bushels of grain during World War II.

Doran

An Industrial Titan, Progress and Romance in the Air

IT PAYS TO BE A FRIEND OF JAMES J. HILL, owner of the Great Northern Railway. The city of Doran was named in honor of Mr. Hill's close friend, Senator Michael Doran from St. Paul. Born in County Meath, Ireland, Senator Doran was elected state senator in 1870 from Le Sueur County, and held the position as chairman of the National Democratic Committee from 1888 until 1896.

Fellow Irishmen J. H. Fitzgerald and E. J. Kelley settled in the area in 1872 and immediately kickstarted the Doran business community. Mr. Fitzgerald opened an elevator and a warehouse while Mr. Kelley bought a farm and stocked it with staple groceries. The city incorporated in 1907, and by 1929 the city boasted the R. O. Harrison Store, Nortz's Lumberyard, Bernard Holmen's Barber Shop and Ice Cream Parlor, the Ed Aasness Garage, a bank, two elevators, the depot, a Standard Oil Station, and Peter Thorsten's Restaurant. Under the direction of M. S. Smith, the Kent-Doran Grain Company began that same year and expanded to several elevators in the area. The post office, established in 1892 for a population of 200, has moved around the community, operating out of homes, grocery stores, the liquor store, and the old bank. (Now the citizens receive their mail from nearby Campbell.)

Another adventurous Irishman, J. J. Brady from Wisconsin, headed north to work in the wheat fields near Fargo and ended up in Doran at the turn of the century. The handsome, lonely bachelor was not lonely for long. A Norwegian girl, Clara Johnson, who owned a millinery shop in her father's hardware store, fell in love with the Irishman, and they married in 1906. Frugal to a fault, Mr. Brady managed the Doran Farmer's Cooperative Elevator Company for ten years, until he opened his own elevator, the J. J. Elevator Company. In addition to the elevator, the conglomerate included a feed mill and a coal sales division. Fortunately, Mr. Brady had four sons, John, Russell, Merton and William, all of whom were essential to the success of the enterprise. Shortly after Mr. Brady sold the business, the elevator burned to the ground.

Romance was definitely in the air. Rueben Harrison, the owner of the R. O. Harrison Store, was also clerk of the school board. One of the teachers, Esther Johnson, assumed the position of school principal when former principal Wallace Rosel left to serve in World War I. The clerk and the new principal fell in love, marrying at last in 1929 in Alexandria, Minnesota. One of their three daughters, Isabel, named her last son Hans Doran to honor the wonderful town of her childhood. But romance was not the only pastime in Doran. Families entertained in their homes, while plays, musicals and dances provided entertainment in the old town hall. First Presbyterian Church and Vukku Lutheran and Stiklestad Lutheran Churches, just east of town, hosted marvelous lutefisk dinners.

Meanwhile in 1941, the elevator reorganized as the Kent-Doran Grain Company with John Oksness managing the Massey-Harris implement business. At the onset of World War II, thousands of farmers enlisted in the armed forces, and millions of people faced potential starvation, when existing machinery began to wear out. The leaders at Massey-Harris promised a new No. 21 one-man self-propelled combine that would cut grain more efficiently and with less fuel. Oksness pioneered the use of the new combine for harvesting grain, and helped organize the "Massey-Harris Self-Propelled Harvest Brigade" in Wilkin County during World War II. The brigade swept the country, harvesting 25 million bushels of grain.

Saint Olaf, a Medieval Battle, and a Church With Foreign Ties

Built in 1898 by Norwegian immigrants, Stiklestad United Lutheran Church joined the National Register of Historic Places in 1980. Norwegian architect Sam Christenson designed the frame church in the Late Gothic Revival style complete with a bell tower. Though not in use today, the church was the focal point for Norwegian Lutherans who settled around Doran. The church is named after the Battle of Stiklestad in 1030, one of the most famous battles in Norwegian history. On that day, King Olav Haraldsson lost his life fighting to regain his throne and to convert Norway to Christianity. His body was secretly buried near the Nidelva River south of Trondheim. A year later, his body was exhumed with the claim that the body remained unchanged, and that former king's nails and hair had grown. The body was then moved to St. Klement's Church in Trondheim, where he was christened St. Olaf for his efforts to Christianize the country. The Stiklestad Church was built on top of the stone in the Verdahl valley where he died, and that stone still rests on the altar of that church in Norway. But the Norwegians had bigger plans for St. Olaf's body. One hundred years later, the Nidaros Cathedral in Trondheim claimed it and enshrined him in a silver reliquary behind the altar. But this was not his final move. In the sixteenth century, St. Olaf's body was moved from the reliquary, which the Dano-Norwegian king ordered to be melted down for coinage. His remains are reburied somewhere in the church, but no one knows exactly where.

Doran Today

Doran is just a mile off Highway 75 and is near the historic King of Trails, which was traveled by Native Americans and oxcarts until the automobile gained popularity. Doran is also only a few miles from Breckenridge, where visitors can see the headwaters of the Red River of the North, a 550-mile river famous as the longest north-flowing river in North America.

In 1970, the Doran Presbyterian Church joined forces with the Campbell and Tintah Congregational Churches to form the United Community Parish. The church originated in 1909 when a circuit preacher conducted monthly services in German in the Woodman Hall in northeast Doran. Two years later, the congregation purchased the former Doran School and remodeled the interior for the present church.

Mother Nature has not been kind to Dovray. Our
Savior's Lutheran Church, initially called Dovray
Norwegian Lutheran Church, opened their doors in
1900, only to lose the building to a tornado eight
years later.

TOP: "Welcome to Dovray"

Dovray

Lunch is at Noon and Everyone in Town is Invited

NO ONE IN DOVRAY EVER GOES WITHOUT A NOON MEAL.
Staffed by volunteer cooks, the Norwegian Community Center and Café
prepares a delicious meal for 20–35 people each day, an idea conceived
in 1993 by the Booster Club. Completely on the honor system, a money
jar on the counter suggests a $5 donation, but no one is turned away.
The freezer is stocked with hot dogs, should the food, God forbid, run
out. Diners donate fresh garden produce to supplement future meals
and the local postmaster stops in to wash dishes over the lunch hour.
The center also hosts meetings for the township hall, the city council,
the local 4-H Club and the Booster Club.

When Nels Taarud emigrated from Norway in 1872, he named the
town after his ancestral home in Dovre, Norway, and for Dovrefjell,
a mountain range nearby. Nels arrived with a handful of fellow
immigrants and settled one mile northwest of the present Dovray. The
arrival of the Chicago Northwestern Omaha Railway in 1899 from
Bingham Lake to Dovray convinced the settlers to move Old Dovray
to its present site. The sale of lots by the Interstate Land Company in
1904 opened with devotions by a Methodist pastor. That day, two lots
were donated for a Methodist church, which was never built in Dovray.
The city waited twenty years to incorporate in 1924, when the desire for
electric lights made incorporation necessary.

In 1908, the railroad depot opened to accommodate the freight
and passenger trains that navigated through Dovray twice a day for

many years. Often the trains would be trapped for days in massive snow drifts until the rotary plow rescued the cars. Children eagerly anticipated the arrival of the rotary plow, a fascinating machine that helped extricate the train from deep winter snow.

A fire of unknown origin in 1916 almost destroyed the entire main street, consuming the Swoffer Hardware Store and the Johnson Mercantile Company, which housed the post office. Three grain elevators, constructed in 1904, were also destroyed by fire. Only one was rebuilt and remains viable in the city. The lumberyard closed in 1935, and the building was converted to an Allis Chalmers and Minneapolis Moline implement business. After the Depression closed the town's bank in 1937, Our Savior's Ladies Aid bought the building for church use, until their new church opened in 1953. Now the old bank serves another purpose as the Log Cabin Restaurant. Dovray Co-op Creamery opened in December, 1923, and developed into Dovray's largest business enterprise.

In spite of the hardships of pioneer life, the good people of Dovray continued to socialize and dancing was especially popular. The dancing style changed somewhat in 1914. "No more weird slides and dips will be tolerated," announced those in charge of the social mores. Distance between partners was encouraged and couples determined to dance cheek-to-cheek were called "neckers." The tango was introduced as a series of walks and turns, with dangerous speeds and whirls eliminated. When the Charleston and the shimmy arrived in the roaring twenties, women put on their flappers, spit curls, and bow lips to shake a leg with the young men with the patent leather hair.

Mother Nature has not been kind to Dovray. Our Savior's Lutheran Church, initially called Dovray Norwegian Lutheran Church, opened their doors in 1900, only to lose the building to a tornado eight years later. Amazingly, the rebuilt church was hit by lightning and burned to the ground in 1931. A testament to their faith, a third church was erected in 1952, and so far, so good. The German Lutheran Church flourished for many years, until membership dwindled and the church closed.

A Center of the Community and Quilting

After 110 years, Our Savior's Lutheran Church has remained a constant force in the community in spite of the ravages of nature. Several women, including Helen Amundson, meet monthly for a full day of quilting, Bible study and singing. Their theme song, "Bind Us Together Lord," testifies to the faithfulness of the centennial congregation.

Dovray's fire department is exceptionally well equipped. Located next to the downtown café in the former American Legion building, some of the extra equipment is stored with local farmers. A huge crowd shows up to the support the hometown heroes at the firemen's annual pancake dinner.

Dovray Today

Neat and clean identical white frame buildings, similar to the type of buildings found in Norway, line Woodman Avenue. Today Dovray revolves around the grain elevator, Dovray Community Center and Café, Log Cabin Restaurant, the Fire Department, and Our Savior's Lutheran Church. Santa Claus Day, an annual event held in the café, brings out the entire city for bags of candy with an apple on top, coffee, cider, and homemade doughnuts.

An active Dovray American Legion Post 632 and Auxiliary meet monthly in the café. Their Memorial Day service at the church, followed by decoration of the cemeteries and a potluck dinner, are an annual tradition. The Log Cabin Restaurant, formerly the Dovray Manor, recently opened with fresh décor and a new menu.

A home-cooked, wholesome meal is guaranteed at noon at the community café, a true testament to community spirit in rural America. The cooks vary, depending on who signed on for duty, but all are excellent chefs.

Dundee's two-story white frame school opened in
1901. An 8th grade teacher set up a boxing ring
in the basement for noon recreation, where Gleva
Uhlkin, known as "Tomboy Gleva," took on the boys.

TOP: Brenda's Gas and Grocery

Dundee

A Full-Service Station

THE FULL-SERVICE GAS STATION is rarely found in Minnesota's smallest cities, but Dundee has that rare commodity: Brenda's Gas & Grocery, home to gas, groceries, gifts, and live bait, open from 7 to 7, seven days a week. This former railroad city has many other gems, too, if you just know where to look.

Even though Dundee would be just a mile down the road from Kinbrae, the St. Paul and Sioux City Railway decided to compete with the Chicago, Milwaukee and St. Paul Railway, and platted another townsite in 1879. Then the company built a branch line along Dundee, and hired Mr. G. Foils as depot agent and postmaster. Initially named Warren, in honor of Joseph Warren, who died in the battle of Bunker

Hill, the name changed to Dundee when the post office opened at the end of the year. F. D. Lindquist and H. A. Scherlie opened the first general store in 1880, but real growth did not happen until the country recovered from the Panic of 1893. When the census reached 187, the city incorporated in 1898 with Mr. Lindquist as president.

By 1900, Dundee's population reached 217, and business boomed. Following a trip to Joe Suding's Barber Shop for a shave and haircut, residents headed to Ernest Cord's Photography Studio, where he recorded their lives from childhood to marriage. A telephone prop in each picture symbolized his trademark. The chicken king of Nobles County, Atwood Poultry featured seventy varieties of chicken, which Mr. Atwood proudly sold to poultry breeders in North America. When H. A. Scherlie put up a "milk fence," with hooks to hang buckets of milk, residents picked up milk for five cents a quart. In 1909, Henry and Haken Johnson organized the Dundee Mercantile Company, which evolved into the Dundee Co-op, the longest running retail cooperative in southwestern Minnesota. Under the management of R. F. Nelson, the store sold general merchandise, along with farm fresh eggs, cream and wool from local farmers. Each year, the co-op hosted an anniversary party that was considered the social event of the season. In February 1969, the Co-op celebrated its 60th anniversary, but finally closed the doors in 1982. After delivering grain to Farmer's Elevator and Hubbard & Palmer's Elevator, farmers left their horses at the livery stable, and hustled to the Dundee House Hotel for Minnie Schmidt's delicious homemade meals and pie.

Shortly after arriving in 1885, Swedish pioneers organized the Swedish Evangelical Lutheran Lund Church, now called First Lutheran Church. When bids for a new church built in 1942 came in too high, the council instituted "God's Acre," and each farmer donated one acre of crop, or the equivalent cash. The fund drive succeeded, and the congregation celebrated their centennial in 2010. In 1901, F. D. Lindquist donated land for St. Mary's Catholic Church, built for the princely sum of $3,500. A beautiful rectory followed in 1918, and is now the home of Bud and Clara Henkle. Due to a shortage of priests, Bishop John Vlazny celebrated a farewell mass on June 17, 1990, marking the tearful closure of the 89-year-old church.

A two-story white frame school, the pride of the community, opened in 1901. Children sent their Palmer method writing books to the county fair to be judged, learned geography from the pull-down globe that dangled from the ceiling, and participated in "recitation" on a daily basis. An 8th grade teacher set up a boxing ring in the basement for noon recreation, where Gleva Uhlkin, known as "Tomboy Gleva," took on the boys.

When the local lodge of the Independent Order of Odd Fellows fell on hard times during the Depression, member Casper Hultquist loaned the club $600 to pay the taxes, with the hall as security, and ended up owning the building. An earlier fall from a telephone pole had landed Casper in a wheelchair, but this did not stop him from opening the hall. Later on, his son and daughter-in-law revamped the hall, ordered 100 pairs of clamp-on skates and opened the Dundee Roller Rink, where you could rent skates for a quarter.

The Teacher of the Year

Minnesota Teacher of the Year in 1977, Ray C. "Spanky" Olson credits growing up in Dundee with his philosophy of teaching: "In Dundee you can't be anonymous. I accept my students where they are. You just never give up. You don't dare because you never know what sparks them." Twenty years later, Ray's sister, Carol Olson Roesner, received the Minnesota School Nurse of the Year award for 1997–98.

Dundee Today

Today Dundee is home to Brenda's Gas & Grocery, Hogan Oil, Dundee Steak House, the Fire and City Hall, Minn-kota Construction, New Vision Co-op Elevator, Pritchard Service Center, the Senior Citizens Center (the former Dundee Hotel), and First Lutheran Church. Surrounded by lakes, the Gas & Grocery store sells everything from fresh eggs to live bait and fishing poles. Owner Brenda's heart is as good as her business—each December she clears out the bait section of the store to host Mr. and Mrs. Santa Claus Day for up to 60 children who arrive for a visit and gift from Santa. Brenda sponsors a continuous garage sale all summer to buy the Christmas gifts.

Ida and Rudy raised four sons in the old Sioux City and St. Paul Railroad Station House. Now known as the Peddycoart house, the structure was placed on the National Register of Historic Places in 1980, in recognition of the connection between the railroad and the development of Dundee in 1879.

Well known for spreading fun and smiles, the Dundee Clowns traveled to parades, advertised for Dundee Nothing Days, performed in the Coliseum Ballroom, and worked the crowd at church services. Former clowns have clowned all over the county, and managed to kiss both Worthington Mayor Bob Demuth and Attorney General Hubert H. Humphrey III.

TOP: "Welcome to Effie" and rodeo sculpture

Early loggers in Effie quickly dubbed the railroad "the Gut and Liver," as weekly carloads of frozen beef livers and sausages arrived for their food supply.

Effie

Chief Busticogan Saves the Future Logging Town of Effie

LIFELONG EFFIE RESIDENT JAMES K. KNIGHT wrote about his father's homestead and life in the Bigfork River Valley in September 1901. Their nearest neighbor, Chief Busticogan of the Nett Lake band of Ojibwe, lived seven miles east of Effie on the Bigfork River. Then 75 years old, the Chief had grown up along the English River in Northern Ontario, Canada. When the beaver supply dwindled and floods destroyed the wild rice, the band migrated to the Effie-Bigfork area. Earlier in 1898, Chief Busticogan gained fame for his peace-making efforts in the Battle of Sugar Point, the battle with the Fort Snelling militia. The Chief didn't just help mediate conflicts; later, the survival of the remote outpost of Effie depended on his humane temperament. While return-ing from a visit to the Rainy River, the Chief and his wife noticed that no smoke arose from the chimney of the logging camp, nor had any ice been cut from the waterhole. They entered the camp to discover the entire logging crew incapacitated with smallpox. Without any thought for their own safety, they buried the dead, cared for the crew, and fed the draft stock until the survivors recovered sufficiently. Later on, the Chief saved a government agent from sure death by an Indian, and was given a grant of land surrounding his camp in 1895 by the "White Chief" in Washington for "as long as the river flowed." In 1910, the Chief traveled to Washington, D.C., to protest the illegal taking of his timber and land by the government. While there, he died in his sleep in a boarding house. Chief Busticogan forgot to turn off the gas when he blew out the light.

Before the railroad came through in 1906, a Civil War veteran from Wright County named John Rahier settled on the Bigfork River, bringing his seventeen children along with him. He wasn't alone. Donning their packsacks, Art Zaiser, Professor F. A. Whitely, and James Knight paddled from Red Lake Falls to the Bigfork River to homestead near the Rahiers. When the government hired Pat Kinney to build a ten-mile trail from Bigfork through Effie, Cap Weanus opened a store and post office on the Kinney Trail in 1904. He promised to name the post office after his oldest daughter, Effie Rose, if she would stay for one year to help run it. John Rahier, whose homestead adjoined the post office, carried the mail by packsack or horseback to Bigfork over the Kinney Trail. Cap's wife, Eva, was the postmistress until 1918, when the post office moved closer to the railroad, now the site of Effie. The business district expanded, adding a large livery barn owned by Walker Matthews, Norman Didiers' General Store and Ed Opsahl's Hotel.

As logging camps opened near the river, a township took shape, and by 1912, Effie had emerged as a railway city, nestled between the Bigfork River and the Minneapolis and Rainy River Railroad. Early loggers in Effie quickly dubbed the railroad "the Gut and Liver," as weekly carloads of frozen beef livers and sausages arrived for their food supply. Loggers cut millions of feet of virgin pine along the Bigfork River and floated the logs to Canada to build the grand city of Winnipeg. Known as "river pigs," lumberjacks followed the exciting drives down the river from dawn to dusk. By 1910, the land opened to homesteaders, but not before every 40 acres with 15,000 feet or more of pine was sold to lumber companies. One early homesteader, Orin Patrow, sat in line at the land office in Cass Lake for over a month to file his claim near Busti Lake.

Effie's Most Wanted: A Murderer at Large

Effie is also the scene for a notable cold case. The unsolved murder of George Herbert Rahier on July 21, 1911, remains a mystery one hundred years later. That day, George left home with his packsack and rifle to search for blueberries. After two days, his wife became concerned and launched a search party, which found his body in the woods. The nature of the two bullet wounds, one through the head and one in the body, pointed a finger at the only two men in Itasca County who owned the caliber of gun used in the shooting. The fire warden had an alibi, but the other man, Ed Erway, did not. A trapper with long trap lines extending to Bigfork, Erway had killed a moose out of season, and another trapper, Gus Soyka, turned him in to authorities. Law enforcement surmised that Erway had mistaken Rahier for Soyka, whom he hated. Erway disappeared and was never seen again. Authorities believe that the murder suspect fled to Canada, fifty miles north, an easy distance for a good woodsman to cover in two days.

Effie Today

Effie welcomes you in style. As you enter town, you are greeted by a pair of sculptures, a six-foot-long mosquito by artist Alvin Dor and a new sculpture of a life-size cowboy riding a bucking bronco in commemoration of the 50th anniversary of the North Stampede Rodeo. Today logging remains a vital piece of the economy, supplemented by beef cattle and tourism. The business district consists of City Hall, Waldron-Flaat American Legion Post #182, Effie Country Service with the attached post office, Tavern on the Edge, and Effie Café, located on the former depot site. The walls of the Effie Café are covered with historical art, including a series of early railroad drawings by Pete Bastiansen (creator of the Hamms Bear) as well as cowboy poetry by rodeo star Harold Pitzen. When asked about retirement, proprietor Kathy Powell responded, "I can't shut the doors. This place is the social hub of the community."

An annual rodeo since 1945, Harold Pitzen's North Star Stampede Rodeo is located on North Star Ranch just outside Effie. Minnesota's largest and oldest open rodeo, the rodeo draws veteran cowboys from the United States and Canada for three days on the last weekend of July.

Shortly before midnight, on June 29, 1947, a
tornado tore through Evan, uprooting trees,
downing electric lines and destroying buildings.

TOP: Morgan Grain & Feed Co.

Evan

A City Full of Norwegians and Danes, A Town Known for Butter and A Mysterious Bell Ringing During a Storm

WHEN THE COMMUNITY OF EVAN INCORPORATED in 1904, the city had 640 acres and 192 people. All the families were of Norwegian or Danish heritage, and everyone's name ended in "-son" or "-sen," depending on nationality. Originally called Hansen Station in 1887, the depot agent, Nels Hansen, wisely chose to honor his wife Eva by adding an "n" and renaming the town Evan.

Longtime resident Anna Peterman, who died the summer of 2010, recounted what life was like in Evan when she was a child: the town boasted a train depot, two grain elevators, Mogensen's General Store, Miller Hardware and Implement, Evan Lumberyard, Paulson's Café,

and Lutheran and Presbyterian churches. Anna's father, Lars Paulsen, ran the butcher shop in their home where Anna and her daughter Kala once lived. When the creamery opened in 1895, seventy farmers joined, netting $17\frac{1}{2}$ cents per pound for grade A No. 1 cream. Their hardworking creamery manager, P. N. Paulsen, won an award at the Pan-American Exposition in 1902 for butter making. In 1936 members voted to drop their affiliation with Land O' Lakes and go independent, with William Hensch as butter maker. A creative entrepreneur, Mr. Hensch designed a butter box with the slogan "Evan Pride," and by June of that year Evan Pride Butter made its debut. The slogan "Evan Pride" was chosen fifty-one years later as the theme for the Evan Centennial.

Located just southwest of Evan, the first school built in 1879 added an addition in 1905 to accommodate 51 pupils. In 1951, a new brick school opened on Evan's south side for grades one through eight, under the direction of teachers Helen Fohl and Gertrude Seifert. When District 58 consolidated with Sleepy Eye in 1970, teachers Helen Hanson and Edna Kalk were the last to instruct Evan students. The old school was razed for lumber, and the new school is now a woodworking shop.

Shortly before midnight, on June 29, 1947, a tornado tore through Evan, uprooting trees, downing electric lines, and destroying buildings. Once believed to be a rock-solid building, the two-story brick creamery lost its top floor that night. The depot roof disappeared, and six steel grain bins blew across the tracks. Unaware that the belfry and bell had blown to the sidewalk below, Reverend Jensen recalled thinking, "Now who is ringing the bell at the crest of the storm?" One oddity of the storm occurred when a two-by-four from the lumberyard pierced the bedroom wall in Grace and Lester Hansen's home, pinning a dresser to the floor. Luckily, no one was seriously hurt.

A Centennial Celebration Led by a Popular WCCO Sportscaster

Under the direction of Leo Scherer, co-chairman of the Evan centennial committee, local residents worked hard to tear down old buildings and beautify the city for their centennial on August 8–9, 1987. Mr. Scherer won the bid for tearing down the town eyesore by outbidding two other contenders when he bid "free." The newly refurbished main street sparkled as Ralph Jon Fritz, popular sportscaster of WCCO-TV and acting Grand Marshall, led the 93-unit centennial parade down Knudson Street to the delight of 3,000 viewers. (Fritz grew up in Evan where his father, Al Fritz, ran the Evan Café.) One of the parade favorites was an Evan Pride butter box replica modeled by Jaclyn Schwint. During the Evan Centennial, the town unveiled a new historical marker that commemorates the early history of Evan. A flag, dedicated by the Sleepy Eye Honor Guard, stands proudly at the Evan Village Hall.

Originally the United Danish Evangelical Lutheran Church, St. Matthew's Lutheran Church observed their 100th anniversary August 12–14, 1977, with a Danish Evening of Costumes and Kaffe. Former Pastor Fred Jensen led the Friday night service, and Pastor George Jensen, whose father, Pastor K. R. Jensen, served the Evan parish from 1942–1952, gave the sermon on Sunday afternoon. Members recalled when women and men sat on opposite sides of the church, and the tornado in 1947 that toppled the church steeple. In 2002, the church celebrated another milestone, their 125th anniversary.

A cemetery near Evan also made the local news when vandals destroyed the gravestone for Ana Knudsen, who was killed by lightning in 1878. Her great-grandchildren united to purchase a new monument for Ana's grave in the little Prairieville Cemetery near Evan.

Evan Today

Today Evan is home to the Rasmussen Body Shop, Evan Auto Repair, St. Matthew's Lutheran Church, MaMa G's Bar & Grill, and the Morgan Grain & Feed Company, a hustling business during the harvest. The Evan City Hall is surrounded by flower beds, a flag pole, and the centennial monument. Evan is also home to a fine city park.

The Evan post office was located in the former Evan State Bank, which was built in the '20s. The post office is gone today, but the main floor retains the original bank teller windows and vault. The interior of the building remains basically unchanged from the thirties when the bank closed during the Depression. In 1977, former Postmaster Alice Radel summed up Evan, "I think it's a good, happy Danish community. They are very friendly—they don't complain." Alice's husband, Donald, ended his military service as a guard at the famous Nuremberg Military Tribunal in 1946. Mr. Radel's responsibilities included escorting the 21 officers of the Third Reich charged for crimes against humanity in World War II.

Donald Radel, the husband of former postmaster Alice Radel, ended his military service as a guard at the famous Nuremberg Military Tribunal in 1946. Mr. Radel's responsibilities included escorting the 21 officers of the Third Reich charged for crimes against humanity in World War II.

Farwell mail carrier Carl Forsberg hauled mail for over fifty years, many years by horse and sleigh in the winter.

TOP: "Welcome to Farwell, est. 1886"

Farwell

A Town Named Goodbye, Midwife Services for $10 and U.S. Mail via Horse and Sleigh

THE STORY OF FARWELL'S NAME BEGINS with the day Swedish settlers met to choose a name for their emerging village. Unable to find a suitable one, the group met a second time, once again without success. Thoroughly disgusted with all the wasted time, one man stood up and exclaimed, "Farval!" (the Swedish word for farewell). The remaining men shrugged their shoulders and named the city Farval, which evolved into Farwell over time. Just west of Glenwood on Highway 55, on a stretch of road known as the Floyd B. Olson Memorial Highway, Farwell is surrounded by miles of cornfields and the best farmland in the county. The city was platted in 1887 and incorporated as a city on June 12, 1905, under Mayor E. J. Johnson and City Clerk Lewis Lund.

When the Soo Line arrived in 1886, G. Carlson and Charles Hansen built a complex containing a hotel, a livery stable in back for horse and buggy rental, and a blacksmith and wagon repair shop. The busy depot, constructed by August and Emil Turnquist, shipped out carloads of grain and shipped in carloads of coal. Alfred Jergen's horse Nellie hauled barrels of apples, coffee, fish and sugar from the freight train to his new two-story general store. The depot was later purchased by William Anderson, who moved the historic structure to his farm.

Upon their arrival from Sweden in 1915, Anders and Stina Anderson bought the blacksmith shop, and Stina worked as a midwife for twenty five years. Her $10 fee included both the delivery and two weeks of care for baby and mother. Under the direction of butter maker Jacob Jacobson, the Farmers Creamery Company churned out thirteen tons of butter in two years. A grain elevator, the Atlantic Elevator Company, located east of the depot, still thrives today under a new name.

In 1909, a new post office opened on Main Street with Alfred Irgens as postmaster. The second postmaster, Louis Lund, was a true entrepreneur, and added an ice cream parlor and candy to the post office. In 1917, a new brick school with a gym and price tag of $6,000 replaced the two-story structure erected in 1893. During the winter months the custodian returned at 2 a.m. each morning to refill the hopper with 24 scoop shovels of coal to keep the school warm. The school closed in 1971 and no longer exists.

At one time Farwell hosted several churches, including Swedish Methodist Church, the Free Church, and Farwell Lutheran Church, all closed today. Only Farwell Lutheran church, erected in 1907, still stands, with a beautiful steeple and wide steps leading into the house of worship. Two other lovely original churches, Lake Oscar Lutheran and Norunga Lutheran, stand outside the city limits and maintain active congregations.

With trucks taking over transportation and business on the decline, the railroad discontinued their shipping service in 1958. Mail trains No. 5 & 6 continued to deliver mail by throwing the mail pouch near the depot, until mail trains were discontinued in 1964. But the real heroes of the post office were the rural mail carriers who delivered mail in the worst kinds of weather. Carl Forsberg hauled mail for over fifty years, many years by horse and sleigh in the winter. From 1957 to 1980, mail carrier Helmer Carlson lost count of the times that farmers pulled him out of ditches during snowstorms. Through sheer determination, Farwell has kept its post office in the community today.

While the citizens of Farwell worked hard to build their village and make a living, many men and women from Farwell went to war in the twentieth century. On July 9th, 1944, World War II serviceman Donald Bollum, stationed in France, wrote a poignant letter to his sister, Helen Bollum: *"Dear Sis, This is being written in my pup tent on a rainy, dreary Sun. afternoon. I have a hole dug in the ground with my tent pitched over it. This way one doesn't have to get out of bed if a German plane flies over. At first the anti-aircraft firing kept me awake, but I must be getting accustomed to it because I sleep right through most of it now. Yesterday we were given five days rations which consisted of 4 packs of cig, 4 packs of hard candy, 2 razor blades, and a choice of soap, shaving cream, or tooth powder. This is given to us free so we don't have any expenses at all. That's a good thing because we don't have pay day very often. Since leaving the States we have been paid only $25 so the gov't owes me some money now. I believe we will get only partial payments until we get back and that's okay with me because a little money will be handy to have when we get back. That's the day I think of so often and I hope and pray it isn't far off. Take care of Dad and don't let him work too hard. You are both in my thoughts. Love, Don."* Donald was killed three months later on October 13, 1944.

An American Legion Post Honoring World War I Veterans

OGMAR American Legion Post #268 was organized in 1919 by several World War I vets, including Tom Thronson, who worked nights at the Depot. The name OGMAR stood for five men from Pope County killed in World War I: Edward Olmein, Magnus Grondahl, Carl Moe, Alfred Anderson and Arthur Rosenberg. During the '50s the post was moved to Kensington.

Farwell Today

Today Farwell holds fast to their City Hall and Community Center, with the post office tucked inside the community center. The B&S Grain Elevator across from the "Welcome to Farwell" sign remains an important outpost for local grain farmers.

Recently the population decreased by two, when Marv and Marie Bjorklund sold their home and all their possessions to open a children's home in Africa. A haven for neglected and abused children, Place of Hope Africa will provide a home for 50 children in Plettenberg Bay, South Africa.

In the space of a week and a half in 1955, over one hundred muskies, weighing from eighteen to forty pounds, were caught in Federal Dam.

TOP: U.S. Army Corps of Engineers dam, Leech River

Federal Dam

The Leech Lake Muskie Rampage

FEDERAL DAM MADE NATIONAL NEWS in 1955 during a hot, dry and calm two weeks in midsummer. On July 16, 1955, fishing guide Danny Chalich, Bob Neururer and his nephews Chucky and Peter set out on their Chris-Craft for a morning's fishing. Ten-year-old Peter decided to troll a Red Eye Wiggler on 40 feet of line, and before long, he had a 35-pound muskie. The crew backed the big boat toward the fighting fish as the young boy held on and won the battle. The "Leech Lake Muskie Rampage" gathered momentum with nineteen muskies reeled in that day, and by the following day, a total of thirty-one muskies lay on the dock. Within a week, over one hundred muskies, weighing from eighteen to forty pounds, were caught.

Federal Dam sits near the Leech Lake Dam, a reservoir dam built by the U.S. Army Corps of Engineers on Leech Lake in 1882. Three hundred men were hired for $1.10 per day to build the dam. Upon completion in 1884, the total cost was $171,805. Following the passage of the Dawes Act in 1887 and the Nelson Act in 1889, the Leech Lake Reservation was divided into individual land holdings. New settlers arrived to claim the land, including T. B. Walker and his Red River Logging Company. By 1902, dam tender William L. Moody owned all the land for the future Federal Dam.

Surrounded by the Chippewa National Forest and located on the Leech Lake Indian Reservation, Federal Dam organized around the arrival of the Soo Railroad in 1910. Once the Soo Line chose Federal

Dam as the terminal for trains traveling from Superior, Wisconsin, and Thief River Falls, Minnesota, the city's future solidified. Despite a heavy snowfall the evening before, depot agent Frank Gustin and residents cheered the arrival of the first train on November 14, 1910. Over one hundred men, typically of Swedish, Czech and Slovakian descent, manned the eight-stall roundhouse, 24 hours daily. Less than a year after the arrival of the train, the city incorporated on October 30, 1911.

Business expanded with the arrival of the railroad. The Corps of Engineers licensed a public boat landing on the reservoir, and in 1912, Ed Warren built the Rex Hotel on land purchased by the Duluth Brewing and Malting Company. Unfortunately, due to a Supreme Court case, prohibition was enacted on all reservations in 1914, and saloons on reservations were forced to close. The Duluth Brewery sold the property in 1918 to Ray and Ella LeMire, who opened the Hotel LeMire, advertised as a "modern hotel with rooms fit for a king." Guests paid $2 a day for a steam-heated, electrically lighted room, located near the best pike fishing in the state. By 1919, fishermen from around the state filled the hotel. After a full day of fishing, the guests played pool and cards in Andrew Lego's pool hall, located at one end of the hotel. Other businesses included the Russell Lego General Store, Soo Line Rooming House, Theo Tobiason Hardware Store, State Bank of Federal Dam, and Federal Dam Motor Company, owned by Venzel Johnson. Mac McCarthy bought the Padgham Lumber Company in 1954, and delighted patrons each St. Patrick's Day by painting certain parts of his bulldog Max's anatomy green. In 1935, the Federal Dam Improvement Club leased land for a campground, and the train delivered tourists from Chicago for fishing excursions on Leech Lake. At the end of the week, the train carried happy tourists along with gutted fish and ice back to the Windy City.

The Sugar Point Indian Day School opened in the late 1800s with teacher Leo Brevik conducting classes. In 1911, the two-story Federal Dam School opened, and the children danced around the May Pole to celebrate the end of the school year. In 1939, a new WPA school was constructed for grades one through eight.

Federal Dam fans took their baseball seriously. Large crowds visited the ball field near the railroad west section house. During one close game tempers flared, and Calla Nelson recalls her mother, Mina, getting so upset that she roughed up the umpire. Folks also played in the brass band and the village band, and in 1916, attended movies at the Palace Theater.

Leech Lake and a Member of the American Indian Movement

The Leech Lake Recreation Area, near the Leech Lake outlet in Federal Dam, offers a wooded campground and a canal for boats. One of the state's premier walleye, perch and muskie lakes, Leech Lake is the third-largest lake in Minnesota.

Co-founder of the American Indian Movement in 1968, Dennis Banks was born in Federal Dam April 12, 1937, to Bertha Banks and Walter Chase. From the AIM's occupation of Alcatraz to the seventy-one day Siege at Wounded Knee, Banks has fought to protect the traditional ways of Indian people and the treaty rights of Natives. The Trail of Broken Treaties, a peaceful march on Washington, turned into an historic six-day takeover of the BIA headquarters. He has also written two books and acted in three movies including *The Last of the Mohicans*.

Federal Dam Today

Today, Federal Dam is home to Machart's Bar, Abe's Bar (the former liquor store), Tonga's Launch Service, My Buddy's Place, City Hall, and the Fire Department. River Side Quick Stop sells gas and groceries. In 1961, Sacred Heart Catholic Church moved St. Cecelia Church from Tobique to Federal Dam, and Our Savior's Lutheran Church built a new church in 1995.

The lone cemetery, Fairview Cemetery, had an unusual beginning. In 1914, when digging a grave for an infant, a family uncovered the body of an Indian child with another body directly below it. The child's coffin contained a tin box with a duck's bill, beads and brass ornaments.

CATCH EM' HERE
BAIT TACKLE ICE SNACKS
FEDERAL DAM LAUNCH SER

TOP: Residential street

In September, 1877, a fire driven by strong winds from Sioux Falls, South Dakota, burned a considerable portion of west Lyon County, including Florence.

Florence

Hardship on the Prairie

WHAT WOMAN WOULDN'T LOVE to have a city named after her? Before Miss Florence Sherman arrived in 1888, Norwegian immigrant families homesteaded in the area; these families included the Ronnings, Myrans, Sandens, Bergs, Johnsons, Blegens, and the Andersons. Escaping the rocky, inhospitable farmland of Norway, their dream of owning profitable farmland came with a huge price.

The early settlers fought against drought, grasshoppers and fire to keep their farms and families intact. But the forces of nature were stronger than even the toughest Norwegians. In September, 1877, a fire driven by strong winds from Sioux Falls, South Dakota, burned a considerable portion of west Lyon County. Farmers H. P. Sanden,

E. K. Ronning, C. P. Myran and Christopher Johnson had just finished threshing, and were hauling wheat with oxen teams to Marshall. Looking back at their homes, they saw the fire closing in behind them, turning the prairie into a charred wasteland. Waiting at home for her husband, Mrs. Myran, her two children, and a friend, Mrs. Hendrick Jorgenson, watched the flames approach rapidly, and were forced to run for their lives. Mrs. Myron and her children reached the dugout, but Mrs. Jorgenson was overcome by the fire. The buildings, grain, and everything except the dugouts were destroyed.

Florence wasn't officially platted until 1888 when the Great Northern Railway arrived. Early settler W. H. Sherman purchased eighty acres of land from H. P. Sanden to plat a town along the tracks, and named the town Florence after his beautiful daughter. The first depot agent, Eugene Jackson, and his family took up residence in the depot until the construction of their first home. Tyler resident Thomas Owens opened a general store to sell supplies to the early settlers, and did double duty as the first postmaster from 1889 to 1894. As service on the railroad improved, the town of Florence added Gorseth's Store, a grain elevator, Jeglum Implement, the State Bank of Florence, a lumberyard, and Andrew Sanden's Hotel and Livery service. When Mr. Sanden sold the business to Erick Erickson in 1910, the Ericksons erected a new hotel to accommodate the increased business. Travelers arriving by train would spend the night, and the next morning Mr. Erickson delivered the well-rested folks by horse and buggy to Tyler to catch the Northwestern train. Florence was also the mail exchange point, with mail delivered by train to Florence and then by truck to Brookings. Mail continued to arrive by train until 1960, when mail routes were established. When the depot closed in 1962, the Russell and Florence stations merged. In 1897, local businessmen organized Modern Woodsman of America, a fraternal organization founded by Joseph Cullen Root in 1883 to protect families following the death of a breadwinner.

In 1884, before the village organized, school district No. 47 opened on the C. P. Myran farm just south of the future Florence. A new school building, now named District No. 78, was erected in the village proper in 1893 under the direction of school board members A. E. Green, H. P Sanden, and Anton Hyndan. By 1911, teacher Edla C. Johnson taught forty-five students of varying ages and abilities in the two-room school. A few years later, the city incorporated February 16, 1920, but declining enrollment in the 1940s forced the school to send their 7th and 8th graders to Tyler, and in 1966 the Florence school district, the last rural school in the county, consolidated with Tyler.

Village life centered around Opdal Norwegian Evangelical Church, a country parish founded in 1878 and moved to the city in 1914.

By the time the church celebrated their Golden Jubilee in 1929, Reverend S. A. Stenseth had agreed to alternate services in the Norse and English languages. Opdahl proudly celebrated their 75th anniversary in 1954, and two honored guests were hometown boys, Reverend Howard Blegen and Reverend Melvin Peterson. In 1959, the church honored Mrs. Inga Riste, daughter of church founders Mr. and Mrs. Cornelius Peterson Myron, for fifty years of service as the church organist. Mrs. Riste continued to play organ for another ten years. Opdal closed in 1975, and the building is now owned by a private party.

A Piece of History Saved

Local resident David F. Van Nevel owns the original town livery stable and post office, both located on his property. He also recently purchased the Opdal church, and plans to recycle the wood and fixtures. Nevertheless, the original organ, made by Fort Wayne Organ Company in Fort Wayne, Indiana, was spared and resides in the Lyon County Museum, Marshall, Minnesota.

Just west of Florence, the Opdal Cemetery formed in 1878 following the death of early settler Peder Sanden in 1875. Still active, it is one of the oldest cemeteries in Lyon County, and some of the county's earliest settlers are buried here.

Florence Today

The city of Florence, with its pretty houses and lawns, keeps its city park just as neat. Someone still runs the flag up the pole each morning and takes the time to tend to a brick planter of marigolds. A trio of brick buildings, one the former State Bank, line Main Street and are now apartments.

Minnesota birders travel to the East-West Twin Lakes area south of Florence for a glimpse of migrating waterfowl. Uncommon species reported on West Twin Lake include Clark's Grebe, the Greater White-fronted Goose, Ross's goose, and the Surf Scoter.

Fort Ripley was originally established as a buffer
zone between the feuding Dakota and Ojibwe tribes.

TOP: Fort Ripley historical marker, Mississippi River

Fort Ripley

A Fort Built to Keep the Peace

LOCATED ON THE EAST BANK of the Mississippi River, Fort Ripley bears the name of Old Fort Ripley, a military outpost on the west side of the Mississippi from 1849 to 1878. The fort was built on a one-mile-square tract, with another 57,000 acres on the east side of the river used for farming and logging. Established as a buffer zone between the feuding Dakota and Ojibwe tribes, the military fort also offered protection to the Winnebago Indians, who had recently resettled in the area after ceding their land in Iowa to the U.S. government. When the post closed in 1877, the city moved east across the river to the confluence of the Mississippi and Nokasippi Rivers. Only ruins of the stone powder magazine remain as a reminder of Old Fort Ripley. Today the site is

included in Camp Ripley, a 20,000-acre National Guard camp for Minnesota soldiers.

Initially named Fort Macy, the fort was renamed in honor of Brigadier General Eleazar W. Ripley, a hero of the War of 1812. Sixteen one-story wood frame buildings formed three sides of the square fort, with the fourth side open to the river. The first garrison from Fort Snelling arrived on May 13, 1849, to find an isolated outpost with few neighbors, apart from the Winnebago and Ojibwe, a farm across the river, and a group of pesky whiskey sellers at Crow Wing. Following the relocation of the Winnebago to Mankato in 1855, the government abandoned the fort on July 8, 1857. Immediately the traders began illegally selling liquor to the Ojibwe. After armed white settlers lynched three Ojibwe men on a suspected murder charge, the fort quickly reopened two months later. In 1862, during the Dakota War, panicked settlers inundated the fort, which was never attacked. Over the years, Indian attacks were not the main threat; the fires needed to fend off dangerously cold temperatures were. A fire in 1868 destroyed several buildings, killing the caretaker, Sgt. Frantzkey, and his four children. Another fire in 1870 destroyed the hospital, the chapel, and the officer's quarters.

By 1873, Fort Ripley was no longer on the western frontier, the Ojibwe were settling on the White Earth Reservation, and there was no need for an outpost in central Minnesota. When the laundry, commissary, and officers quarters were destroyed by a chimney fire on January 14, 1877, the War department decided to close the post. Old Fort Ripley was abandoned on July 11, 1877, and only a caretaker remained behind to tend to the buildings. Over time, buildings in the old fort disintegrated; in 1931, Adjutant General Ellard A. Walsh selected a 12,000-acre site, including old Fort Ripley, for a new National Guard training facility.

The town of Fort Ripley incorporated March 19, 1927, and in 1934, it suffered a setback when ice destroyed the bridge crossing the river. People living on the west side were ordered to move, and many businesses folded. A second blow occurred in 1955 when the State of Minnesota notified the city of plans to widen Highway 371. All homes and businesses along the highway were moved to make way for the new divided highway, which did not materialize until 2005, fifty years later.

Minnesota's "Civil War" and the first American woman to land on Guadalcanal during World War II

On August 17, 1862, a Dakota hunting party killed a white family near Acton, Minnesota, in retaliation for the repeated failure of the government to provide promised food and supplies to the starving tribe. This marked the official beginning of the Dakota War, also known as Minnesota's "Civil War." Further attacks occurred at the Lower Sioux Indian Agency near New Ulm, the Episcopal Mission at Gull Lake, the Lutheran Mission at Lower Mission Lake, and at Fort Ridgely. Most federal troops were off fighting the U.S. Civil War, and Fort Ripley was defended by troops of the Minnesota Volunteer Infantry. In a bid for power, the renowned Ojibwe Chief Hole-in-the-Day threatened to attack in retaliation for government fraud. Frightened settlers rushed to Fort Ripley, where the fort's occupants prepared ammunition for their rifles by candlelight and dug trenches outside the stockade. Mille Lacs Chief Migizi (Eagle) and his head warrior, Niigaanigwaneb (First Seated Feather), refused to support Chief Hole-in-the-Day, and sent more than one hundred Mille Lacs warriors to protect Fort Ripley. The attack never materialized, and attempts to arrest Chief Hole-In-The Day failed.

Army Nurse Corps Captain Mae Olson Pruitt, of Fort Ripley, was the first American woman to land on Guadalcanal in March 1943, and earned five air medals for her efforts to evacuate United States Marines in the Solomon Islands during World War II.

Fort Ripley Today

Despite its troubles, the city refused to quit. Today it boasts a new city hall, the renowned Fort Ripley Rebels baseball team, and Patnaude City Park, which features the Gladys Nelson Pavilion, donated in 1990 by the local snowmobile club. The town is also home to the Fort Steak House, which offers great food by a cozy fireplace. Next door, the Fort Ripley Store covers the community necessities with groceries, gas pumps, and a tiny post office.

Just north of Fort Ripley, the Nokasippi Historical Marker notes the confluence of the Mississippi and Nokasippi Rivers, where ferryboats dropped off passengers and cargo. If you couldn't afford the ferry rate, a bucket with a rope allowed you to pull yourself across the Mississippi.

Visitors need a camp escort to visit the remnants of the stone powder house at Old Fort Ripley, located on the grounds of Camp Ripley. The Military Museum at Camp Ripley offers a complete history and model of the old fort in its "Forts on the Frontier" exhibit.

In the 1980s, Funkley promoted the imaginary Hiney Wine, the only wine in the country sold in a flip-top aluminum can.

TOP: Funkley Bar

Funkley

One of the Smallest Minnesota Cities and Its Big Fight Against Cancer

OVER THE YEARS, FUNKLEY AND TENNEY have held a long-running contest to claim the title of the smallest city in Minnesota. Now that Tenney has voted to dissolve as a city, Funkley will soon own the title outright. Though there are only a handful of residents in Funkley, it has a larger-than-life story to tell. Tiny Funkley achieved national fame on June 5, 1953, when the entire village boarded a plane for New York City to receive an award from the American Cancer Society for their work recycling old sheets into cancer dressings. Twenty-five citizens and eight women from surrounding farms, including one-year-old Nancy Louise Nagle and 78-year-old Mayor E. J. Woodin, flew to NYC on

Northwest Airline Flight 208. Northwest nicknamed the flight "The Funkley Fight Cancer Special." Even the town dog, "Blackie," was invited on the trip. The group met with New York dignitaries, appeared on TV and radio shows, attended receptions, and in their spare time enjoyed the sights in the Big Apple. From New York, the guests flew to Washington, D.C., where Minnesota Congressmen Harold Hagen and Walter Judd, Senator Edward Thye, and Governor C. Elmer Anderson introduced the people of Funkley to President Dwight Eisenhower. Unfortunately, Mayor Woodin missed meeting the President, as he had slipped in the hotel bathtub the night before and cracked two ribs. He arrived home on a stretcher. Only the Minnesota Highway Patrol and two elderly men stayed behind to protect the community. Richard

Smith, age 72, stated that his feet were on the bum, while 80-year-old Hank Huffstutler reported that he had already visited New York City in 1900 and, "It's just a lot of concrete."

Drive thirty miles northwest of Bemidji on highway 71 and you will find the Funkley Bar and a new business, Funkley Log Furniture. Once a Northern Pacific railroad stop and a logging community, the city's population plummeted following the decline of the logging industry in the 1920s. Platted in 1903 by Matt Fisher on his homestead and called Hovey Junction, Matt decided to name the new village Funkley after his attorney and good friend, Henry Funkley. Mr. Funkley waived his fee in exchange for the honor. Matt's wife, Belinda, did not get to be the town namesake, but she was appointed the first postmaster in 1903. She also started the *Funkley Bugle*, a newspaper which circulated from 1903 to 1907. By the time the city incorporated on January 14, 1904, fifty families called this lively logging community home. Main Street bustled with a post office (closed in 1967), three saloons, a church, two hotels, and a general store. Today, the Funkley Bar provides over half of the city's $2,000 budget with the liquor license fee.

It pays to be the smallest city in Minnesota. Based on the 1980 census, Funkley defeated Tenney for the title of smallest city with 18 residents to 19 in Tenney. Once again, Funkley hit the road when WCCO honored Minnesota's smallest city in 1989 with a chartered bus trip to the Cities. Citizens were interviewed on a WCCO radio show, ate dinner at the Chanhassen Dinner Theater and took in a Minnesota Twins game.

You Bet Your Hiney You'll Like This Wine

In the 1980s, Funkley promoted the imaginary Hiney Wine, the only wine in the country sold in a flip-top aluminum can. Supposedly sold by owner-brothers Big Red Hiney and Thor Hiney, here is how the '80s promotion worked: T.J. Donelly Enterprises provided a 60-second radio commercial script promoting the Hiney Winery in a small, nearby town, drawing customers who were looking for the winery. The commercials were hilarious, making liberal use of double entendre: Their sister Ophelia Hiney was the bookkeeper, and a cousin, Seymour Hiney, was a distributor. Owners Thor and Big Red offered to help you start your own distributorship with two free cases of wine, a bicycle to pedal your Hiney around town, and swizzle sticks with your name on them, so no one would accidentally grab your Hiney. When customers noted that they liked to chill their wine with ice cubes, the brothers widened the opening in the pop-top can, resulting in a new commercial: "Hiney Wines, now in the new wide cans with the big ice hole!" When the promotion ran its course, the writers announced that the winery had burned down, but not before a lot of folks in Funkley had a lot of fun.

Star Tribune writer Bob von Sternberg alerted readers in 1997 to the financial troubles facing Funkley when the Funkley Bar, the main source of income, closed temporarily. Members of the Waverly Lions Club, led by Pat Borrell, from Waverly, Minnesota, (home of Hubert Humphrey) remembered hunting and fishing in the area and decided to sponsor a benefit softball tournament to raise $1,000 to keep the city alive. The event was a success and kept Funkley on the map.

Funkley Today

You will have a hard time finding a seat in the Funkley Bar during deer hunting season. If you can't find a spot, you can join Hagar, the wooden bartender, who used to preside over the old bar counter, but now relaxes on the deck. His leather vest, hat, and bottle of Bud Light in his hand symbolize the rollicking good fun in Funkley.

Funkley is known for an impressive hunting record. In 1918, near Funkley, John Breen shot the largest "typical" whitetail buck ever taken in Minnesota. Nearly thirty years later, the buck was determined to have a net Boone and Crockett score of 202" 0/8 (a measurement of key antler parameters), and is still the "typical" state record.

Population: 75 **Incorporated:** 1915

INSETS L to R: Campground • Horseshoe Barn •
Bison ranch • Soo Line Trail

TOP: Red Rooster Bar

In 1981, tiny Genola drew twelve hundred contestants to the Preimesberger Arena for the World Horseshoe Championships.

Genola

The World Horseshoe Championships—in Genola

IF YOU BUILD IT, THEY WILL COME. In 1981, tiny Genola drew twelve hundred contestants to the Preimesberger Arena for the World Horseshoe Championships. Henry and Dolores Preimesberger erected the 80-by-220-foot building with eighty horseshoe pitching courts in 1978, one of the finest horseshoe arenas in the world. The tournament put Genola on the map for good.

Genola has lived up to author Clara Fuller's description of the settlement as "a good small trading point—a hamlet of good promise," in her book, *The History of Morrison and Todd County*, written in 1915. Platted in 1908 as a railway station for the Soo Railroad and initially named New Pierz by John Stumpf, the city was renamed Genola in 1915. Although officially named after a village in Piedmont, Italy,

Genola's German Catholic citizens don't buy it. They believe that the city was really named after a railroad worker's beloved daughter.

Following the arrival of the first passengers on the platform of the gold-painted depot in 1909, Genola quickly expanded and was soon home to the First State Bank, Peter Beckka's Blacksmith Shop, Handy Litke's Saloon, Harsh & Grell Hardware and Grocery, Peter Kelgenberg's Hardware, F.O. Bolster General Merchandise, the New Pierz Grain Company, and the McGentry Potato Warehouse. The rich prairie land produced vast amounts of grain and potatoes for shipment to larger cities. When a fire of unknown origin swept through Main Street on August 13, 1923, it completely destroyed nine buildings and almost wiped Genola off the map.

In 1910 the post office opened and continued until 1956, when many of the smallest post offices closed nationwide. Until the co-operative creamery organized in 1911, the Bridgeman-Russell Company controlled the market share of cream stations in every small town in Morrison County. Determined to get a higher price for their product, the German farmers formed the Pierz Farmers Co-operative Creamery.

Unlike other small cities, Genola never had a school or a church, but they have always maintained a lumberyard. What was once Preimesberger Lumber is now Loidolt Lumber, owned by Bob Loidolt.

A Trophy and a New Arena for Horseshoes

In 1981 Henry and Dolores Preimesberger and their thirteen children were honored with the Stokes Memorial Trophy for promoting the sport of horseshoes. Their effort to successfully secure the 1981 *National Horseshoe Pitchers Association World Championship* in Genola, Minnesota, achieved national acclaim. Established in 1958, the Stokes Memorial Trophy commemorates the memory of Arch Stokes, four-time president of the N.H.P.A and the man who is credited with rescuing the game from oblivion following World War II. Although the original arena is gone, the legendary horseshoe capital lives on in a new horseshoe arena located in Memorial Park.

Genola Today

Downtown Genola sports the Red Rooster Bar & Grill, the Double Deuce Bar & Grill, Loidolt Lumberyard, Genola Grain Company, Dale's Farm Repair, and Rich Prairie Livestock Exchange. Jolly Jack Food Products, producer of a garlic cheese spread, is once again headquartered in Genola after Rick and Kim Lyons purchased the business from Jean and Bob Pace of Sartell. Genola is also home to a new business: The Unity Bank, which opened in 2006 with Rick Wiersgalla as President. Needless to say, a new bank for a community of seventy-five is somewhat astonishing. In addition to this new business, Genola is also home to a family business over one hundred years old—the Genola Grain Company. Built in the center of town in 1910, it has been owned and operated by four generations of the Sollinger family. The original feed mill was destroyed by arson in 2002 and rebuilt in 2003 to continue 100 years of service to local customers.

Like Genola's population, Genola's City Hall is small—a building with just enough room to seat the six council members, and to house the original city bell, restored by Chuck Storkamp.

Genola is close to a variety of recreational opportunities. The 17-acre Genola Memorial Park offers lighted softball diamonds, a playground, an indoor horseshoe arena and volleyball court for community celebrations. In addition, the former Soo Railroad track is now the Soo Line Recreation Trail; it begins in Genola and ends in Superior, Wisconsin. Spanning 114 miles of scenic forests, farmland and streams, the trail draws outdoor enthusiasts of all sorts to Genola. The Genola Campground is also a destination. Nestled along the Skunk River, it is filled with campers all summer. Genoa is also known for golf; golfers from all over the state visit Genola and enjoy the many beautiful golf courses in the area.

Visitors can have a good time in town too. Genola's Red Rooster Bar & Grill is home to one hundred ceiling inflatables, "Polish horseshoe," and terrific homemade cucumber horseradish pickles. It also hosts Bologna Days every Wednesday. Freshly cooked bologna from world-famous Thielen Meats in Pierz arrives hot out of the cookers in time for the noon crowd. Since the corner cafe closed, the bar has also offered a full breakfast menu for the morning crowd. Each Saturday the bar holds a meat raffle conducted by the Eastern Morrison County 4-Wheeler Club, with all money donated to community projects.

At one point, Genola's sister city, Pierz, approached Genola with the idea of consolidating, but Genola declined the offer.

Following incorporation, over thirty main buildings,
all painted white, were constructed, lending Goodridge
the title of "White Village."

TOP: Country Store Museum and Goodridge Area Fire and Rescue

Goodridge

A Rare Sort of Small Town

GOODRIDGE STANDS OUT as a unique little city in many ways.
This proud community is the only little city in the state with a school
that houses students from kindergarten through high school. They also
have that rare historical building, the depot, a structure that has gone
the way of the dinosaur. And last, but not least, the city boasts their own
historical society, second to none in Minnesota.

When homesteaders Carl Lindstrom and John Guinan sold sixty
acres to Northern Townsite Land Co. in 1914, the Minnesota Northwestern Railway developed the village of Goodridge. Named for the broad,
low ridge surrounding the community, the city of 300 incorporated on
August 15, 1915. Jay Payne served as Mayor and his wife, Jennie, born in

New York in 1875, officiated as the first postmaster until 1934.

Following incorporation, over thirty main buildings, all painted
white, were constructed, lending Goodridge the title "White Village."
The Farmers Elevator, owned by A. B. Mandt, had the capacity to grind
fifty barrels of flour a day, a treat for area farmers who had previously
traveled many miles to have wheat ground into flour. An electric light
plant in back of the elevator supplied electricity to forty-one village
homes. Lights came on at dusk and were turned off at 10:00 p.m., much
to the dismay of children who yelled, "Light the lamp!" followed by their
mother's joyful reply, "Go to bed!"

A typical day in Goodridge started with two blasts from the horn
of the "Potato Bug," an electric train. As students debarked from the

train, agent R. H. McDonald unloaded the mail into a two-wheeled cart, and delivered the goods to Postmaster Jennie Payne. Citizens patronized the O.K. Restaurant, managed by Ole Kirklie, and Dairy Lunch, where teens met after dances for ice cream at the soda fountain. Both Halvor Christianson & Son and the Goodridge Mercantile Company supplied dry goods, groceries, and shoes. Severt Anderson's Harness & Shoe repaired worn out leather goods, and the Farmers State Bank took care of your money, until the Depression forced the bank to close in 1930. In 1918, the Enterprise Co-op Creamery moved into town, and was renamed the Goodridge Co-op Creamery Association. Three years later, the creamery produced 90,000 pounds of butter. On November 8, 1932, the night Franklin Delano Roosevelt won his first term as President, fire destroyed the Mercantile Store, Dairy Lunch, and the post office.

A Superb Historical Society and Schools Setting an Example

The Goodridge Area Historical Society maintains the original Woodrow School, the Telephone Exchange Office with the 1910 switchboard, the Country Store Museum, and Settlers Center, all in mint condition. The society also carefully restored the 1914 Brown House, donated by Dr. David Brown, Superintendent of the Goodridge School for twenty-five years. When Historical Society President Norma Hanson heard that their old depot in Grygla would be replaced, she and her husband picked the depot up in the dead of night, and brought the historic treasure to Goodridge. On February 26, 2011, Norma Hanson was inducted into the Northwest Minnesota Women's Hall of Fame for her efforts to improve life for farmers, women and schools statewide. Under her leadership, much of Goodridge history has been preserved through the Goodridge Area Historical Society.

Goodridge School District 561 excels in many areas from football to tolerance. In an era of segregation, Superintendent Brown hired three African-American teachers. Roland Samber, music teacher from 1953–1960, writes about his experience in Goodridge: "I remember the honor, respect, and opportunity afforded me by Superintendent David Brown. I remember that I wished all of America could take notice of the Pennington County school system. It was the most meaningful experience of my life. I believe it was an equal and fair exchange. I was fully accepted as an educator and a person and, as a result, I never hesitated to do my utmost to meet the needs and demands of the students, parents, community and the school system. How can I ever forget Goodridge, Minnesota!"

Goodridge native Kirk Hibbert, legendary Arctic Cat racer and designer, was inducted into the Snowmobile Hall of Fame in St. Germain, Wisconsin, in 2006.

Goodridge Today

Today Goodridge is home to the Municipal Liquor Store, the post office, C & J's Café, a fire department, Farmer's Union Cenex Station, Farmer's Co-op Creamery, Goodridge Community Center, and Goodridge School. Led by manager Dale Hanson, the Farmer's Co-op Creamery Association celebrated their centennial July 20, 2008. Although train service ended March 15, 1940, when conductor Joe Zavoral stepped off the Minnesota Northwestern Electric Railway for the final time, the depot remains in the same place. A lovely City Park, named for A. C. Tvedt, the first Mayor in Goodridge, is faithfully maintained by the Deer Park Garden Club. Faith Lutheran Church and St. Ann's Catholic Church, both modern structures, reside within the city limits.

John Franzman, a master woodcarver born in Austria in 1866, settled around Goodridge in 1897. He designed four church altars for Grygla and Goodridge, and two are still in use. The altar from Faith Lutheran Church was returned to the family, and was displayed at the Minnesota History Center for the MN150 Exhibit.

The unusual stained glass windows at Faith Lutheran Church, crafted by artist Lavonne Forsberg, reflect the hobby of benefactors Ulrich and Hilda Hoffman, who collect John Deere memorabilia. A John Deere combine, Case International Harvester tractor, and a 1944 Massey-Harris tractor embedded in glass frame the church entrance.

Gully loves a party. Three months after the centennial
celebration in 2010, Gully celebrated Leftover Days,
another party to auction off leftover souvenir items
and feed the city leftover beans and bratwurst.

TOP: Gully city park, bandstand

Gully

A Town That Knows How to Throw A Good Party

IF YOU WANT TO HAVE FUN, head to Gully. This little city, named
for a gully next to the highest beach ridge of Glacial Lake Agassiz, loves
to throw a party, just for fun. Three months after the centennial celebration in 2010, Gully celebrated Leftover Days, another party to auction
off left over souvenir items, showcase local musical talent, and feed the
city leftover beans and bratwurst. The homemade pies, however, were
baked that morning at the Gully Café, and you could go back for a
second slice. Winning numbers under plates, chairs, and tucked into
napkins were redeemable for prizes. Couples could not resist dancing
to music by cousins Vernon Wold and Melvin Churness and residents
sang their hearts out on the Gully Hall stage. To balance out the sing-

ing, Leftover Lars brought out his bag of tricks, including a reading on
Norwegian wit and wisdom.

Homesteaders first arrived in Gully in 1896, shortly after the Red
Lake Reservation land opened for settlement. In 1905, the local newspa-
per, *The Sunbeam*, advertised Lydia Pinkham's Vegetable Compound,
"the great woman's remedy for woman's ills," and flour from the 24-hour
Gully Flouring Mill, owned by Richard Ohm. The Soo Railroad arrived
in 1909, and new Gully moved a quarter-mile closer to the railroad.
Then named the *Gully Advance*, the newspaper advertised Gust Strande's
Cash and Produce Store, the Gully Hotel, and Thor Moen's Meat
Market, also an exclusive dealer in hides. The Farmer's Elevator sold
their home brand flour, C-A-P-I-T-O-L, and another brand, V-I-V-O,

made by competitors Hanson & Barzen Milling in Thief River Falls. Local citizens enjoyed membership in the Sons of Norway and the Modern Woodmen of the World. In 1916, Gully lost a few citizens, when the Soo Line offered special "Homeseekers Fares," for tickets to North Dakota, Montana, Idaho and Western Canada.

Over the years, the mainstay of Gully has been the Gully Co-op. In 1912 local farmers purchased the elevator owned by Hanson and Barzen, and developed a strong Farmers Union. The entrepreneurs expanded the cooperative to include a credit union, a service station, a general store, a bulk oil plant, a lumber and machinery business, and a trucking business, all vital to the success of the city today. By the time the city incorporated in 1924, a full business section included Wieberg's Sanitary Bakery, Lars Nylund Motor Service, and Bob's Place, which sold both poultry and radios.

When Gully School opened in 1897, enrollment peaked at one hundred students, and by 1965, a new school was needed to accommodate the growing district. When the school closed in 1977, the city created the Gully Mall out of the vacant building.

Gully History Day, and a Centennial Spelling Bee

On May 17, 2008, Gully celebrated "Gully History Day" in conjunction with a grant from the state of Minnesota. All gathered in the Gully Hall for a full course lunch prepared by the Lutheran Church followed by speeches from residents who grew up in early Gully, and keynote speaker, historian Art Lee. History buffs enjoyed military displays, family histories, handmade quilts, antique farm and household goods, and a reproduction of an old schoolroom, all perfectly staged by artist Cindy Kolling.

One hundred years after the railroad arrived, Gully celebrated their centennial in 2010 with a royal court and city-wide spelling bee. The reigning royalty in the Gully Area Centennial were LuVerne Fore, Woman of the Century; Halvor Rikje, Man of the Century; and Honor Court Vernon Wold and Bernice Oftelie. Ramona Emerson defeated 23 contestants in the Centennial Spelling Bee with the word *ostensible*.

Gully Today

The former school is now The Gully Mall, and is home to the post office, Schoolhouse Grocery, Gully Hair Lounge, and Gully Café, famous for Betty's potato klub. Several apartments in the school provide housing for the elderly, and for those who like living downtown. The former movie theater, Gully Hall, hosts parties as well as city council meetings. Other businesses include Agassiz Hills Guest House, Gully-Cenex Tri-Co-op Association, Tri-Coop Elevator Company, Tri-Coop Lumber & Supply, Hill River Electric, and Shorty's Place, host to a smear tournament every Tuesday. The Gully Trail Lutheran Parish rests serenely across from City Hall. A monument in front of City Park honors Edwin H. Christianson, who organized the Gully Cooperative in 1932, and several other cooperatives throughout Minnesota. The Cooperative Builder Magazine wrote that under Mr. Christianson's leadership, "co-operatives at Gully grew like mushrooms after a rain." Artist Cindy Kolling, owner of Northwind Productions, sells her stationery products out of her mother's barn. The American Legion Gully Post 603 and Auxiliary maintain an active post in this remarkable city.

Built in 1938 by the WPA and local carpenters, the Gully Hall is used for community gatherings, dances, auctions, rummage sales and Senior Meals. In 1990, Gully gathered all their resources, including the City Council, American Legion & Auxiliary, Gully Township and the Community Club, to remodel the hall.

Carol Torgerson remodeled her mom's 1930s bungalow into the Agassiz Hill Guest House, a cozy retreat on the Pine to Prairie Birding Trail.

When Glacial Lake Agassiz receded, it left behind unique habitat suitable to over 275 species of birds. There is more birding nearby. Gully Fen Scientific and Natural Area, a 1,610-acre site managed by the DNR, along with nearby rice paddies, attracts birds endemic to lowland conifers, as well as migrating waterfowl, shorebirds and hundreds of swans.

"WE'RE SPREADING THE WORD"

GULLY CAFE

"HOME COOKING"

Jan, Don, Jodi, Carole & Bett...

The Hadley Buttermakers' annual Fan Appreciation Day is a free-for-all—free watermelon, free corn-on-the-cob, free root beer floats and free beer.

TOP: Hadley on Summit Lake

Hadley

Gamblers Beware: Don't Bet Against Hadley's Baseball Team

HADLEY IS ALL ABOUT BASEBALL. Home to the Buttermakers Baseball Team, Hadley sports one of the first baseball teams in Minnesota. Organized in 1882, the talented Buttermakers put Hadley on the map. The local butter makers at the creamery churned out highly prized butter, hence the name of the team. Over the years, the team won four trips to the state tournament in the forties, and again in 2001. The citizens in Murray County took their baseball very seriously and were not above betting on a game now and then. When the Iona baseball team lost to Hadley, Leo McDonald from Iona lost his bet on the game, and had to push Hadley supporter Ben Wagner in a wheelbarrow all the way to Hadley.

Overlooking beautiful Summit Lake, Hadley sits on a hill in the center of Murray County surrounded by prairie grass and cornfields. The first settlers, Hans Simonson and Christian Christiansen, arrived from Norway in 1872. They were closely followed by Gilbert Johnson, Theodore Knutson, Claus Clausen, L. O. Solem, Peter Thompson, Nels Sevenson, Hans Jacobson, Olus Johnson and Sven Nilson. Initially called Summit Lake, the city was re-named by railroad officials on the arrival of the St. Paul and Sioux City Railroad Company in 1879. However, the city waited to incorporate until 1903. The patience of the settlers was immediately tested the following year, when a devastating blizzard hit in mid-October. Forced to leave their threshing undone and with cornfields under several feet of snow, farmers could not pay their bills. By February 1881, food and fuel supplies dwindled to a frightening low as the trains were locked in for six weeks. Kerosene was non-existent and hay was scarce.

The town survived, and like all railroad towns, several businesses followed the railroad, including the oldest business in Hadley, the Clauson Well Company, founded in 1900 and open until 1995. Carl Clauson also jumped in on the automobile craze, and started Hadley Motor Co., where he sold Essex, Terraplane, and Hudson cars. Another longtime business, the Hadley Lumber Company, founded by B. H. Larson in 1904, operated until 1962 and is now the location of Hadley Steel. On opening day, May 5, 1905, the Hadley Co-operative Creamery churned out 628 pounds of Hadley Gilt Edged Butter, and by 1946, the creamery had produced over 26,000,000 pounds of butter. In the mid-sixties, the creamery went out of business, and the Hadley Sportsman Club, under the leadership of Allan Stuckey, bought the building for their headquarters in 1967. Today the building is a lovely home overlooking the lake. Built in 1914, the Farmer's Co-op Elevator remains a busy drop-off point for corn and soybeans.

Baseball, Free Beer, and a Political Powerhouse

The Hadley Buttermakers continue to embody small town baseball at its best. Manager of the Summit Bar and the baseball team, Myron Bennett runs a well-coached team on the Laurie Mahon Memorial Baseball Field, a perfectly kept field with new dugouts and fences, compliments of a grant from the Minnesota Twins. Season passes are $25, and include a free drink or brat at the home games. The annual Fan Appreciation Day is a free-for-all—free watermelon, free corn-on-the-cob, free root beer floats and free beer. Even the opposing team and fans are invited to the party. The baseball field sits on the site of the former school, demolished in 1963 following consolidation with Slayton.

Hadley is known for its politics. The first female mayor in Minnesota in the early 1940s, Mrs. Elizabeth Bishir, also led the Hadley Study Club, a group of women whose purpose was to the study the political development of the nation. Hadley has also produced four state legislators: Herman Nelson, John G. Johnson, Alex Lowe and Trigg Knutson.

Hadley Today

Today Hadley is home to the Farmer's Co-op Elevator, Camp Summit Campground, Hadley Steel, Pavlis Auction & Realty, Mt. Cavalier Kennels and the Hadley Community Center. A brick and block structure, the Summit Bar & Municipal Liquor Store opened in 1964 with managers Ted and Zelda Ruppert in charge of sales. A Buttermakers baseball jersey hangs from the ceiling. Chartered in 1984, the Hadley Lions Club works tirelessly to support the community. One member, cowboy poet and auctioneer Dale Pavlis, just returned from a 235-mile horseback trip to raise $5,000 for the Lions Club Eye Bank. Hadley also maintains an active Lioness Club, one of three left in the country.

Only one church remains in Hadley—Hadley Lutheran Church, organized in 1873, with the present building erected in 1907. A horrific grasshopper invasion in 1874 destroyed all the crops and led to widespread poverty. In spite of this, the church persevered, and it is the oldest Lutheran church in Murray County.

Hadley is well known for Buffalo Ridge, an awe-inspiring natural formation that shapes the area's weather. Buffalo Ridge consists of sixty miles of rolling hills and features the second-highest point in Minnesota at an elevation of 1,995 feet. Because of its high altitude and wind speed, Buffalo Ridge has over 200 wind turbines harnessing energy for southwestern Minnesota.

The new Hadley Community Center hosts meetings for both the Lions Club and the Hadley Golden Club. Bring a few jokes, a potluck dish, and ten nickels for bingo, and you are guaranteed good conversation and lots of laughs. Socialization continues at the Liquor Store attached to the Community Center where a burger bar and 30-ounce margaritas entice the hungry traveler.

TOP: Eidsvold Lutheran Church quilters

Halma's quilters consistently meet their goal of producing one hundred quilts a year to warm people around the globe.

Halma

From the Hills of Norway to the Fertile Red River Valley

IN 1875, JOHN EDWIN HOLM left the hills of Norway for the fertile Red River Valley farmland near Halma. Holm began farming, and in 1902, he assumed the position of postmaster. Initially named Lofgren, the post office was changed to Halma, either to honor the railroad president's wife, or perhaps the name is a derivative of Holm. Nearby, a settlement named Beaton formed in 1891, with a store and post office opened by entrepreneur B. M. Bothum. Swampy land changed the run of the Soo Line tracks from Beaton to Halma in 1904, and Beaton packed up and moved to Halma. During the slow move of the Beaton Store by horsepower and manpower, the T. L. Spilde family, who lived in the back of the building, carried on with business as usual, selling everything from coffee to harnesses.

The arrival of the Soo Line spurred the platting of the village, but incorporation waited until September 24, 1923. By that time, Halma had three general stores owned by the Bothums, Spildes, and Holms, the Halma State Bank, Folland Hardware, Braaten's Feed Mill, the *Halma Pilot* newspaper, Farmer's Elevator, Bertram Lumberyard, and the Halma Cattle yard, operated by M. P. Halbert. The creamery sold butter for 12½ cents a pound. When the log Lundeby Lutheran Church burned, a new church, Eidsvold Lutheran, was built in 1897. The church was moved to its present location in 1910.

After the Holmberg Act passed in 1912, a new schoolhouse was constructed. The legislation covered twenty-five percent of construction costs for the building, allowed $750 annually for two teachers, and contributed state aid for instruction in manual training, domestic science and agriculture. In addition, the Farmers Club Organization sold candy and hosted basket socials to purchase the school bell, two clocks, and two desks. Fun-loving folks gathered in the school or hall above the restaurant to play "Flies in the Sugar Bowl," "Four in the Boat," "*Der krommer et par ifra vesten*," and "*Di vilde sall sall gjerne el presenten*," and ended the evening with a grand march at twelve o'clock. Singers would gather around the piano to harmonize on the hits of the decade: "Happy Days are here Again," "K-K-K-Katy," and "When Johnny Comes Marching Home Again." The school consolidated with Karlstad in 1961, and is now owned by Jeff Folland, who maintains the original school bell in the tower.

Mail came from Donaldson by route delivery, until the "Flier" started running on the Soo Line in 1904. The postmaster hung the mailbag on a crane near the track platform each evening for the train postal clerk to snag with a hook as the Flier soared by. Originally located in the Spilde store, Nels Oien built a new post office in 1925. Despite a valiant attempt by the community to keep their post office, the office closed in 2008.

An annual Fourth of July celebration drew people to Halma for baseball, sack races, and high jump competitions. A homemade merry-go-round, run by a pulley and horse, and later a gas engine, delighted the children and young at heart. Spectators cheered on tug-of-war contests between the Soo Line boys and the Great Northern boys. When the Trianon City Hall opened in 1936, the hall filled to capacity for weekly movies, basketball games, dances, and rollerskating.

Two Great Baseball Players from Halma, For Hire

Halma boasted a first-rate baseball battery with catcher Severt "Shorty" Spilde and pitcher Louis "Silver" Spilde on the mound. Area teams would hire the two aces to play with them. Fans drove their Fords, Hupmobiles, Imperials, Overlands, or Krits to the ball field to watch their guys play ball.

Halma Today

Today Halma is home to the Halma Community and Senior Center, Fish Construction, Folland Construction, American Legion Post #315, Halma Ideal 4-H Club, Jon's Bar & Grill, and Carlson Prairie Seed Farms, located in the old creamery building. Eidsvold Lutheran Church celebrated 125 years of active service in 2011, with an anniversary service, dinner and live music.

Hop on in to Jon's Bar and Grill, the former Spilde General Store built in 1934, for a great burger. Weekend entertainment by local performers and the Annual Frog Fest in July keep the bar hopping.

Lovely Eidsvold Church, with its well-kept cemetery, recalls the town of Eidsvoll, Norway. On May 17, 1814, in Eidsvoll, the Norwegian Constitution was adopted and Christian Frederik was elected King. The day is now celebrated as Constitution Day, or *Syttende Mai*. Each fall the church hosts a Fall Harvest Festival at the Halma Hall complete with a turkey dinner and music such as the Popple Ridge Pickers, a gospel singing team from Lancaster. Every Wednesday, quilters Audella Stamnes, Helen Rickenberg, Lorraine Prosser, and Joydis Folland meet for a quilting bee. The quilters consistently meet their goal of one hundred quilts a year to warm people around the globe. As the photographer took multiple photos of the group, Joydis asked why he needed so many photos. He replied that he hoped to get at least one really good picture, to which she replied, "You should get a better camera."

Built in 1935 by the WPA and local labor, the Halma Community Center is a classic example of building construction in Minnesota during the thirties. A flag waves proudly on a rock pedestal with the inscription, *Halma Centennial 1904–2004.*

By the '40s, the Hollyhock read like a Who's Who of the Music World, hosting a dance every night of the week to the big band songs of live performers Duke Ellington, Tommy Dorsey and Guy Lombardo.

TOP: Hatfield Bar & Grill

Hatfield

A Music Destination during the '50s, '60s and '70s

WHEN THE HOLLYHOCK BALLROOM OPENED in 1933, owners Don and Effie Shadeck put Hatfield on the map. By the '40s, the Hollyhock read like a *Who's Who* of the Music World, hosting a dance every night of the week to the big band songs of live performers Duke Ellington, Tommy Dorsey and Guy Lombardo. After Alvin Kirby bought the Hollyhock from the Shadecks, he maintained the same schedule except for a brief respite during Lent, when he closed the doors for six weeks. Hatfield continue to rock in the fifties, sixties, and seventies. Big names like Neal Sedaka, Fats Domino, Lawrence Welk, Bobby Vee, Bobby Vinton, Del Shannon, the Everly Brothers, Jerry Lee Lewis, Conway Twitty, Lou Christy, and the Beach Boys played to apprecia-tive and lively audiences. Myron Lee and the Caddies from Sioux Falls played fifty shows at the Hollyhock to well over 1,000 fans for each show. A seven-piece rock-and-roll band from Concordia, Kansas, the Sensational Showmen, and a band named The Beautiful People from Columbus, Nebraska, played to standing-room-only crowds. Harold Paulsen, Hatfield mayor for 26 years, recalls the heydays of Hatfield: "Some nights in the 1960s and 1970s, there were upwards of 1,500 young people at the Hollyhock on Friday and Saturday nights. Every street was crowded with parked cars, and the line to get into the ballroom stretched two blocks."

When the first train passed through Hatfield on December 5, 1879, the engine conductor had three views: a vast landscape of fields and prairie, one windmill, and the sign "Hatfield." The windmill went up in 1880, the first structure in town, followed by several businesses.

Surveyed in 1882, the 13-acre townsite developed with organization of the Union Sabbath School, Colman Lumber Company, Converse General Store (with the post office tucked in a corner), and Bonner & Hyde wheat warehouse. In 1890, School District #13 opened with a fine two-room building complete with a steeple bell and six-column entryway. That same year, a new Woodmen of the World Lodge provided the perfect venue for dances, basket socials and political speeches. School children practiced for the Christmas program on the Woodmen Hall stage, and used ropes to raise and lower the canvas curtain on a roller. When the depot, with living quarters upstairs, burned in 1910, depot agent F. A. Widmayer lost all his possessions. By the time Hatfield incorporated September 9, 1919, Adolph Smallfield (no kidding) had erected a modern concrete elevator, and William "Chicken" Smith ran a chicken incubator, and a hand-operated printing press. He printed the election ballots for the village elections, and served as the village clerk from 1919 to 1938. After the Farmer's State Bank closed in 1926, the building housed a pool hall, grocery store, municipal liquor store, and finally Kor's Café before closing for good.

In 1983, longtime resident Walter Weiner offered a glimpse into life in early Hatfield when he wrote about people who helped define Hatfield: "George Grover was so bow legged he couldn't stop a pig in an alley. Dreese DeBoer migrated to this country with his family from Holland, and wore the traditional wooden shoes. George Fleming retired in Hatfield after an active family life. Rudolph Boomgaarden, a section hand, had the name Rickety, which seemed to be very appropriate for him. Fred Hintze was a skilled carpenter, and built many of the buildings in and around Hatfield, but he never let driving nails interfere with his fishing. William Smith had a small hand-operated printing press, and did a lot of printing in his home. Charles Kerkove operated a steam threshing machine for many years in the area. William Haubrick took pride in his fine garden, vineyard and orchard. Jack Lynch, everybody's friend."

In the late 60s, Hatfield's heydays came to an end, as the school had closed in 1955 and rail service ended. With attendance on a downward slide and the building in disrepair, the Hollyhock was razed in the late 1980s. Another blow to the city was the loss of a seventy-foot cottonwood in front of the ballroom. Renowned for the beautiful Christmas lights strung on its limbs each year, the Hatfield landmark was removed in 1984 by the county to make way for a wider street.

The Hollyhock—The Best Ballroom of Them All

In his memoir, *Myron Lee and the Caddies—Rockin' and Rollin' Out of the Midwest*, the former Myron Wachendorf writes about his favorite ballroom, the Hollyhock: "Hatfield was the epitome. It was perfect. There was a lot of drinking, a lot of fights and a lot of dancing. It was one of the most popular dance halls in the area, and every time we appeared there, we packed the place. It was raucous but enjoyable. A hollyhock, my mother told me, is a hardy flower popular in this area in the 1920s and 1930s, that many old-timers say could survive here on the flatlands even with conscious neglect. That pretty well sums up the Hollyhock Ballroom at Hatfield. It was hardy and it survived, that's for sure."

Hatfield Today

Five sets of deer antlers on carved posts adorn the front of the Hatfield Bar & Grill, a historic bar across from the former ballroom. Owner Deanna Smith, who moved to Hatfield in 2004, displays wildlife mounts of geese, ducks and pheasant in the newly decorated bar.

Why the name Hatfield? In 1879, on an extremely windy day, one of the men on the railroad grading crew kept retrieving his hat from a field, and jokingly named the area Hatfield. The name stuck, and the station of the Southern Minnesota Railroad evolved into the city of Hatfield.

Before a gas engine furnished power to the town's grain elevator, an old blind horse, "Sam," did the work. Clara Thorpe earned her first nickel by coaxing Sam to pick up his speed.

TOP: Jolly Workers 4-H Club City Park

Hazel Run

A Farm Town That Loves Music

YOU CANNOT TALK ABOUT HAZEL RUN without mentioning grain and music. Named after the Hazel Run Creek, a tributary of the Minnesota River, the village was platted in 1884 by Norwegian settlers. The post office opened with Ole Fostvedt as postmaster. When the Minneapolis and St. Louis Railroad arrived the same year, farmers could now haul grain, livestock, and machinery to Minneapolis, the top milling center in the country. Surrounded by rich farmland, area farmers established the Hazel Run Produce Company (a grain elevator), one of the longest-running cooperatives in Minnesota. Initially a flat shed for storing sacks of grain, the newly erected elevator loaded 3,320 bushels of grain in one day. Before a gas engine furnished power to the building,

an old blind horse, "Sam," did the work. Clara Thorpe earned her first nickel by coaxing Sam to pick up his speed. Farmers were paid in gold for their grain, the gold shipped by express.

And those farmers were first-rate musicians, too. In 1918 the Hazel Run Cornet Band formed with thirty-one men, and the Ljom Male Choir began with thirteen members. When the band equipment burned in a 1923 fire, the community rallied to replace the music and instruments. In 1934 the band was selected to play at the Minnesota State Fair, but none of the members had any money during the Depression to travel to St. Paul. Band treasurer Johnny Jurgenson drove to Clarkfield to request a $200 loan from the bank, and with the borrowed money and the $100 in the band treasury, each member had $10 in his pocket for the three-day gig. Determined to raise funds for a bandstand, the band played Wednesday night concerts, attracting music lovers from around the county. That memory-filled bandstand now stands on the bank of the Minnesota River, a donation to the Yellow Medicine Historical Society from the community of Hazel Run. A square dance club, the Hazel Run Fiddle Footers, met for ten years in the village hall to carry on the tradition of early American dance.

By 1887, the city had three grocery stores, two blacksmiths, five elevators, two saloons and the Jertson Hotel, owned by James Jertson. A Norwegian immigrant and founder of Hazel Run village, he began building businesses, homes, and the Norwegian Lutheran Church, including the altar, pulpit, and baptismal font, while his wife Clara ran the hotel. Meanwhile, his father, Herman Jertson, managed the Hazel Run Produce Company from 1897 to 1932. The city incorporated in 1902, the same year the Hazel Run State Bank opened. Fire was the nemesis of all towns and Hazel Run was no exception. On July 19, 1910, a gas tank exploded at the Jertson Store and five businesses were destroyed, including the post office. This fire was one of many over the years, including one in the fire hall itself in 1940.

In 1898, a two-story wooden schoolhouse was built in town to educate 77 students. Without an auditorium, the plays, operettas, spelling bees, and graduations were held in the village hall. Forty-one years later, the WPA built a two-story brick schoolhouse, complete with an auditorium, stage, kitchen and a library. The school consolidated with Clarkfield in 1970.

A Virtuoso Violinist and a Very Old Grain Elevator

Steiner Odden, a famous Hardanger fiddle player born in Telemarken, Norway, immigrated to Hazel Run in 1911. He married Marion Hagen in 1918, raised six children on their farm, and performed all over the country with his rare eight-stringed violin, the Norwegian national folk instrument. Steiner repaired his own fiddle bows using hair from the tail of a white horse, and replaced missing mother-of-pearl ornamentation with clam shells from the Minnesota River.

Now a privately owned elevator used for storage, the Hazel Run Produce Company grain elevator was the second-longest running co-op elevator in the state. Only Underwood, Minnesota, has an older elevator still in operation, and only two other co-op elevators in the United States have a longer record of existence. When the company celebrated its Diamond Jubilee in 1961, 331 shareholders and guests were treated to a steak dinner and an open house at the elevator. Mrs. Waldrum displayed her antique dishes; her husband, Arlen, exhibited his old 1900 Maxwell.

Oliver C. Wilson, born in 1849 to Norwegian immigrants, helped found the Norwegian Mutual Insurance Company. He served as the first president until his death in 1916, when his son, Clarence, took over as president for 35 years. Oliver Wilson was also elected to the state legislature from 1890 until 1893.

Hazel Run Today

Today Hazel Run is home to City Hall and the Fire Hall, Dyrdahl Lumber Construction, the Hazel Run Elevator (now privately owned) and Anderson-Tongen American Legion Post 559. An annual Memorial Day service is held in city hall. The bell from the old fire hall holds court in front of the new city building. According to a local source, the clapper was removed from the bell because pranksters liked to ring the bell at midnight. The Hazel Run Lutheran Church rests near a lovely cemetery, located on a hill and surrounded by a cornfield. A small chapel adorns the entry to the cemetery.

Each year, Hazel Run Lutheran Church hosts a well-attended dinner and quilt auction following the Memorial Day program at the community center and cemetery.

TOP: City view, St. Scholastica Catholic Church

Population: 122   Incorporated: 1894

INSETS L to R: Stars & Stripes Garage • Odenthal Meats •
City Hall • Friedens Evangelical Lutheran

Founded in the late 1850s by two German immigrant farmers, the town fathers were smuggled to the United States by hiding in wine barrels.

Heidelberg

The Town Fathers Smuggled into the U.S. via Wine Barrels

FOUNDED IN THE LATE 1850S by two German immigrant farmers, Frank Heil and Frederick Ihrig, Heidelberg is named in honor of the German city widely known for its famous university. The story is told that Frank Heil and his two younger brothers, Joseph and Thomas, were smuggled to the United States by hiding in wine barrels. Shortly after their arrival, Frank Heil and F. W. Ihrig opened a sawmill, until Frank sold his share and bought a brewery in Jordan. Although the railroad lines bypassed Heidelberg for New Prague, Heidelberg thrived as an inland city due to rich black soil suitable for bumper crops of wheat, oats and corn.

In 1878, Andrew Thompson platted the city and recorded a population of 130. When the city officially incorporated June 26, 1894, several businesses lined Main Street. Joseph Heil, by now a veteran of the Civil War and the Dakota Sioux Conflict, and his wife Sophia, opened a general store to sell groceries, seeds and patent medicine. Frank Hauber and Albert Zika, an immigrant from Bohemia, each opened a blacksmith shop. Ihrig's flour mill paid area farmers $200,000 for their wheat, which shipped to the International Milling Company in New Prague for production into *Seal of Minnesota* brand flour. Each day Rose Holub baked bread for eleven hours at the mill office to make sure that flour shipped that day met company standards. Farmers socialized at F. J. Weiland's coffee and schnapps bar, and Albert Ambroz built a business block named the Ambroz Hall.

The year 1906 was good to Heidelberg. The community danced to music by the Heidelberg band in their new hall, and also celebrated the dedication of St. Scholastica Church by Archbishop Ireland. By 1882, the parish counted 137 families: 70 Czech, 53 German and 14 of Polish descent. Parents chose among three schools for their children's education. Two miles north of the village, Frieden's Evangelical Lutheran Church operated a private school; a Catholic school opened under Father Simonik, and everyone else attended public School District #7. In 1913, the creamery added a cheese factory, the only one in Le Sueur and Nicollet County.

Early in the twentieth century, the sugar beet harvest was the mainstay of farmers. Later, farmers switched to growing wheat, which required threshing. Backbreaking work and time intensive, threshing was only slightly easier with the help of a wood-fired steam engine and threshing machine. Both John Guessen and Frank Ambroz traveled with their threshing crews from farm to farm to assist with the harvest. Frank was an ambitious man. After a long hot day on the threshing rig, he helped his father tend bar at the Ambroz Hall. Later on, Frank owned a sawmill, and in the winter he cut ice by hand to supply the saloons in the area. Many of the homes in Heidelberg were built by Frank Ambroz. After his father, Albert Ambroz, retired as Mayor of Heidelberg in 1949, Frank became Mayor until his death in 1973.

A Bicentennial Game of Euchre

Heidelberg claimed fame as the smallest official bicentennial Minnesota city in 1976. Lieutenant Governor Rudy Perpich presented the city with a bicentennial flag in a memorable celebration recorded by WCCO television. The County Sheriff's Posse escorted the Lieutenant Governor and State Senator Clarence Purfeerst from the south city limits to the Heidelberg Liquor Hall. Mayor Gerald Odenthal accepted the official flag from Mr. Perpich on behalf of the city. In return, Frank

Ademmer, the longest serving member of the city council presented the Lieutenant Governor with a Heidelberg beer stein. After the ceremony, the church ladies served sauerkraut and bratwurst to hundreds of people.

Heidelberg is the Euchre Capital of the entire world. Following the presentation of the bicentennial flag to the city, a game of euchre started and continued for 200 hours, one hour of euchre for each year of the United States. Lt. Governor Perpich and Mayor Odenthal teamed up to defeat Tony Lambrecht and Betty Odenthal, co-chairmen of the Bicentennial Committee, proving once again that you cannot win against politicians. The Heidelberg Euchre Tournament received international recognition in newspapers and interviews from all over the world.

Heidelberg Today

Today Heidelberg is home to KZ Plumbing, the artistic Stars & Stripes Garage, Heidelberg Bar & Liquor (the former Ambroz Hall), City Hall with the original school bell, Odenthal Meats, Theresa Hlavac's Beauty Salon, and St. Scholastica Church. Frieden's Lutheran Church, a majestic brick structure, stands two miles north of town. A community park, created for the city bicentennial celebration by the Heidelberg Athletic Association, borders St. Scholastica Cemetery. On the north side of town, a new 80-acre development of homes lends an air of prosperity and growth in this German and Czech city. Longtime resident Theresa Hinderscheit welcomes each new baby with a gift and a cake.

St. Scholastica Catholic Church, built in 1905, is an architectural testament to the hardworking Czech, German and Polish families who pledged everything they had to build their house of worship. The stately brick building showcases a beautiful hand-carved altar and communion rail built by artists Reverend Ralph Muehlstein and his father in 1953.

Considered one of the best meat markets in Minnesota Czech country, Odenthal Meats, owned by Randy and Laura Odenthal, offers natural beef, pork, and chicken raised by local farmers. Customers drive from the Twin Cities to buy their specialty bratwurst and bacon.

On one memorable day during the early 1920s, the
Henriette logging crews sawed 300,000 feet of
pine near Isanti.

TOP: "Welcome to Henriette"

Henriette

Want Lower Prices? Burn Down the Creamery

AS LUMBER CAMPS HARVESTED virgin timber from the
Minnesota wilderness in the 1800s, the Eastern Minnesota Railroad
followed the cleared land to build a depot in 1898 near Cornell,
which was named after a local sawmill. In 1913, the name changed
to Henriette to avoid confusion with another Minnesota town named
Cornell. By then, over 250 people had cashed in on the Homestead Act,
and struggled to remove stumps and rocks near Henriette to make the
land tillable.

When Henriette incorporated on March 10, 1920, Art Gustafson
operated the lone creamery in town after local farmers, unhappy with
unfair prices for their cream, rode into town on horseback one night,

and burned the Cornell Creamery. Main Street prospered with First
State Bank of Henriette, a central telephone office, a pool hall, and
Thorstenson's Grocery and the post office. Eager to trade business for
adventure, Edward Peterson sold his grocery store to George Morton,
and bought two Ford touring cars to travel to Seattle, Washington. His
14-year-old son Dale, drove the car that carried camping equipment
on gravel roads the entire way. Henriette's only barber, Algot Randall
opened his shop in 1917, took time off to serve in World War I, and continued to cut hair until his death in 1975. When potatoes emerged as the
main industry, Ed Peterson, Gust Norlander and Mr. Butterfield opened
potato warehouses along the railroad tracks. Potatoes were shipped to
the Twin Cities for sale as food or used in starch factories. Meanwhile,

the Henriette Band erected a bandstand in a park near the railroad and furnished music for Honorable Allen Cox from Detroit, Michigan, who rendered a speech on why Pine County should not vote away its right to issue liquor licenses.

Two churches took root in the village. In the early 1900s, John Thomas experienced a conversion in a train boxcar en route from southern Minnesota to Henriette. After settling on a farm near town, he held revival meetings in their home, the school, and even in the potato warehouses. His dream was realized in 1913 when Mrs. Charles Hart, a wealthy widow from Iowa, donated land to build the Free Methodist Church. That same year, a Methodist Episcopal Church was erected, and in 1922, it was purchased by Zion Lutheran Church. The church closed in 1959, and was dismantled in 1966.

In 1910 the village erected a two-room schoolhouse in Henriette on land purchased from Andrew and Christina Swanson. As enrollment surged, in 1916, the school was enlarged by removing the roof and adding a second story for a lovely red brick structure. Former student Leslie Olson recalls the end of a school day, when he slyly remarked to teacher Anna Berglin, "Good night, don't let the bed bugs bite." She made him stay after school for two weeks. When the school consolidated with Pine City in 1967, the school was dismantled. The last graduates from Henriette District #46 were Darryl Dickinson, Caroline Fore, Margaret Kupsch, and Duane Hawkinson. Caroline Fore Hall purchased the bell at auction as a reminder of her school days, and now a piece of District #46 history stands in front of her house.

A Sawmill and a Family of Lumbermen

Swedish immigrant Joseph Steward Olson opened Olson's Sawmill in 1910, and his sons, Leonard and Maynard, continued the business until 1970. A portable rig with a steam engine traveled to area communities every spring to saw logs for farmers, until improved roads allowed transportation to the mill. On one memorable day during the early 1920s, the crew sawed 300,000 feet of pine near Isanti. During World War II, the steam engine was sold for scrap for the war effort, and the mill converted to a diesel-powered engine.

Henriette Today

Today Henriette is home to Ryders Bar & Grill and a sparkling new city hall with separate restrooms for each gender, unheard of in much of little Minnesota. The old Free Methodist Church housed city hall until arson destroyed the building. The original bell from the church, which rang in the New Year and also alerted citizens to fire, now stands in front of the Henriette Community Church. The church, north of town, welcomes visitors with a sign, "Hello! Would the person who has been praying for rain . . . please stop!"

Ryders Bar is home to Ryders Sliders hamburgers, live bands, and the sixth-oldest liquor license in Minnesota. Civic minded owner Sue McNeil offers parking space for a road construction crew, and sells tickets for a television as a fundraiser for the Henriette Area Lions Club.

Melvin "Rasty" Thorson maintains the Henriette Cemetery, a pretty piece of farmland full of lilac bushes and oak trees. Next to city hall, bicyclists on their way to Mille Lacs Lake can enjoy lunch in the new pavilion, built by the Grasston-Henriette Area Lions Club. Each August the community gathers in the park for an annual pig roast and potluck picnic. Although the train doesn't stop, the Burlington Northern blows through town on the way to Duluth.

A skilled inventor and teacher, Henriette resident Joseph Olson patented a set of mill "dogs," a device used to hold logs on the carriage, and he also taught sawmilling courses for the University of Minnesota. The original lumberyard buildings still stand on the south side of town, along with the Olson home.

On his first day of work at St. Rita's church, Father Schoenberg stepped into the church and found that the building was on fire.

TOP: City center, looking south

Hillman

On His First Day of Work, the Priest's Church Burns Down

FATHER MARTIN SCHOENBERG, a Crosier priest and native of Spring Hill, had an inauspicious start in Hillman. Three years following his ordination, he was appointed to St. Rita's Catholic Church ten miles west of Onamia's Crosier Seminary. You can imagine the shock when on his first day of work on March 7, 1943, Father Schoenberg stepped into the church and found the building on fire. The frame church, which was built with great care in the 1920s, was totally destroyed. Undaunted and under the leadership of their new priest, the parishioners gathered to worship in the grade school until the completion of a basement church. The underground church held mass for 24 years until 1967, when the beautiful split-granite and stone church replaced the basement church.

The new church also signaled a new era, as the Second Vatican Council decreed that churches be designed to allow the priest to face the people while presiding at mass.

Originally a logging village, the city was named for Hillman Creek, a nearby creek used to transport logs. Although the Soo Line Railroad laid track through Hillman in 1906, the first train did not come through until 1909 due to the intensive labor needed to lay tracks through the swampy terrain. Not long after the arrival of the Soo Line, Osmar Leigh opened the first general store in Hillman. For much of his life, Osmar was missing a finger, but his family never knew why. This mysterious absence was not solved until Osmar was in his nineties and an acquaintance finally told the story. Apparently, he and his buddies got caught in a tavern brawl and during the ruckus, someone bit Osmar Leigh's finger off.

A bank opened in 1915 followed by Gorse Lumber Company and the Hillman Co-op Creamery, managed by William Haggerty until the business closed in 1958. After several years of standing on the road waiting for the postman to come by, the city rejoiced at finally having a post office in the lumber building. 1917 was an exciting year, as the Gedney Pickle Company of St. Cloud opened a plant in Hillman. Local families contracted with the company to grow cucumbers on a set number of acres and Gedney provided the seeds. One dry summer, snakes slid out of the swamps to drink juice from broken cucumbers, and Mrs. Walter recalled hearing the sound of frogs as the snakes ate them. The pride of Hillman, a new school in town opened in 1920 with three classrooms and indoor plumbing and heating. Students completed their 8th-grade education in Hillman and took the train to Onamia to finish high school.

St. Rita's Church began in the Diedrich brother's farm home May 22, 1920, when Reverend Pringle offered the first mass on the feast of St. Rita. Two years later, a new church opened at a cost of $1,000, the money raised through church picnics and an annual assessment of $12 on families and $6 on bachelors. Through the zealous efforts of Father Stiegler, *Extension Magazine* donated $500, a statue of St. Rita, a chalice, a ciborium, and a white vestment. Hot on the heels of the Catholics, Immanuel Evangelical Lutheran Church organized on October 13, 1921, at the Community Building of Hillman. In spite of early deaths, fire and snowstorms, the church persevered. The first funeral in the fledgling congregation was for a founding member, 33-year-old Charles F. King. One pastor's wife remembers singing "Jesus Savior Pilot Me" as they traveled home through multiple snowstorms. When the Community Building burned down in 1923, the members met in the school until the new church opened in 1930 on land donated by Louis Strauch and Gust Carlson. The task of excavating the basement went to J. E. West, who used his Fordson tractor and a handheld breaking plow.

The city incorporated in 1938 with George McDonald as first mayor and a population of 71.

A Priest Recruited by the Saint Paul Saints

St. Rita's Catholic Church celebrated their Golden Jubilee in 1970 and their 75th anniversary in 1995 with an anniversary mass and open house. In a true sense of unity, members of Immanuel Lutheran Church provided the anniversary lunch so that all St. Rita's parishioners could celebrate their 75th. One attendee, Father Raymond Schulzetenburg, pastor from 1949 to 1952, enjoyed playing shortstop and pitching for the Hillman baseball team. The St. Paul Saints recruited the athletic priest for their professional team, an offer the opposing teams understood. Father Schulzetenburg recalls an inordinate number of intentional walks by opposing pitchers. The church continues to celebrate with two gala events each year: the fall auction with quilt bingo and the church picnic.

Immanuel Evangelical Congregation celebrated their 60th anniversary on September 13, 1981 at 122 members strong. A new church structure opened in 2005, and the small church built in 1930 is now a private home.

Hillman Today

Today the city boasts the Hillman Bar & Grill and the American Legion Wojciak-Talberg Post #602, an award-winning post with a state-high membership of 182 members. Post Commander Ronald Rinkel leads the post in the original 1920 school building, repurposed as a home for the legion since 1976, two years after the school closed. A very active Richardson Lake Lion's Club holds their monthly meetings at the legion.

No smallest city hosts a better Fourth of July than Hillman, and the event is always held on the 4th, rain or shine. Three to five thousand patriots fill the city for the parade, food, softball tournament and horseshoe tournament.

Rationing cards became a way of life in Holt during World War II. Earl and Christine Carlson borrowed sugar rationing stamps to make a wedding cake, and family members pooled their gas stamps for the newlyweds' honeymoon trip to International Falls.

TOP: Holt Community Park

Holt

An Idyllic Setting, and Holt Orders a Moose from the Eskimos

WHEN THE SANDRIDGE POST OFFICE opened in 1901 on a ridge trail near what is now Holt, the Indians had traveled the trail for centuries. Old Lake Agassiz melted and drained into the Hudson Bay, leaving behind ridges for early travel. Indians traveled to Sandridge to trade their fish, black snakeroot, and furs for milk, butter, eggs and potatoes from the settlers. Abundant oak and aspen forests provided a natural habitat for wildlife, while the bogs supported cattail, sarsaparilla and berries. Vast quantities of waterfowl, fish, beaver, mink, caribou, deer and moose flourished in the remote area. In 1904, the Great Northern Railway arrived to enlist the help of men and mules to haul sand from the ridge to build the railroad track. The village then

officially changed its name from Sandridge to Holt in honor of Norwegian pioneer Halvor Holte, and incorporated on March 16, 1915.

A May 31, 1914, issue of the *Minneapolis Journal* described Holt: *"Holt is a thriving little town situated in the heart of eastern Marshall County with a population of 200. It is in the midst of a rich and well developed farming district. It has two banks, two good hotels, a weekly newspaper, four general merchandise stores, a hardware store, excellent public schools, a blacksmith shop, two lumberyards, two grain elevators, a first class creamery and a livery barn. There are Lutheran and Free Mission churches there. The principal industries are farming, dairying and stock raising.*

Holt began to boom. Local farmers counted 500 milk cows in the area and opened the Holt Cooperative Creamery in 1907. A typical Saturday in downtown Holt included a stop at the creamery to deliver cream to receive cash to spend in the stores on Main Street. Children eagerly anticipated a stop at Ma Nyhus' for penny candy, and the entire family enjoyed a treat at the Bennes Café. On a dance night, you could swing to the music of Tiny and His Toe Teasers from Red Lake Falls. By the time three Minneapolis men opened the Holt State Bank in 1922, Holt listed a population of 232. A meticulous general store, Sollom Brothers Store sold everything from cigars to chicken feed during the '30s and '40s. Emilie Carlson Peterson recalls her mother choosing chicken feed sacks with the prettiest prints in order to sew dresses for her daughters. In 1911, *The Northern Light* began publication. Renamed *The Holt Weekly News* in 1914, it continued until May 30, 1952, when Western Union discontinued its Ready Print Service. When publisher Hans Hanson died in 1946, his wife Mabel was the first woman to both publish and edit a newspaper in Minnesota.

The people in Holt took action when the moose population declined. By the time the legal moose season closed in 1922, the moose population was almost extinct and only farm cows were left. The city garnered the support of the Minnesota Department of Fish and Game, who contracted with the Eskimos for a live bull moose, which they hauled two hundred miles by dog sled and then flew by plane to the nearest airport. Placed in a pen fourteen feet high near Holt, he successfully cleared the fence to breed in the wild.

When the United States entered World War II on December 7, 1941, rationing cards and Victory gardens became a way of life. Earl and Christine Carlson borrowed sugar rationing stamps to make a wedding cake, and family members pooled their gas stamps for the newlyweds' honeymoon trip to International Falls. The economic strain eased a bit when the lowly cattail that grew in the marshes around Holt spawned a new business during World War II. Prior to the war, the United States imported 90% of its kapok (silky down from a kapok tree) supply from the Dutch East Indies for insulation in mattresses, sleeping bags and life preservers. When the islands fell to the Japanese, the kapok supply was cut off, and the cattail proved an excellent replacement for Navy life jackets and aviation jackets. Two to three hundred pounds of cattails were picked a day around Holt for use as insulation. The cattails were fed into a hammer mill which blew the cattails into settling chambers. Fans would separate the lighter fluff which was then baled by using an old paper press. The business provided much-needed income before closing when the war ended.

As dairy farming decreased due to higher costs, the creamery sold in 1958. The post office closed in 1969, and the Holt School followed suit in 1970. Although the depot doors shut in 1960, the freight train still rolls through Holt.

The Creation of Agassiz National Refuge

Former farmland for early settlers in Holt, the Agassiz National Wildlife Refuge was established in 1937. Marshes were drained into arable land in 1909, with approximately one million dollars spent on the drainage system by 1933. By 1937, the government had declared sixty thousand acres suitable only for wildlife and farmers were forced to vacate their farms. Ten square miles of land in the Mud Lake area were condemned by the state in the largest single condemnation proceeding in United States history.

Holt Today

Today Holt is home to Nazareth Lutheran Church built in 1906, Mary Ann Swan's Beauty Shop and Davidson Ready Mix and Construction, which occupies the former creamery. The old federal-style schoolhouse, built in 1914, hosted the Once in a Blue Moon Reunion and parade on July 3, 2007. Now the owner of the building, Ron Davidson towed his 727 airplane behind a tractor along with sixty-five other parade entries.

The Agassiz National Wildlife Refuge offers beautiful hiking trails to view the resident moose herd, waterfowl, and other migratory birds. The refuge supports 287 species of birds and 49 species of mammals.

TOP: Old School Bell, on former school grounds

A champion long-distance runner, resident Ephraim Clow made a running track in the Hill Farm Barn, where he held racing contests for local youth.

Humboldt

The Bread Basket of the World and a Town Renowned for Athletes

DESCRIPTIONS OF THE FERTILE FARMLAND around Humboldt sound like Paul Bunyan legends. The founding of Humboldt by the great railroad builder James J. Hill only adds to the legend. Platted in 1889 as the town of Fairview, the rich soil of the Red River Valley is called "the breadbasket of the world." In 1896, Hill changed the name to Humboldt in honor of the great German naturalist, Baron Alexander Von Humboldt, and the many German people who had invested in railway bonds.

Excitement reigned over the area in 1878 when the Great Northern Railway snaked through Humboldt, and joined the Canadian Railroad in Emerson, Manitoba. For the first time, wheat could be shipped on a continuous track from Winnipeg, Manitoba, to St. Paul, Minnesota. James J. Hill, the owner of 45,000 acres along the tracks from Northcote to Humboldt, decided to sell 80- to 160-acre lots to encourage settlement along the tracks. Always the businessman, he paid $2.75 an acre and sold the farm lots for $5.00 to $6.00 per acre. Highly profitable in both land sales and grain sales, James J. Hill's own Humboldt farm was planned around diversification: raising stock in addition to wheat.

The first settlers in Humboldt, Charley Clow and Nels Finney, arrived by boat on the Red River from Canada's Prince Edward Island. Another early settler, James Diamond, stepped off the train south of Humboldt where the tracks ended. Although Mr. Hill is given credit for the settlement of Humboldt, the true developers of the village were brothers Edward "Ted" and James Florance. In 1897, Edward organized the First State Bank of Humboldt, the only bank in Kittson County to remain open after the Depression, out of 17 in all. The bank moved to Hallock in 1936, but the original bank safe resides at the Kittson County Museum in Lake Bronson, Minnesota. In 1911, James Florance and N. J. Nelson bought Nels Finney's store, and the new E. Florance & Co. housed the first electric light system in the county. On the second floor, the first movies in Kittson County were introduced to an appreciative audience.

However, the city of Humboldt was not all business, and the settlers made time for sports. Another Prince Edward Island native, Ephraim Clow, along with his three brothers, moved to Boston, Massachusetts, in 1854, and then to Humboldt to buy farmland. A champion long-distance runner, he made a running track in the Hill Farm Barn, where he held racing contests for local youth. He died July 26, 1927, in Humboldt, and is buried on his farmland, now the Humboldt-Clow Cemetery. Another sports great, Cal Farley, moved to Humboldt at age 16 to play on Walter Hill's semi-professional baseball team. Born December 25, 1895, in Saxton, Iowa, Cal left an unhappy home at age 16 to fend for himself in Humboldt. When he left Humboldt in 1917 for World War I in the Third Army Division, he won both the American Expeditionary Forces and Inter-Allied Games wrestling titles. Farley continued in professional wrestling after the war, and also played baseball in the minor leagues. Another Humboldt athlete, Flora Bockwitz, hunted with her father as a young girl, and gained fame for her ability to shoot a hundred clay pigeons with a .22 caliber rifle without a miss. An extraordinary sharpshooter, Flora and her husband represented the leading manufacturers of shotguns and rifle ammunition, including the Peters Cartridge Company. Flora thrilled the crowds by shooting a cigarette out of her husband's mouth. Neighbors recalled Flora stepping out the front door and shooting a chicken that was on a dead run in order to cook it for the evening dinner.

By the time Humboldt incorporated in 1919, a farm family lived on every quarter section of land. The city had emerged as a wheat shipping center, and five grain elevators lined the railroad tracks, including the first cooperative elevator in Kittson County. That same year, seven students graduated from Humboldt High School, and when the school closed in 1991, the final class once again graduated seven students.

The Greatest Foster Father

Humboldt citizen from 1911 to 1917, Cal Farley is called "America's Greatest Foster Father," for his work with troubled youth. A champion wrestler and baseball player during World War I, Farley counted Jack Dempsey, Roy Rogers, J. Edgar Hoover and Gene Tunney among his staunchest supporters. In 1939, he founded Boys Ranch in Amarillo, Texas, and Girlstown, U.S.A., near Whitefish, Texas, for homeless children. For his efforts, the United States Postal Service honored Farley with a 34-cent stamp in the Great Americans stamp series. In 1989, the city of Amarillo renamed the Amarillo Civic Center the Cal Farley Coliseum.

Humboldt Today

Today, Humboldt claims CHS Agriliance, the post office, Johnson Oil Company, Bakken Construction, Viking Gas Transmission Company and Humboldt-St. Vincent Elevator. In 2010, the United Methodist Church burned down, but natural disasters haven't stopped this city. Led by board chairwoman Lorna Hemmes, a new church opened in June, 2011, and a new city hall sits next to the church.

Members of the band "The Charms," Maury, Al, and Louise Finney, Arlo Dinusson, Gary Emerson, and the late Doug Renaud were inducted into the Minnesota Rock Country Hall of Fame in 2007. Another Humboldt boy, Jerry Diamond, released four of the Charms records with hit singles, "O Mercy," "Rambunctious," and "Dig Yourself," under his record label "Jay D Records." In 1977, the Country Music Association nominated Maury Finney Instrumentalist of the Year.

On Thanksgiving Day, 1934, Albert and Glen Dahlmeier walked along Split Rock Creek and envisioned a recreational lake and park. Now a 228-acre park, Split Rock Creek Park hosts over 100,000 visitors a year.

TOP: Ihlen city park and playground

Ihlen

A Lake Amid the Prairie, A Railway Hub, Bank Robberies, and More

IHLEN HAS ALWAYS DARED TO DREAM BIG. On Thanksgiving Day, 1934, Albert and Glen Dahlmeier walked along Split Rock Creek and imagined a recreational lake and park that could be developed by expanding on a dam built earlier by the Great Northern Railway. The men drew up plans for their dream, and along with a group of Ihlen businessmen, drove to St. Paul to lobby for money. Amazingly, the Split Rock dam was one of eleven projects approved for construction by the Works Progress Administration and the State Department of Conservation. Now a 228-acre park, Split Rock Creek Park hosts over 100,000 visitors a year.

Split Rock Creek has been good to the city of Ihlen. In 1888, the Wilmar and Sioux Falls Railroad bought land from Carl Ihlen for a village next to the railroad. Twenty-eight years later, when the Great Northern Railway planned to build a million-dollar freight division center, James J. Hill chose Ihlen over Pipestone because of easy access to water in Split Rock Creek. The twenty-stall roundhouse, the new depot, and the coaling station was the largest facility of its kind west of Chicago. Designated a point of registry, the depot required all trains to stop there to record the number and type of train cars. In the early 1900s, a general freight train hauling grain and coal went through Ihlen each day, and a livestock freight train followed a few hours later. Four passenger trains also stopped in Ihlen, two northbound and two southbound. Area citizens could hop the train to Sioux Falls for a day of shopping and arrive back in Ihlen that evening. Community elders remember the director of the Ihlen Municipal Band taking the train to Ihlen for rehearsals, and returning to his home in Marshall on the late train. Following the expansion of the railroad facility, the old depot was converted to the "Beanery," a railside restaurant where the Great Northern Railway workers and passengers could eat breakfast or pick up snacks. The city of Ihlen boomed until the advent of diesel-powered locomotives made the stop for coal no longer necessary.

Ihlen's oldest business, John Olson's general store, was built in 1885 and reorganized as the Ihlen Mercantile Company in 1903. When Lewis Wilson bought the store in 1924, he remained the president of the business until he died working at the store in 1960. His daughter, Lucille Mertz, worked in the store for forty-eight years, before selling the business to Bruce and Joyce Rodman in 1977. In 1985, the Rodmans moved the store into their home to save costs. Albert Olson's hardware store opened in 1894 and the Bank of Ihlen followed in 1904. Three grain elevators operated in Ihlen at the turn of the century, their success partially due to the low freight rates on the Great Northern freight line. Sadly, in 1918, the Northwestern Elevator burned, and both the Farmer's Co-op Elevator and the Cunningham Elevator burned in the 1930s. They were never replaced.

The State Bank of Ihlen opened in 1908, and survived two robberies in 1933. The first heist involved the theft of $2,000, but the second robbery resulted in two wounded employees. Both Ted Arp, the bank cashier, and Joe Evenson, the bank president, were seriously wounded, but luckily, both fully recovered. The two masked men grabbed four hostages, placed them on the car running boards and finally released them unharmed a mile out of town. The thieves were never apprehended.

The only church in the city, Norwegian Zion Lutheran Church, kept the doors open from 1900 to 1960. A grandson of a former charter member, Curt Sabies purchased the church and, along with community members, restored the church for the Ihlen centennial in 1988. Now known as the Ihlen Chapel, the church serves as a venue for weddings and special occasions. The original one-room schoolhouse built in 1898 closed after serving students from Ihlen for 63 years. The school bell rang for the last seventeen students in May 1961. Their teacher, Mrs. Eva Bork, was still using the original teacher's desk and chair from 1898.

Gone are the days when the Greek immigrants lived in boxcars and worked for the Ihlen railroad division. In the early years, the Greeks, dressed in their native apparel, strolled Main Street, playing their concertinas.

A Manmade Lake in the Middle of the Prairie

One mile south of Ihlen, Split Rock Creek State Park is an unusual park set in the middle of agricultural flatland. Starting as a reservoir of water formed by a natural dam on Split Rock Creek, the WPA built a stone dam and stone bridge to form an 80-acre lake and a 238-acre park. A small hill just before the campground retains the original prairie grasses and plants, a rare example of what the land looked liked before agriculture. Constructed in 1938 of Sioux quartzite stone from nearby Jasper, the Split Rock Bridge exhibits the largest stone arch span of any active highway bridge in Minnesota.

Ihlen Today

Today, the Ihlen business district is home to the Glass Restaurant, the Cutting Junction, Olsen Electric, Ihlen Chapel, Ihlen Eden Community Center, and Split Rock Creek Park. Joyce Rodman runs the post office from the front porch of her home, where residents arrive for coffee in her cozy kitchen.

Even though the church had been closed for 25 years, Jode Rodman was determined that she and her fiancé, Dennis Bjerke, would be married in the old The Ihlen Chapel. After much sanding, cleaning, and repairing, Jode and Dennis were married in the historic landmark on May 25, 1985.

TOP: Railroad switchyard, southwest of Iron Junction

During World War II, all the iron ore needed for combat material went through Iron Junction on the Duluth, Missabe & Iron Range Railway.

Iron Junction

A City Perfectly Positioned for Success as a Railroad Hub

IN THE SUMMER OF 1890, the Duluth Missabe and Northern Railway laid track and erected a two-stall roundhouse and depot in Iron Junction, in order to connect the port of Duluth with Mountain Iron and Biwabik. The city's future looked promising, as it looked likely that Iron Junction would become an important railroad intersection. Overnight, multiple homes, thirteen saloons, and four hotels opened up for a sudden population of three hundred and sixty-five. Railroad men filled the large thirty-room Downey Hotel, owned by Dixon and Laury of Duluth, and Hotel Missaba, owned by M. R. Johnson. On July 25, 1893, at P. J. Clure's store, the village elected to incorporate with one hundred forty-two unanimous votes. Due to the strategic location of the site, the

city changed the name from Ryan Junction to Iron Junction, and over the next seven decades, millions of tons of "red rust" were mined in the area. City prospects for long-term prosperity and growth were lost, however, when Stephan Ryan rejected an $18,000 offer by the railroad for land needed to build a railroad yard and headquarters. The railroad moved the entire project to Proctor.

In 1897, Charles Zacher and family moved from Hibbing to take the job as section foreman for the railroad. Several families welcomed the new family including the Griersons, Ryans, McKaiges, Fitzpatricks, Dougals, and Ansleys. Due to the proximity to water, the city functioned as a fuel and watering station for the railroad. A large coal dock holding ten coal cars drew water for the engines from Elbow Creek with a steam-operated McIntosh pumper. A storage tank near the depot leaked continuously, and inebriated men were often placed beneath the tank to hasten the process of sobering up. Iron Junction also functioned as a service center for the many logging camps in the area. Food, grain and other necessities were shipped by train and stored in a warehouse behind the Ansley Saloon. In 1915, Emanuel Moline purchased Kingensmith Grocery and post office. The business continued until his death in 1957 and Mrs. Moline's retirement in 1961.

School District #25, a one-room building with a bell tower, rang the bell in the morning, at noon and after school. Early teacher Etta Young, who lived in the Downey Hotel, recalls the simple entertainment in a railroad town. "Our life revolved around the activity and fortunes of the railroad. From early spring to late fall the ore trains rumbled through town. Six times a day there was a passenger train on the main line. The early morning hours were filled with the noise of freight trains loading and unloading. In summer a circus train offered some variety. All the kids gathered to watch and wish they could have seen more. Social life in the early days was pretty much homemade. There were frequent dances held in the hotel, and they were gay and lively enough to bring handcar loads from Eveleth, and they stayed and danced until dawn. I recall one rather unusual evening which had us all entertained. A man, whose name I have long forgotten, drove a team of moose harnessed to a sleigh around town. He had trained the animals himself and later went on tour with them."

Everyone looked forward to Sundays in Iron Junction. Sunday afternoon, the town gathered at the baseball field to watch Iron Junction take on the Forbes team, who typically arrived by handcar on the railroad tracks. On Sunday evening the young people gathered at the railroad station to meet the trains as a precursor to an evening of singing around the piano at someone's home.

Following the loss of the potential railroad headquarters in 1895, the population quickly declined. In spite of this, Iron Junction remained busy with two passenger trains running daily from Virginia to Duluth. Several students hopped the "Flyer" to attend high school in Virginia. By 1919, the population had settled at ninety-two: the assessed valuation of the city was $1,575. However, once again in 1962, E. W. Anderson, General Superintendent of the Duluth, Missabe and Iron Range Railway recognized the strategic importance of Iron Junction as a railroad center: "The D. M. & N. Railway began its service in 1892 with operations headquarters at Iron Junction, and this year, 1962, with the completion of a long-range study, the Duluth Missabe and Iron Range Railway will come full circle. Once again operations headquarters for the Northern portion of the railroad will be located at Iron Junction." Sadly, Mr. Anderson's prediction did not come to pass.

The City That Helped Launch a Thousand Ships

During World War II, all the iron ore needed for combat material went through Iron Junction on the Duluth, Missabe & Iron Range Railway; trains traveled around the clock, seven days a week. Now named the Canadian Northern Railway, Iron Junction is still quite the railroad town, with 20 trains passing through daily.

Iron Junction Today

Today, Iron Junction is home to City Hall, the post office, and Frank's Taxidermy. City Hall now stands on the former site of Emanuel Moline's General Store and post office, a city fixture until 1961. Mr. Moline's son-in-law, Frank Klabechek Sr., served as postmaster for forty years, and built the present brick post office in the 1940s with money out of his own pocket. The family line continues with Mr. Moline's grandson, Frank Klabechek Jr.

Frank Klabechek Jr. owns Frank's Taxidermy in town. Klabechek played hockey for Eveleth High School, served in Vietnam, got his degree in zoology, and now owns Frank's Taxidermy, a two-building gallery of animals ranging from a fisher to a full-sized bear. When the talented artist isn't working, Frank plays hockey in an over-fifty league in Eveleth.

TOP: Historic cabin and horse-drawn road grader

Johnson Resident David "Andy Bear" Anderson
collects old fire trucks. He often give town
residents a free ride on birthdays, anniversaries
and other special days.

Johnson

A Free Ride in a Fire Truck for Your Birthday

TWO CAREFULLY RESTORED FIRE TRUCKS catch your attention when you drive into the city of Johnson. No, this is not the city fire hall, but the collection of resident David "Andy Bear" Anderson, who collects old fire trucks. The former owner of the Bears Den Bar, Anderson travels to auctions to bid on aging trucks, and takes the fire engines on the road for parades and celebrations. He recently traveled to Casselton, North Dakota, for the Casselton Fire Truck Parade, and took home the "Staff's Favorite Choice" award. He often gives town residents a free ride on birthdays, anniversaries or other special days.

Once a vast treeless prairie, where ducks, geese, coyotes and prairie chickens filled the land, settlers arrived in this area, which was called

Johnson Station as early as 1880. Located on the Saint Cloud and Traverse Railroad Line (later the Great Northern Railway), the city was named in honor of a section foreman. In 1880, Mary Burns opened the first store and post office, later called Duffy's Store following her marriage to Steve Duffy. The post office closed in 1897, and reopened in 1903. Herman Jaenisch opened the first hotel, and in 1905 future liquor store owner Jacob Luchsinger paid his hotel bill with nickels and dimes. Entrepreneur S. L. Duffy built the first elevator, known as the West Elevator, and two others followed: the Cargill and the Northwestern, which later burned. A bank, a cream station, a school, Jones Lumber Company, Fred Andrew's livery stable, two churches, and a depot quickly filled the city. Postmaster from 1913 to 1927, Ted Nerenz also operated Nerenz & Rixe Store in Johnson. The city incorporated on November 12, 1903.

School District 43 held classes in a two-room building west of Johnson from 1882 until 1903, when the school was moved into the city. Teacher Blanche O'Hara's records noted, "No school November 11, 1903—our schoolhouse moved to town of Johnson." Long before scores of teaching manuals and seminars were available for teachers, one of Johnson's early teachers, Mrs. Agnes Hickey, figured out how to teach to a wide range of ages and abilities. She wrote in her 1885 records: "Rule by Kindness. Manners are the happy ways of doing things. You will find the pupils in all grades good workers if you take an interest in their work, and you will have no trouble in governing them if you give them plenty of seatwork to do." District 43 continued with two rooms and two teachers until 1945, when declining enrollment demanded only one teacher. When the public school closed in 1965, the building took on a new life as the Trinity Lutheran Church Parochial School until that school, too, closed in 2001.

About 1907, the German Lutheran Church opened under the leadership of Reverend Fischer and organist Anna Rixe. As a compromise to life in America, the church services were conducted in German and Sunday school classes were held in English. With a growing membership, the congregation moved into a building vacated by the Evangelical Church, which had disbanded in 1923. Later the church combined with Trinity Lutheran Church, 2 miles north of Johnson.

A Guinness World Record—The Most Fire Trucks in a Parade

David Anderson put the city of Johnson on the map with his collection of fire engines. He drove one of 181 fire trucks in the Casselton, North Dakota, Fire Truck Parade to help set a Guinness World Record for the most fire engines in a parade. On a beautiful October day, the bright red engines sit next to his perfectly tended garage.

The Johnson community celebrated Minnesota's Centennial in style. On May 27, 1958, Ed Heuer Sr. and his horse, Old Babe, ferried folks in a two-seated buggy to the schoolhouse to view window displays and artifacts from the history of Johnson. Following the viewing, the pupils and adults, dressed in period attire and clothing worn in the "old country," gathered in the town hall for a program with the following theme: "What has made Minnesota GREAT? Its PEOPLE—they're Minnesota's greatest asset!"

Johnson Today

There are no businesses left in Johnson. Andy's Pop Store on Highway 28 was the last business to close. A corner building with a square turret, the former grocery store inscribed with the name *J. Luchsinger 1912*, faces the railroad track. A concrete slab between the tracks and the town suggests the location of the former elevator. A three-block section of houses is all that remains in this still proud former railroad town. Located two and a half miles north of Johnson, Trinity Lutheran Church celebrated its 125th Anniversary in 2007.

The former school building still stands in town, now owned by a private party and used for storage. A partial playground envisions the past when children ran around during recess.

The Johnson Community Club, with the help of the Great Northern Railway, created a playground for the local children. While the railroad leased land to the community and provided trees and shrubs to beautify the area, the local club sponsored card parties and bake sales to finance the playground equipment and additional flower gardens.

In 1923, Hugo Roeska purchased the old German Lutheran Church and remodeled it for his home. The home is still a residence in Johnson, now known as the Running House.

Mayor Donald Johnsrud reports that Burlington Northern is rebuilding the rails to accommodate a large grain handling system six miles west of Johnson. The mayor and his wife, Elaine Johnsrud, city clerk since 1982, faithfully keep the city in good condition. Don't even try to get map instructions to their house on the computer. The Internet directions lead you a spot in a plowed field in Dumont, seventeen miles away.

TOP:Centennial monument, 1900–2000, with old school bell

A unique structure built in 1901, the Kenneth
School has a slide for a fire escape.

Kenneth

A Farm Town with Promise

TUCKED AWAY IN ONE OF FOUR COUNTIES in Minnesota without a natural lake, Kenneth manages to maintain the past and plan for the future. The youngest and smallest city in Rock County, Kenneth was planned for several months before the Chicago, Rock Island & Pacific Railroad laid track between Worthington and Hardwick in 1900. The new city was founded due to the rich farmland surrounding the area and in the hopes that it would become a service center and a hub for the area's agricultural economy. Land agent J. A. Kennicott worked diligently to choose a desirable site for the city, and the town site company rewarded his effort by naming the city after Mr. Kennicott's son, Kenneth. Before the year was over, three elevators were completed and prepared to handle the corn harvest.

On May 3, 1901, the *Rock County Herald* described Kenneth: *Peopled by enterprising, thrifty and progressive citizens, its business enterprises in the hands of public spirited and far-sighted men, and surrounded by a rich and productive agricultural country, Kenneth enters the list of Rock county towns with every promise of growth and prosperity. Where one year ago was but a fertile field are now two well stocked general merchandise stores, a hardware store, a commodious hotel, a lumberyard, a blacksmith shop, three elevators, livery stable, restaurant, two dray lines, a farm machinery and implement business-all housed in handsome and substantial buildings.* Postmaster James Hogan tucked the post office in a corner of his general store. Before long, A. D. Parker started a second general store, and a new bank was established. Classes began in a handsome two-story school building with 32 students and teacher Nellie Morse. That same year a physician from Holland, Dr. Van Krevelen, moved to town and hung his shingle on a drugstore, along with his medical practice. An attempt to incorporate the city in 1902 failed, due to opposition from farmers who objected to the proposed inclusion of their land into the city limits. The city finally incorporated July 20, 1921.

A School with a Slide for a Fire Escape

Erected in 1901, the Kenneth School is listed on the Registered Historic Places in Minnesota. A unique structure, the school has a slide for a fire escape, and is positioned on a wide expanse of green lawn and is flanked by a playground on one side and a picnic shelter and band shell on the other. The unique band shell sits on antique wheels and is painted with musical notes.

The city of Kenneth celebrated their centennial in 2000 with a parade, a beer garden, a fireman's dance, and an outdoor church service at Kenneth Lutheran Church. Next to the fire hall a granite monument inscribed "Centennial 1900–2000" depicts an engraved train. The old school bell sits next to the monument.

In June of 2010, Nora Halvorson, owner of the Kenneth Bar, spearheaded the first annual Kenneth Fun Day, the first city celebration since the centennial in 2000. More than forty locals chipped in $10 for a 6-mile lawnmower run around two sections of farmland, and gamely drove their mowers in spite of rain and mud. Those without a four-wheeled vehicle rode on the hay wagon. All the participants put their name in a hat, and the winner won a weed eater, compliments of Dave's Repair. Local cooks grilled burgers and brats, and donated bars for the picnic lunch in City Park. Even the old school opened its doors to shelter the wet and hungry party crowd. A planned rodeo was cancelled due to the muddy conditions.

Kenneth Today

Kenneth is home to the Kenneth Bar, Dave Groen Repair, the post office, the Fire Department, Land O' Lakes Fed-Cenex, and Kenneth Lutheran Church. Plans are underway to convert the Kenneth Community Center, formerly the grocery store, into the Kenneth Café. Founded in 1947, the State Bank of Kenneth closed in 1993 after a buyout by the State Bank of Edgerton. Rather than tear down the old bank, the city repurposed the bank into an apartment building. Although the train tracks are gone, local farmers have bought the elevator and use the bins to store corn. Kenneth has no empty houses, and several homes are being remodeled.

Visitors can also stop by the Kenneth Bar, a cozy pub on Main Street, which has been a bar for as long as Nora, the current owner, can remember. Patrons enjoy a brew at the original long oak bar, backed by an art deco mirror and woodwork. Collections of antique cars, a train, telephone liquor bottles, and ceramic wildlife fill the high shelves around the room.

A vintage church is also a sight to see. Built in 1906 by Norwegian immigrants, the Kenneth Lutheran Church maintains the original pulpit and altar. The unaltered church, including the original steeple and weather vane, is now a three-point parish with Hadley, Zion and Kenneth all sharing a pastor.

Kenneth is also home to a unique repair shop. Located in the old hardware building on Main Street, Dave Groen Repair fixes lawnmowers in the spring and snowblowers in the winter. Lawnmowers converted into ceiling fans hang from the rafters above the original hardwood floors. But if anything is broken, Dave or his daughter, Kristy Vander Ziel, can fix it.

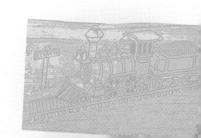

If you're passing through, don't forget to look for the town's sporty fire engine, the *Fast Attack,* which sits proudly in front of the three-stall fire department, ready to respond quickly to a fire call.

Who knew that sand could be so valuable? Over the years, the Kerrick Sand Pit shipped more than 2,500 train car loads of red sand.

TOP: First National Bank of the North

Kerrick

The Most Valuable Natural Resource in Kerrick? Sand.

WHO KNEW THAT SAND could be so valuable? While employed by the Eastern Minnesota Railroad, Swedish immigrant Louis Hultgren discovered sand with the same granular texture as the sand in the foundry where he worked in Sweden. Recognizing the value of sand for industrial use (in casting molds), he purchased 40 acres of land from the railroad, and opened the Kerrick Sand Pit in 1894. When the steel plant opened in Superior, Wisconsin, the plant used sand from Kerrick. Over the years, more than 2,500 train car loads of red sand were shipped from Kerrick, some to destinations as far away as British Columbia.

The city of Kerrick could just as well have been called Little Sweden. Settled by Swedish immigrants, the city was instead named for master

mechanic Cassius Kerrick, an employee of the Great Northern Railway in 1889. Born in Greensburg, Indiana, in 1847, Cassius Kerrick constructed many local railroad bridges while under contract with the railroad.

Hogan was another prominent name in Kerrick; the Hogan brothers, William and James, arrived in 1900 to open the Hogan Mercantile Company. By 1926, the store had sales from $65,000 to $80,000, with most of the groceries sold in bulk form. Pickles arrived in barrels and crackers in large wooden boxes. Herring and lutefisk, holiday specialties, were put up in pails and soaked for three weeks in wood ash lye and several changes of water before broiling or baking with cream and butter. Tobacco came in bars, sugar in one-hundred-pound bags, a coffin cost $16, and syrup was available in gallon pails. After the syrup was used, these pails were perfect for the children's school lunches. In 1901, William began his tenure as postmaster for 42 years. He was also vice-president of the Kerrick State Bank, organized in 1915, while his brother James held the position of president. The bank remains active in the community today. James Hogan also formed a sawmill business with Matthew McGrath, which experienced a boiler explosion in 1909, killing six men. Their sister, Mary Agnes Hogan, was the first female telegraph operator, a position that she held for 25 years.

In 1916, the entire community came out to celebrate the dedication of the Kerrick School, District 88, constructed for $7,800. A complete program included speeches by W. P. Hogan, several students, and Miss Schallon of the State Rural School Department along with much praise for the four-room brick building. In the words of the local newspaper, "a most enticing lunch was served, and after the doings in the schoolhouse were over, most all the folks moved to the town hall and made the rest of the night merry with a dance." Once the joy of the city, the school consolidated with Askov in the early 70s, and the structure no longer exists.

The year 1935 was good to Kerrick. Due to an outbreak of Bang's Disease infecting the cattle around Herbster, Wisconsin, Arnold Fuhrmann transferred his cheese factory to Kerrick where he built a two-story tile structure. The cheese factory closed in 1954, the last in Pine County, and the building is now a private residence.

When Kerrick incorporated in 1946, the city housed a station of the Great Northern Railway. Both Canadian Pacific and Burlington Northern trains carrying taconite still pass through the center of town several times a day, now without stopping. The post office sits on the site of the former depot.

A Historic Home and Two Generations of Politicians

The first home built in Kerrick in the 1880s, Swedish immigrant Louis Hultgren's house, has been on the National Register of Historic Places since 1980. The two-story, T-shaped clapboard-covered log house has roof boards from the Willow River and porches on both levels. Hultgren's grandson, Jeff Hultgren, now lives in the historic home.

Although inactive, the Kerrick Sand Pit is a historic landmark of Louis Hultgren's entrepreneurial vision. After a long day at work, Louis would walk up to 8 miles with his guitar to provide music for dances held in people's homes; of course, he charged no fee for this service.

Former Minnesota State Senator Becky Lourey, who farms with her husband in Kerrick, served as a State Representative from 1991 to 1997, and in the state senate from 1997 to 2007. While in office, Senator Lourey worked hard to expand MinnesotaCare, a state program providing health care coverage for low income Minnesotans, and earned a reputation as an expert in health care. When she declined to seek another term in 2006, her son, Tony Lourey, won the election and holds her former seat.

Kerrick Today

Today Kerrick is home to the post office, First National Bank of the North, and the original general store building on the east side of the tracks. On the west side stands Pracher's Pub, Kerrick Fire & Rescue, and the former Louis Hultgren sandpit. Beautiful old birches and cedar trees tower over the tiny city park next to the post office. The Kerrick Community Church keeps the door open for area residents.

The Kerrick Volunteer Fire Department hosts an annual ice-fishing contest the second Saturday in February. In May, the firemen whip up an annual turkey dinner with all the trimmings to raise money for the community.

The historic Kerrick State Bank, now named the First National Bank of the North, anchors Main Street, and has provided excellent service for almost a century. The building facade remains untouched from its 1915 construction.

TOP: Historic Farmers Coop Elevator Co., Kinbrae Lake

Located on the high, rolling banks of Kinbrae
Lake and surrounded by rich farmland, Kinbrae
is picture perfect.

Kinbrae

The 10th Earl of Airlie Visits Kinbrae

IT'S EASY TO UNDERSTAND how David Ogilvy, the 10th Earl of Airlie, fell in love with beautiful Kinbrae. Located on the high, rolling banks of Kinbrae Lake and surrounded by rich farmland, Kinbrae is picture perfect.

In 1879, the Chicago, Milwaukee and St. Paul Railroad planned a route from Heron Lake to Fulda and proposed a station in the Graham Lakes region. David Ogilvy, the 10th Earl of Airlie, formed the Dundee Land Company of Scotland for the express purpose of building a railroad town, and planned to name the site Airlie. He invested $15,000 to build a steam elevator with a capacity of 16,000 bushels, a three-story hotel, and a general store. Unfortunately, a jealous rival, the St. Paul

& Sioux City Railway, platted the village of Dundee only a mile away from Airlie, and their proximity restricted the growth of both. David Ogilvy is of historical significance for another reason; his granddaughter Clementine Hozier was married to Winston Churchill from 1908 until his death in 1965.

Only three months later, in December 1879, the townsite was surveyed, and the name changed to DeForest, which also became the name of the railroad station. Although home to only nineteen residents, a post office and depot opened in 1880. Tiny DeForest was almost obliterated in 1883 when fire nearly destroyed the steam elevator. Perhaps to change their luck, and at the request of the railroad, the town was renamed Kinbrae, and then sold to Hanson & Graeger, a Chicago land firm.

The first issue of the *Kinbrae Herald* on September 20, 1894, claimed a population of 150, two general stores, a hardware store, a lumberyard, a blacksmith shop, one stock buyer, two grain elevators, a hotel, a post office, the railroad depot, a newspaper, a millinery store, a Presbyterian Church and a school.

Once again Kinbrae was sold in 1895 to W. N. Bickley and W. E. Fletcher, two businessmen who invested $13,000 in an effort to build the community. Building improvements included a bank, a creamery, an elevator and a Methodist Church. Kinbrae reached the height of prosperity in 1895 with a population of 178, and voted to incorporate February 17, 1896. An impressive two-story brick school building was completed in 1915, including indoor plumbing, a library, and a full basement. Teachers living in Fulda commuted by train to Kinbrae to teach 50 students per year, until the school closed in 1957.

The last passenger train passed through Kinbrae on September 1, 1963. Passenger service ended after the railroad testified at an Interstate Commerce Commission hearing that receipts totaled $11.45 on eastbound trains and $9.08 on westbound trains in all of the previous year. When the city failed to grow, the founding fathers sold off all but 20 of the original 640 acres to two neighboring farmers. The farmers promised to sell land back to the city if needed it for expansion.

One of the Best Steakhouses in the State

You can expect a five-star dining experience at the family-owned Kinbrae Steakhouse, and you'll also get a glimpse into the early days of Kinbrae. Located in the former Kinbrae Bank building, owners Dwight and Robin Meintsma offer their hand-cut bacon-wrapped steak, second to none, in your choice of three dining rooms. The largest dining room, named the Airlie Room, features a 30-foot mahogany bar. The middle dining room is called "The Main," and the back room, the Segar Room, honors the Segar family who owned the Segar General Store in Kinbrae

until 1987. The original bar from the Segar General Store remains in the dining room. The history lesson continues with a horse-drawn Kinbrae fire truck, which is tucked in the restaurant and was manufactured by Waterous Engine Works Company in St. Paul, Minnesota. Uniforms from the first Kinbrae baseball team adorn the interior, a reminder of the excellent baseball once played in the village. At the meat counter (where items from the menu are sold) stands the former bank vault, now a wine cellar. In 2001, *Minnesota Monthly* magazine voted the Kinbrae Steakhouse one of the top six steakhouses in Minnesota, and that tradition of excellence continues today.

Kinbrae Today

Now the oldest and smallest city in Nobles County, Kinbrae consists of the Kinbrae Steakhouse and City Hall, a well-tended building of graduated brick. The old Presbyterian Church still stands, and is now used for storage. Just half a mile south of town, the Kinbrae Cemetery sits on virgin sod near Jack Lake by Maka-Oicu County Park, a historic site with Indian burial mounds.

On a given morning, a steady stream of tractors and trucks move grain though town, a vivid testament to the lush farmland of this lovely, small city. Mayor Glen Gruenwald, and city council members Tom Gruenwald, Dwight Meintsma and Hollis Chepa elected to remain a municipality, however small.

Now abandoned, the grain elevator is a wonderful example of elevators at the turn of the century. Attached to the elevator is a Quonset building with a *Farmer's Co-op Elev. Co.* sign flanked by two circular signs, each with the words *Golden Sun Feeds*. The photo-op on a warm October day was priceless.

Formerly called Clear Lake, Kinbrae Lake lures fishermen to the public access on the south shore to catch bluegill and crappie, two species well stocked in the lake. The Sisseton Indians of the Dakota camped on the lakeshore long before settlers arrived in the area.

TOP: Lake Henry baseball field

Population: 103   Incorporated: 1913

INSETS L to R: Lake Henry Implement • St. Margaret's Catholic Church • L. H. Bullpen • Sportsman's Den

Long before the Lake Henry Lakers baseball team joined the Stearns County League in 1939, local men invited opposing towns to join them for a game in a cow pasture.

Lake Henry

A Town Built Upon Baseball

ACCORDING TO DAVE HESS, a former player and manager of the Lake Henry Lakers, "Baseball is the heart and soul of Lake Henry. If baseball in Lake Henry would fold, the town would struggle. Baseball keeps the town together." Long before the Lakers joined the Stearns County League in 1939, local men invited opposing towns to join them for a baseball game in a cow pasture. The first Lake Henry team included nine men of the Hess family, and for fifty consecutive years, a Hess boy played on every Laker team. After three years, the team moved from the cow pasture to land donated by Werner Kraemer, with the agreement that the team would clear another three acres of woods for Werner's crops. In 1959, the Lakers made it to their first state amateur baseball tournament. Before facing Shakopee in the first round, tragedy struck when starting left fielder John Lieser died in an electrical accident. The Lakers lost 4–1 in a great game, and Shakopee went on to win the state title that year.

Long before baseball ruled in Lake Henry, thirty-six year old Governor Alexander Ramsey sought shelter during a snowstorm in the Lake Henry woods after signing an Indian treaty at Pembina on October 21, 1851. His entourage included twenty-five dragoons and a small official party, including guide Pierre Bottineau, clerk J. Wesley Bond, Dr. Thomas Foster, special agent Hugh Tyler, and Father Lacombe, who led the troop in prayer that evening. They also named the lake, calling it Lake David. Four years later, Prussian immigrant Xavier Poepping and his wife Christine settled on the east shore of the lake. When Mr. Poepping platted the town in 1857, he called the lake "Henre Lake." Around this time, Father Francis Pierz was traveling from town to town conducting mass and stopped at the Poepping's home to offer mass to a growing contingency of German and Austrian immigrants, including Michael Kraemer from Bavaria, who settled on the south end of the lake. With thirty-five families living around the lake, Michael Kraemer donated land for a church in 1881, and named the church St. Margaret's Church, after his wife. A Catholic school, staffed by Benedictine nuns from St. Joseph, and a convent were built soon after.

Gradually, as businesses opened, the hamlet of Lake Henry grew up around the church. Postmaster Michael Kraemer built a hotel and he was followed by postmaster Edward Hess until 1905, when the post office closed. Local farmers ran the Lake Henry Cooperative Creamery Association from 1900 to 1963, now headquarters for Harvey Neubauer and Kevin Weller's feed store. Peter Schmitz opened a blacksmith shop, and Farmers State Bank operated from 1920 to 1930. On July 4, 1922, the city celebrated the construction of a new St. Margaret's Church with a picnic, a baseball tournament, and a bowery dance featuring the St. Martin Band. Parishioner Tony Stalboerger recalled the story of church members hauling bricks by horse and wagon from the train in Regal to build the church. Father Joseph Linz led the church through the building process and remained their priest for forty years until he retired in 1955. Edward and Al Hess opened a general store, now home of the Sportsman's Den, a combination bar, restaurant and dance hall. Under the leadership of Fire Chief Ray Chalupsky, a new village hall and fire station were built in 1959. A state-of-the-art pumper truck and water tanker completed the renovation.

100 Years and Counting for St. Margaret's Church

St. Margaret's Church celebrated their centennial in 1982 under the direction of Father Frederick Kampsen. The Most Reverend Bishop George Speltz presented the Bishop's Medal of Honor to longtime St. Margaret's organist Adella Wuertz and Alfred Spanier, a trustee for many years.

Organized in 1947 by veterans of World War II, the Othmar Braun American Legion Post 612 is named after Othmar Braun, a young navy man killed in action during the battle of the Marshall Islands. Under the leadership of Post Commander Peter Ludwig Sr., the members formed a drill team and firing squad of twenty members who participated in area parades and military funerals. When the ladies auxiliary formed in the late 1960s, the Legion bought the former District 1966 schoolhouse for a permanent home.

The Lake Henry Lakers retired the first jersey in team history when longtime player and former manager Lynn Hemmesch died in a farm accident in August 2002. A star left-handed pitcher for Paynesville High School, a sign in the shape of a baseball with his number (#6) hangs on the left field fence.

Lake Henry Today

Today, Lake Henry boasts Othmar Braun American Legion Post 612, Lake Henry Lions Club, the Sportsman's Den, Lake Henry Implement, Lake Henry Fire & Rescue Department, Lake Henry Body & Automotive, Lake Henry Ag Service, and L.H. Bullpen On and Off-Sale. Right across the highway from the Lake Henry Lakers baseball field, magnificent St. Margaret's Parish thrives after 89 years of service to the community.

Watching the Lake Henry Lakers play baseball is pure pleasure. In 2010, the Lakers advanced to the state tournament for the eighth time before bowing to Raymond 11–6.

Every year since 1995, Lake Henry celebrates the annual *Lake Henry Hay Raze* on the third Saturday in June with a full day of baseball, volleyball, lawnmower racing, and dancing to live music. Competition for the Hay Raze Olympics is stiff, as competitors alternately toss bales and jump bales in a test of strength and speed.

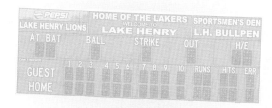

TOP: Site of capture of the Younger brothers, September 21, 1876

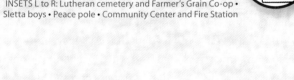

Population: 87   **Incorporated:** 1921

INSETS L to R: Lutheran cemetery and Farmer's Grain Co-op •
Sletta boys • Peace pole • Community Center and Fire Station

A large granite marker just south of La Salle marks
the spot where the Younger brothers, Cole, Bob
and Jim, surrendered after a famous gun battle on
September 21, 1876.

La Salle

Jesse James, Bank Robberies, Gun Battles and La Salle

A LARGE GRANITE MARKER just south of La Salle marks the spot where the Younger brothers, Cole, Bob and Jim, surrendered after a gun battle on September 21, 1876. Two weeks earlier, the James-Younger gang had robbed the First National Bank in Northfield. After pursuing the criminals for weeks over several counties, a local posse cornered the gang. One of the gang members, Charlie Pitts, died during the shootout near La Salle. Jesse James and his brother Frank escaped in the swamps and high grass of the Watonwan River bottom. Each fall since 1997, a group of men on horseback re-enact the event and haul the robbers back to nearby Madelia in a horse-drawn cart.

The town's history wasn't always so dramatic, however. In August 1899, a large advertisement appeared in the *St. James Gazette* announcing lots for sale in the new city of La Salle, one of two villages in Watonwan County planned in conjunction with the developing Minneapolis and St. Louis Railroad Company. Prices were low (lots sold for as little as $50) and hopes were high, as the census predicted a population of at least 750 people in two years. When the passenger trains began their daily run in December, both the city and railroad anticipated great growth and prosperity. Land agent Harry L. Jenkins, who was of French descent, grandly named the city in honor of the French explorer, Robert Cavalier Sieur La Salle.

Two of the original pioneers, John and Rena Sundt, purchased the first two lots in La Salle from the Iowa and Minnesota Land & Townsite

Company, and within a few months opened the Country Store Grocery. The post office opened next door, with Mr. Sundt appointed the first postmaster. Determined to develop the city, he persuaded the Eagle Roller Mill Company of New Ulm to build an elevator in La Salle and worked hard to open the La Salle Cooperative Creamery in 1901. John Sundt's dream of a local school was realized in 1904, and two years later, he assumed a position on the board of the newly opened La Salle State Bank in 1906. Honored at the Watonwan County Fair in 1958 as a "Centennial Pioneer," John Sundt was referred to as "The Father of La Salle, a most honest and progressive individual who gave so freely of his wisdom, time and talent." In 1910, Alfred Sletta purchased the general store from Mr. Sundt and ran the family business for 68 years.

Ole and Anun Halvorson arrived the same time as the Sundt family and opened the La Salle Hardware and Implement Store, a business well known for stocking everything from stoves to tractors. When the Halvorsons weren't selling merchandise, they sponsored dances in the hardware store on Saturday evenings, with the Madison Orchestra providing the music.

Reaping a banner corn crop of 2,500 to 3,000 bushels in 1914, La Salle's farmers and the business community enjoyed tremendous pros-perity. The farmers purchased more machinery and built new barns.

La Salle's local baseball team didn't have a nickname, but who needs one when you have the talent of the 1936 team? The local boys defeated everyone, including the defending state champion, Stephens Buick Team. When Olaf Hanson wasn't managing the team, he and Blake Sifford umpired the games, and were referred to by other teams as the "hometown Norwegian umpires."

Blizzards constantly tested the will of the citizens, including a severe blizzard that hit in December 1927, putting the entire city in total isolation for one week. In the storm, a passenger train was stranded, essentially doubling the population of La Salle. Undaunted,

the hospitable locals opened their doors to the unexpected guests. With so many extra people, provisions began to dwindle, and Mayor Alfred Sletta traveled to St. James through stormy weather for help. Unfortunately, the blizzard of January 30, 1920, did not turn out so well. The heavy snow and severe cold stranded a freight train with 23 carloads of cattle, and many cows perished.

The original school, built in 1904, served the community until 1960, when a new three-room elementary school replaced the one-room schoolhouse. When the new school closed in 1977, the building was eventually remodeled into the La Salle Community Center. The former gymnasium is now home to the Volunteer Fire Department.

By 1929, La Salle Lutheran Church had opened with the altar, a baptismal font and narthex all handcrafted by Andrew Barton.

War Heroes from La Salle

Jesse Markeson, an apprentice at Halvorson's store and later the owner of the store, was one of forty-eight World War I survivors in his division of the 319th Machine Gun Battalion, who successfully battled the Germans in the Argonne Forest, France. Another survivor in Markeson's division was Sergeant Alvin C. York, the most decorated soldier in World War I and recipient of the Congressional Medal of Honor. The battle is immortalized in the 1941 film *Sergeant York*, starring Gary Cooper, who won an academy award that year for best actor.

La Salle Today

Today La Salle proudly boasts the Village Inn Restaurant, La Salle Farmers Grain Co., the Community Center, La Salle Meats, La Salle State Bank, Jordahl Repair, Western Pet Treats, and La Salle Lutheran Church.

Following the death of local soldiers in World War I, the community donated money for a flagpole on a concrete base, which stands today as a tribute to the local men who sacrificed their lives. The pedestal stands directly behind the bank in the middle of the road. A large chunk of concrete is missing from the base, as an elderly citizen crashed into it while driving to church directly into the sun.

TOP: Residential area, Ash Avenue

A century farm is really the history of a city.
When Virgil and Evelyn Ortman won the coveted
Century Farm Award in 1981, the award symbolized the story of their families and the settlement
of Lastrup.

Lastrup

A Century Farm

A CENTURY FARM is really the history of a city. When Virgil and Evelyn Ortman won the coveted Century Farm Award in 1981, the award
symbolized the story of their families and the settlement of Lastrup. Over
one hundred years earlier, Virgil's maternal grandparents, Frederick and
Angela Wolke, had purchased 420 acres "on the edge of the wilderness"
in 1878 for $1.76 an acre from the Western Railroad Company. Around
the same time, Virgil's father, Theodore Ortman, arrived with his parents, the Bernard Ortmans, from Damme, Germany, when Theodore
was just six years old. Like so many émigrés, the Ortmans fled Germany
to escape the conscription of their sons into military service. The promise
of rich farmland in America helped seal their decision to leave Germany.

Following graduation from St. John's University in St. Cloud in
1892, young Theodore accepted a job offer at Lastrup District 36, where
he taught for thirteen years. The student master boarded at the Wolke
home, and eventually married one of the Wolke daughters, Katherine.
The marriage proved to be a lasting legacy for them and for Lastrup.
Together Katherine and Theodore helped organize St. John's Church
where Ted was church organist and choir director for fifty years. Theodore also assumed the role of postmaster in 1900 following the first
postmaster, William Hoheisel. In the meantime, the couple raised nine
children. When the city wanted to name the site Ortman after Theodore,
he suggested Lastrup, after his relative's hometown in Germany. Lastrup
means "last town" in an obscure German dialect and the city was located

in the farthest province from the capital. Likewise, the sister-city was the farthest settlement from the diocesan center in St. Cloud.

Established as a post office point in 1898, Lastrup is one of a few small cities not connected to a railroad. Grain was hauled to the railroad in Pierz or Genola for shipment. Composed of two earlier settlements, East Lastrup in Granite Township and West Lastrup in Buh Township, the city incorporated as one March 1, 1916. The heartbeat of the city, St. John's Catholic Church, was erected in 1901 by brothers Wessel, Anton, and Frederick Wolke. These skilled carpenters also constructed St. Joseph's Church in Pierz, Seven Dolors in Albany, and the Morrison County Courthouse in Little Falls. Later in 1951, the church opened St. John's School. Until then, District 36 School educated students in two rooms with four grades per room.

Business took off when the church steeple rose above the village. Gross Implement & Hardware Co. opened in 1911, and owner Peter Gross expanded his business interests when he bought the grocery store in 1912, which operated under various owners until 1981. Vincent Dombovy opened the blacksmith shop in 1903 followed by F. X. Steger's Saloon in 1908. Although all the businesses contributed to the economy of Lastrup, the Farmer's Co-operative Creamery, organized in 1915, accounted for the economic prosperity of the community. Excellent black loam topsoil combined with clay subsoil produced bumper crops of clover and corn to support the numerous dairy farms surrounding Lastrup. By 1922, the creamery produced $65,000 worth of butter. A later addition to the creamery sold feed and farm supplies. Steve Gross opened a gas station and sold the business to his son Don, who then sold the station to his son, Steve. The station remains a vital business today.

Closed in the early '80s, the 1909 brick creamery building adjacent to the Sunrise Co-op was recently dismantled, as the number of dairy farms has dropped precipitously—from ten farms every five miles to one farm every five miles.

A Saint Watching Over the City and Mass in a Shed

St. John's Church has held center court ever since the first mass was offered December 2, 1900, in a shed. Dedicated to St. John Nepomuk, a national saint of the Czech Republic, the Catholic Church claims the allegiance of most the German families in the city. The church's namesake, St. John of Nepomuk, christened John Wolfin, was drowned in the Vltava River as ordered by the King Wenceslaus IV, in 1393. Serving as confessor of the queen of Bohemia, John refused to divulge the secrets of the queen to her jealous king. On this basis, John of Nepomuk is the first martyr of the Seal of the Confessional, and was canonized in 1729 as the Patron Saint of protection against floods and slander. The church chose their saint well; unlike many other small cities, Lastrup has never experienced flooding or fires.

Lastrup Today

Today Lastrup is home to Herald's Bar & Grill (the former bank building), Lastrup Implement, Tiny's Tavern, and the Sunrise Ag Cooperative with a community post office in the corner. The old village hall is now Thomas Welding. The original blacksmith shop is located next to the new Village Hall, and is now owned by Clyde and Joelle Hayes, a reminder of when the blacksmith was essential to Lastrup.

Steve Gross puts in one-hundred-hour weeks at his full-service gas station, Lastrup Implement, a family run enterprise passed down from his father and grandfather. His great-great-grandfather, Matt Gross, an original settler in Lastrup, shot a deer in 1898, and the mounted head proudly oversees the action in Steve's station. On a Sunday afternoon, Steve is busy answering the rotary dial phone, waiting on customers and watching the Vikings football game with local farmers.

The Lastrup Lakers thrilled area fans with ten trips to the state tournament. In 2008, manager Paul Froncak took the Lakers to the Class C State Tournament and defeated Stewart-Racine 10–3, before bowing to Isanti 6–3. Two years later, the Lakers won the 2010 Region 8C title, and advanced to the state tournament.

Lengby butter maker P. M. Scott took a four-year hiatus to return to Denmark for "a very charming bride"; the community sighed with relief upon his return. The much-loved butter maker continued his work at the creamery until his death in 1933.

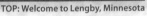

TOP: Welcome to Lengby, Minnesota

Lengby

Like Living in a Norman Rockwell Painting

LENGBY IS LOVELY. Just west of Bagley on Highway 2 lies the Swedish village of Lengby, set on the shores of pristine Spring Lake. The ambiance begins with the *"Welcome to Lengby"* sign, surrounded by a flower garden and a banner announcing the Centennial 1898–1998. Just past the railroad tracks and Main Street, a graceful church steeple draws you into the heart of this scenic community. Fridhem Lutheran Church overlooks the lake and town, projecting a sense of calm and integrity. Each little road offers up another delight—two more beautiful churches, an old brick school, lovely gardens throughout the community, and finally, the crown jewel, Spring Lake Recreation Park. The perfect sand beach and picnic area, complete with an old-fashioned band shell, is reminiscent of a Norman Rockwell painting.

Bountiful lakes and plentiful timber welcomed Swedish settlers William and Charles Hilliard in 1883. Five years later, James J. Hill's Great Northern Railway extended track between Fosston and Duluth, and more settlers arrived to start a new life in northern Minnesota. Originally named New Town by two Fosston businessmen who owned the town site, the railroad renamed the town Lengby. Another theory is that Lengby is a distortion of Lindby, the name of a local settler. Either way, Lengby incorporated on March 9, 1904.

Business flourished with Argall's General Store, the Lengby Hotel, the Spring Lake Hotel, O. M. Olson's Hardware Store, A. Bye and

Lindberg Blacksmith and Carpentry, and the Saterstrom and Olson Mercantile. In 1904, Frank C. Johnson began publishing a weekly newspaper, *The Lengby Star*. When Ole K. Ringstad bought the general store in 1902, he became the official postmaster until his death in 1908. His widow, Cora, assumed his duties until 1945, when their son, Knute, carried on the family tradition. A fire in 1908 almost destroyed the entire business district and took the life of Simmie DeMarre, who fell from a burning building while fighting the fire.

Business boomed when clay suitable for masonry bricks was discovered on the shores of Spring Lake. The Lengby Lumber, Brick, and Fuel Company produced 40,000 bricks per day, including bricks used to build both the Lengby School and the Beltrami Courthouse. A sawmill opened next to the brickyard where thousands of logs were stacked on the lake ice waiting for the ice to thaw. Progressive farmers formed the Lengby Co-op Creamery in 1908, and hired P. M. Scott as butter maker and bookkeeper. When Mr. Scott took a four-year hiatus to return to Denmark for "a very charming bride," the community sighed with relief upon his return. The much-loved butter maker continued his work at the creamery until his death in 1933.

A Civil War Veteran and the Grand Army of the Republic

An early settler and businessman of Lengby, William Hilliard served as a Union soldier in the Civil War and later, as Commander of the Minnesota Department of the Grand Army of the Republic, a Union veteran's organization. Today Elaine Kildal lives in the original William and Mary Hilliard home on Main Street.

The Lengby Improvement Club, organized in 1915, is the oldest active community organization in Minnesota. Plans are underway for the club's centennial in 2015. The twenty members maintain Spring Lake Recreation Park, keep the flower gardens beautiful, and prepare dinner for as many as four hundred people at the community Memorial Day picnic. Each year in May, they also join forces with the Sunday School children to clean up Lengby, followed by a picnic at the park. This year the children dipped their hands in paint and put their handprints on all the garbage cans in town as a testament to their efforts.

Lengby Today

Today Lengby's Main Street includes the Community Hall, the VFW Post 2759, the Clinic Bar & Grill, PD Graphics, Nelly's Salon, and the Lengby Oil Company, a full-service gas station. The old Village Hall, with a bell tower and red water pump, completes the street. A modern post office proudly waves both the American flag and a POW/MIA flag.

Just south of Fridhem Lutheran Church lies the perfect sand beach at Spring Lake Recreation Park. If you're lucky enough to be there for Memorial Day or the Fourth of July, you can share in the community barbecue. Members from the Lengby Improvement Club are renovating the split-rock bathing house, a WPA Project from 1940.

Organized in 1887 by Reverend Ylvislaker and sturdy Norwegian pioneers, St. Paul's Lutheran Church held their first services in different farm homes. In 1898, the Ladies Aid gave the pastor $96 to buy forty acres of pine from state land near Crookston. All able-bodied men in the congregation took two-week shifts to cut and haul logs to the sawmill to build their church. Norwegian artist August Klagstad painted the church altar painting, typical of rural church art at the turn of the century. Nestled in a grove of trees next to the church, St. Paul's Cemetery holds the tombstones of the original Norwegian pioneers including the tombstone of Harry Hilliard, Civil War Veteran.

Lengby is home to a Baptist church as well. Originally named the Queen Swedish Baptist Church, the Lengby Baptist Church lies on the east side of Main Street. Built by members and friends, it was dedicated on June 12, 1944.

The old Lengby School, built with Lengby bricks in 1905 at a cost of $3,000, still stands next to the town baseball field. The school closed in 1969, and is in the process of renovation as an artist's retreat.

Population: 41   **Incorporated:** 1922

INSETS L to R: Leonard Café • Reichert's Saddlery •
Landon's in Leonard • Strand's Store

A two-story frame school replaced Leonard's
one-room school in 1915, with stacks of wood for
fuel piled next to the building. Teachers were paid
$30 to $40 a month to fire up the stove, do the
janitorial work, and teach all grades.

TOP: Amish horse and buggy, Reichert Saddlery

Leonard

A Strange Visitor from Siberia

SHORTLY AFTER WORLD WAR I, a man from Siberia clad in
Eskimo clothing appeared on the street in Leonard. Introducing himself
as Dr. Spears, he announced that he wanted to set up a medical practice
in Leonard. Due to his cold origins, he chose to reside in the basement
of the bank, where his colorful furs and leggings kept him comfortable.
On the side, Dr. Spears planned to construct an expensive Eskimo igloo
at Clearwater Lake, but his shipment of gold was lost somewhere between Siberia and Leonard. When a financial dispute arose between the
doctor and the community, someone stuffed a wad of hay in the top of
the chimney and the doctor was smoked out of his basement home. He
disappeared that evening and was never seen again.

Over the years, Leonard has been home to many remarkable men
and women. Nels Strand and his son, Ernest, opened a general store in
1926 that remains the hub of the community, and Donn Reichert owns
a saddle and tack store second to none in Minnesota. With such an
impressive business district, Leonard is surprisingly the ninth-smallest
city in Minnesota. Located in the northeastern part of the county near
Four Legged Lake, this secluded city boasts rolling farmland, pristine
lakes, and woods full of deer and fowl—an Eden for the residents who
enjoy the quiet side.

Prior to settlement in 1896, T. B. Walker and his son began active logging in 1883 along the Clearwater River. Majestic white pines
covered thousands of acres of prime forest, the perfect opportunity for

a land agent to make his fortune. According to Rueben Holm, who worked felling trees from 1899 to 1903, "After fifty five years in the woods, I will still say that it was the best timber I ever worked in."

Named for the son of early settler George French, Leonard incorporated on June 12, 1922. When Mr. French established the first post office in 1899 on Four Legged Lake, Leonard joined the mail route between Bagley and Neving. At that time, mail was carried by swift teams of horses for twenty-four miles over the Red Lake Indian Trail, the only wagon road in the county. A lack of transportation limited development until the Soo Railroad arrived in 1911, with Ben Titus as first depot agent. Now logs, supplies and mail could be transported by rail.

As the timber industry phased out, agriculture and dairy replaced logging as the main industry. Due to rocks and stumps in the fields left over from logging, farming was a difficult and slow process. Fortunately, the heavy clay soil supported hay pasture which enabled almost every farm to sustain a dairy herd. When the Leonard Creamery organized in 1916, the business bought milk and cream from the farmers, and also ran a top-notch meat locker until closing in 1989. Today Reichert's Saddlery and Feed Store thrives in the original creamery building.

In 1899, thirty-five children ages five to twenty started school in Leonard School District 23, a one-room log building. A two-story frame school replaced the one-room school in 1915, with stacks of wood for fuel piled next to the building. Teachers were paid $30 to $40 a month to fire up the stove, do the janitorial work, and teach all grades. Mae Barness, County Superintendent for over fifty years, tells of driving a two-wheeled cart over terrible roads to travel to the area schools. She preferred to stay in the Leonard Hotel rather than travel at night over rutted trails with only the moon to guide her way. One dark cold winter evening on her way to another county school, she grew weary and stopped at a house to ask for lodging. Only when Miss Barness spoke in Norwegian, "I do not like to travel any further at this time of the night," was she welcomed into her new friend's home.

Other early businesses included Stokes Hotel, Leonard Bank, Ernest Strand's Store, Hans Bye's Livery Barn, Marvin Monson Oil Company, Leonard Cafe, and Max Postier's Blacksmith Shop. Adventuresome folks hopped the 9 a.m. train to Bemidji to shop and returned to Leonard at 5 p.m. The busy little town celebrated the Fourth of July with a large bowery dance, and filled the street between the hotel and railroad tracks for the annual circus and Chautauqua (a type of lecture circuit).

All Roads Lead to Leonard

Early maps indicate twenty-five towns existed in Clearwater County, of which five incorporated towns remain today. Leonard is unique, with five main roads intersecting the community. Strand's Store, the original general store built in 1915, is where you pick up the mail, buy a raffle ticket for the Ladies Aid quilt, purchase groceries, and order lefse and lutefisk for the holidays. Manager Diana Gerlot needs extra help in the store during deer hunting season—"one to check in the bounty and one to run the till." Bear season also brings in ample customers.

Leonard Today

Today Leonard boasts five businesses on Main Street and one church: Strand's Hartz Store which houses the post office, Reichert's Saddlery and Feed Store, Landon's in Leonard gas station, Dyrdahl Construction, Side Track Tap Bar, and Our Savior's Lutheran Church. Our Savior's Lutheran Church hosts a church picnic at Harvey Miller's farm the last Sunday in August every year, complete with musical entertainment, horse and buggy rides, and a potluck dinner. The Leonard Café serves a good home-cooked meal at a great price. Reichert's Saddlery boasts the best selection of saddles, tack supplies, western boots and clothing in northern Minnesota. Owner Donn Reichert serves customers from all over the world.

You can still see traces of the Red Lake Indian Trail on the south edge of Leonard, where the Indians traveled by foot from White Earth to Red Lake.

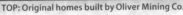

TOP: Original homes built by Oliver Mining Co.

Mr. and Mrs. Fred Williams, some of the first residents in the town, chose their home based on the least number of boulders in the yard.

Leonidas

Lumber and Iron Ore

AN EXPERT TIMBER CRUISER AND LUMBERMAN, Leonidas Merritt grew up in a family of eight boys in Duluth. On a trip through the Mesabi Range in northeastern Minnesota in the mid-1860s, his father, Lewis Howell Merritt, saw what he believed to be outcroppings of iron ore. Convinced that one day the area would be home to great mines, Leonidas led brothers Cassius and Alfred on a long search for iron. Using a dip needle, a compass with a magnetic needle that dipped down towards ore, the men mapped the area from the Gunflint Trail on the Canadian border to Grand Rapids. The first large body of iron ore was discovered lying only 12 to 14 feet below the surface in an area now known as the Mountain Iron Mine. Efforts to obtain financing were hampered by rough roads and the presence of only two distant railroads, the Northern Pacific and the St. Paul & Duluth, neither the least bit interested in building a branch to Mountain Iron. Determined to ship their ore to the steel mills on Lake Superior, the brothers commenced construction of the Duluth, Missabe & Northern Railroad Company in 1892, a 48.5-mile track from Stoney Brook Junction (Brookston) to the Mountain Iron Mine. On October 15, 1892, the Merritt family celebrated the completion of the line and the 80th birthday of the Merritt's mother, Haphzibah Merritt, with a special excursion on the new railroad from Duluth to Mountain Iron. The *Duluth News Tribune* reported that fifty-five members of the Merritt family and 200 guests traveled by train to the mine pits, where Reverend Dr. Forbes entertained the group with an oration. Instead of champagne, the devout Methodist family served twenty-five gallons of milk to the guests. A year later, the Merritt family faced financial ruin and lost the company to John D. Rockefeller.

In 1910, the Oliver Iron Mining Company leased the Leonidas mine from the state and developed Leonidas, a company mining camp with thirty-four homes and a boarding house for miners and their families. Mr. and Mrs. Fred Williams, some of the first residents in the town, chose their home based on the least number of boulders in the yard. As mining operations expanded, 150 men worked underground, but without enough housing, many walked three miles home to Eveleth. The Leonidas mine, a small and very deep mine, was named the "Rat Hole" by the men who stood in ankle deep water. Pumps worked continually to keep the men in the shafts from drowning.

The modern age arrived when running water and three water hydrants were installed for the residents. In the depths of winter the hydrants froze until someone would brave the cold and pour hot water over the top to thaw the hydrant. The women were especially pleased when concrete sidewalks replaced the wooden ones, where they were forever losing heels between the boards.

The company took care of the recreational needs of the city. Tennis courts were laid, with free racquets available at the Mining Company's warehouse. Company workers provided all the maintenance for the courts, and in winter, the courts were flooded for a large skating rink. Over Christmas, the skaters spun under brightly colored lights hung around the rink, and on Christmas Eve, Santa Claus drove a mule-drawn sleigh, with the mules wearing deer antlers to replicate reindeer. Each child's home in town received a visit and candy from Santa in his sleigh.

In 1910, at a cost of $12,000, a new two-room school opened for grades one to eight. Miss Jensen and Miss Pfeiffer taught classes, and Mr. Stetzler served as principal, custodian and teacher. As enrollment increased, a beautiful brick school replaced the earlier structure, and in 1919, a large addition was finished. By 1945, the Leonidas School closed following consolidation with Eveleth, a colossal disappointment for the community.

Seven Iron Men and a Hockey Great

Led by Leonidas Merritt, the Merritt family is credited with the discovery and development of the Mesabi Iron Range. Five of the Merritt brothers and two nephews are immortalized as the legendary "Seven Iron Men."

Wally Grant, born and raised in Leonidas, grew up skating on a small rink that his father, an immigrant who worked in an open-mine pit, had created. Grant went on to play left wing and captained the Eveleth High School hockey team in 1945, the year they won the first Minnesota state hockey championship, scoring the game-tying and game-winning goals within a span of 61 seconds. Later he played for the University of Michigan. In 1948, he played in the first NCAA Men's Ice Hockey Championship where the famous "G" line, Wally Gacek, Ted Greer and Wally Grant, each scored a third-period goal to defeat Dartmouth. Grant was inducted into the U.S. Hockey Hall of Fame in 1994.

Leonidas Today

Today Leonidas has 26 households, 52 residents, a beautiful city park, a paved walking path, a tennis court, a baseball field, and a skating rink with a warming house. The Leonidas Community Center is often used for wedding receptions and other social events. Leonidas boast three streets of nearly identical houses, distinguishable by various additions and all painted different colors. The immaculate homes were once owned by the mining bosses of John Rockefeller's steel company.

The Leonidas Overlook, created by mining overburden (surface materials that covered the ore body), offers a 15-mile view of breathtaking scenery over the Iron Range, including the active mine, U-Tac, in Eveleth. On the Fourth of July, you can watch the fireworks from Chisholm, Buhl, Virginia, Eveleth and Gilbert.

Population: 47   Incorporated: 1905

INSETS L to R: Louisburg Lutheran exterior • Interior of Louisburg
Lutheran • Louisburg Reed and Cornet Band •
Centennial Monument

Prior to incorporation, illegal liquor establishments in town were called blind pigs. When the *Appleton Press* featured the headline "*A Blind Pig Is About To Be Butchered*," everyone understood that the perpetrator had been caught and sentenced.

TOP: Third Avenue, Louisburg's main street

Louisburg

Destroyed by a Tornado, and then a Fire, Louisburg Lives on

THE CITY OF LOUISBURG and its Lutheran Church are a determined pair. Completely destroyed by a tornado a century ago, and destroyed again later by a fire, both have persevered and stood the test of time.

Louisburg, a small Norwegian city founded in 1887 by Ole Thompson and William R. Thomas, developed after the St. Paul, Minneapolis and Manitoba Railway constructed a railroad siding in the area. Railroads typically developed markets within a seven-mile interval, the distance a farmer could travel to deliver a horse-drawn wagon of grain and return home in the same day. Due to low financial returns, the railroad delayed building a depot until 1893. Constant com-

plaints about the lack of a depot may have contributed to the early death of the first depot agent, Mr. Clifford, who transferred to South Dakota in 1891, and committed suicide there by drowning himself in a barrel of water.

In December 1891 the first public building, school District No. 92, opened and a money-order post office followed the next year. Businesses who boasted the largest inventories in 1894 included: Anderson and Siverson General Store, $2,750; Benson General Store, $2,200; Northwestern Elevator Company, $1,600; and the Interstate Grain Company, $900. Louisburg citizens loved both sports and the arts, spending their leisure time on the baseball field, playing in the Louisburg Reed and Cornet Band, and studying for the Literary Society. The Knights of

Pythia formed in 1893, the first fraternal lodge in Louisburg. Bitterly opposed by the local pastor who objected to secret societies, the pastor was gone by the end of the year, and the lodge remained.

Not long after the arrival of the first immigrants, Minnesota Valley Lutheran Church opened in 1891. That same year, the Norwegian Evangelical Lutheran Church formed when several members of Minnesota Valley withdrew to begin a church closer to the railroad site. Without an organ or song books, Tollef Hovden was elected as *klokker* to sing a solo verse to teach the congregation the music. The forces of nature tested the faith and fortitude of the solid members of the new church. After the destruction of the Norwegian church and the entire community by a tornado in 1905, members built another church, only to have lightning strike the church spire and burn the building to the ground. Determined to rebuild a church to resist storm and fire, a new brick building with slate shingles rose in 1927.

Prior to city incorporation, Tom Winger, owner of a local restaurant, was arrested for selling liquor. Illegal liquor establishments were called blind pigs. When the *Appleton Press* featured the headline "*A Blind Pig Is About To Be Butchered,*" everyone understood the meaning that the perpetrator had been caught and sentenced. On September 25, 1905, the village voted to incorporate and quickly set up liquor ordinances. Now the incorporated village could regulate liquor licenses and other misdemeanors as well, such as riding autos or animals more than six miles per hour, breeding animals in public view, and injury to trees.

Three years later, a new community hall celebrated their grand opening with dancing and music by a St. Paul orchestra. With an auditorium and stage on each of two stories, the unusual hall hosted traveling shows, rollerskating, church, and lodge events. However, the city fathers drew the line at ragtime dancing in 1913, forbidding "Ragging Dances" and opting for a horse show instead. A grand two-story brick schoolhouse opened in 1911.

A Deadly Tornado

On March 27, 1905, a tornado cut a 1,500-foot swath and demolished the entire city of Louisburg. In less than a minute, every building in the village was damaged or destroyed. Amazingly, only one child, seven-year-old Jennie Winger, died in the storm. The Louisburg Lutheran church exploded in the vacuum along with the lumberyard and the grain elevator.

Louisburg Today

On June 20–21, 1987, Louisburg celebrated their centennial with a parade, contests, music, and tasty Norwegian treats. A large granite centennial marker with an etching of the historic school stands in front of the Fire Department. Louisburg is also home to the Farmers Elevator Company, an active train stop for loading grain and the coffee stop for local farmers. The Burlington Northern Santa Fe travels through daily, carrying ethanol from the plant in Watertown. The prettiest Lutheran church in Minnesota, Louisburg Lutheran celebrated their centennial in 1991, and remains firmly anchored in the community. The church displays beautiful hand-carved wood panels and other art pieces made by Rev. Allen C. Erickson, pastor of the church from 1973–1981. Upstairs, the $650 bell purchased in 1927 by Christ Sundahl and his mother, Bertha, calls the parishioners to worship. A beautiful stained glass window graces the altar in memory of Ole and Kari Kolkjen. Two additional windows on either side are in memory of Ole Anderson and Mr. and Mrs. Aanund Dalen. Limited to 100 reservations, the annual Lutefisk & Swedish Meatball Supper is a hot ticket item.

The Louisburg School, added to the National Registry of Historic Places in 1986, is one of the best examples of Victorian school architecture in Minnesota. Designed by Kilroy Snyder and constructed by Fred Knepfer, the impressive building closed its doors in the sixties, but stands as proud reminder of education at its best.

TOP: Manchester Evangelical Lutheran Church

Population: 57   Incorporated: 1947

INSETS L to R: Paul Jensen at Jensprint • Bend in the Road • Manchester-Hartland Telephone • Jordahl Meats

Tornadoes remain an annual threat in the Manchester area. On June 17, 2010, a tornado funneled through the area, destroying several farms around Manchester.

Manchester

Antique Tractor Manuals, Wind Farms and a City with Three Different Names in One Year

SURROUNDED BY CORNFIELDS and wind farms, the last thing that you expect to find in little Minnesota is a highly successful and unusual printing business. Owner Paul Jensen of JenSales & Print reproduces original tractor manuals for aging tractors that need repair. Recently, Paul shipped a 1940 Minneapolis Moline manual for a Model Z tractor to Turkmenistan. Boasting a progressive city council and business community, this little city consistently pushes beyond the ordinary.

In 1858, the city went through three different names in the span of a year. Initially called Buckeye, the name changed to Liberty in May. Finally, Mathias Anderson suggested Manchester after the county in

Illinois where he once lived. In 1877, Anton Anderson opened his blacksmith shop with an attached five-horsepower steam engine house. The same year Cosgan & White erected a grain elevator for storage. H. R. Fossum and E. H. Stensrud opened a general store and post office with Mr. Fossum as postmaster. The Manchester Creamery Association formed in January 1891 under the leadership of President Claus Flindt, and butter maker C. F. Meyer. After the original creamery was destroyed by fire, a brick structure with 16-foot walls, a concrete ceiling, and a steel roof was constructed in 1910. Farmers from around the area brought in milk, and the creamery had an average daily butter output of 500 pounds.

By 1910, Manchester bustled with a railroad station on the

Minneapolis and St. Louis Railroad, a bank, the Farmer's Mutual Insurance Company, a brand new creamery, and a large 1909 Fire Hall also used for plays and other social events. Tragedy struck the community when the Manchester train station burned to the ground in 1914. The body of depot agent Mrs. Irene Coleman was discovered in the rubble. One of the few women trained at Barry's Telegraph School in Minneapolis, she held the Manchester position for only three months. Her husband had arrived in Manchester just three weeks earlier.

Both the Evangelical Lutheran Church and a two-room school opened in 1916. When the school closed in the 1960s, the students were bused to Albert Lea. The city waited until 1947 to incorporate, and that meant waiting for state funding for new city water mains. Life had gone smoothly for Manchester until a tornado hit the city in 1952, destroying several homes and businesses, including the creamery. The Manchester tornado was one of the top news stories in the state of Minnesota that year.

Antique Tractor Manuals Produced Amid the Relics of the Old Creamery

JenSales & Print occupies the site of the former creamery building, which was destroyed during the tornado of 1952. Some relics remain; the original smokestack stands in one of the closets, and the pass-through door in the butter room remains as well. Following a nine-year stint as a navy diver and EOD (Explosive Ordnance Disposal Technician), Paul Jensen bought the business from his father in 2009, and secured the original office door for his office. The unique business offers over 200 custom tractor manuals for out-of-print and rare models.

After many years of fund raising through raffles and dances, the new fire hall, with three stalls and a meeting room, opened in 1982 at a cost of $32,000. Trained EMTs and firemen respond to fires and traffic accidents along busy Highway 13. An annual soup and pie supper keeps the coffers full.

Manchester Today

Today Manchester's forward-looking community includes Jordahl Meats (home of the best dried beef in the county, according to one source), JenSales & Print, Jensen Manufacturing, Farmer's Mutual Insurance, City Hall & Fire Department, and Bend in the Road Bar. The highly esteemed Manchester-Hartland Telephone Company, led by manager Omer Emstad, serves more than 500 customers north of Albert Lea in Freeborn County, and recently replaced underground copper wire with 122 miles of fiber optic cable for high-speed internet access. City Clerk Angie Hannegrefs closed out the post office in 1998, but the building still stands. If the railroad tracks are replaced with a rumored state recreational trail, bicyclists will find their way to Manchester. The sole surviving church, Evangelical Lutheran, remains active in the community.

Tornadoes remain an annual threat. On June 17, 2010, another tornado funneled through the area, this time destroying several farms around Manchester. Luckily, the Bent Tree Wind Farm project had not installed their wind turbines prior to the tornado. Today the 69-square-mile farm powers approximately 50,000 homes, another sign of a progressive city that continues to move ahead.

Lifelong residents Mike "Bass" Skov and Scott "Mule" Juveland completely remodeled the Bend in the Road Bar, home to free pool on Fridays and guest pool on Mondays, where one person, or guest, gets to play pool for the entire evening against any challenger. Summers are busy with horseshoe, volleyball and bean bag leagues. The location of a snowmobile trail next to the bar invites snowmobilers in for a convenient stop.

Manchester Lutheran Church celebrated their 75th Anniversary in 1991 on the same land lot donated in 1916 by Betsy Ingebritson. The original building has never been altered, but the stable at the town creamery used for the horses of members attending church is gone.

TOP: City Hall

Population: 57   Incorporated: 1941

INSETS L to R: Manhattan Beach Lodge Bell • Restaurant • Winter scene • Beach

In the 1920s and '30s, the Manhattan Beach Lodge was visited by some of the most famous criminals of the era.

Manhattan Beach

Mobsters in Manhattan—Manhattan Beach, Minnesota, that is

MANHATTAN BEACH: the name conjures up sophistication and elegance, and this tiny city 28 miles north of Brainerd lives up to your expectations and more. The Manhattan Beach Lodge is the heart of the city of Manhattan Beach, and when you step into the historic Spanish Mission-style lodge, you will want to stay. An original two-sided stone fireplace, perfectly prepared meals, and immaculate tables overlooking Big Trout Lake welcome you. The original log bar next to the new ballroom overlooks the tiki bar on the lakeshore, a popular hangout in the summer. Unlike any of Minnesota's smallest cities, this unique city developed solely on the back of a beautiful vacation lodge and the tourism industry.

Before Manhattan Beach Lodge opened, there was no semblance of a village in Allen Township, the precursor to the city. The first permanent European settlers, John Stees and his wife, moved from the east to cook in area lumber camps. While her husband worked at camp during the winters, Mrs. Stees remained behind at the homestead, ten miles from the nearest European neighbor. Horace Butterfield's family and Freeman Doane, a wolf trapper, followed. A school, organized in 1898, was followed by a second school, which burned in 1915. Attempts to mine the township in 1907 by Pittsburgh businessman E. M. Haukill proved unsuccessful. Since then, tourism has served as the sole economic basis for the area.

During the '30s and '40s, central Minnesota became the vacation playground for the Hollywood elite. Ahead of their time, Ed and

Al Kavli, under the name Kavli Realty, began a large advertising campaign to sell the concept of a summer vacation community, with Manhattan Beach Lodge as its anchor, in remote northern Minnesota. Built in 1929 for well-to-do folks from Minneapolis and Chicago, the guest list included Bob Hope and his entourage. Trains rolled through the Midwest to St. Paul, where passengers transferred to the express to Brainerd. Lodge employees met the guests in Brainerd, and loaded their steamer trunks into wagons for the final twenty-eight miles to Manhattan Beach. Guests such as John Dillinger, who owned a home on the lake, waltzed and danced to the Charleston, performed by big bands of the era, who traveled by bus to the resort. For guests with two left feet or other interests, the gaming room in the basement offered high rollers a chance to win big money at the slot machines and poker tables. Even the onset of Prohibition did not change service at the Lodge, as nothing was denied the "gat-toting boys" from out of town. The isolation of the area was perfect for John Dillinger and bootlegging gangsters like Baby Face Nelson, Pretty Boy Floyd, and Legs Diamond, who headed north to "escape the heat." During the day, guests fished, swam in the pristine lake, played tennis, or rode a horse from the lodge stable.

On June 24, 1941, the city separated from Allen Township and incorporated, in order to provide a liquor license for its growing tourism business. Across the road on Highway 66, the Kavlis expanded Manhattan Beach Lodge with a four-lane bowling alley, restaurant, barbershop, grocery store, bar, gas station, motel rooms, a post office, and a riding stable. Buildings next door housed a puzzle factory and gift shop. During the long winter months, children and adults flew around the community skating rink. The long time caretaker of Manhattan Beach Lodge, nicknamed Wally-A-Frame, died of a heart attack in the early '80s in one of the motel rooms where he lived. Without Wally's diligent supervision, the complex across from the lodge burned to the ground on October 8, 1984, and over time, all of the buildings disappeared. The firefighters who responded to the call that night still talk about seeing Wally deep within the flames, in a rocking chair, smoking a cigar.

A Renovation and the Ghost of a Saxophone Player?

Manhattan Beach Lodge underwent a major renovation from 1995 to 1999, adding eighteen new guest rooms, a gourmet dinner menu, and a lakeside ballroom for wedding receptions. Created from locally harvested wood, the log and stucco lodge recalls an era of elegant vacations. According to legend, a saxophone player from one Big Band era band disappeared while staying at the lodge, and while his belongings remained, he was never seen again. Over the years, guests have claimed to hear the plaintive cry of a saxophone late at night. Then again, perhaps it was a loon.

Of course, the Lodge is famous in part to Big Trout Lake. At the head of the 15-lake Whitefish Chain, it is perhaps the most accessible spot for lake trout in Minnesota, with a boat landing on County Road 66 on the east shore and a channel from Whitefish Lake on the southwest. Home to lake trout, northern pike, largemouth bass, panfish and walleye, the clear, 1,342-acre lake is 128 feet deep at its deepest point.

Manhattan Beach Today

Each Halloween, the lodge basement becomes a haunted house, and the public is invited to view the former gambling room and speakeasy. At one time, all the walls were painted in vivid scenes, but with multiple renovations over the years, much of the artwork has disappeared. Today various coats-of-arms, dragon heads, and a Viking ship scene await visitors. Several of the staff claim to have found objects misplaced, a reminder that the lodge may remain haunted. One original cabin, named the "haunted shed," remains untouched out of the first cabins built in 1928.

Manhattan Beach is part of the Paul Bunyan Scenic Byway, covering fifty-four miles of stunning scenery. Interpretive kiosks along the tour tell the history and folklore of each community.

TOP: Soo Line Trail, old railroad station house

In early McGrath, Pete BaDour ran the tonsorial parlor (also a pool hall) despite suspicion among authorities that he was selling moonshine and allowing minors to play pool.

McGrath

An Entrepreneurial Vision

JAMES E. MCGRATH FORESAW A FUTURE IN LOGGING near McGrath after other timber cruisers passed up the heavily wooded area near the Snake River and its tributaries. Several logging companies thought the Snake River was too small to float logs, but in 1895, McGrath built a system of dams that created a large enough reservoir to float logs to Pine City, and then on to the St. Croix River and the mills at Stillwater. Without a railroad in the area, all the white pine, spruce, oak, birch, tamarack, and balsam logs were stacked near the river and rafted to the mill in the spring. By 1906 eight logging camps were developed north of the future city of McGrath, and lumberjacks built

their reputations on being the best skidder, hauler, top loader, notcher, blacksmith, or timber cruiser.

Just two years later, in 1908, the Minneapolis, St. Paul and Sault Saint Marie Railroad (Soo Line) arrived, and James McGrath donated 40 acres for town development. When McGrath convinced the Soo Line to build a spur to his White Pine Mill, business boomed for 12 years. With an ambition equal to the lumberjacks, the railroad men tied their reputations to the number of railroad ties (up to 300) one could load into a boxcar. Several sawmills opened in McGrath, including one owned by Robert Zempel and Ernie Zempel; Ernie operated the sawmill until his death in 1974. Logging remains a vital part of the economy in McGrath today.

Once the king of transportation, the river lost importance as rail cars carried the hardwood ties, timber, and posts needed by farmers who were clearing their land. Main Street bustled with a saloon, the McGrath Mercantile, the Shamrock Hotel, and the Anderson Hotel, which housed the post office. The McGrath State Bank opened under President O'Connors in 1912. Pete BaDour ran the tonsorial parlor (also a pool hall) despite suspicion among authorities that he was selling moonshine and allowing minors to play pool. In 1916, Ed Vivant delivered pupils by horse-drawn school buses, with skis or wheels, depending on the season, to the grand two-story brick school. Unfortunately, a large fire in 1921 destroyed the entire block of stores on the north side of Main Street. In 1969, fire reared its ugly head once again, destroying the school. A new single-story grade school opened in 1973 and closed in 1988.

James McGrath was also well known for his strong Catholic roots. Tending to the spiritual needs of his men, he encouraged frequent visits from Father Reiger, who traveled by train, buggy and finally horseback for the last leg into the logging camps. In 1910, the Church of St. Anthony went up in downtown McGrath with financial support from railroad workers, lumberjacks and farming families. Built by John Zempel, each pew had the name of the family who donated $25 to the church. By 1958, the old church was abandoned for a larger facility named Church of Our Lady of Fatima. The old pews were installed in the new church. Three other churches opened their doors: Zion Lutheran, erected in 1921, Grace Lutheran, built in 1939, and Calvary Presbyterian Church. Zion Lutheran Church hosts an annual Memorial Day dinner and Veterans Day dinner for the local VFW Post #2762, which was founded in 1932.

McGrath finally incorporated in 1923. Ed Vivant, owner of the blacksmith shop, was elected as the first Mayor. That same year, the McGrath Creamery hired F. P. Worm, a graduate of the University of Minnesota Dairy School, as manager. Within six years, Mr. Worm increased butter production by 40% and won awards from the Minnesota Creamery Operators and the Minnesota State Fair for his outstanding butter. The building hosted several other businesses after the creamery closed in 1949, but it burned down in the early 1990s.

The End of a Logging Legend

By 1902, James Edward McGrath operated the largest logging business on the St. Croix River. With a workforce of over 1,200 men and 600 horses, his crews logged thirty million feet of pine. When Mr. McGrath died in 1940 at age 79, he and his son Jay were in the woods searching for timber stands. When he did not return, a search party found his body against a tree, an appropriate death for a man who built a town out of his logging business.

McGrath Today

Today the city is home to the post office, VFW McGrath Post 2762, Senior Citizen's Center, Grace Lutheran Church, Zion Lutheran Church, and Our Lady of Fatima Catholic Church. On Highway 65, Vie's Place and Pour Lewey's Saloon sit side by side, with Vie's place residing in the original White Pine school building. The impressive McGrath Fire Department and the City Office & Public Works are located next to a pavilion and playground. The South Soo Line Trail, once the railroad tracks, draws ATVs and snowmobiles to explore the city.

On Labor Day weekend, visitors flock to McGrath for the annual White Pine Logging and Threshing Show hosted by William and Sylvia Langenbach on their farm. Participants experience grain threshing, lumber sawing, shingle making, and observe a water-powered feed mill and a working blacksmith shop. More than 250 tractors line up for the daily parade, and each evening the barn is filled with dancers. A polka service at the church wraps up the unique weekend.

McGrath City Park hosts an annual Fourth of July celebration. The festivities begin with a pancake breakfast and continue with a log-sawing contest, a pie social, and a beer garden in the fire hall. Members of Our Lady of Fatima Catholic Church typically win the food vendor's contest with a terrific barbecue sandwich, served all day long. A spectacular fireworks display ends the memorable day.

TOP: City Hall and Library

McKinley may have gone the way of many mining
ghost towns had not the Minnesota Iron Company
opened the Elba Mine one mile west of McKinley
in 1898.

McKinley

A Daring Move

TYPICALLY, A MINE WAS FULLY DEVELOPED before the mining camp evolved into a village. But McKinley dared to incorporate as a village before their mine was secure. Similar to the Merritt brothers who found iron ore in Leonidas, the McKinley brothers, John, William and Duncan, discovered iron ore in December and platted 80 acres of their exploration camp as the townsite of McKinley.

The Mesaba Lumber Company hitched their wagon to the McKinley star, and constructed a small lumber mill near the townsite to build a mining camp. Early residents S. L. Johnson, W. G. Dundas, Jack Smuk, George Lestic and 189 others petitioned to incorporate the following year. The county commissioners ordered that notices be posted at the McKinley Iron Company boarding house, the logging camp, J. Ford's boarding house, and S. L. Johnson's store, the first store in the new village. On October 12, 1892, 127 unanimous votes were cast for incorporation at Duncan McKinley's store. The first city council was then elected.

Elisha Morcom, a native of Tower, Minnesota, was captain of the mine, and developed a new way of mining ore by sinking a shaft through the soft ore, building a main level under the ore, and mining it from below. The ore would be pumped through chutes into ore cars waiting on a track. Though it was described as a brilliant invention and a model for mining, not one ton of ore came out of the mine. By the time fire wiped out the camp buildings in 1893, followed by the Panic of 1893, the McKinleys were out of money, and lost the property to John D. Rockefeller and the Lake Superior Consolidated Mines. The McKinley Mine closed until 1907, when the Oliver Mining Company took over, mining the ore with two steam shovels.

McKinley may have gone the way of many mining ghost towns had not the Minnesota Iron Company opened the Elba Mine one mile west of McKinley in 1898. A wooden boardwalk connected the mine and the city, and in 1899 the beautiful two-story Elba-McKinley Public School went up on the boardwalk halfway between the two cities. The Sigurd Moe School opened in 1920, and the classes performed many plays over the years including the May 1951 operetta *Joy for the Rose-Tree Kingdom*.

After the McKinley Mine reopened in 1907, the city reached a peak population of 411. Mr. H. J. Millbrock opened a bank, the city erected a town hall with a courtroom and a jail, and Dr. J. C. Farmer operated a private hospital in an old mining company building until his death in 1921. Under the competent leadership of Village President Ed Olson, the city built a water and light plant along with a fire hall staffed by a volunteer fire department. Despite attempts to advertise McKinley as the "future hub of the iron range," the city did not grow.

Tempers exploded on the iron range when miners demanded higher wages and better working conditions from the Oliver Mining Company, which controlled more than 75 percent of the ore resources on the Mesabi Range. Language difficulties made things problematic too. In 1907, fewer than 300 out of 10,139 employees of the Oliver Mining Company could speak fluent English. The workforce consisted mainly of Finnish, Slavic and Italian immigrants, and the men worked ten-hour shifts, six days a week, for $12.50 to $20.00 a week. In addition to the low wages, the workers were forced to pay bribes to the mine bosses in order to retain their jobs, and morale reached an all-time low. Despite union backing from the Western Federation of Miners, a strike in 1907 failed when the Company imported new immigrants to replace the strikers. Once again, in 1916, 20,000 miners walked off their jobs, this time led by the Industrial Workers of the World, whose members were nicknamed "The Wobblies." After considerable violence, this strike also collapsed, but the miners did attract national attention, and the company improved wages by 20–30 percent. Night schools for immigrant parents were instituted in all the mining towns in the 1920s to teach English and American cultural mores. Children were encouraged to wear pins that read, "We only speak English in our Family." When Congress passed the National Labor Relations Act (Wagner Act) in 1935 to protect workers' right to unionize, the unions took control of the iron range, and secured a better life for the miners and their families.

Iron Mining, Then and Now

Open pit iron ore mines, old and new, dominate the landscape around McKinley, just as they do on the rest of the Iron Range. The original McKinley mine was followed by the Elba and LaBelle mines in the early 1900s. By 1918, when C. K. Quinn developed the Wistar Mine, Minnesota was producing 43 million tons of iron ore per year, 60 percent of the nation's total. As the high-grade ores, containing 50–60 percent iron, have been exhausted, mining and enriching taconite, with 20–30 percent iron, has taken over.

McKinley Today

Today, McKinley is home to the McKinley Volunteer Fire Department, City Park, and a rare utility—their own water tower. City Hall, a beautiful WPA stone building erected in the 1930s, is also home to a public library. West of the city, the active Laurentian Mine is owned by ArcelorMittal Steel USA; the East Reserve mine, developed by ArcelorMittal in 2007, is a 476-acre project which can be seen by taking a short drive west of McKinley.

The longest paved section of the Mesabi Trail, a paved bike trail, spans seventy-five miles from Grand Rapids to McKinley. When completed, the trail will traverse 132 miles and connect 25 communities.

Population: 111   **Incorporated:** 1857

INSETS L to R: Street mural • Carven Critters •
remaining insets from Harvey Langseth Woodcarving

A city that straddles two counties, Minneiska
belongs to both Wabasha County and Winona County.

TOP: Welcome to Minneiska, looking south

Minneiska

A City in Two Counties

A CITY THAT STRADDLES TWO COUNTIES, Minneiska belongs to both Wabasha County and Winona County. Nestled in the bluffs on the Mississippi River, this beautiful river city on Highway 61 lies close to the Whitewater Management Area and several sections of state forest. Minneiska means "water white," a name given by the Sioux Indians, who used the river for travel and the bluffs as a lookout for game and enemy tribes.

Michael Agnes, Louis Krutely and Charles Reed were the first settlers and arrived in 1851 to cut wood for the steamboats traveling up and down the river. Subsisting on fish and fowl, these hardy men climbed a tree to watch for boats carrying much-needed supplies. By 1857, when the city incorporated, Main Street claimed a post office, a hotel, a steam sawmill, many saloons, and two breweries. Halfway between Wabasha and Winona, Minneiska served as the natural stopover to change horses for the stagecoach between La Crosse and St. Paul. Boasting one of the finest landing spots on the Mississippi, Minneiska planned to use the river boat traffic to build industry and economic growth.

The following year, the village school, St. Mary's Catholic Church, a Lutheran Church, and a Methodist Church all opened their doors. After the arrival of the River Branch of the Chicago, Milwaukee & St. Paul Railway in 1870, the Farmer's Co-operative Elevator and lumberyard opened for business. The Farmer's State Bank organized in 1917, handling farm loans, insurance, and general banking business.

Minneiska was almost wiped off the map when old Highway 61 was converted to a four-lane highway in 1960. Up to that time, Minneiska provided all the amenities for travelers including seven gas stations and a brewery, but the new construction led to the demolition of almost every downtown business and twenty-five homes, all of which were torn down to make room for the new highway. Also on the list of casualties were the Lutheran Church and the two-room schoolhouse. The city has recovered, is growing again and now has a panoramic view of the Mississippi River.

A Haunted Castle and a Bob Dylan Song

Just south of Minneiska on the river side of Highway 61, Putnam Gray built a bizarre ten-room home out of driftwood in the nineteenth century. Three stories high with a tower, steeples, verandas, and pagodas, the house was named "Crazy Man's Castle," an apt description for the tourist curiosity. Legend states that when the steamboats meandered by the castle at night, Gray's sisters would dance covered with white sheets for the passengers of the river boats, who delighted in the haunted castle. Needless to say, the dancers were a major attraction for the Diamond Jo river cruise line. Putnam Gray is also believed to have invented the precursor to the first Ferris wheel, which was later adapted by George Ferris Jr. Mr. Gray is buried in the local cemetery.

Highway 61 and the Minneiska area are immortalized in Bob Dylan's 1965 album *Highway 61 Revisited*. Dylan was born in Duluth along Highway 61, and began his musical career in Minneapolis. An important north-south connection before the interstate highway system, Highway 61 followed the Mississippi River from New Orleans, through the Mississippi Delta and Memphis blues country, all the way to Grand Portage, Minnesota. Designated the *Great River Road* and "The Blues Highway," the highway now officially ends in Wyoming, Minnesota.

On July 10, 2008, at the Winona County Fair, the city of Minneiska received recognition as a Minnesota sesquicentennial city.

Minneiska Today

The stubborn spirit of Minneiska's first pioneers remains alive with Buck's Bar & Grill, Eagle View Bar & Grill, and Konkel Consulting, which all line Main Street. Two world-class woodcarvers work side by side on Bennett Avenue in downtown Minneiska. Langseth Norsk Woodworking, owned by Harvey Langseth, specializes in Kubbestoles (carved chairs) and Scandinavian furniture. A picture of his great-grandfather, Hans Langseth, hangs in the shop. Hans is listed in the Guinness Book of World Records for growing the longest beard, an incredible stretch of nineteen and one-half feet. At Carven Critters and Carousels, owned by Todd Pasche, the art focuses on gnomes, trolls and carousel horses. Their unique artistic partnership draws a steady stream of customers into both stores.

The spiritual bedrock of this remarkable city, St. Mary's Catholic Church, celebrated their centennial in 1989, and shows no signs of slowing down. The mayor, city clerk and city council allocate money to worthy causes. Lucky recipients include the Rollingstone Snowbankers Snowmobile Club, who groom the beautiful trails that meander directly into scenic Minneiska, and the Annual Minneiska Charity Golf tournament, with proceeds donated to cancer research. In cooperation with the Winona State Art Department, the progressive council plans to extend $500 to the winning design for a mural on the city's retaining wall on Bennett Avenue. Plans are under way for Fourth of July fireworks show too.

Blessed with a clear, three-mile view of the Mississippi River, Minneiska residents watch eagles, tundra swans and pelicans feeding and nesting near the highway.

In 1985, a new fish weathervane was mounted high on the bluffs above Minneiska. Originally made of wood in the 1800s, the weathervane provided wind direction to the log rafters as they navigated the Mississippi River.

One of the town's first settlers, Walter Potter donated land for the First Baptist Church, with the stipulation that the doors remain unlocked to anyone without shelter.

TOP: Old Mizpah General Store, now Steinhorst residence

Mizpah

Lucille's Life: A North Woods Story

SURROUNDED BY FRIENDS, FAMILY AND GUESTS, ninety-year-old Lucille Schue plays her accordion, while guests sing along in a cozy corner of Rose Heim's log and stone studio near Saum, Minnesota. Typical of the resourceful and talented pioneers who settled in Mizpah, a logging village at the southern tip of Koochiching County, she grew up milking cows, stacking hay and picking blueberries on the family farm. After graduating from high school, Lucille stayed on the farm to help her father, and also worked for the Mizpah Lumber Company. Her musical parents encouraged her to play the piano and accordion, and this talent helped pay the bills when her husband, Dutch, died at a young age and left her with three small children to support. At age 50, she beat out three

men for a job as custodian and bus driver for the new Head Start program, and eventually earned her teaching degree and taught for 21 years, before retiring at age 74. A musician for over seventy years, this amazing woman is the church organist, plays the piano on Fridays at the Bigfork Nursing Home, and recently played accordion for Octoberfest at the Kelliher Liquor Store. In 2010, Rose and Gretchen Heim's *Places & Faces of North Beltrami* tribute honored Lucille as one of fifteen outstanding artist/citizens in remote Northern Minnesota. Her photo, taken by New York City photographer Peter Zander, was unveiled November 20, 2010, in Rose's studio. Lucille still lives on her original homestead in Mizpah.

Mizpah, the Hebrew word for watchtower, was named by Reverend Potter, a traveling Methodist minister. The word is used as a parting salutation in Genesis 31: 49, *"Therefore was the name of it called Galeed and Mizpah, for he said, Jehovah watch between me and thee, when we are absent from one another."* The Reverend surely believed that he was saying farewell when he landed in remote Koochiching County, a vast area of over 3,000 square miles, 90 percent of which was once covered by Glacial Lake Agassiz. When the great lake receded, it left behind poorly drained bogs with deposits of peat up to 20 feet deep. Unless drained, peat bogs cannot support much agriculture, but they do sustain black spruce, aspen, balsam, cedar, tamarack and birch for a vital lumber industry. Thankfully, Mizpah sits on higher ground and has soil suitable for farming. Incorporated as a village on March 13, 1903, Mizpah was in Itasca County until December 1906, when the city became part of the newly created Koochiching County.

The first recorded settlers, Will, Walter and Sam Potter, arrived in January 1900 and reported signs of previous habitation, including several deserted cabins. Walter opened the post office in 1901. He donated land for the First Baptist Church, with the stipulation that the doors remain unlocked to anyone without shelter. Will built a sawmill in 1904, and later, the first electric light plant in the county. Several homesteaders and businesses followed the Potters that year, including the Grindall Hotel, "the largest this side of Blackduck," and the *Mizpah Message*, owned by George Cowen. John Cowan established the Bank of Mizpah, which operated until the "Bankers Holiday" in 1932. Reverend Actwood formed a Presbyterian Church, and maintained a lively ministry in logging camps. But the most famous preacher, Frank Higgins, known as Sky Pilot, traveled by dog team and sled throughout two hundred square miles of forest, to spread the good message to unruly lumberjacks.

Early pioneer Lillian Vaughan, a young schoolteacher, walked twenty miles from Blackduck to Mizpah in August 1902 to stake a claim on eighty acres of free government land two miles north of Mizpah. Her diary tells of traveling four days to teach the winter term and returning to Mizpah in February, this time wading through icy water to build a shanty on her claim. She returned in June, only to find plants growing through the floorboards. That fall Miss Vaughan began teaching in an unfinished hall over the Mizpah post office. During the winter, snow drifted over the children's heads through wide cracks in the walls, while cracks in the floorboards allowed the students to watch patrons in the post office below.

In 1906, the Minnesota and International Railroad arrived in Mizpah, although not without considerable effort. Due to the peat bogs and sinkholes, laying track was a slow process, with most of the grading done in the winter. At one point, the train moved so slowly between Blackduck and Bemidji that it was said a passenger could hop off the train to pick a quart of berries and hop back on. Fire swept through Main Street in 1910, reducing fifteen buildings to ashes in three hours. Unfortunately, the fire hall was the first to catch fire. Bucket brigades, dynamiting several structures, and a lucky change in the wind kept the fire to one block.

A Lumber Mill Fills the Town

Opened in 1939 by the Rajala Brothers of Big Fork, the Mizpah Mill covered twenty-five acres of land and employed one hundred and fifty men. The mill operated continuously at its peak, closing in 1944 when all the timber was gone. During its operation, every hotel room and spare room in town was full.

Mizpah Today

Today the city is home to the Community Center, Reinarz Station and Licensing, Mizpah Precision Manufacturing, the post office, Mizpah Liquor Store, and the Bear Bar. Formerly the Englewood Town Hall, Bethesda Lutheran Church celebrates 85 years of service in Mizpah.

The town's simple and touching Memorial Park was erected in 1948 to honor the servicemen and women from the area who served in World War I and World War II. Hand-etched on stone tablets, each name lives on in this tiny town. Nearby, a cannon stands watch.

TOP: Corn delivery Progressive Ag Co-op

Before the Illinois Central Railroad arrived in 1900,
Miss Myrtle Lane ran the town post office out of
a log home.

Myrtle

A Terrible Series of Tornadoes

SUNDAY EVENING, APRIL 30, 1967, started out warm and windy in Myrtle. Mr. and Mrs. Ruben Nelson were eating their dinner when suddenly, the wind came to a complete standstill. Frightened, they hurried to the southwest corner of their basement where they hung onto the water pipes while the house disappeared over their heads, all in 15 seconds. The barn and 21 cattle were gone, and the silo reduced to a quarter of its size. A large grove of trees on three sides of the house were toppled like bowling pins. East of Myrtle, David Ziebell, 16, and George Pacovsky, 17, were milking cows when the barn tipped over. By the time David dug George out from beneath the timbers, the house had blown apart, and Mrs. Ziebell lay 75 feet from the house, alive, but

seriously hurt. Six of the cows died in the barn. Southeast of Myrtle, Mrs. Herbert Bauer and her three-year-old son rode out the storm on the living room floor while her husband was in Albert Lea picking up fried chicken for dinner. They lost their barn, granary, garage, and all other buildings on the farm. Miraculously, everyone in Myrtle survived the four tornadoes that passed through Freeborn County, two of them originating in Iowa. Not everyone was that lucky—thirteen people died that day in surrounding communities.

The city of Myrtle began with a post office. Before the Illinois Central Railroad arrived in 1900, Miss Myrtle Lane ran the post office out of a log home, one mile east of Myrtle, from 1886 to 1900. Early postmasters tended to give emerging cities their name, and the names reflect the history of Minnesota's earliest businesswomen. After the tracks were laid, connecting Cedar Rapids, Iowa, to Albert Lea, Minnesota, William A. Morin bought forty acres for the railway station, and the city developed on Albert Schuhmacher's farm next to the station.

The earliest business developed in 1892, when the Myrtle Cheese Company, under the management of Otto Radloff, manufactured the first brick cheese ever made in Freeborn County. When the railroad station opened in 1900, Bertie Burtch and Daniel Hoyt opened a general store, followed by the Hanson Brothers Grocery. Carl Hanson managed the post office out of his store for 21 years until the building burned in 1927. Soon after, the post office was run once again by women. Mrs. Mollie Kral erected a small post office on Main Street acting as postmistress from 1922 to 1963. Mrs. Sylvia Dahlum continued the tradition until she retired in 1987 while Ray Machacek served as rural mail carrier for forty years.

By 1910, Myrtle boasted a full main street, including a bank and a creamery. The village directory included: two general stores, the Eclipse Lumber Company, A. Lang, who was a stockbuyer and also the agent for Speltz Brothers Elevator, blacksmith Carl Johnson, a feed mill, a harness shop, and a hardware store. When train service stopped during the February blizzard of 1916, passengers, businessmen and farmers alike all pitched in to clear the tracks for the Illinois Central Railroad to resume rail service. At one time, both the United Brethren and the Danish Lutheran Church called residents to worship. A new two-room school, built in 1916, housed grades one to six until 1971, when District 71 consolidated with Glenville.

The Myrtle Museum

Myrtle celebrated their 75th Centennial and the U.S. bicentennial when local citizens opened the Myrtle Museum on July 11, 1975, one of three museums in Freeborn County. Under the direction of curator Edna Belshan Johnson, city residents renovated the building, and filled it with donated maps, documents and other memorabilia. Elmer Pederson donated an old cookie case from the former grocery story to showcase glassware. The old school bell sits proudly on a brick foundation built by Frank Nerad next to a flag pole erected by Verner Schilling. In 1975, approximately 1,000 visitors enjoyed the delightful museum.

Myrtle put on a grand party in honor of the U.S. bicentennial on June 12, 1976, with a parade, ball games for the adults and contests for the children. Once again, the museum stole the show with over 1,000 visitors in 1976.

Myrtle Today

Today Myrtle is home to an active fire department, Hunter's Bar, CJ's Revenge Theater, a bustling Progressive Ag Co-op, a city park, Lawson Tree Service, and the Myrtle Museum. The old creamery still stands next to the elevator. Although Myrtle no longer has an active church, there are six cemeteries in the town, all of which are reflective of the diverse migration to the area: the National Bohemian Cemetery, Danish Cemetery (seven graves), Kestner Cemetery (one grave), Krikva Cemetery (a private cemetery), Pilgrim's Rest Cemetery, and Wanders Rest Cemetery.

The Hunter's Bar sports a large outdoor picnic area with bean bag toss games set up for tournaments. A small brick building, the former fire department, sits next to the bar. A well-cared-for City Park with a softball diamond, picnic shelter and playground equipment is home to the local coed softball team.

Agriculture is still the core of Myrtle's economy. The railroad tracks are lined with grain elevators, and streams of tractors transport grain to and fro in order to keep the cars on the freight trains full.

Founded in 1882, the National Bohemian Cemetery near Myrtle is evidence of the large number of Bohemian settlers in the area in the mid-1800s. A walking history lesson of Freeborn County, most of the headstones are written in Czech. Each year, a Memorial Day service at the cemetery is followed by a potluck dinner in the brick hall on the grounds.

TOP: Original Nash home, now Wood residence

Local teacher Florence Engen Aldrich taught hundreds of local children to play piano at 25 cents a lesson, a sum almost everyone could afford to pay.

Nashua

Leaving for Texas or Minnesota, whichever Train Arrives First

WHEN REVEREND FRANCIS AND MATHEW NASH, brothers from Greenfield, Iowa, decided to move either to Texas or to Minnesota to take advantage of free land advertised there, they couldn't agree on the state. The year was 1879 and land sold for as little as $3.50 an acre. Leaving the choice up to fate, the men decided to take the first train to arrive at the station. As it happened, a northbound train arrived first and Nashua was born, named after the Nash families and their home state, Iowa. That spring, they returned with their cattle and seed to plant wheat.

The Soo Line Railroad came through in 1887, built a small flat-house for grain purchases on the Nash property, and moved the depot from Elliot to Nashua. A large contingent of German settlers arrived in the early 1900s: the Roecks, Wilkes, Hasses, Toelles, Arfstens, Brauses, Steens, Bremers and Everts, followed by settlers of English stock: the Hosfords, Maces and Crosses. The village incorporated in 1902, prompting the first liquor license, street lamps, and wooden sidewalks. A former wheat field surrounding the railroad tracks soon held the P. S. Stickney General Store, Tony Prohosky's Hotel and Saloon, Mike Schuster's Blacksmith Shop, and the Atlantic Elevator, powered by a $3\frac{1}{2}$ horsepower Fairbanks Morse gas engine. Mr. Stickney was also the first postmaster, and his friend, George Mace, the first mayor. One of their leaders, Herman Hasse, along with Font Nash, helped open the State Bank of Nashua in 1914 with Hilmer Lundquist as

Cashier. In 1929, a new creamery and community hall supported the flourishing village.

In 1892, Miss Constance Helen (Nelly) Lewis and her sister Amy arrived from England to live with their brother Charles on his claim in South Dakota. Amy taught school while Nelly, who had never cooked a meal or washed clothes, faced the rigors of housekeeping in a small shack. When Charles Lewis married the daughter of an English family near Wheaton, Nelly was a bridesmaid for the wedding. A year later, Phillip (Font) Fontaine Nash, younger brother of Mathew and Francis, married Nelly on February 15, 1984. The couple raised four children: Helen, Fontaine (Maury), Dorothy and Harry. The couple worked hard to build the community. Font brought settlers to Nashua through his real estate business. He helped found the Farmer's Elevator, the First State Bank and the Nash Lumber Company. Mrs. Nash promoted the Farmers Club, the Nashua Improvement Club, the Red Cross, and the Congregational Ladies Aid of Tintah. She also had the gift of hospitality, and opened her home to many friends and relatives. Their son Maury helped organize the Nashua Cooperative Creamery in 1929, and followed in his father's footsteps as mayor of Nashua from 1940 until his death in 1964.

Students attended a small wood schoolhouse until 1914, when a new brick school, the pride of Nashua, opened its doors. Local teacher Florence Engen Aldrich, who married businessman Fred Aldrich, also taught hundreds of local children to play piano at 25 cents a lesson, a sum almost everyone could afford to pay. Mrs. Aldrich vividly recalls her first spring visit to Nashua when the town was covered with water from the swollen Red River, and had very few trees to break the wind.

When drought and depression hit in the '30s, Nashua, along with the other prairie towns, lost business and population. A disastrous fire on October 27, 1961, destroyed the hotel, Kapitan's Store, and Mohagen's Store. City clerk Sharon Rittenour writes, "When we moved here forty-four years ago, Nashua had an elevator, a school, post office, grocery story, hardware store, and a liquor store. Farmers now farm a lot of acres with big machinery, and the smaller farms are gone. Many people milked cows, and now, none can be found for miles. My personal thought is that big wasn't good for the small towns, it killed us. But I still think Nashua is a great place to live, almost like living on a farm, but I can still see people moving around." Today the Canadian Pacific passes through Nashua to unload fertilizer, while Nashua's lone business, Wendell Agronomy, stands guard along the tracks. On the outskirts of town, the Haus Plant stores beets for local farmers. The city contracts with Tintah for fire protection.

A Rat-catching Contest

Along with breaking prairie sod for wheat and oats, many of the men were avid hunters and trappers. Roy Brown, who operated the cream route for 33 years, tells the story of a rat contest held in Tenney, where the team who brought in the most rat tails won a barbecue supper from the losers. When they discovered that the official counter, Nellie Delgarno, a clerk in Klugman's Store, could not bear to touch the tails and used a stick to count them, the men began bringing in any vegetable root that resembled a tail. That ended the contest.

Nashua Today

Phillip Fontaine (Font) Nash and his wife Constance Helen (Nelly) Lewis Nash built two beautiful homes in Nashua. Font landscaped a large artificial pond and garden fed by two artesian wells in his yard. The couple worked tirelessly to improve life in the city, and all of Nashua were recipients of their generous spirit.

Although vacant and with windows and trim somewhat the worse for wear, the old brick school still stands and waits for a new purpose in Nashua.

The original Nash residence on the north end of town, now owned by Sally and Mark Wood, recently hosted their daughter's wedding in the garden. During the ceremony, the mailman delivered the mail, and the neighbor honked his horn as he drove by the house.

Immediately following Nassau's incorporation in 1887, an application for a legal liquor license was granted with the provision that there would be no dice, cards, pool, gambling, or curtained windows on Sundays.

TOP: Vintage merry-go-round on the old school grounds

Nassau

A Small Town Buzzing with Activity

NASSAU HUMS WITH ACTIVITY. Harvest time finds the city full of grain trucks hauling soybeans and corn to the grain elevator, and there is a steady stream of customers going in and out of the implement dealer. Wildung Implement not only sells machinery, they host a coffee corner where the local wives take turns providing treats for the coffee group. Spirits are high and the money is good with a record harvest in Minnesota's finest farmland.

The name of the city is a mystery. However, with the majority of the settlers of German descent, the name may have originated from the title of the Duke of Nassau in Germany. When the Great Northern Railway arrived in 1887, John Macy sold his farmland to the railroad

for a dollar, and began construction of a grain elevator. That same year, Michael and Kate Mason arrived in a covered wagon drawn by oxen, and found a job managing the elevator and a home in the elevator loft, where they slept on straw ticks (a form of mattress). Immediately following incorporation in 1887, an application for a legal liquor license was granted to Herriges & Co. with the provision of no dice, cards, pool, gambling, or curtained windows on Sundays. Frank Schliep jumped on the bandwagon with a pool hall, and J. C. Rourke opened a bowling alley. When a new post office was built in 1987, the city celebrated the 100th birthday of the Nassau post office with a party on May 27, 1988.

After the city was platted by Isaac Macy and William Thomas on December 26, 1893, many new businesses followed, including W. G.

Mix Hardware, Michael Mason's Hotel, Kanthak's Blacksmith Shop, and Nelson's General Store and post office. A. S. Randall and l. H. Macy sold farm machinery, and Helmer & Herriges was the headquarters for buggies and wagons. Both the Nassau Farmers Elevator and the Village Hall were built in 1899. The Nassau State Bank opened in 1901, and the following year, the *Nassau Gazette* sported multiple ads for a thriving business community.

In 1902, school board members voted unanimously to build a new two-story brick school with a bell tower. Twenty-three years later, the board voted to erect a school barn with four stalls to house the horses of the children, who traveled to school by horse and buggy. When the school closed in 1968 to consolidate with Marietta, the school was dismantled, but the barn remains on the Ed Struck farm east of Nassau.

Like most small towns, fire and storms took their toll on the community. On January 27, 1915, the north side of Main Street went up in flames, including Nassau Lodge No. 186, Independent Order of Odd Fellows. The lodge rebuilt a two-story brick building that fall, and the former I.O.O.F. is now the local bar. Two months after the first fire, the south side of Main Street met the same fate. The elevator burned down in 1931, was rebuilt, and a second elevator opened in 1953. In January 1969, a steady series of snowstorms kept the school closed for a month.

Two of the three churches that formed in Nassau remain. St. James Catholic Church erected a new church in 1967 and sponsors a sauerkraut festival each year. Built in 1909, St. Paul's Lutheran celebrated their 60th anniversary in 1969. The Congregational Church, organized in 1898, consolidated with a church in Marietta in 1963. A beautiful granite monument stands in the city cemetery; it is dedicated to all veterans and was erected by the Meyer-Thompson Post 536 of Nassau.

A Little Town That Throws Big Parties

Nassau knows how to throw a party. The city celebrated their 60th anniversary in 1952 with a street carnival, a baseball tournament, and a street dance. Under the leadership of C. A. Hewitt, the *"Nassau Old Timers"* gathered early on June 16 to reminisce about life in Nassau at the turn of the twentieth century. Several elders reflected on growing up in the city; Mrs. George Baker read a poem, "It's Just a Street Where Old Friends Meet," and Mrs. Hewitt rendered a solo, "A Little Bit of Honey." Members of the choirs throughout the years came forward and led the group in singing "Auld Lang Syne." Everyone was reluctant to leave at the end of the day. In 1967, the city drew a huge crowd for their 75th anniversary, perhaps to admire all the local men who grew beards for the celebration. The 90th Anniversary party eased the way into their centennial celebration in 1993, where the all-male Miss Nassau contest raised money for the Centennial fund.

Santa Claus Days rule in Nassau. Local merchants offer free movies in the town hall and promote store drawings for free turkeys. Everyone takes home a sack of candy, peanuts, and due to the small population, everyone's guaranteed a turkey. Sirens blaring, the shut-ins receive their treats via delivery by the fire truck. Even the bar gets in on the festivities, offering free Tom & Jerry drinks to the party crowd.

Nassau Today

The lively city of Nassau is now home to the Farmer's Elevator, Farmer's Oil, City Hall & Senior Center, the Fire Hall, Bordertown Bar, and Wildung Implement. Chartered in 1945, American Legion Post Meyer-Thompson #536 honors the first men from Nassau to lose their lives in World War II. The post hosts an annual Bingo Poultry party each November and a mulligan stew fundraiser each spring. Led by Agnes Tobias and Marcella Kelley, the women formed an auxiliary in 1946, with membership reaching a record 52 in 1993.

The site of the Nassau Public School District is now a large city park. The original school steps and walkway, anchored by the school bell, lead into the park, which includes the original merry-go-round and swing set, a reminder of great memories.

The 1819 Battle of the Little River near Nielsville
between the Dakota and Ojibwe capped decades of
fighting over wild rice and territory.

TOP: Greeting on Nielsville's east side

Nielsville

The Battle of the Little River

BEFORE 1736, THE DAKOTA OCCUPIED much of northern
Minnesota, with its extensive lakes and waterways. The Ojibwe
depended on wild rice *(Mahnomin)* as it was their most important food
source and considered sacred. They fought repeated skirmishes with
the Dakota over this resource. The 1819 Battle of the Little River near
Nielsville between the Dakota and Ojibwe capped decades of fighting
over wild rice and territory. Yankton Dakota chief Wah-nah-ta was
leading a war party toward Red Lake, when he ran into an Ojibwe band
led by Wash-ta-do-ga-wub opposite the mouth of the Goose River, just
south of Nielsville. The resulting bloody, all-day clash caused such great
losses that at sundown both sides retreated from the battlefield—the

Dakota back to the mouth of the Goose River, and the Ojibwe north to
the Sand Hill River. The battle influenced the 1825 Treaty of Prairie
du Chien, which established boundaries between various tribes in the
upper Midwest. In this area, land to the west and southwest was identi-
fied as Dakota land, with the Ojibwe controlling the wild rice beds of
northern Minnesota.

In 1869, Nels O. Paulsrud left Norway and settled near the battle
site to begin the community of Nielsville. An old deed reveals that Mr.
Paulsrud's actual name was Nils Olson and that the surname Paulsrud
was adopted from his landowner in Norway. The promise of owning
their own farmland lured land-hungry Norwegians to the fertile fields in
the Red River Valley. Before Norwegians were allowed to leave Norway,

United States officials insisted that they submit a certificate of good character from their pastor, most of whom were solidly opposed to anyone leaving Norway. Twenty-five brave families followed Nels, and they named the community after him in 1882. Nels was elected sheriff of Polk County and served from 1886 to 1890.

By the time the Great Northern Railway laid tracks through Nielsville in 1896, the city was thriving and featured multiple businesses, all essential to a city located in one of the best farming sections in the Red River Valley. The Northwestern Elevator Company, the Kolden Lumberyard, and the State Bank of Nielsville all helped farmers operate top-notch farms. Over the years, Charlie Bye's Store, Sundet's Place, Landgaard's Cash Mercantile, and Eidsmoe's Café served up exceptional food and service to the locals. In 1970, Landgaard's Cash Mercantile celebrated their 50th anniversary with a dinner for 350 guests in appreciation for community loyalty. Stores remained open as late as midnight to accommodate farmers' families who bought supplies, traded goods and caught up on local news. Entertainment was just around the corner at the Nielsville Hall where you could watch a basketball game, catch a movie, dance to live music, or rollerskate for 25 cents, including skates.

In 1918, a new school opened in Nielsville and remained open until 1971, when the school consolidated with Climax. After it closed, the two-story brick building served as an apartment for years, and remains occupied as a private residence. John Dahl, owner of the lumberyard, served as the first mayor when the city incorporated in 1920.

A Trail Used by Indians and Settlers Alike

Nielsville sits on Highway 75, designated "the Historic King of Trails" by the state of Minnesota in 2001. Originally Highway 75 was a Native American trail. Later, pioneers followed the route in wagons and oxcarts to settle in the Red River Valley. With the arrival of the automobile and improved roads, travelers took to the road stretching from Winnipeg to the Gulf of Mexico. Originally named "The King of Trails" in 1917, the name changed to highway US 75 in 1926. Since 2002, communities along the trail celebrate the Annual King of Trails Fall Market on the second Saturday in September with a farmer's market, flea markets, an antique and collectibles fair, and a local artists' showcase.

Nielsville Today

Today Nielsville boasts a post office, the Nielsville Fire Department, City Hall, Fabian's Tavern, Spokely Potato House, O Zone Bar, Hubbard American Legion Post #336, and two churches: St. Petri Lutheran Church and Living Water Assembly of God. St. Petri Lutheran Church celebrated their centennial in 1975 with the original church still used for the sanctuary. A large playground and meticulous baseball field lie just behind the old Nielsville Hall. The rural character of the land is still very much in evidence around Nielsville, with fields planted right up to the edge of town, and forested areas, one with an active eagle's nest, nearby.

In 1939, to honor the 120th anniversary of the battle between the Dakota, led by Chief Wahnahtah, and the Ojibwe, led by Chief Wash-ta-do-ga-wub, a marker was placed on the school grounds with the inscription: *Battle of the Little River. Near this spot on the Little River the Chippewa and Sioux fought a major battle in 1819 leading to the treaty of 1825 ending tribal wars in Minnesota*. This rock cairn monument can be found near the Living Waters Church.

Nielsville Hall, a plated tin-covered hall built in 1915, still stands in Nielsville. Citizens recall the local piano players who accompanied the movies shown there. Nielsville also staged an outdoor movie theater by showing movies on the side of the elevator.

Sundet Cemetery, located three miles north of Nielsville, is now the site of the "Smallest Church in the World." Completed in 2010 by Bruce Larson, the tiny church is nestled in the corner of the cemetery, surrounded by rich Red River Valley farmland.

STIGMAN'S MOUND
PICNIC AREA
BUILT BY
ORTON GRANGE 802
CROW WING
RAMBLERS 4H

On the Fourth of July in 1934, over 3,000 participants showed up to watch a mile-long parade that featured a life-sized mechanical cow built by Bert Marshall, which ate and gave milk.

TOP: Stigman's Mound Picnic Area

Nimrod

Only You Can Prevent Forest Fires

THE HISTORIC NIMROD FIRE TOWER has held watch over Nimrod and the surrounding area since 1928, the year the Minnesota Forest Service erected the structure. Each day in May and June, from snow melt to green up, a "spotter" makes the slow climb up the 94-foot ladder to the octagonal crow's nest on top of the tower. Smoke spotters always keep a close watch for smoke during peak fire season, but also keep vigil in the fall and summer during dangerously dry periods. On September 6, 1976, during a bad drought, a smoke spotter from the Nimrod tower discovered the historic Huntersville-Badoura fire that consumed more than 23,000 acres and cost almost a million dollars to control. Over the last 83 years, the watchful eyes of the spotters in the tower have caught many wildfires and prevented another disaster like the 1976 forest fire.

Wheat was king in 1870, and its production brought the Northern Pacific Railway north to Wadena to capture the wheat shipping business. As new settlers arrived, the demand for lumber skyrocketed. In 1879, loggers found the perfect setting for a camp near Nimrod on the Crow Wing River, surrounded by a great pine forest. Nimrod also provided a respite for wheat haulers traveling from Shell City to Verndale on the "Wheat Trail." In 1880, Jacob Graba constructed a hotel on the banks of the Crow Wing in Nimrod to accommodate Wheat Trail travelers and passengers on the Stageline. When Pac and Mary Williams bought the hotel from Graba in 1885, the newly named Williams Landing became the center of the local social scene.

A passenger stagecoach run by Sheriff John and Frank Eddy carried the mail from Verndale to William's Landing. Passengers were treated to lunch prepared by Mary Williams, who also was the first postmistress. A post office demanded an official name, and in 1891 Mrs. Williams sent the name Luedma to St. Paul postal authorities. Lu-Ed-Ma stood for Luther McClure, Ed William, and Mary McClure, the first children born in Nimrod. An unpopular name with St. Paul, the authorities instead chose the name of the biblical figure Nimrod, named for the grandson of Ham, and called "a mighty hunter before the Lord" in Genesis.

In the '20s to the '50s, Nimrod was home to two cafes, one owned by Lydia Jenson, three grocery stores, Tomlinson Lumber Mill, a blacksmith shop, a used car lot, Stigman & Frame Skelly Station, Emil Stelck's barber shop, and a feed store. Marion Tomlinson started the Nimrod Creamery, where the Nimrod Farmer's Club organized in 1919. In 1934, the club sponsored a Fourth of July celebration second to none. Over 3,000 participants showed up to watch the mile-long parade, and the hit of the parade—a life-sized mechanical cow built by Bert Marshall, that ate and gave milk.

Although logging and wheat were the major industries, two large swamps surrounding Nimrod provided another interesting business in the 1920s. Manufacturing wiregrass mats and rugs was a thriving industry in Wisconsin, and the swamps in Minnesota were covered with wiregrass. Both the American Wire Grass Co. and the Waite Grass Co. headquartered near Nimrod and competed for the lucrative wiregrass.

A Town Celebration, a Rodeo and a Minnesota Twin

Every Labor Day weekend since the city's centennial in 1979, the community hosts "Nimrod Jubilee Days," a family celebration complete with a pageant, a parade, a big truck mud run, mud volleyball, and a softball tournament. Sixty-nine high energy citizens put on a party for five thousand friends and extended family.

Troy and Peggy Meech, owners of Meech Bucking Bulls, sponsor the Nimrod Labor Day Bull Bash, a bull ride that draws top riders from all over the country. Winner of many awards in the Professional Rodeo Cowboys Association, Troy also offers a bull riding school Memorial Day weekend.

The Stigman Mound City Park and Stigman Field are named for a local, Dick Stigman, who was a relief pitcher for the Minnesota Twins on the 1965 American League Championship team. The field is also home to the Nimrod Gnats, three-time state tournament participants and the pride of Nimrod. Dick's mother, Ann Stigman, held the job of postal clerk until she was 90 years old. Stigman's Mound along the Crow Wing River is a rest stop for canoe enthusiasts who meander along the scenic river at four miles per hour.

Nimrod Today

Today Nimrod is home to J & J's Bar and Grill, Nimrod Community Center, Nimrod Lutheran Church built in 1950, Stigman Mound City Park, and the Stigman Baseball Field. The creamery resurfaced as Riverside Grocery until owner Jeanne Tellock sold the store in 2002 to Reese and Melanie Meech, who renamed the business Nimrod Gas, Grocery & Off-Sale. The store closed in December, 2010, along with the post office located in the store. That sad day officially ended Nimrod's 56478 zip code forever, but there is talk of reopening the grocery store.

Nimrod is close to some great boating opportunities; the Crow Wing River, one of 19 designated Canoe and Boating Route Rivers in Minnesota, flows through Nimrod to the Mississippi River in Brainerd. An abundance of wildlife and birds await the canoe enthusiast. Visitors are also encouraged to take a dip in the Swimmin' Hole by the bridge. The river transforms into a popular snowmobile highway during the winter months.

Standing in a long line with very few possessions, Ole Birkland was informed by the immigration officer that he couldn't settle in Minnesota unless he changed his name to Ole Olson. He did and many of his descendants still live in the area today.

TOP: Norcross Community Park and Gardens

Norcross

Norwegian Immigrants and a Real Ole Oleson

IT IS NOT SURPRISING THAT NORWEGIAN immigrants chose to settle in Norcross. Located near both the Red River Valley and the Lake Agassiz Plain, the Norwegians chose one of the best farming regions in the state. Lacking any sizable farmland in Norway and accustomed to mountainous terrain, the new settlers had truly found a farm paradise in Norcross.

In 1882, Norcross began as a large grain ranch owned by N. F. Griswold and Captain J. N. Cross. They convinced the Great Northern Railway to build the depot at their ranch rather than two miles north at the planned town of Gorton. The train regularly stopped at the ranch to pick up wheat, and the railroad officials agreed to build the depot and grain elevators there. Why the name Norcross instead of Griscross? The two gentlemen and an old army career man, called Norton, donated the land for the town. Norton and Cross teamed up for the city name, Norcross, and Griswold settled for main street, known as "Griswold Avenue."

The town incorporated in 1913 with 140 people. Lund and Sellseth started a bank in 1909, which closed in 1931, a victim of the Depression. The first school, named "New School," opened in 1903, and later was home to the Norwegian Lutheran Church when a newer school was built. In 1928, a great fire destroyed all the buildings on the south side of town. Refusing to give in to the forces of nature, the citizens opened a creamery, the town hall, and a liquor store, which later was converted to a pool hall during Prohibition. George Houps from Iowa bought the stockyards and started a general store.

The population continued to grow, with the majority of the new citizens arriving from Norway. A story is told of Silas Olson's grandfather, Ole Birkland, who arrived from Norway via Ellis Island in 1866. Standing in a long line with very few possessions, he was informed by the immigration officer that he could not settle in Minnesota with a name like Birkland. He must change his name to Ole Olson, and he did. Many of his descendants still live in the Norcross area today.

At one time Norcross had three churches. Our Savior's Lutheran Church celebrated their 75th anniversary in 1976 and their 90th anniversary in 1991, and is now a beautiful private home. Before the church was built, early pioneers walked 17 miles to a church northeast of Norcross in order to be confirmed. St. Mary's Catholic Church opened in 1905 and closed in 1923. The Faith United Methodist Church began services at the Amundson School in 1919, erected a church in 1952, and closed in 2007.

American Legion Hillestad-Borgeson Post #410, based in Norcross, established a veterans' memorial in Norcross Park on Highway 9. The monument erected by the post is dedicated "In memory of all the men and women who have served their country in all wars." A National Guardsman and 2005 veteran of the war in Iraq, Norcross native Jacob Veldhouse's name is inscribed there, as is the name of his uncle, Dennis.

The Town Hall as the Social Center

The Norcross Town Hall, built in the late '20s, was the place to be when growing up in Norcross. People danced to the Lawrence Welk Band, Tiny Little, Lem Hawkins and Willie Whistle, Al Mikesh, the Don Strickland Band, and later, The (Unbelievable) Uglies. Other events included rollerskating Friday nights, funerals, wedding receptions, church fundraiser dinners, and basketball games. No longer in use by the '90s, the large brick building fell into disrepair and was dismantled in 1997. Bricks were offered free to the public, a reminder of the great memories shared by the fun-loving people of Norcross.

Organized in 1929, the Norcross Women's Community Club meets monthly at members' home to discuss biotechnology, tornado and flood relief, or whatever topic piques their interest. Members also maintain the Norcross Park, and decorate the park shelter with lights and a nativity scene each Christmas. For many years, the club held Santa Claus Day at the Norcross Café following their annual holiday dinner. Sarah Bowden has been a member since 1936.

Norcross Today

Today, the post office, open from 8:00 a.m. to 12:24 p.m., represents the only storefront still active on east Griswold Avenue. The city office and Norcross Fire Department share a white frame building in the center of town, and Grant County maintains a county garage. A dozen cars line up in front of the fire hall each morning for coffee prepared by the local women. Each year, the coffee drinkers pool the free-will offerings, and put on a community pizza party and Christmas party. A distinctive aqua and silver water tower marks the entry to a pleasant residential neighborhood on the west side of the tracks. Once a barren strip of land between the railroad tracks and the highway, Norcross Park is now an oasis of flowering crab trees, tulips and bushes. Picnic tables, an old railroad bell, the Veterans' Memorial, and a windmill complete the lovely park. The Great Northern Railway ceded a one-hundred-year lease to the Norcross Women's Club in 1929, and donated a carload of cinders to fill in the low land. Over the years, the women have volunteered countless hours of hard work to maintain the park.

The Norcross school building is a worthy candidate for the National Register of Historic Places. Built in 1938 by the WPA, the building is made entirely of poured concrete, a fine example of Art Deco architecture. For over thirty years, students from first through seventh grade were educated in the three-room school. The school consolidated with Herman in 1971, and the building is privately owned.

*No single event made a bigger impact on the
citizens of Odessa than the disastrous train wreck
on December 18, 1911.*

TOP: "Welcome to Odessa" city park

Odessa

The Great Train Wreck of 1911

NO SINGLE EVENT MADE A BIGGER IMPACT on the citizens of Odessa than the disastrous train wreck on December 18, 1911, at 4:28 a.m., when a new all-steel train of the Chicago, Milwaukee & St. Paul Railroad crashed into the rear of a Columbian Flyer bound for Chicago. Carrying live silkworms bound for eastern markets, the silk train was traveling at 70 miles per hour around a curve when the engineer saw the passenger train on the tracks. The engine crushed the sleeper car with every berth full of sleeping passengers. Twelve passengers were killed and another dozen seriously injured. The sound of crashing steel awakened the community, who rushed to the aid of the injured. Three more train accidents occurred over the next sixty years, but none as dramatic as the crash of 1911.

Now located on Highway 7 near the Big Stone National Wildlife Refuge, Odessa first settled as a city in 1879, when the Chicago, Milwaukee & St. Paul Railroad opened a depot and post office under the direction of A. D. Beardsley. Although Odessa Township is named after the Ukrainian city, Odessa, where wheat seed used in the area originated, it is believed that the city is named after Mr. Beardsley's beloved daughter, Dessa, who died from diphtheria at age three. Around 1880, a general store opened in Odessa, and in 1883, Herman Kollitz moved from his farm in Akron to start a legendary mercantile store. By the time the city incorporated in 1895, Odessa thrived with two grain elevators (the Empire and the Crown), the Odessa House Hotel, and

Boetcher Lumber Co., managed by Richard Menzel. When Mr. Menzel built his own lumberyard in 1902, he bought the stock of his former employer. Newspaper editor Irv Townsend printed the *Odessa Tribune* from 1898 to 1908, and in 1917, another newspaper, the *Odessa Signal*, published a weekly paper for one year. A local flour mill opened to produce "Odessa Best Flour," an extremely popular brand of the era. Sadly, the landmark mill exploded just after World War I and burned to the ground. A man with many careers, J. W. Lenz opened a furniture store and also worked as the town barber, the town marshall, a night watchman, and manager of the Odessa baseball team.

Water frequently inundated the original school, so a new brick school was built on top of a hill in 1914. Although the high school consolidated with Ortonville in 1966, students in kindergarten through grade 6 continued to use the building for several years. Bob Kollitz was the first high school graduate of a total of 509 graduates over the history of the school. Author Arlo Janssen writes about Leander Strei, former owner of the gas station, who was a top-notch basketball player at the high school. In January, 1932, Leander set a basketball school record when Odessa defeated the big city, Ortonville, 12 to 11. Leander scored all 12 points.

Odessa has had many churches over the years but only Trinity Lutheran Church, a German-speaking congregation for many years, remains after serving the community for more than one hundred years.

A Mercantile, Lumber, Bees, and a Century-Old Company

Herman Kollitz opened his general store in 1883, constructed a new building on Main Street, and continued in business until 1971. One of the oldest businesses in Big Stone County, the historic building remains a proud legacy of the family's history on Main Street. In 1902, Richard Menzel built the town lumberyard, and bought out three competitors over the years. As business prospered, he added a hardware store to offer better service to the early settlers. His son, Chip Menzel, eventually took over the company until the business closed. In 1952, the Herman Ellingson family moved to Odessa with 800 beehives and increased that number to 4,000 hives by 1979. A honey and beeswax producer, the honey business recently closed, but the Triple D Wax Rendering business remains in the community.

Over 120 years old, the Agassiz of Odessa Mutual Insurance Company formed in 1888 when a small group of farmers established their own insurance business. From 1934 to 1983, the company operated out of the Farmer's and Merchant's Bank building until a lack of space fueled the need for a new facility in town.

Odessa Today

Today, Odessa is home to Tom's Service and Repair, the Agassiz of Odessa Mutual Insurance Company, the Farmer's Elevator, the Refuge Bar, Cha Ches Café, Big Stone Western Art, the post office, Ellingson's Wax Rendering, Club 7-75, and a new fire hall sided with red and gray metal. The Odessa American Legion Post 520 maintains their headquarters on Main Street. In 1979, Odessa celebrated their centennial, but on June 21, 2011, the closed elevator auctioned off more than one hundred years of equipment and memorabilia. The Burlington Northern train sailed by without stopping.

The Yellow Bank Church Campground Bridge over the Yellow Bank River is also one of Minnesota's historic bridges. Built in 1893 by the King Bridge Company in Cleveland, the single-span through-truss steel structure is significant as an example of experimentation with bridge truss configuration during the late nineteenth century.

The Odessa Jail, a Minnesota Historic Site, was built in 1900 and functioned as a jail until 1924. A square brick structure with a flat roof, the historic building on Main and Second Street was listed on the register of historic places on July 24, 1986.

Darold and Paula Bailey, owners of Big Stone Western Art, house their studio in the former Methodist Church. The last couple married in the church in 1980, the Baileys remodeled the building for a home and studio for their original bronze, stone, and wood sculptures, as well as handmade baskets.

TOP: Quilt display, Kirkebo Lutheran Church

The spring Flood of 1969 almost wiped Perley off the map. With the exception of the church, elevator, and a few homes, every building filled with water on the main floor.

Perley

A Love-Hate Relationship with the River

SURROUNDED BY A DIKE TO PREVENT FLOODING in this fertile agricultural community, Perley has a love-hate relationship with the Red River of the North. Long before the railroad, the Red River was the major artery for transportation and settlement in the area. Along the river, early Norwegian entrepreneur Andrew Aabye opened a general store and post office next to an elevator for grain storage. Three river barges, the *Grandin*, the *Alsop* and the *Pluck* transported 40,000 bushels of grain from the elevator, as well as passengers to and from the site. When the Great Northern arrived in 1883, two hundred men camped near the Aabye Store to help lay track as far as Perley. Mr. Aabye promptly decided to move his store to the new village, and cut down two large oak trees to use as skids for transportation. Thirty-six horses pulled the store to Perley, while Mrs. Aabye prepared meals in the store during the move.

In 1883, Solomon G. Comstock, land purchaser for the railroad, platted Perley, and named the village for his good friend, George E. Perley, a Moorhead attorney and state legislator from 1905 to 1907. By the time the village incorporated on November 22, 1906, Ole Wiig operated the Perley House Hotel, butter maker N. C. Blow earned $70 per month at Lee Cooperative Creamery, and Hovden & Anderson sold general merchandise. Two elevators, the Monarch and the Minneapolis & Northern, went up along the railroad tracks. First State Bank of Perley opened for business in 1912, followed by the Farmer's and

Merchant's State Bank in 1914. Children attending country school could now attend Perley Public School District #25 with an additional three year high school. When the Red River flooded the city in 1969, the school was heavily damaged, and the district consolidated with Hendrum in 1974. The building was torn down, but the original school playground equipment coexists with brand new equipment across the street from the former school grounds.

Initially located on John Jacobson's farm, Kirkebo Lutheran Church (*Kirkebo* means "church home" in Norwegian) moved to the village in 1890, following the arrival of the railroad. By 1943, church services were mainly conducted in English, women gained the right to vote, and the church decided to build a home for the elderly in Moorhead, today known as Eventide. After the church building burned in 1955, the congregation erected a new building in 1957. Dedicated sandbaggers saved the church from flooding in 1969, and services were suspended only temporarily. In 1981, Kirkebo celebrated their centennial at 304 members strong, including the oldest member, 95-year-old Ingeborg Hoganson.

The Flood of 1969

The spring Flood of 1969 almost wiped Perley off the map. With the exception of the church, elevator and a few homes, every building filled with water on the main floor. All but five residents out of 165 were evacuated out of the city. An emergency levee built around the city kept the city dry during a summer flood in 1975, but damaged the countryside. A record 117 inches of snow fell in the winter of 1997, and ended with an ice storm in April that knocked out electricity for 127 hours. All-time high Red River water levels were recorded, and only the diligent efforts of the twenty people left in town and neighboring students kept the town dry.

Farmers are the lifeblood of Perley, and are honored as such. Tucked in the back of the Community Co-op Store, the Perley Café serves breakfast and lunch to farmers, and the rest of us eat only if we happen to stop at the right time. A hand-painted mural of two farmers, one skinny and one stout, sitting at a café counter, graces an entire wall.

Located on US Highway 75, the Historic King of Trails, Perley joins forces with other cities on the highway to celebrate Labor Day weekend with a meal at the community center, an antique car show, a farmer's market and a quilt auction.

Perley Today

Today, the city is home to Perley's Place, the post office, American Crystal Sugar Company, Interstate Roofing & Construction, Perley & Lee Township Fire and Rescue Station, Ron Nelson Masonry, Triangle Agronomy Service, Perley Community Hall, Riverside 4-H Club, and Kirkebo Lutheran Church. In 1997, the Perley Farmer's Elevator and Farmer's Union Oil Company merged to form Perley Community Co-op, a full-service "mini-mall," on Highway 75. High water is an ongoing problem, and in 2011, the streets were badly damaged by heavy trucks hauling supplies to build a higher dike. But this resourceful and progressive community meets challenges head on. A new wastewater system, future new streets, and a higher dike will provide a solid infrastructure for Perley. Through all its trials, Perley celebrated their centennial in 1983, a 125th celebration in 2008, and plans on a grand party in 2033.

Kirkebo Lutheran Church quilts all year long for an auction at their annual spring supper. During the auction, quilts are draped over each pew, and are priced from $25 to $600.

The Perley Community Hall, built in 1936 and completely refurbished by residents and the fire department, hosts weddings, reunions and a recent auction. During the 1940s the building was used as a roller rink, and performances were held on its original stage.

Mayor Anne Manley leads the fight against a 1.7-billion-dollar flood diversion project that will save one thousand homes in Fargo-Moorhead, but wipe out several small cities south of the metro area. Mayor Manley comments that the diversion project is "just not neighborly," a solid virtue in this neighborly small city.

Population: 34   **Incorporated:** 1940

INSETS L to R: Regal ball field • "Cornstalk 04" barn • Heather,
Denise and Ashley at the Pilgrim Inn • Exterior of Pilgrim Inn

TOP: Rail crew, Regal elevator

For over a decade Regal was home to the Cornstalk Festival, which featured Mel Tillis, Conway Twitty, George Jones, Charlie Pride, Loretta Lynn, Waylon Jennings, Tammy Wynette, Willie Nelson, Merle Haggard and Johnny Cash.

Regal

Johnny Cash and Cornstalk in Regal

IN 1989, MIKE AND KATHY KAMPSON, owners of the County Line Bar, promoted the first Cornstalk Festival, initially named Regal Music Fest. Johnny Cash, who headlined the first fest, stated, "Twenty years ago there was a Woodstock. I'm going to call this Cornstalk!" Many memorable events happened on that magical evening. When Cash sang, "I Hear the Train a Coming," a train rolled through on the Regal railroad tracks and blew the horn. The highlight of the concert was when Johnny Cash called Hermie Kampson, Mike Kampson's father, to sing on stage with him. A lifelong fan of Johnny Cash, Hermie grew up singing along with Cash on the radio on their farm near Elrosa. At the end of the evening and following a long drought, Cash sang his last song, looked up at the sky, and said, "Now Lord, you can let it rain." The heavens opened up and it poured. When the festival ended in 2003, Regal's County Line Bar had hosted all the big names: Mel Tillis, Conway Twitty, George Jones, Charlie Pride, Loretta Lynn, Waylon Jennings, Tammy Wynette, Willie Nelson, Merle Haggard, and of course, Cash. Attendance peaked at 20,000 fans in 2002.

Located six miles west of Paynesville in west-central Minnesota, Regal's unusual name makes a good story. Initially called Linton after one of the Soo Line contractors, it was soon discovered that another town in Minnesota had the same name. To simplify mail service, the name was changed to Lintonville. However, the post office objected as there were too many towns ending in "-ville," which only added to the confusion of mail delivery. A local farmer, Leo Neutzling, suggested the name "Ford" following his recent purchase of a Model-T Ford, but local Postmaster George Weidner, who owned a Regal, protested the idea. With neither party unwilling to bend, Mr. Weidner submitted three names for consideration to the post office—Ford, Regal and Harvard. The Harvard is gone, the Ford still roams the highway, and the Regal is commemorated in a tiny town.

When the Minneapolis Sault St. Marie Railroad arrived in 1886, the post office opened with Ole Halvorson as postmaster. The following year early pioneers, George and Eva Weidner, arrived from Illinois to farm near Regal and made an enormous impact on the community. After twelve years on the farm, they moved to town to open a general store, a lumberyard, a coal shed, an implement shop and a cream station. Four of their sons took over the operation of the businesses. In 1896 the Regal Creamery Association formed with support from 36 patrons and 300 cows. J. H. Flat served as the first butter maker and B. F. Gray was selected as the first president. The creamery continued for several decades before closing down.

Early school records from 1874 indicate that the first school was a log structure with 21 students, and a lone teacher who earned $25 per month. A new grade school was built in 1924. Students now attend school in Paynesville, and the old school building functioned as the County Line Bar until closing in 2003.

In 1935, Highway 55 was built through the north end of the city. The following year, St. Anthony Catholic Church erected a basement church. The former community hall was moved on top of the basement foundation to form a simple but beautiful church. When membership dwindled to just a few, St. Anthony's closed on July 31, 2005.

The Regal Eagles Baseball Club

The Regal Eagles baseball team keeps a winning tradition going since battling their way to the state tournament in 1933. Second only to Wolf Lake in trips to state, the Eagles team slugged their way to the Minnesota State Baseball tournament in 1933, 1986, 1987, 1989, 1991 (Class C Champ), 1992, 1993, 1994, 1995, 1996 and 1997 (Class C Runner up). Pitcher and outfielder Tim Haines won the 1991 MVP State Tournament award, winning three games while pitching 11 innings in relief, and hitting 10 for 22 for a .455 batting average. This well-coached team is led by Joe Beier and Tim Beier and also has Chris Beier, Josh Beier, and Jordan Beier on the roster.

In 1992, Buddy Beier was inducted into the Minnesota Amateur Baseball Hall of Fame, and in 2010, he was awarded the Mike Downes Memorial Award for outstanding service to Minnesota Amateur Baseball.

Regal Today

Today Regal supports the Regal Elevator, The Pilgrim Inn, Regal Starter and Generator, and the St. Anthony Catholic Cemetery. Regal boasts two beautiful baseball fields, side by side, with a playground for the young fans. A sign on the back of the bleachers proudly lists all eleven years that this amazing team has represented Regal at the state tournament. The Pilgrim Inn opens at 9:30 for coffee and freshly baked pastries, a haven for area farmers who gather six days a week to discuss the weather and local baseball. On a lovely April 2011 day, 150 railroad workers using heavy equipment began replacing the railroad ties on the tracks in Regal.

The outstanding Pilgrim Inn Restaurant serves homemade food on their handcrafted bar, which features wildlife etchings carved by Kathy Gustafson. Owner Denise Wuertz bought the business from Larry and Janet Fleck in 2000 after working for them for 22 years.

On New Year's Eve, The Pilgrim Inn draws kids from across the area for their annual Kid's Junk Food Buffet, a plethora of drummies, pizza and cookies. Kids get the party hats and noisemakers, a bow to a non-traditional New Year's Eve celebration.

TOP: City park, Revere Elevator Co.

In 1840, three-year-old Anders O. Anderson traveled by ship for four months with his family from Norway to Minnesota. He eventually worked his way to Revere to claim 160 acres of homestead land.

Revere

An Immigrant's Story

IN 1840, THREE-YEAR-OLD ANDERS O. ANDERSON traveled by ship for four months with his family from Norway to Minnesota. He eventually worked his way to Revere in 1871 to claim 160 acres of homestead land on the vast prairie. The industrious Norwegian and his wife, Gunhild, built a two-story house, and in 1875 he added a lean-to for a school for the settlers' children. Following the opening of the Chicago and Northwestern Railway station in Revere, Anders O. Anderson and partners Lewis J. Rongstad and Norman Nelson operated a general store with a post office from 1892 to 1895. Prairie fires, grasshoppers and blizzards took their toll on the early settlers. Because so many defaulted on their bills at the store, it closed. To pay off his

debts, Anders sold 40 acres of his farm, which his son Oskar eventually bought back. Undaunted, four years later Anders hired stone mason Christ Nordsiden to lay the foundation for a twelve-sided barn, the only one in Minnesota. The stone construction allowed wagons to drive into the upper wood level and unload grain, hay, straw and feed down to the livestock in the basement. Along with their son, Oskar, the Andersons raised a niece, Helen Colbo, whose parents died at an early age, and a nephew, Arthur Swanson, whose father disappeared when Arthur was three years old. Arthur recalls the day that his mother placed him on a rug in the middle of the living room at the Anderson home, also leaving him forever. Mrs. Swanson left two other children with relatives. Shortly thereafter, she gave birth to twin girls who did not survive. After burying her daughters on the prairie, she left Revere to find work.

The Chicago and Northwestern Railway planned Revere as a stopping place between Lamberton and Walnut Grove, where farmers could deliver their wheat and corn. By 1900, farms covered 90 percent of the land, one third of which was tilled for wheat. When the city voted to incorporate in 1899, the village drew outlying farms into the city limits to boost the census to 177 in order to be eligible for incorporation. A newspaper, *The Revere Record*, printed by C. W. Folson, ran from 1901 to 1915. Charles, Raymond and John Sawyer founded the State Bank of Revere, but when the Bank Holiday of 1933 closed its doors, they never reopened. Central to Revere's business community, John Brudeli's Department Store sold groceries, clothing, furniture, and offered his undertaker services. John and his family of nine children lived above the store until they built a new home on Main Street. Generous to a fault, Mr. Brudeli extended credit to his customers during the Depression years. He once told his grandson that he didn't have any money, but had a lot of friends.

Revere built a series of schools, with the final school a WPA project erected in 1938 for $20,000, with the government paying half the tab. By 1969 enrollment had dropped to twelve pupils, and the school consolidated with Walnut Grove.

In 1907, the Revere Lutheran Norwegian Church vacated a rural schoolhouse to move into a former Methodist church building that they purchased from a German Lutheran Congregation. When Pastor Henry Bruns arrived in 1920, the church had two members and a $475 debt. Until his death in 1928, Pastor Bruns worked hard to pay off the debt and to build membership to sixty. The church celebrated a 75th Anniversary in 1974 with a new narthex, and a new silver communion set donated for the occasion by charter members Mr. and Mrs. John Brudeli. After the final worship service on June 3, 1993, Revere Lutheran Church was converted to the Revere City Hall, where the good work of the community continues.

Two Historic Destinations in Revere

Listed on the National Register of Historic Places in 1980, the Revere Fire Hall on 2nd Street is a frame construction station with a bell tower built in 1900. One of the few surviving railroad depots from a small city, the old Revere depot was rescued from the dump ground and donated to the Laura Ingalls Wilder Museum in Walnut Grove.

Revere Today

Located on the Laura Ingalls Historic U.S. Highway 14, Revere is home to the post office, Francis Harnack American Legion Post #582, the Revere Body Shop, Warren Parker & Sons Farm Tiling, and Country Drieds. The former John Brudeli home is now an assisted-living facility. A large city park and Community Hall, the former Norwegian Lutheran Church, complete Main Street. A brick monument at the park reads, "In tribute to all the men and women of the Revere Area who have or will serve in the defense of our country. Each Memorial Day, Post Commander Martin Kleven, post members, and the auxiliary present a full memorial service, complete with the advancement of the colors, a memorial address, and taps.

Revere is the only little Minnesota city named after a patriot in the American Revolution, Paul Revere. A Massachusetts silversmith, Paul Revere was immortalized 1860 when Longfellow wrote the poem, "The Midnight Ride of Paul Revere."

Warren Parker, who sets drain tiles in fields around Revere, works magic in his shop. One year he made a replica of a 1910 Sears buggy car "from scratch" and his version of "The Little Engine That Could" pulls six train cars and delights spectators in parades throughout the area.

Revere resident Warren Parker's wife, Ollie, achieved national recognition when the creator of the Precious Moments empire named his Norwegian doll "Ollie" after her. Ole Blegen, Ollie Parker's father, was famous for another reason. He celebrated each New Year's Eve by blowing up a stick of dynamite.

TOP: "Richville Welcomes You"

Population: 96   **Incorporated:** 1904

INSETS L to R: St. Paul's Lutheran • Wagon Wheel Grocery •
remaining insets from Community Park

The first business in Richville was a bootleg joint,
typical of many towns' thirsty beginnings.

Richville

A Settler's Life: Taking a Covered Wagon to a Log Cabin

IN HER MEMOIR, MRS. TREAN WHITNEY HOOVER recalls
the late October evening in 1898, when her family of nine traveled three
hundred miles by covered wagon to settle on a land filled with huge trees
and dotted with log cabins. The following day, her father, V. A. Whitney,
began to cut timber and clear land. Mr. Whitney turned the sod with a
jumping plow, a name derived from the numerous stumps that must be
avoided to prevent the plow from jumping and the driver going over the
top. Placed in a sack around the farmer's neck, the seed was painstakingly
laid by hand in the furrows. Corn was cultivated with a small plow drawn
by one horse. As it was difficult to guide the plow and horse at the same
time, Trean rode the horse while her father held the plow.

In 1903, settlers excitedly prepared for the arrival of the Soo Line,
and a new townsite was platted for 152 citizens in an area of 960 acres.
Named for an engineer on the Soo Line, Richville incorporated October
25, 1904. Mrs. Hoover writes that the first business was a bootleg joint,
typical of a town's thirsty beginnings. C.A. Friberg's General Store and
post office followed the saloon. Both the Johnson brothers and Henry
Burgess opened sawmills for an expanding lumber industry, while
Northern Cooperage Company opened a stave mill to build barrels for
beer, vinegar, wine, crackers, apples and china, all shipped by barrel.
Fred Heinecke managed the depot, and John Kapell built the Corner
Saloon, later known as the Jensen Store. Although business was on
everyone's mind, Richville made time for romance, too. Bartender

Andrew Hilckosky married Miss Mary Kapell, the proprietor's daughter, and Charles Friberg Jr., bookkeeper for his father's general store, married the village belle, Miss Nellie Atherton. An ongoing rivalry between city and country folk extended even to marriage.

Life in Richville was not without peril. Editor F. E. Harris, owner of *The Richville Leader*, reported a close call in 1905, when Mrs. H. B. Johnson fell into her well while fetching a pail of water. Just as she stepped up on the platform covering the well, the platform collapsed, and Mrs. Johnson plunged thirty-five feet into ten feet of water. Luckily, she instantly rebounded to the surface, grabbed the water pipe, and hung on until her husband arrived on the scene with a ladder. Once Mrs. Johnson had ascended to terra firma with only minor bruises, she entertained many folks over the years with the story of her "high dive." Unfortunately, Mr. Jones and Mr. Zimmer, owners of the Bank of Richville, were not so lucky. Anxious to try out a new gasoline launch, the two men and friends took the boat out that evening. While filling the tank with gasoline, a lantern on the floor of the boat came in contact with the gas and exploded, severely burning Mr. Jones and destroying the boat. Editor Harris chided the men in his newspaper: "Grown up people should have more sense than to monkey around gasoline with a light of any kind." On a lighter note, the following ad appeared under *Lost*: "Lost, between Richville and Bill Mack, a young man's heart. Finder, please return to Fred Friberg."

By 1920, over 400 citizens called Richville home. A school opened in 1905 with forty-six pupils, and closed in 1970 when enrollment dipped to twenty-three. Country folks herded their livestock through town to the stockyard, past well-fenced yards. When farmers increased their dairy business, a well for a new creamery was drilled by horse power. Cal Mielke opened his renowned general store in 1926, and eventually bought almost every building in downtown Richville. Initially a hobby, Vincent Sundberg started an apiary (beekeeping) business that continues today. A disastrous fire in February, 1937, destroyed an entire block of buildings, including the fire hall, and marked the end of growth for the city.

Find Your Thrill in Richville

The Richville Community Club and the Richville Tractor Pullers Association teamed up to celebrate the Richville Centennial August 27–28, 2004. The Centennial Slogan, *"I found my thrill in Richville,"* aptly reflected a weekend of dancing, turtle races, tractor pull races and fireworks.

In 1926, Clarence "Cal" Mielke erected his general store, named the "Biggest Little Store in Northwestern Minnesota," and rebuilt the store after fires in 1935 and 1959. A shrewd investor, he owned 1,000 acres of farmland, timberland and lakeshore property including Cal's Rainbow Resort and Head Lake Camp. He also purchased the Royal Neighbors Hall in 1959, a large dance hall that easily held one hundred couples. In 1960, the community honored Cal, "Mr. Richville," with a "This is Your Life Day," a gala event still talked about today. For sixty years, Cal took responsibility for the Otter Tail County booth at the Minnesota State Fair, and was named to the Minnesota State Fair Hall of Fame in 1992, the year after he died.

Richville Today

Today, Richville is home to Wagon Wheel Gas & Grocery, the post office, Rockin' Horse Café, Larry Sundberg Apiary and Hoffman Apiary. Arv Widness and Richard Loerzel led the Richville Community Club in a fund drive for new park playground equipment on land where the former school once stood. A Little League team, the Richville Rockets, and the Richville Rock-a-Boosters 4-H Club contribute to the upkeep of the park. St. Paul's Lutheran Church, a dollhouse-sized building, and United Methodist Church serve the spiritual needs of the community.

Spanning five counties, the Clothing Redistribution Center at the Richville Methodist Church donates bedding, household items and clothing, including a wedding dress and veil for a young bride-to-be.

One of the more sensational events in Mower County occurred on May 17th, 1939, when the four "Cream Can Bandits" attempted to rob the Sargeant bank.

TOP: "Welcome to Sargeant," United Methodist Church

Sargeant

Sargeant and a Bank Robbery Make National News

ONE OF THE FEW BANKS IN LITTLE MINNESOTA to survive the Bank Holiday in March, 1933, the State Bank of Sargeant remained financially sound under the leadership of President George Bartel and Cashier Ted Knutson. One of the more sensational events in Mower County occurred on May 17th, 1939, when the four "Cream Can Bandits" attempted to rob the Sargeant bank in the early morning hours. The would-be bandits were trapped in the bank after locals notified authorities, who sped to Sargeant. When the robbers came out shooting, the officers emptied their guns and wounded three robbers. On July 11, the F.B.I. found another culprit secluded in a cabin on Lake Vadnais, Ramsey County. For a year the men had robbed banks and post offices in Minnesota and other Northwest states, despite an extensive hunt by federal agents and crime bureaus. The unusual name of "Cream Can Bandits" came about as the robbers carried water in cream cans to cool cutting tools while breaking into the vaults. When the Associated Press discovered the story, the capture of the "Cream Can Bandits" in the little village of Sargeant, Minnesota, became national news. And in the *Austin Daily Herald*, the robbery took precedence over the scheduled visit of the King and Queen of England to the United States. The attempted robbery took the front page, and royalty settled for the second page.

Sargeant is named for pioneer farmer Harry N. Sargeant, a native of Quebec, Canada who settled in Mower County in 1865, and organized Sargeant Township in 1873. Fellow pioneer Samuel King, a native of England, purchased a farm in New York before heading west with his wife and seven children. In 1869, Mr. King settled on a farm near Sargeant, erected a frame house on a knoll, and grew wheat. The failure of the wheat crop in 1878 compelled him to turn to raising stock and dairy farming. This crop failure also had a disastrous affect on settlement, as many moved away, and others decided not to move to the area. However, the Chicago Great Western Railroad saw a future in the open prairie farmland perfect for grain crops, and established a station in Sargeant in 1887. A post office opened the same year.

Following incorporation in 1900, business bustled in Sargeant as the town was home to Siegel Farm Implements, a dance hall, Henry Beck's Blacksmith Shop, Heydt Hardware Company, and Jeffers Hotel. Mrs. Jeffers watched the noon train arrive each day to count the traveling men debarking, and would fill waiting pie shells as needed for dinner. When the post office was located in Grimm Hardware, Frank Grimm sold stamps and bought cream from local farmers in the back of the post office. Led by the Siegel brothers, the Sargeant Coronet Band played twice a week in the band shell, and the city council reimbursed the band $20 for "musical services rendered during the summer of 1907." Sargeant had its share of excitement. One muddy spring in the early 1930s, a circus from the east arrived in Sargeant, and the wagons full of animals got stuck in the mud. Circus officials tried to convince the elephants to pull the wagons out of the mud, while other animals escaped their cages and went on the loose. When Annie Knutson breathlessly told her brother, Ted, that she saw elephants coming up the road, he thought her "looney."

The only church in the city limits, Zion United Methodist Church erected a wood frame church in 1899, and later added a bell and basement as the church prospered. Church liturgy continued in the German language, until Reverend Schmidt directed a difficult adjustment to services in English under his reign from 1913 to 1918.

125 years of Zion Methodist Church

Zion United Methodist Church loves to celebrate its heritage. On April 29, 1984, the congregation observed Heritage Sunday, which involved a discussion about the church history. This continued every Sunday until the final culmination on November 18, 1984, when the church celebrated their centennial with an anniversary service and fellowship supper. Several talented members rendered musical selections, and the women unveiled a beautiful Centennial quilt. On August 23, 2009, the church celebrated 125 years of service to the community. On June 30, 2001, Sargeant residents celebrated their 125th Anniversary at the Sargeant Community Center with games, music, and a re-enactment of the Cream Can Bandits robbery. All commemorative souvenir items carried the theme, "You can count on your neighbors in Sargeant."

Sargeant Today

Today, Sargeant is home to Wayne's Auto, Northwoods Credit Union, Sargeant Agri-Service, Larson Products, the Fire Department, Sargeant Grain Co. and Commercial Service of Sargeant, and the First Farmers and Merchants Bank. The school closed in 1975, and the building now serves as the Sargeant Community Center, with a volleyball court and basketball hoops bordering a cornfield. St. John's Lutheran, Zion Lutheran, and Evanger Lutheran Church reside outside the city limits. In 1992, St. John's and Zion Lutheran suffered severe damage after an arsonist attempted to burn down both churches. Both rebuilt and are stronger than ever.

In 2011, a renewable energy project, the Pleasant Valley Wind Farm Project, will build close to 200 turbines on 70,000 acres near Sargeant. The largest wind farm planned for construction in Mower County, over a million megawatt hours per year from the turbines will transfer onto the national energy grid.

Seaforth has been called "Smallest Polka Town in the Nation." Every July the Booster Club sponsors two days of polka bands, softball and horseshoe tournaments, and plenty of food and beer. The festivities also include a Catholic Polka Mass, which is strictly BYOC (bring your own chair).

TOP: Angie's Park

Seaforth

A Polka Capital

EVERY JULY SINCE 1974, polka dancers have headed to Seaforth, the smallest polka town in the nation, for the annual Polka Fest. Little did the town fathers know that Seaforth's claim to fame would be the polka. Eager to cash in on profits from the wheat grown in this area, the Chicago and Northwestern Railroad, along with the Western Land Company, developed small towns along the railroad in 1899. The railroad developed towns at regular intervals—the distance a farmer could travel in half a day to deliver crops. Initially Seaforth was named Okawa, the Chippewa word for pike, a fish caught in nearby Clear Creek. The name was later changed to Seaforth by a Canadian land developer after his hometown Seaforth Island in the Outer Hebrides of

Scotland. Grain elevators, creameries and lumberyards quickly followed, as well as a post office and business district. By 1900 the city census was 185, and incorporation followed on March 12, 1901.

Prosperity and good fortune favored Seaforth and soon the town had a local newspaper, a highly successful bank, and the very accomplished Seaforth Cornet Band with 22 remarkable musicians. Two of the three Stanek brothers went on to play with the Barnum and Bailey Circus band. Seaforth had thirty good years until World War I, the Depression, and drought all took their toll on this farming community. During the '30s, crop prices fell to an all-time low of 7 cents for a bushel of oats, 14 cents for barley, 9 cents for corn, and 19 cents for rye. Farmers burned corn for heat, as it was cheaper than coal. Over 150 farms were unable to make their mortgage payments and were foreclosed. In 1933, the Seaforth State Bank quietly closed, but not before secretly repaying all their investors before locking the door. Within two years all the depositors were fully compensated.

A two-story wood structure functioned as School District 104 from 1900 to 1962 before consolidating with Wabasso. The two rooms on the main floor housed grades 1–8, but plans for a high school upstairs never materialized. The large school bell with an attached rope frequently tipped over if the teacher pulled too hard at the end of recess or noon hour. Herb Winn Jr. now keeps the bell securely placed in his yard. One of many hilarious school stories involved Ervie Bliss, former mayor of Seaforth. While in grade school, Ervie brought a small, round siren whistle from a cereal box to school. Throughout the day, the teacher was puzzled to hear a siren noise in the classroom as Ervie put the whistle in his mouth and discreetly drew in and out through it. At one point he drew in harder and inhaled the whistle. From then on he would whistle a little each time he took a breath.

Only one church remains in Seaforth. St. Mary's Catholic Church evolved from a mission church of 1900 to 1935 to a self-supporting new brick church built in 1963. Started by German immigrants, St. Paul's Evangelical Lutheran erected a new church in 1973, celebrated their centennial in 2000, and closed. The First Presbyterian Church closed in 1962 and is now the home and studio of Jerry and Joni Woelfel.

The last train rolled through Seaforth December 22, 1978, and the rails were removed a year later.

The Smallest Polka Town in the Nation and a Polka Mass

KNUJ Radio of New Ulm named Seaforth the "Smallest Polka Town in the Nation." Every July the Booster Club sponsors two days of polka bands, softball and horseshoe tournaments, and plenty of food and beer. The festivities also include a Catholic Polka Mass, which is strictly

BYOC (bring your own chair) on Saturday afternoon. All proceeds are donated back to the community.

On July 5, 1996, in celebration of 100 years of rural mail service, Leonard Bernardy and Ken Kovtal delivered mail to Seaforth residents using a horse-drawn wagon. All the area radio stations converged on Seaforth to cover the event and partake of refreshments in Woelfel's Garage, which also housed the post office.

Seaforth Today

Today the Seaforth Tavern, the Fire Department, Angie's Park, American Legion Ralph Lamb Post 275, and the Community Legion Center line Main Street. A historic gas station and the original yellow post office remain intact.

On June 24, 2009, the community celebrated the grand opening of Angie's Park, on the site of the former Bergen Café owned by Angeline Bergen, a much loved businesswoman and friend. A merry-go-round and basketball, horseshoe and volleyball courts, as well as a gazebo, remind the citizens of Angie's generous spirit.

The "C4th" Fire Department shares a corner with the Community Legion Center. Like all the well-tended public buildings in Seaforth, the fire department exhibits the tremendous pride that the citizens have in their city. An old depot sign, an American flag, an antique fire pump, and shrubbery surround the tidy cement block building.

In 1925, Ralph Lamb American Legion Post (#275) purchased a fifteen-foot tall memorial monument in Washington D.C. to commemorate local servicemen. Forty veterans from Seaforth served in World War I alone.

TOP: Immaculate Conception Church

Population: 45   Incorporated: 1897

INSETS L to R: Julie's Greenhouse • Original Pope County Courthouse •
Playground near Sedan Fire and Rescue • Rooney's Bar

On March 21, 1953, a tornado hit Sedan's
Main Street and demolished or heavily damaged
every building.

Sedan

*"It is the fate of every generation not to know that they are living in history,
however humble their role, until both they and their time are part of it."*
—Francis Gannon, Sedan, from a letter from January 16, 1968

A Naming Mystery, Train Wrecks and Depot Disasters

NO ONE SEEMS TO KNOW WHY this farming community, surrounded by vast prairie in eastern Pope County, was named Sedan, after
the city Sedan in France. History may have something to do with it.
The Prussian army defeated Napoleon III and his army on September
1, 1870, during the Battle of Sedan. The decisive German victory ended
the Second French Empire, and Germany celebrated *Sedantag* (Day of
Sedan) each September 2 until 1919. Perhaps the high percentage of
German immigrants in Sedan explains the choice of Sedan as a name.

Initially named Thorson in 1887, the name changed to Fowlds in
honor of the first postmaster Jim Fowlds, and finally to Sedan when the
Soo Line established a station there in 1893. The city incorporated in
1897. Rail lines from Minneapolis to Bismarck, North Dakota, allowed
easy transport of local grain to flour mills in Minneapolis, and Sedan was
positioned as the water station for the steam locomotives between the two
cities. Shortly after the station was established, a train tragedy shook the
community to the core. One evening the brakeman left the switch open,
and without a passing track, a freight train came through with nowhere
to go but the sidetrack, killing five people. Sedan has been notoriously
unlucky with their depots—the first depot burned, as well as the second depot, along with three elevators. On August 2, 1934, an explosion

leveled the elevator near the third depot. Determined to save the depot, watchman Ralph Tacklind stood over the site for three days and nights, until he believed the site was safe. That night, August 5, sparks ignited and once again leveled the depot. Without the grain elevators, business slowed to such an extent that the railroad closed the depot in 1940.

In 1913, a beautiful two-story brick school, constructed on a gently winding road up the hill, replaced the old school, which was repurposed as a hotel. By 1920, Sedan boasted a complete main street including a Modern Woodmen of America Hall, the H. W. Ross Lumber Company, the T. S. Gannon Blacksmith Shop, and the Farmers and Merchants State Bank. The hotel was full, farmers lined up at the creamery, and entrepreneur Martin Bremness sold Columbia phonographs and Wear-U-Well shoes out of his general store. On December 22, 1921, the Glenwood Herald reported that a well-attended play, *Hiawatha*, was performed in Sedan, followed by a dance. The Sedan boys' basketball team lost 18 to 2 to a strong Farwell team on December 17, 1925, while the girls prevailed over Farwell 5 to 4. However, the glory days were short-lived, as fire demolished the hotel and three other businesses in December 1925. Johnny Peterson, an employee of the grain elevator, rescued cobbler Henry Jacobson, but Henry died two days later at Sonnenburg Hospital in Brooten. The Farmers and Merchants State Bank closed in 1931, a victim of the Depression, like most small banks in that era. Sedan never fully recovered from the fires and the Depression.

Built in 1918, the Immaculate Conception Church closed in 1998. Early records of the congregation indicate that many of the first settlers were from Donegal, Ireland. The Presbyterian Church, erected in 1904, anchored the community until 1953, when a tornado completely destroyed the building. The congregation voted to rebuild, and celebrated a 50th anniversary in 1954, though tight finances forced closure in 1965. Now the building serves as the Scandia Lutheran Church on Lake Scandia. The fire hall and community center sit solidly on the former site of the Presbyterian Church.

A Log Cabin Courthouse and a Tornado Wreaks Havoc

Pope County's first courthouse, a small log cabin built by the Schluter brothers and Nick Koob, was moved from Scandia Lake to Sedan, and finally to Glenwood, where the building resides at the Pope County Historical Society. In 1867, Daniel Pennie carried all the court documents in a sack on his back from Sedan to Glenwood. A replica of the courthouse, restored by Ray Hawn, resides in Glenwood in a park just up the hill, on the north side of the railroad track.

On March 21, 1953, a tornado hit Main Street and demolished or heavily damaged every building. The twister picked up the Presbyterian Church and dropped the building on the lumberyard. Both the Standard Oil Station and Poverud's Garage and Service Station were destroyed as well. But the most unusual incident happened at the Catholic Church when a board five feet long by four inches wide drove through the wall of the sacristy into a chalice cabinet. Unbelievably, the wood did not splinter and was like a knife through butter.

Sedan Today

Main Street has held onto Rooney's Bar, Clausen Auto Body, Sedan Fire and Rescue building, and Bremness Park. A brick two-story structure, Sedan's third school opened in 1913 and closed in 1966. Anchoring Main Street, the once-proud school is now a private residence. Flowers have replaced the students at the school, as the owner now operates Julie's Garden Center in front of the building.

The Sedan Fire Hall and Community Center is a testament to the efforts of former Mayor Bob Hawn, Walter Skeates, and the senior citizens of Sedan, who persevered to secure funding and labor for the building.

The last passenger train, the Winnipeger, made its final run on March 25, 1967. On that day, Beverly Hawn and her father, Stanley Hawn, rode from Glenwood to Sedan, the last people to arrive in Sedan by train.

In January 1899, the Solway Mercantile Store
had receipts totaling twelve thousand dollars, a
remarkable sum when you consider that veal
sold for nine cents pound and butter for sixteen
cents a pound.

TOP: Martin Sorenson's miniature stone village

Solway

A North Woods Medley

WHERE WOULD A TRAVELER in northern Minnesota find a fully
stocked Asian food market, an organic dairy farm, and a Danish miniature stone village? Solway, of course. A modest community on Highway 2
between Shevlin and Wilton, Solway is home to this unusual combination.

At the suggestion of a Scottish train engineer, the town was named
after Solway Firth, the wide inlet from the Irish Sea between England
and Scotland. When the Great Northern Railway arrived in 1898, the
town's location between Red Lake and Itasca placed Solway as the
nearest rail point for freight to the Red Lake Agency. All the supplies
to build schools in Red Lake were shipped to Solway via the Great
Northern, and then hauled by wagon to the agency. Solway was also

headquarters for twenty logging camps, all in need of food, clothing and
other supplies for the men employed by the camps. In January 1899, the
Solway Mercantile Store had receipts totaling $12,000, a remarkable sum
when you consider that veal sold for nine cents a pound, butter for sixteen
cents a pound, and land sold for two to five dollars per acre.

Local Indians dug snakeroot and picked blueberries to sell to the
merchants, who then dried, baled and shipped the snakeroot by rail to
St. Paul for sale to pharmaceutical companies for medicinal purposes.
On August 4, 1899, the Solway Press reported, *"As many as 500 crates of
blueberries were shipped out of Solway this week. A ton of snakeroot was dug by the
Indians in ten days."*

When the village incorporated on June 27, 1898, a shopper on

Main Street could visit Burke's Mercantile Store, Hildreth's General Merchandise Store, the Underwood Hotel, a livery and feed store, a blacksmith, and the Solway Bank. Two women, the misses Kirch and LeMasurite, bought *the Solway Advocate* and later changed the name to *the Solway Press*. The press kept local citizens informed of international news as well as local events. On August 25, 1899, the *Solway Press* reported, *"Prairie chickens are reported plentiful. The hunting season opens September 1st, so boys are ready for a few days of sport."* From July 28, 1899, we learn that *"Rudyard Kipling was bitten by a dog in London, and carries his hand in a sling."*

After shopping, the weary logger could find respite in the many saloons including the Blue Front Bar and Whipple's Saloon. Medical attention was just around the corner in a hospital, operated by the Benedictine Sisters until 1910, when fire destroyed the building along with most of the village. The fire engine was inoperable because someone had stolen a valve.

The first permanent schoolhouse was a large two-story building with a dance hall on the top floor. Invitations for the dedication of the new schoolhouse on October 27, 1899, read as follows:

Yourself and the ladies are cordially invited to attend a Grand Ball at the opening of the new schoolhouse, Solway, Minnesota on Friday evening, October 27, 1899. Music by the Moose Full Band. Raffle for a horse, tickets one to one hundred cents. Dancing free. Given by Baxter and McRae. Charles Dickenson, Master of Ceremonies. Bring this with you. Grand March 8:30 P.M. Listings for Quadrille, Virginia Reel, Two Step, Shotische, Lancers, Waltz and Polka.

When fire destroyed the school in 1921, the community erected another school, and later added a WPA addition in 1937. As the number of students declined, the upper grades consolidated with Bemidji in 1969. A beautiful new elementary school, home of the Solway Tigers, sits proudly on the east side of town, providing lucky children the increasingly rare experience of small town education.

Twenty Million Logs Sent Down the River

During the winter of 1898–1899, Lammers Logging Camp shipped twenty million logs, the largest drive ever made down the Clearwater River. The following year five hundred men worked nine months to cut sixty million logs, shipping the logs by rail from Solway as well as floating them down the river.

Solway Today

Today the business district includes Thompson's Auto Repair, the Asian and American Mini Market, Solway Bar and Grill, Jacobson Body Shop, Collectors Central Antiques, a new post office, and two churches: Solway Lutheran and the Solway Bible Chapel. The Asian and American Mini Market, the only Asian food store in northern Minnesota outside of Duluth, opened on Main Street in 2003. Owners Tom and his wife Mimi, who grew up in Korea, serve a Korean dinner on Friday evenings, and also offer cooking classes. They set tables in the store to accommodate up to thirty guests hungry for fare other than potato dumplings and lutefisk.

Martin Sorenson's miniature stone village is one of little Minnesota's best kept secrets. Each building is approximately three feet high and built as a replica of the village in Denmark where Martin's parents were born. The perfectly rendered church, complete with a tower and bell, a schoolhouse, a town hall, a storm shelter, a village fireplace, and a stone mountain delight young and old alike.

Rod and Sue Cloose and their cows make milk and yogurt the natural way at Blackstar Dairy. Free of growth hormones, their products attract customers who want un-homogenized milk and cream fresh from the farm. The Cloose cows lead the good life. They each have their own choice of bedding: wood shavings, paper, straw or sand. "Cows are like people," Sue says. "They have their own preferences."

TOP: St. Michael's Catholic Church

Population: 85   **Incorporated:** 1900

INSETS L to R: Mark Kurtz sculpture • Schwagel's Grocery •
City view • Horseshoe Ballroom

Two separate grasshopper plagues in the 1800s destroyed everything in Spring Hill. The insects were so thick on the railroad tracks that they actually stopped trains.

Spring Hill

A Different Sort of Holy Trinity

CHURCH, BALLROOMS AND BASEBALL are the holy trinity in Spring Hill. This picturesque city of German immigrants is located one mile west of Highway 4, sits peacefully amid fields, a lovely church, a lively ballroom, and a first-class baseball field.

When John Schoenborn followed the Middle Trail of the Red River Oxcart Trails in 1860, he stopped at a fjord, later called Schoenborn's Settlement, and opened the first general store. Eventually located one mile south of the settlement, Spring Hill is named for an artesian spring found on the Schoenborn property. In 1873, as he drove a team of horses home with son Henry at his side, Mr. Schoenborn and both horses died after a lightning strike; oddly, the forelegs of one horse bored six to eight inches into the ground. Miraculously, Henry survived.

A log church erected in 1864 burned, and a new church went up a mile southwest on the present site of St. Michael's Church. Spring Hill evolved around the church, including a new general store and post office opened by Michael Hogan in 1873. In 1880, School District No. 38 opened near the blacksmith shop, and the following year, a brick rectory was added to the church. The 1890s brought new business to the city by adding the Spring Hill Creamery Association, James Bock's Hotel & Saloon, and Henry Ley's General Store.

The early settlers truly suffered catastrophes of biblical proportions. However, neither grasshoppers nor smallpox could destroy the faith of the hardy German settlers. Two separate grasshopper plagues between

1857 and 1877 destroyed everything, even the priest's vestments. During mass, the altar boys frantically beat the insects away from the chalice, sacred host, and any piece of cloth. One of the religious brothers hung his coat on a fence while plowing and returned to find a pile of buttons. The insects on the railroad tracks actually prevented the wheels from gripping the track and stopped the trains. By 1877, the plague was serious enough to warrant the full attention of Minnesota Governor John S. Pillsbury and the legislature. At the request of the church, April 26th was declared a day of fasting and prayer for deliverance from the locust. Divine intervention seemed to work, and the grasshoppers disappeared, never to return again in the same destructive numbers. In October 1881, the city called on Governor Pillsbury, who sent Dr. D. W. Hand to check out reports of smallpox in Spring Hill. Dr. Hand found four households with a total of twenty-four people infected with the disease. Reports revealed that the virus had arrived in Spring Hill via a Hungarian family who had crossed the ocean three months earlier on a ship infected with smallpox. By January 1882, about one hundred twenty-four people had contracted the disease, and twenty-one died, the majority of them children.

Spring Hill celebrated the city's incorporation on February 7, 1900, and that same year, the construction of the elegant St. Michael's Catholic Church. Determined not to lose another church to fire, the city council formed the Spring Hill Waterworks, a committee directed to build a water tower in 1905. The tower served the community well until the structure was removed in 1933.

During the '20s, Michael Spaeth bought the Bock Saloon, and ran the business for forty years. He even managed to keep the "soft drinks" parlor open during Prohibition. Nick Laubach opened a general store behind the saloon and added the Spring Hill Ballroom in 1933. He and his son, Matt, continued the business well into the 1950s. The Farmer's State Bank, founded in 1922 with Anton Schmitt, president, and Henry Moser, cashier, closed during the 1933 Bank Holiday.

St. Michael's Church and Baseball

Dedicated in 1903 by Bishop James Trobec, St. Michael's Church is the glue that holds the community of Spring Hill together. Over the years, parishioners have stepped up to provide the funds and labor to keep the beautiful structure intact. When Bishop Trobec arrived for the church's dedication, he was met at the edge of town by Arnold Loehr's surrey and a team of ceremonial horses, accompanied by "dressed to the nines" escort riders. The high altar, imported from Europe, is made of oak and basswood, and a beautifully carved angel and boy, carved by Mark Kurtz from a 200-year-old tree, stand watch over the cemetery directly behind St. Michael's Church.

The Spring Hill Chargers, a local baseball team since 1982, play on a first-class baseball field funded by the Spring Hill Recreation Club. Coached by team managers Randy Schoenberg and Gordon Barten, the club hosts an annual dinner in March to fund park improvements, including an automatic sprinkling system. In 1979, Urban Spanier was inducted into the Minnesota Amateur Hall of Fame, and in 1992, he was awarded the Mike Downess Memorial Award for outstanding service to Minnesota Amateur Baseball. The Chargers won a trip to the 2007 Class C State Tournament, and also won the hearts of the fans by taking home the J.M. and J.D. Brennan Sportsmanship Trophy, an annual trophy awarded by the St. Paul Baseball Club.

Spring Hill Today

Today Spring Hill is home to Jim Klassen's Spring Hill Garage (the old creamery building), St. Michael's Community Center (the former 1957 St. Michael's grade school), the Horseshoe Bar and Spring Hill Ballroom, Nancy's Small Town Salon, Schwagel's Grocery, Extra Innings Bar, Spring Hill Ball Park, and St. Michael's Church.

Owners of Schwagel's Grocery for 46 years, John and Dorine Schwagel offer everything from fresh Easter hams to religious icons, all in a tiny space. Purchases are handwritten in a receipt book. Dorine's 97-year-old mother, who previously owned the business for 18 years, still lends a helping hand. Without any signage, look for several bottles of laundry detergent sitting in the window.

TOP: Danielle and Jan, The Hill Restaurant

Each Christmas Eve in Squaw Lake, families make
ice candles and light them on the graves of loved
ones in the cemetery, creating a beautiful sight on
that special night.

Squaw Lake

A Finnish Cemetery and Ice Candles on Christmas Eve

A FINNISH CEMETERY AT EDNA'S ISLAND on Round Lake
made national news in 1986. Four-year-old Edna Haamalainen died
in the early 1900s, and was the first person buried on the tiny island,
owned by John and Minnie Haamalainen. For over twenty years,
coffins carrying the dead were carried by boat in the summer and by
horse-drawn sleigh in the winter. When water erosion exposed the
graves in 1986, archeologists arrived to remove the burials and send
the artifacts to St. Paul. The bodies were reburied in the Squaw Lake
Cemetery, and artifacts were returned to relatives. Although the little
cemetery on Edna's Island is no longer used, another Finnish tradition
continues in the Squaw Lake Cemetery. Each Christmas Eve, families

make ice candles and light them on the graves of loved ones, to create a
beautiful sight on that special night.

Squaw Lake is uniquely situated on the Leech Lake Indian Reservation between two lakes, Nature and Round Lake, an early homestead
site for Finnish immigrants in 1903. The Haamalainens, Hyttinens,
Gustafsons, Sakus, Lepistos, Kallroos and Niskas arrived in a territory
that the Dakota and Ojibwe had hunted and fished for thousands of
years. When the settlers found that the railroad track ended in Bena,
the edge of the wilderness, they were forced to hire wagons to haul
their goods farther north to Squaw Lake. One early settler, Mary
Haamalainen, homesteaded on the shore of the Popple River in Squaw
Lake, where she built a log cabin. Later she married Paul Hyttinen, and

their daughter Selma was one of the first children born in Squaw Lake. A popular stopping place for folks traveling on the Popple River, the Hyttinen cabin still stands today. The first mail carrier between Max and Rosy, Paul Hyttinen made the trek by foot or rowboat three times a week for $24 a month in wages.

Originally a station on the Great Northern Railway, you can still see parts of the old railroad in the cut between Round Lake and Alice Lake. In low water years the "dead heads" of sunken logs are visible, remnants of the early logging industry. In 1937, the Kananen brothers erected a store operated by Eino Leino, a butcher and musician, who indulged his musical talents on the second floor dance hall. The first post office opened in 1923, and the city incorporated December 17, 1940.

Surrounded by lakes and the Chippewa National Forest, the logging industry and the resort business anchor the economy in Squaw Lake. Early resorts catered to fishermen in the summer and hunters in the fall. Charlotte Stangland Morsch recalls working at a duck camp with 20 to 30 hunters who bagged mallards, teal, bluebill, and goldeneye, while she bagged a husband. Charlotte owned a duck cleaning business for 40 years, and in a record year, she alone cleaned 1,557 ducks. All the feathers went into down pillows, another source of income for the entrepreneur. While Charlotte cleaned ducks, George Kananen cleaned bullheads. During the 40s, George, also known as the "Bullhead King," ran a bullhead fishery, selling millions of pounds of bullheads.

An Historic Ranger Station and an Ancient Intaglio

Old Cut Foot Sioux Ranger Station, listed on the National Register of Historic Places, is the oldest ranger station in the Forest Service's Eastern Region. Between 1994 and 1998, the interior was restored to the original early twentieth-century condition present when Horace Lydick and his young bride were sent to run the station and build roads for the loggers in 1908.

A rare variety of intaglio, the Turtle Oracle Mound is located on the Cut Foot Sioux Trail near Squaw Lake. The Dakota carved this turtle into the ground rather than building it into a mound, as most intaglios are created. Constructed in the 1700s after winning a battle against the Ojibwe, the head and tail of the animal originally pointed to the enemy, with its body curved into a "C." The Ojibwe later reversed the direction. A snake mound surrounds the turtle. The site, which has been used as a council area, is on the National Register of Historic Places.

The Avenue of the Pines Scenic Byway stretches for 46 miles from Northome through Squaw Lake to Deer River, and cuts through the center of the Chippewa National Forest. Lined with stately red pines growing straight as arrows, the pines are home to the largest nesting site of eagles in the contiguous United States.

Squaw Lake Today

Today the city is home to Squaw Lake Community Center and City Hall, the Fire Department, the post office, The Hill Restaurant and Motel, and Mertes Garage. Just outside the city limits, the Crow Bar & Grill and Max Mini Store sit side by side on Highway 46. The Leech Lake Tribal Council owns a facility for tribal meetings and events. Two churches, Centennial Lutheran and St. Catherine's Catholic Church, remain active in the community, and an old Indian cemetery lies on the north side of Round Lake. Numerous excellent resorts surround the city.

Built in 1945 by the Cut Foot Sioux POW Camp #707, the Centennial Lutheran Church has a unique history, unlike any other church in little Minnesota. After two unsuccessful attempts to build a church, the Lutheran congregation approached the prisoner of war camp commander, Captain F. K. McClintic, who agreed to allow the prisoners to build the church. The last German POW camp to close in Minnesota, the prisoners of war returned to Algona, Iowa, for repatriation in late 1945.

Since 1974, Squaw Lake celebrates St. Urho's Day, the legendary day that St. Urho drove the grasshoppers out of Finland and saved the wine grape harvest. On the Saturday closest to March 16, Squaw Lakers celebrate with a parade and a dance at The Hill Restaurant and Motel.

Population: 86   Incorporated: 1911

INSETS L to R: St. Anthony Church stained glass window •
Exterior of Schiffler's Liquor • Mixing a drink at
Schiffler's Liquor • St. Anthony Church interior

The road leading into St. Anthony is so lovely
that it was chosen to grace the cover of Garrison
Keillor's book, *In Search of Lake Wobegon.*

TOP: City view, St. Anthony Catholic Church

St. Anthony

The Town that Graces the Cover of *In Search of Lake Wobegon*

THE ROAD LEADING INTO ST. ANTHONY is so lovely that it was chosen to grace of the cover of Garrison Keillor's book, *In Search of Lake Wobegon.* Beautiful dairy farms border St. Anthony Catholic Cemetery on one side of town, and Schiffler's Bar on the other, adding to the pastoral setting of the picturesque city.

Surrounded by rich farmland, St. Anthony's Catholic Church is named in honor of early settler Anton Gogala and the Catholic saint, St. Anthony of Padua. Five years before the church opened in 1870, immigrants from the Austrian province of Krain, called Krainers, flocked to the lush farmland to claim a homestead in the land of plenty. Among the early pioneers were Joseph and Mary Gasperlin, Mathias and Cecelia Pogatchnik, Joseph and Mary Cremers and George and Margaret Urbaschich. Most of the city's original families remain in the village and on the surrounding farms.

For the first five years, the mixed population of Austrian, Slovene, Dutch and German settlers met monthly in Anton Gogala's log cabin for mass offered by a missionary priest. A frame church was built in 1870 and succeeded by a new brick church in 1901, and the village formed around the church. Initially named Gates after a small store and post office in a private home next to the church, the village adopted the name of the church following incorporation May 31, 1911. Ben Blume established a general store to save settlers a trip to Albany and Holdingford, and to provide refreshments after church on Sundays. In 1895, the St. Anthony

Band boasted 70 members, just under the population today. A village school for grades 1 to 8 served next to the church, until the district consolidated with Albany in 1968. Business boomed in 1925 when farmers brought their milk and cream to the new creamery.

While war raged throughout the world in 1918, the families in St. Anthony were battling the great Influenza Epidemic of 1918. Within thirteen days, the Gerads family lost six children at the peak of the epidemic: All the children are buried side by side in St. Anthony Catholic Cemetery, St. Anthony.

In 1932, Wilfred Schiffler bought the Green Lantern, a popular ballroom during Prohibition in the early 1930s. Once located a mile east of town, the Schifflers moved the Green Lantern next to their bar in town. In 1976, a new Schiffler's Bar replaced the landmark building. That same year, fire leveled another landmark, the two-story general store, owned for forty-seven years by Charlie and Helen Schmoll. After the March blaze, the Scmolls rebuilt and sold the business to David Heinen, who renamed the store St. Anthony Market, which is now used for storage.

A Church with a Congregation Bigger than the Town

St. Anthony Catholic Church continues to pack the pews on Sunday morning. Over 400 parishioners claim membership in the century church. A statue of St. Anthony graces the pathway to St. Anthony's Catholic Church, a spectacular brick church with a stone foundation and stained glass windows and doors. Three beautiful ornate altars and original pews reflect the deep devotion of the early settlers to their house of worship. Saint Anthony of Padua, born in 1195 to a wealthy family in Lisbon, Portugal, gained fame for his exceptional oratory skills. Only a year after his death in 1231 at age 36, Pope Gregory IX canonized the young priest as the Catholic patron saint of lost items, the poor, and travelers.

Listed on the National Register of Historic Places, the Anton Gargola Farmstead honors the immigrants from the tiny country of Slovenia, formerly a part of Yugoslavia. With the collapse of the agrarian economy, Slovene missionary Francis Pierz championed the first Slovene settlements in the United States including the German Catholic colonization of Stearns County. The Anton Gargola Farmstead represents the typical pioneer farmstead of the immigrants from Slovenia.

St. Anthony Today

Today, St. Anthony is home to St. Anthony Catholic Church and Cemetery, Schiffler's Bar, Cremer Construction, and a city park with new playground equipment. Resident Jeff Wenning likes living in safe, quiet St. Anthony just off Interstate 94 and Highway 17, with easy access to work in St. Cloud. A sense of place, tradition, church, and the family farm are rooted deep in this small inland city, the heart of small-town Minnesota.

Home to the first liquor license in Minnesota, a brand new Schiffler's Bar draws families together as they have done for generations. On weekends, the bar fills with patrons who dance to live bands and disc jockeys, attend snowmobile and motorcycle runs, and play darts, pool, and kickball. A private party room draws weddings and family celebrations. New owner Stacy Meyer, Erv Schiffler's daughter, continues the 80-year family tradition.

In April 2011 St. Anthony's Men's Society and St. Anthony's Christian Mothers celebrated the 40th Swanycake & Sausage Supper, an annual church festival and fundraiser that uses flour from the Swany White Flour Mill in nearby Freeport. Family owned and operated since 1903, the mill is famous for their Swany White Buttercake Pancake & Waffle Mix.

TOP: St. Leo's Church

Population: 100   **Incorporated:** 1940

INSETS L to R: Community Center • Fertilizer plant •
remaining insets from St. Leo's Church

On November 3, 1921, in the early hours, the residents of St. Leo jumped out of bed after hearing a loud explosion. Safecrackers had blown the vault's six-hundred pound door off the hinges and destroyed the bank.

St. Leo

A City Centered around a Church

A BEAUTIFUL BRICK CHURCH built in 1940, St. Leo's Catholic Church, anchors this German Catholic community named for St. Leo, a pope who was also known as St. Leo the Great. The city has always centered around the church, and until recently, the St. Leo Catholic School. Built in 1881 on five acres, the first humble frame church, which was donated by Anton Baierl, drew Father Lee and Father Victor Hugo for mass once every six weeks. Two years later, the parochial school opened with Peter Nosbush teaching catechism classes in German for the children.

The growing mission parish continued until 1885 when Archbishop Ireland appointed Father Francis Jaeger as the first resident priest. With a membership of over one hundred families, a new church was dedicated in 1896 in the presence of two thousand joyful celebrants. A new school followed in 1902, with dinner, dancing and a raffle for prizes, all organized by the Christian Mother's Society. By 1964, a new rectory and five-room school were needed to accommodate the expanding parish. Once again 95 women from St. Leo's Catholic Women's Society gathered to sew new blue plaid uniforms for the next school term.

While life revolved around the church and school, the business district originated in 1880, when the post office opened in Valentine Lenz's farm home. Frank Antony, the first businessman in St. Leo, opened a general store in 1885, followed by Jacob Gieb's building in 1890. Like many of his peers, Jacob Gieb was born in Germany and moved to

America. The ambitious, hardworking immigrant platted the townsite of St. Leo in 1900. Other businesses soon filled Main Street. When Peter Tholkes and son Matt opened Tholkes Brothers, a general merchandise store right next to the church, the business became the heartbeat of the community. Open from 7 a.m. to 10 p.m. six days a week, farmers delivered eggs packed in oats to prevent them from breaking, and brought their butter in molds to the store. Local philosophers and cracker barrel politicians solved the problems of the world, and the neighbor ladies exchanged gossip and recipes. Matt Tholkes served on the first city council and served as mayor for six years. When he retired after 54 years in the store, his son Fabian bought the third-generation business.

Optimistic that the railroad would lay track near St. Leo, the *Canby News* reported in 1910, "Mayor Schnittgen was in from St. Leo and reports the new railroad survey to his burg among the current events." The community remained hopeful when the Luce Line planned a new railroad from the Twin Cities to Watertown in 1923. Unfortunately the line ran out of money, and the line stopped at Gluek, eight miles north of Maynard, Minnesota. Despite all efforts to bring a railroad to town, St. Leo has never had railroad service and remains an inland city. Meanwhile, the bank had its own problems. On November 3, 1921, in the early hours, the residents jumped out of bed after hearing a loud explosion. Safecrackers had blown the vault's six-hundred pound door off the hinges and destroyed the bank. Luckily, the hole blown in the inner door was too small to put a hand through, and the thieves could only reach the bank's note pouch which held a registered $50 Liberty bond and $6.15 in cash. Times were tough during the Depression, and bank robbers struck again in February, 1931, this time in daylight. Two unmasked bandits robbed L. P. Funke of $715.00, but the cashier kept his wits about him and memorized the license plate numbers on the car. Even Radar's General Store took a hit the following year, and lost $50 worth of food, clothing and smokes.

In June 1940, the village cast all 36 votes in favor of incorporation for assessment and taxation. The first official city council convened and the St. Leo Fire Department organized in February 1951, and sits next to a new community center.

Pope Leo the Great

St. Leo's Catholic Church is named in honor of Pope Leo I, also known as Pope St. Leo the Great. Born an Italian aristocrat in the year 400, he served as pope from September 29, 440, until his death on November 10, 461. The first pope in the Catholic Church to be called "the Great," Pope Leo I is best known for persuading Attila the Hun to turn back from his invasion of Italy in 452. He also waged a successful campaign to assert the pope's authority over all his bishops.

St. Leo Today

Today St. Leo is home to the American Legion St. Leo Post 524 & Auxiliary, Sue's Photography, Double D Bar, Larry Braun Trucking, West Con Elevator, the Fire Department, and Community Center. Tucked behind St. Leo's Catholic Church, a large city park with a baseball diamond, pavilion, and playground draws the community together for picnics and baseball. Church secretary Carol Antony recalls the story of how Father John Gores from St. Leo's Catholic Church walked up and down the streets every day saying the rosary to protect the men from the congregation who were serving in World War II. No one died from St. Leo in war, and the community attributes their safety to his prayers.

When you are not in church, the citizens hang out at the Community Center where coffee and rolls are served for a donation. Anyone with a birthday or anniversary brings a cake to celebrate with friends, and the center is open for parties at no charge. On Wednesday afternoon the tables fill with rummy players, and the fire department also meets in the center.

Each Memorial Day St. Leo's Catholic Church joins with St. John's Lutheran Church, east of St. Leo, for a service at both churches and cemeteries. A memorial mass followed by taps and a twenty-one gun salute ends with a potluck dinner.

When the city wanted to secure a liquor license, Joseph Silbernick approached Father John Stiegler to ask for his blessing to incorporate the city in order to apply for a license. The vote passed with 24 in favor and none opposed.

TOP: St. Rosa, city center

St. Rosa

The town is in central Minnesota, near Stearns County, up around Holdingford, not far from St. Rosa and Albany and Freeport, which is sort of the truth, I guess.—Garrison Keillor

The Model for Lake Wobegon?

WHEN GARRISON KEILLOR "REVEALED" the location of his famous fictional city, he avoided the mistake that Sinclair Lewis made in his novel *Main Street*. The characters in Lewis's book unflatteringly resembled the citizens of Sauk Centre, while Keillor portrayed his people and places as endearing and homey. Indeed, St. Rosa embodies everything above average, and is a worthy model for the subject of one of Minnesota's most famous writers.

The story of St. Rosa begins with a church. Early pioneer farm-ers donated eight acres surrounded by woods, farms and hills to begin a new parish in Millwood County. As luck would have it, the Freeport parish just down the road planned to build a new church and donated their building, a simple unadorned structure, to St. Rosa. Placed on a high hill, the church was christened St. Rose of Lima, the first church in Stearns County named for a female saint.

Moritz Hoeschen, a German immigrant and the first businessman in what would become St. Rosa, recognized opportunity when he saw it and established a general store and a post office across the road from the church. Strangely he chose the name Isabel for the one-store community, a name unknown in his family or in the area. One possible explanation is that Isabel was the baptismal name of St. Rose of Lima before she entered the convent. The mystery goes on as no record exists, but the name Isabel did remain on the map for twenty years. By 1920, the city voted to officially name the city St. Rosa after the church, but used the German name, Rosa, while the church retained the English name, Rose. When the city wanted to secure a liquor license, Joseph Silbernick approached Father John Stiegler to ask for his blessing to incorporate the city in order to apply for a license. The vote passed with 24 in favor and none opposed. One week later both Joseph Silbernick and Edward Czerzek applied for an on-sale liquor license while Helen Czerzek applied for an off-sale license.

Along with the church, Hoeschen's Store was the heartbeat of the community. A combination post office, livery stable, and distribution center, farmers and their wives exchanged butter, eggs, meat and other commodities for staples. Noted for her exceptional butter, Mrs. Louis Zimmerman sold three-pound jars for fifty cents a pound. Following mass on Sunday mornings, families gathered at the store to share recent births, deaths, and perhaps most important of all, weather news, the lifeblood of farming families. One funny story recalls the Sunday after church when Hubert Korte set his pail of syrup on the store floor and someone knocked the pail over. People tracked the syrup all over the floor and Mr. Hoeschen was so angry with Mr. Korte that Mr. Korte refused to enter the store for a few years. Eventually, all was forgiven and Mr. Korte, like all patrons of the store, ended up with a Christmas gift from the Hoeschens, a piece of china with the St. Rose rectory etched in the middle. Mr. Hoeschen was also instrumental in starting the St. Rosa Cooperative Creamery in 1912 to save farmers the effort of hauling milk to Freeport. By 1937, butter maker Joseph Dufner pushed butter production to an all-time high of 217,394 pounds. A steady decline of patrons signaled the end of the creamery in 1954.

In 1926, future Mayor Stephen Engelmeyer erected St. Rosa Hall, another social hub of the community. Patrons enjoyed soft drinks on the main floor, while local polka and schottische bands played for the dancers on the second floor. A warm, fun-loving man, Mr. Engelmeyer never took the Volstead Act and Prohibition seriously, and the locals knew they could always get a brew at the back door. During Prohibition the feds continued to raid bars, and during one visit, the feds even dumped the holy water from the church, which Mrs. Silbernick stored at the bar. The feds probably assumed the water was high-quality moonshine.

Organized in 1901, St. Rosa School opened with teacher Peter Stradther under contract for $45 per month. By the time organist Henry Stoetzel began teaching, the salary topped $62 a month. Besides reading, writing and arithmetic, he taught Bible history to Catholic and Protestant students. Protestant students used their own Bibles and stood with heads bowed, while every noon the Catholic students recited the Angelus in German, *"Der Engel des Herrn brachte Maria die Botschaft."*

St. Rose of Lima Church and the Country Polkateers

St. Rose of Lima Church Festival hosts an annual gala celebration on the beautiful grounds of the church the first weekend in September. Participants look forward to an outdoor polka mass led by the Country Polkateers. A chicken and ham dinner with homemade pies catered by the All Stars Sports Bar and Grill showcases the great cooks in the community. The perfect day ends with an incredible quilt auction followed by an evening dance.

St. Rosa Today

In 1987, the St. Rosa Jaycees and the St. Rosa Lions Club joined forces to build the St. Rosa Sky Dome, an outstanding sports complex on the edge of town, which provides recreation for everyone.

Formed in 1969, the Roving Hillbillies Snowmobile Club of St. Rosa rides the wooded trails of Stearns County. The club made history with the first snowmobile blessing in the U.S. in 1970, with Monsignor Vincent A. Yzermans officiating.

TOP: St. Vincent city view, spring

Population: 64   **Incorporated:** 1857, 1881

INSETS L to R: Former school • Spring flooding •
Christ Episcopal Church • City Hall

A historical treasure trove was discovered when the town depot was being demolished. Bundles of old telegrams were discovered in the depot attic, including many from the "Empire Builder," James J. Hill, that were dated from 1879 to 1881.

St. Vincent

A Small City Unlike Any Other

THERE REALLY IS NO OTHER SMALL CITY quite like St. Vincent. Geographically located in the northwest corner of the state and bordering both Canada and North Dakota, the Red River of the North separates St. Vincent from Pembina, North Dakota, and the United States-Canadian border separates the city from Emerson, Manitoba.

One of the oldest settlements in Minnesota, the XY Fur Company operated a trading post near St. Vincent before 1800, on the site of Peter Grant's fur headquarters, established in 1794. Only marriage to Ojibwe and Cree women secured the French-Canadian fur traders' survival in the remote outpost. Their children, called the *Metis*, meaning "mixed-blood" in French, developed superior skills as voyageurs, buffalo

hunters and interpreters. Most importantly, they navigated the cultural gap between Europeans and Indians, and were comfortable in both worlds. The *Metis* were strongly influenced by Catholic priests, like Father Belcourt, who traveled throughout North Dakota and northwest Minnesota. The fur traders named their settlement St. Vincent after St. Vincent de Paul, founder of missions and hospitals in Paris. When Norman Kittson improved transportation with his oxcart business in 1844, followed by his steamboat line in 1859, the fur trade prospered.

The Indian Treaty of 1863, or the Treaty of Old Crossing, expanded white settlement. Under the treaty terms, the Red Lake and Pembina bands of Ojibwe ceded their rights to the Red River Valley and nearly 11,000,000 acres of rich prairie and forest. Following the treaty, Norman

Kittson and James Hill collaborated to revitalize the bankrupt railway in St. Paul, and succeeded when the Great Northern Railway laid track all the way Winnipeg, Manitoba, in 1878. Hill and Kittson were highly motivated to transport the hard spring wheat of northern Minnesota to market in the cities. Before 1870, only winter wheat grown in southern Minnesota could be made into fine flour, as the red spring wheat grown in the north was too hard for the existing mills. A new milling process developed in 1870 used porcelain rollers to crush the spring wheat into satisfactory fine flour, thereby leveling the playing field. James J. Hill also backed the building of a roundhouse in 1900, with a turntable to turn the train engines around, just east of the city on Lake Stella.

The arrival of the railroad brought a large influx of Canadian immigrants from Prince Edward Island and Ontario to settle on the best land in the Red River Valley. As the fur trading business faded, the deep rich loam soil, free from sand and gravel, produced large-scale grain harvests. The Bank of St. Vincent opened in 1880, followed by Ryan's Livery, Mason's Blacksmith Shop, the St. Vincent Elevator Company, the Ontario Hotel, and the Green & Russell Department Store. A new fire hall, built in 1903 by Edward Cameron and his three sons, boasted three steam fire engines to protect the citizenry. But fire was not the deciding factor in the decline of St. Vincent. Like all cities perched on the Red River, St. Vincent almost perished in the Flood of 1897. Despite James Hill's offer to move the entire village to the "Y" Junction of Highways 75 and 171, the city rebuilt on the same site. After two more floods in 1948 and 1950, the railroad moved the depot to the highway junction. Another flood in 1966 followed by the Flood of the Century in 1997 put all of Northwest Minnesota in a national disaster zone. Even a dike built in 1967 could not keep the city safe from the forces of the angry Red River.

By 1880, St. Vincent boasted a population of 500, and fully expected to win the county seat over Hallock. The oldest settlement and first in both industry and enterprise, St. Vincent citizens were shocked when the honor went to Hallock, and went to court to fight the decision. To their dismay, the majority of county residents felt that St. Vincent was too far north, so Hallock remains the county seat today.

A Treasury of Telegrams

On March 3, 1883, an Act of Congress declared St. Vincent a port-of-entry for border trade and customs in lieu of Pembina, in the Territory of Dakota. Three deputy collectors and inspectors manned the Customs House in St. Vincent, and records show that the city functioned as a port through 1916.

The rich history of St. Vincent was fully realized when their historic 1878 depot was dismantled. Deep in the depot attic were bundles of old telegrams, including many from the "Empire Builder," James J. Hill, dated from 1879 to 1881 and all written in elegant longhand. Depot agent Charles Gooding sent or received all telegrams and had the foresight to tuck the treasured documents away in a safe place. On August 8, 1879, Mr. Hill sent a long telegram to the railroad superintendent in Winnipeg, requesting that "all merchandise be moved by boat from St. Vincent to Winnipeg before winter," and petitioned that "three barges from Selkirk, Manitoba, be sent to Grand Forks to store grain brought in by farmers."

St. Vincent Today

St. Vincent is now home to the Canadian Pacific Railway, Chale's Service and Oil Company, and Mid Central Medical, a first-class company that fabricates operating room equipment. Trish Lewis, the city historian, is spearheading the 155th Anniversary Celebration for St. Vincent in 2012.

The Red River of the North is renowned for its trophy catfish, drawing anglers from around the country. Although the channel catfish is in the northern part of its range here, some catches have exceeded 30 pounds. The Red also has good populations of walleye, sauger and northern pike. Just across the river, Pembina City Park has a public access, a boat ramp, a fish-cleaning station, restrooms and parking.

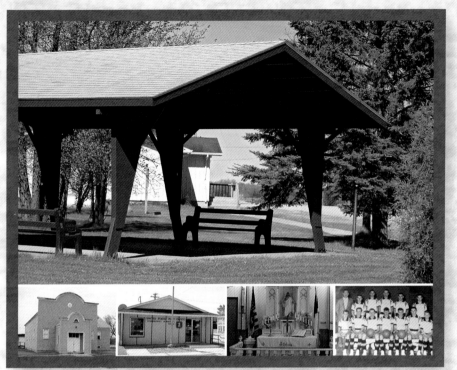

Strandquist's first businesswoman, Miss Anna Ottina Rokke opened Ottina's Variety Store, an unusual mix with a switchboard, post office, millinery and firecrackers.

TOP: City Park and Senior Citizen's Center

Strandquist

A Swedish Town in the Northwest

FRESH OUT OF COLLEGE ON THE G.I. BILL in 1956, Jim Musburger, packed up his family of four to begin his first year of teaching and coaching in Strandquist, 150 miles north of his home in Bemidji. At that time, this Swedish settlement boasted a complete Main Street with two grocery stores, a barbershop, two cafes, a creamery, a train depot, two gas stations, a school, a city hall, a grain elevator, a post office, a tavern, and two churches.

Initially named the Village of Lund in 1902 after Mr. Lund, who ran the post office, John Strandquist, a business owner and politician, renamed the village *"Townsite of Strandquist."* When the Soo Line Railroad arrived in 1904 and wanted the village named Winslow, Mr.

Strandquist prevailed. New businesses popped up, including the Portland Hotel, Myszkowski's Store, Huset Co. (later Carlson's Café), Stodala Confectionary, Bill Warde's Barber Shop, the creamery, and Gust Anderson's blacksmith shop. Farmers sold their cream to creamery workers Ole, Boyd and Oscar Nyflot to be churned into butter, which was then shipped in ice-cooled railroad cars to New York City for Bridgeman's Dairy. The first businesswoman, Miss Anna Ottina Rokke opened Ottina's Variety Store, an unusual mix with a switchboard, post office, millinery and firecrackers. Born in Norway in 1878, and a graduate of Concordia College in Moorhead, she also taught and served as Postmaster. George and Delores Wikstrom bought the telephone company in 1947, and today Wikstrom Telephone Company serves all of northwestern Minnesota. From 1909 to 1937, the Strandquist State Bank served the community well, until N. O. Folland moved the bank to Karlstad.

In 1915, two rural districts consolidated to form Strandquist District No. 65 in a new brick building with 150 students. A basketball team formed in the 20s and a new gymnasium was added in 1956. The 1946 team faced a difficult year with only eight players, five of whom were Andersons, and no coach. The boys coached themselves through a successful season. Tragedy hit the community on January 31, 1959, when defective wiring caused a fire to destroy the entire school except for the new gymnasium.

Strandquist also had a top-notch high school band. In 1960, the John Philip Sousa Award was given to a top musician from Strandquist, Ina Lou Nelson; another resident, Jennifer Anderson, won the final award in 1991. Under the baton of Paul Bacigalupe, the Strandquist High School Concert Band recorded an album in 1968.

Strandquist loves a good party. In 1990, the town celebrated its centennial with a parade, hog roast, and auction. A new sign and deer statue, "*Strandquist, Home of the Whitetail Deer,*" were purchased in conjunction with Minnesota's Celebrate '90 projects. Both the school and the post office joined the century club—the school in 1992, and the post office in 1999. And yes, you can come home again to Strandquist. In 2004, the city celebrated their centennial with an hour-long parade and community meal. Families gathered from all over the world to share stories of growing up in Strandquist.

The Polish Team from a Swedish Town with a German Coach

The 1959 Strandquist Warriors basketball team, called the "Polish team from a Swedish town with a German coach," was honored as the "*Team of the Week*" on Grand Forks' KNOX radio. Coach Jim Musburger was honored as "*Coach of the Week*" and Jim Larson as "*Player of the Week.*"

Superintendent Leon Orcutt collected the spectator fees at the gym door before each game and reportedly commented, "It'll be a hot time in the old town tonight!" The girls' teams did well too. Coached by John Rokke, the team won the Northern Lights Conference Championship in 1978 with 10 wins and no losses.

Strandquist Today

Today, Strandquist is home to the Rainbow Club & R.B. Sizzle, the post office, Bethesda Lutheran Church, and the Senior Citizens Center, which houses the school trophies, and a German machine gun brought back by World War I veteran Nils Sundberg. Father Fraling and parishioners erected St. Edward's Parish in 1920, and celebrated a 50th anniversary in 1970. In 1994, the church closed, and in 1997, a new church was built in Karlstad. Following the disastrous fire in 1959, a new school opened until consolidation with Karlstad in 1998. The one-story brick building now manufactures Elkhorn Valley Honey. Built in 1904, the Strandquist Elevator holds 162,000 bushels of grain for shipment to market.

Sunnyside School, the original schoolhouse, was restored by the high school industrial arts class of 1990 in time for the statewide "Celebrate 90" celebration. The honeybee factory, just south of the restored schoolhouse, still has the original school gym that was saved during the fire of 1959.

Built as a WPA project during the Roosevelt administration, the City Hall & Royal Theater is a reminder of another time, when businessman Theodore Roner showed silent movies to a rapt audience. Another WPA project in 1935 added the stage and a maple floor for basketball games. Upon completion, the building was reported to be the grandest building in the county.

In 1905, the Swedish Bethesda Lutheran Church moved from Lincoln Township to the city of Strandquist. The original structure, made from logs hauled by oxen from Strathcona, held services in Swedish until 1943. A community icon, the century church sponsors Memorial Day services, followed by dinner served by the Legion Auxiliary.

WELCOME To The STRATHCONA COMMUNITY PARK

TOP: Strathcona Community Park

Population: 44   **Incorporated:** 1904

INSETS L to R: Strathcona Café • Grace Evangelical Church • Strathcona Mini-mall • Gustav Adolph Lutheran

The highlight of late summer in Roseau County is the Northland Threshing Bee, held yearly in Strathcona since 1965.

Strathcona

The Threshing Bee: The Event of the Summer

THE HIGHLIGHT OF LATE SUMMER in Roseau County is the Northland Threshing Bee, held yearly in Strathcona since 1965. Anyone interested in agriculture, great food, and a good time shows up in Minnesota's tenth-smallest city for an education in pioneer life. The first Northland Threshing Bee took place on a farm owned by Marshall and Viona Wiskow, and Marshall's restored Case steam engine was the star of the show. Today, instructors demonstrate grain threshing, cultivating with horses, and pioneer survival skills. The event wraps up with a horse and buggy parade.

Along a remote stretch of Highway 32 in northwestern Minnesota lies the once prosperous railroad town, Strathcona, named for Lord Strathcona, who was originally from Forres, Scotland. Lord Strathcona migrated to Canada and was a principal financial promoter for the construction of the Canadian Pacific Railway. He was also a good friend of James J. Hill, builder of the Great Northern Railway, who named the town after his friend. In October, 1904, the Great Northern Railway came steaming into town and Strathcona, formerly known as Jevne, began as a community. Early settler Knute Jevne moved his general store from the outskirts of town to a new building on Main Street in Strathcona, while Hans Lerum established the first post office, which later became the Hartz Store. Following close on their heels, Johnson's Blacksmith Shop opened, which doubled as the Strathcona Opera House. Built in 1912, the bank closed during the Depression but had multiple lives as a print shop, pool hall, grocery store, tavern, telephone company and a village hall. The original bank building still stands.

On New Year's Eve, 1905, a group of men gathered at the Knute Jevne Store to discuss the organization of a Lutheran Church, and elected Hans Lerum, Ole M. Olson, M. N. Grondahl, Ole Holmested and Severt Gjovik to lead the church. Under the direction of the first official pastor, A. N. Skogerboe, Gustav Adolph Lutheran Church was constructed in 1912. Pastor Skogerboe led services for six congregations in the synod, all in Norwegian. When the church was completely destroyed by fire in 1962, the congregation purchased and remodeled the WPA building that housed the Strathcona School, which had closed that same year. Typical of the times, the Swedish contingency wanted their own church and organized Evangelical Gustaf Vasa Lutheran Church in 1908; for over 20 years, services were conducted in Swedish. Fire destroyed their church and the Swedes later joined the Norwegians at Gustav Adolph. Volunteers for the proposed Grace Evangelical Free Church moved a church from Christine, North Dakota, board by board to Main Street, where each member took numbered boards and reassembled the entire building.

Outside of work and church, the fun-loving people in Strathcona danced, sang, played hockey, and worked to beautify the city. Couples danced until midnight to the music of local musicians: the American Legion Stephen Gust Post No. 350 sponsored a masquerade ball at the Strathcona Hall to the music of the Bemidji Jazz Orchestra. Beginning with the Daughter of Ceres Club (goddess of vegetation) in 1919, the Strathcona Club formed fifty years later to make the Community Park, a must-stop for tourists en route to Lake of the Woods on Highway 32. Rasmus Lorenson, Roseau County Senior Citizen of the Year in 1980, found time to play guitar and sing, while farming his original homestead for 75 years. In 1989, another Strathcona citizen, Victor Westlund, won that honor. He played trombone for the community band until World War II occupied most of the musicians.

A Fall Festival and a Pair of Snowmobile Racers

Each year on the second Sunday in August, the City Council, Men's Club, and Women's Club join forces for the Strathcona Fall Festival. In 2010, over two thousand folks attended dinner at City Park and enjoyed music from noon to sundown.

Strathcona boasts famous snowmobile race drivers Larry Coltom and Jomar Bernat, who learned to race on the local track. The icy oval track is also headquarters for a vintage snowmobile racing series called S.L.E.D.S. (Still Legends but Extremely Dangerous Series), which is open to pre-1993 snowmobiles.

Strathcona Today

Under the leadership of 81-year-old Mayor Harvey Hanson, Strathcona is home to Home Town Tax, a new city hall, Gustav Adolph Lutheran Church, Grace Evangelical Church, and a mini-mall, which includes the Paradise Café, a service station, and the post office. Don't miss out on lunch at the Paradise Café, an eight-table restaurant with a NASCAR racing theme. The café was built after the last restaurant closed in 1972, and the people of Strathcona volunteered the time and materials to build the establishment. It quickly got great reviews, even on the national scene. When *New York Times* reporter Dena Kleiman wrote about the café in 1990, she raved about the simple and delicious soups, sandwiches and pies. The reporter was equally impressed with the can-do attitude of the local residents. While you're there, enjoy the food, conversation, a game of dice called "horse," and the spirit of a town that refuses to quit.

For those wanting to stretch their legs, Strathcona Community Park features a lovely pavilion, a baseball field and camping sites. An American flag flies over a monument honoring local Navy veteran Roy Oliver Nelson, who loved the area around Strathcona.

For many years, City Clerk Shirley Ryden's grandparents owned Hanson's Grocery. One morning a few years ago residents awoke to find that the final owner, a "suspicious out-of-stater," had locked the doors, pulled the shades, and left town. All the goods, including the meat and perishables, remained in the building. They checked with the Post Office, but Postmaster Laddie Forst said Mr. Stovkis left no forwarding address. He was never seen again.

Population: 100   **Incorporated:** 1951

INSETS L to R: Kaffestua (Creamery Sign) • Kultur Hus and
Barber Shop • Kaffestua • Skindelien Hardware

The quintessential Norwegian community, Sunburg is home to the Kaffestua and Sunburg Creamery Café, famous for Norwegian cuisine like *klub*, lutefisk and *rømmegrøt*.

TOP: George Carter's Barber Shop

Sunburg

The country town is one of the great American institutions; perhaps the greatest, in the sense that it has had and continues to have a greater part than any other in shaping public sentiment and giving character to American culture.
—Thorstein Veblen, Norwegian-American social critic, 1923

The Quintessential Norwegian Town

SUNBURG IS THE QUINTESSENTIAL Norwegian community. It is a town that celebrates *Sytennde Mai* every May 17th, and a town where Norwegian remained the dominant language until well into the 1950s. Located on the Glacial Ridge Trail along Highway 104, the signs *Velkommen til Sunburg* and *Sunburg Proud FFA Community* are shadowed by grain storage bins, a church and a baseball field.

In 1866, when the first settler, Torger Gunnufson, homesteaded the farm on which Sunburg now stands, the Dakota War was over and the area declared available for settlement. In 1872, the first post office opened in Ole Eliason's home between two lakes or a strait (in Norwegian, a *sund*), hence the name Sundburg. The Stoutland Brothers managed their store for three years until 1892, when Kolbjorn Moen walked to Sunburg from Glenwood and bought the building. Later, his brother-in-law, Peder Anders Gandrud, joined forces with Moen, and the business stayed in the family for 70 years before closing in 1962. After a fire destroyed the Moen & Gandrud store in 1926, the community rallied to rebuild the store with volunteer labor. Mr. Gandrud went on to fame as a three-term state representative from 1899 to 1905, and two-term state senator from 1913 to 1921. The two excellent businessmen, along with Erick Olson, also started a private creamery in 1909. Under the capable management of Carl Gulsvig for 42 years, the highly profitable Farmer's Co-operative Creamery remained open until 1985.

Sunburg citizens enjoyed the arts and sports, too. Local farmers and businessmen organized the Sunburg Band, who played at celebrations and once at the State Fair. A very popular contest named "Spelldown" pitted adults against one another in a spelling bee. The last contestant standing was required to spell "down," hence the name "Spelldown." Today, the community gathers in the former elementary school, now the community center and fire hall. An immaculate baseball field, playground, and Hope Lutheran Church surround the 1955 building. The Community Bible Church also resides within the city limits, with several small rural congregations skirting the community.

Unlike most small cities, Sunburg has no connection to the railroad. While the majority of small towns were established by land companies promoting the railroads, Sunburg survived because of its central location in rolling farm country between other railroad towns, each 20 miles away. Until incorporation in September, 1951, the village was governed by an active Citizens Club and a Commercial Club. Volunteers erected a new fire hall for the city in 1955.

A Celebration on May 17th and Authentic Norwegian Cuisine

Every year on May 17th, this Norsk outpost hosts over one thousand people to celebrate Norway's independence from Sweden. The busy one-day event includes a church service at Hope Lutheran, an antique tractor pull, music at the Kultur Hus, and the chance to cheer on the Sunburg Lakers at the baseball field. The party ends with the firemen grilling burgers and a dance at the fire hall.

Famous for Norwegian cuisine like *klub*, lutefisk and *rømmegrøt*, the Kaffestua and Sunburg Creamery Café draws in local citizens to drink coffee and socialize, in Norwegian, of course. Local rosemaling instructor Judy Christianson painted the Telemark rosemaling on the outside of the café.

Senator Knute Nelson, a former Civil War wounded veteran, a County Attorney, a State Senator, and the Governor of Minnesota in 1892, kicked off his fifth campaign for U.S. Republican Senator in Sunburg in 1918. Born in Voss, Norway, in 1843, he was the first Norwegian-born governor of any commonwealth in the United States. He also authored the Bankruptcy Act often referred to as the "Nelson Cure."

Sunburg Today

While cities of all sizes across the country are struggling to keep Main Street alive, Sunburg has succeeded where other cities with more resources have failed. Like a city preserved in a time capsule, the downtown businesses remain in the original buildings surrounded by whiskey barrels full of flowers. The charming city is home to the Kaffestua and Sunburg Creamery Café, Jorgenson's Auto Dealership, Lake Region Bank (formerly the Farmer's Bank), Sunburg Funeral Home, N & J Foods, the Kultur Hus, Skindelien Hardware and the post office. The barbershop is straight out of an old western movie set and open every day except Sunday and Monday. You can still get a tank of gas at Tollefson Oil, and also get your tractor repaired.

The Kultur Hus, an organization to preserve the Nordic arts, is a direct descendant of the folk schools in Norway. In an original frame building on Main Street, students learn Nordic heritage through music lessons, rosemaling, language lessons, dancing and woodwork.

Sunburg is also home to something of a mystery: a mysterious Viking runestone was discovered beneath the surface of Norway Lake near Sunburg by farmer Elmer Roen in 1938. He described the stone as 20 feet square and covered in runic letters. Other witnesses have spotted a large, curved rock in the center of the lake during droughts. Divers have tried to locate the stone several times without success.

On October 11, 1918, depot agent George Brand furiously pedaled his three-wheel velocipede up and down the railroad tracks to warn residents that a fire, which had started on October 9th north of McGregor, was headed for Tamarack.

TOP: Welcome to Tamarack, Main Street

Tamarack

A Terrible Trio: World War I, Influenza and Fires

THE YEAR 1918 WAS A TERRIBLE YEAR for Tamarack and the surrounding area. On top of fighting World War I and influenza, the village fought fire. On October 11, 1918, depot agent George Brand furiously pedaled his three-wheel velocipede up and down the railroad tracks to warn residents that a fire, which had started on October 9th north of McGregor, was headed for Tamarack. The next day, business-man Marcus Nelson's wife, Mamie, shut down the family sawmill and sent the workmen to plow firebreaks around the town. She also wired Governor Joseph Burnquist, who sent Home Guard troops from Aitkin on the train to assist. Both the troops and a rescue train arrived late October 12 to load fleeing refugees, while Mamie sequestered forty

people safely on her farm. Tamarack, along with 27 other villages, was wiped off the map. Over 1,500 square miles of land surrounding the Cloquet/Moose Lake area lay in ruins. By October 15 searchers had discovered 569 bodies, many of whom had hidden in root cellars or wells and suffocated. Those who survived hung onto rafts in lakes or crouched in the water with wet blankets over their heads. Although Tamarack lost everything in the fire, the rebuilding of the city testifies to the courage and strength of the people who lived there.

Originally located two miles east of its present location, Tamarack grew up out of peat and tamarack covered bogs along the Northern Pacific, when the railroad laid track from Duluth to Brainerd in 1874. One of the original settlers, Bill Sicottes, established a trading post and turntable for servicing trains, and lumberjacks and businessmen flocked into the new village. An adventuresome family from London, England, the Rowbottoms arrived in 1891 to build a large hotel and church from salvage material gleaned from an old sawmill. Martin Tingdale, owner of Tingdale Bros. Realty in Minneapolis, and Marcus Nelson set up a general store in 1899, stocking the store with "Hiawatha" and "Empress" brands of canned goods, teas, coffees and spices. Tingdale was appointed Postmaster and Nelson assistant postmaster for the new post office. The following year, E. L. Douglas, founder of the Aitkin Lumber Company, and Marcus Nelson opened Sandy River Lumber Co., and a lumber dynasty was born. As stores and lumber companies flourished, the village attained a solid economic base to attract new residents. A tough businessman, Marcus also cared deeply about his employees. When a young man developed a drinking problem, Marcus sent him to the *Keeley Institute for the cure of Liquor, Opium & Tobacco Habits, and Nerve Exhaustion* in Minneapolis. The man recovered and went on to open his own general store. The city incorporated July 26, 1921, with a population of 165.

Tamarack was once home to the smallest airmail delivery service in the area, and the post office has the commemorative stamp and envelope to prove it. Sometime during the 1930s, Orvis Nelson landed his plane on a level stretch of soggy sod in Tamarack, and the Snader-King Airport began its brief existence. The two-runway airstrip, commemorated in a cancellation stamp during airmail week, May 15–21, 1938, clearly states: Snader Airport, Tamarack, Minnesota. Deeply influenced by family friend and Little Falls aviator Charles Lindbergh, Orvis Nelson went on to achieve fame in the aviation world.

Movie Reels from Hollywood, Delivered by a Greyhound Bus

After the Rowbottom Hotel burned in 1923, Mrs. Koplen opened a new brick hotel on the same site, with a quonset building in back. In 1952, an enterprising widow, Mamie Nelson, and her son, Orvis, painted beautiful murals on the walls of the quonset, installed theater seats and a curtained screen, and opened the Marcus Theater in memory of her husband. The A.R.T.S organization took over ownership in 1980 with support from the Tamarack Activities Club and the Lions Club. Kathy Haugse recalls calling Paramount and Columbia Pictures to order films, which arrived in Tamarack via Greyhound Bus. One delivery mixed up the reels for *Coal Miner's Daughter* and *The Pink Panther*. Movie watchers watched the first half of each film the first week, and the second half on the following week. The old brick hotel was later dismantled, and the quonset now stands alone.

On October 12, 2003, at the Thunderbird Hotel in Bloomington, Minnesota, Orvis Marcus Nelson, son of Marcus and Mamie Nelson, was inducted into the Minnesota Aviation Hall of Fame for his contribution to the progress and development of aviation. Orvis went on to form Transocean Airlines, an air transport company, and helped establish the Airline Pilots Association as well as airlines in the Middle East. He never forgot his roots, returning to Tamarack to buy back the Nelson Store, the family farm, a sawmill, and also to open a broom factory.

Tamarack Today

Today, Tamarack is home to Sam's Grocery, Hanni Plumbing and Heating, Lucky's Landing Bar & Café, Armour Fuel & Save, and the post office. Old schoolhouse #53 has been restored as the Tamarack Community Center. Both the First Presbyterian Church and Tamarack Church of Christ call the residents to worship. An exceptionally sociable city, local residents participate in the Tamarack Sportsmen's Club, Tamarack Activities Club, Tamarack Sno Flyers Snowmobile Club, and the Tamarack Golden Agers (the first Golden Agers Club in Minnesota).

A possibility for a second economic windfall occurred in 2001, when the Kennecott Rio Tinto Exploration, a company dedicated to nickel and copper exploration throughout the world, discovered high grade nickel-copper mineralization on 120 acres near Tamarack, and mineral exploration in the area is ongoing.

TOP: "Taopi, Heart of the Prairie," Shooting Star Trail

The unusual name of the city derives from Chief Taopi (wounded warrior), a Farmer Chief of the Mdewakanton Dakota who was opposed to war and saved the lives of 250 white and mixed-blood settlers held hostage during the Dakota War of 1862.

Taopi

A Settlement Named for an Indian Chief

SURROUNDED BY RICH FARMLAND and a fascinating history, Taopi was platted in 1875 by the Taopi Farming Company, a corporation which farmed 5,200 acres of the best land in the state. The main line of the Chicago, Milwaukee and St. Paul Railroad ran through the farm with the depot and village located on the farm. Under the management of J. W. Wood, his employees cared for the stock, multiple spacious homes and the granaries located on both sides of the track. Early on, the company erected the largest steam flouring mill in the southern part of the state, with a capacity to grind over three thousand bushels of wheat a year. After repeated failures raising just wheat, the farm expanded to corn, soybeans and other grains. The farm also initiated raising livestock including Shorthorn Durham Cattle, hogs, sheep and Percheron-Norman horses.

The unusual name of the city derives from the Dakota War of 1862, when 800 people were killed during the New Ulm Massacre. When the government reneged on treaties offering the Indians money in exchange for their land, Little Crow and Little Six of the Mdewakanton Dakota tribe left the reservation to wage war against the settlers. Taopi (wounded warrior), a Farmer Chief of the Mdewakanton Dakota who was opposed to war, saved the lives of 250 white and mixed-blood settlers held hostage by the Little Crow band. Chief Taopi's heroic efforts to save the settlers did not soften the government's land aggression, but did earn him the gratitude of the people and a city namesake. Reports are that Chief Taopi would have starved except for the intervention of Bishop Henry Whipple, whom Taopi had invited to establish an Episcopal mission on the reservation.

Taopi reached the pinnacle of success and a population of 400 when the big farm employed many men to run the various operations. By 1900, the city had a bank, two elevators, a church, a city hall, a school and three general stores. A new creamery opened in 1907 and churned 700 pounds of butter a day. Later on, home to two railroads, the Chicago Western and the Pacific, Taopi was a union depot and the only depot outside of St. Paul where you could purchase a ticket for anywhere in the United States. A handsome two-story brick school opened the doors in 1914, and operated until 1962 when only ten students enrolled for the year. In 1923, Carleton College student E. A. Conover organized the Community Church of Taopi, which evolved into the Taopi Community Covenant Church before closing its doors. The fortune of this small city rose and fell with the farming corporation and when the farm dissolved into smaller farms, employment decreased and the population dropped.

Chief Taopi and the Dakota War

Chief Taopi died on March 5, 1869, at age 56. A simple white marble slab in Maple Lawn Cemetery in Faribault reads, "Taopi—A brave Christian chief of the Dacotahs who saved many white women and children during the Indian War of 1862." Named the chief of the farmer band of Sioux by the U.S. government, Taopi refused to go along with Chief Little Crow's attacks on white settlers. He dug trenches around the tepees where white captives were held to protect them from attack, and smuggled letters to Henry Sibley requesting help for the captives. His name lives on in the history books and in this small city in southern Mower County.

Taopi loves a party. In 1975, they celebrated 100 years of incorporation with a Horse Pull event, a greased pig contest and rooster chase. Doo-Dah Days followed in 1995 with the only non-motorized parade in the country, and the annual Chief Taopi Bar Auction and Box Social. Taopi orchestrated a near perfect celebration for their 125th anniversary on August 26, 2000, with a pork chop dinner, an antique tractor pull, a car show, and an old-timers softball game. Competitive contests included the Ugly Cake Contest, the Rubber Chicken Throwing Contest and the Mom Calling Contest. All but 7 residents showed up at the city park for their 125th anniversary photo.

In the 2008 General Election, Taopi Mayor James Kiefer and his sister, City Clerk Mary Kiefer Huntley, ran for each other's office: Kiefer for clerk and Huntley for mayor. Kiefer was elected mayor of Taopi in 1984, and Huntley was elected treasurer in 1976. The pair remain in office, and have served as mayor and clerk the longest period of time in any Mower County city.

Taopi Today

Now this historical city along Highway 56 is home to a one-room post office built in 1979, the Taopi City Park, Taopi Women's Club, and 58 determined citizens. The old railroad track has evolved into the Shooting Star Recreation Trail and the Taopi Prairie Project. A steady stream of trucks hauling grain to the elevator, owned by local farmers, lends a sense of purpose to the city. Incorporated in 1878, Taopi is the oldest city in Mower County.

Marjorie Meier, secretary of Prairie Visions, helped secure grant money to designate Taopi along with three neighboring towns as Minnesota's first Scenic Byway. She also provided leadership for the Shooting Star Recreation Trail, the abandoned Milwaukee railroad track now paved for biking and walking, which has run through Taopi since 2003.

The old Taopi railroad area on the west edge of town is home to one of the few remaining native prairie sites in Minnesota. With assistance from grants, the citizens of Taopi cleaned up the site and preserved the 7.5 acres of original tallgrass prairie and wildflowers. The Taopi Prairie Project is now a wayside rest with an informational kiosk and walking trail.

U.S. POST OFFICE
TAOPI, MN. 55977

TOP: Wheaton-Dumont Co-op Elevator, Canadian Pacific Railway

A once-thriving railroad town with a peak
population of 120 citizens, Tenney is now home
to five citizens.

Tenney

WHERE DO YOU FIND THE SMALLEST incorporated city in Minnesota and in the entire United States? In Tenney. Tenney lies on Minnesota State Highway 55, 167 miles west of Minneapolis. A once-thriving railroad town with a peak population of 120 citizens at the turn of the twentieth century, Tenney is now home to five citizens. Soon, the city will cease to exist, as residents voters voted 2 to 1 to dissolve, thereby handing the title of Minnesota's smallest city to Funkley, MN. Mayor Kristen Schwab and City Clerk Oscar Guenther both voted to dissolve the town, while Guenther's sister voted no. "She voted that way because she knows how hard I've worked to keep the town alive," states Oscar. He hopes to retain the two mowers and a weed whip to maintain Main Street. When German immigrants fled their homeland and sought land

of their own, they found a new life in the rich wheat and cattle country of Wisconsin and southern Minnesota, including the farmland of Tenney. Named after John P. Tenney, a Minneapolis lumberman who sold land to the Soo Line Railroad in 1885, the village incorporated in 1901 with an original plat of four square miles. The arrival of the Soo allowed regular shipping of livestock and grain to St. Paul, and equally as important, the delivery of goods to start a thriving business community.

By 1910, Tenney supported a church, three grain elevators, a hardware store, two mercantile stores, a bank, a butcher shop, a machine and implement shop, a blacksmith shop, a pool hall, a lumberyard, the Hotel Tenney, which housed the post office, and 200 citizens. On a typical Saturday night, you would find the men playing cards and pool at the pool hall, while the women bought provisions at the A. N. Larson General Store or G. A. Klugman's Store, and caught up with the latest news. In the late twenties "Lawrence Welk and His Hotsy Totsy Boys" thrilled the locals with their now famous dance music. The 1907 brick school remained open until 1956 when Irene Doyle and Doris Raguse taught the final year in the Tenney School.

The post office closed in 1980 when the population dipped to 19. All that remains today on Main Street is a shell of the old schoolhouse, and the Tenney Church and Social Hall (the social hall is the former Frieden Church). Like many small towns in the Red River Valley, small farms disappeared as corporate farms purchased large tracts of land. The lack of jobs and steady migration to the cities triggered the loss of all businesses in Tenney except for the Wheaton-Dumont Cooperative Elevator, the largest grain shipping terminal in the region.

Area Best Known For:

Tenney still has a Canadian Pacific Railroad terminal to ship millions of dollars worth of grain out of the area. As many as 32 million bushels of corn, beans and wheat are trucked into Tenney each year and shipped out by rail. The Wheaton-Dumont Co-op Elevator recently underwent a three million dollar expansion to accommodate the rising supply of grain from area elevators. Completed in April 2011, the three additional bins and new grain dryer will help keep the Tenney elevator the largest single origin shipper in the Canadian Pacific system.

On May 23, 1989, KSTP-TV declared Tenney the smallest town in Minnesota, a title that the city of Funkley once claimed. A plush limousine picked up the entire city: Al and Lou Manthie, Opal Hardic, Al Hungerford, Lorraine Church, Willie Rossow, Marian Harrington and Leo Berg. The Tenney clan appeared on the "Good Company" television show, toured the Summit Avenue mansions in St. Paul, and rode the "Josiah Snelling" riverboat on the Mississippi River from

Harriet Island to Fort Snelling. When asked what they liked best about Tenney, they responded, "It's quiet." A group picture taken on the steps of the Tenney Church now hangs in the Lake Wobegon Store in the Mall of America.

Tenney hosted their 125th year celebration on May 29, 2010, with a silent auction, classic car show, lawnmower races and the Tenney quilt on display. Mayor Kristen Schwab and City Clerk Oscar Guenther dedicated a new city office in the old church and offered city tours. A pork loin dinner and street dance, with the live rock band, Roxbury, ended a perfect day in Tenney.

While You Are There:

Check out the old Tenney United Methodist Church built at the turn of the century and purchased by the Methodist Conference in 1916. The town's only church, the city bought the building for $11.00 in 1999. City council meetings and reunions continue to hold court at this historic landmark. Antique stained glass windows adorn the building and a signed proclamation from Governor Rudy Perpich proclaiming May 23, 1987, as "Tenney Day" proudly hangs on the wall. The Tenney Church and Social Hall remain open on a daily basis. Visitors are encouraged to sign the guest register in the church, which now functions as the community center and city hall.

Listed on the National Register of Historic Places, the Tenney Fire Hall was recently razed for safety concerns. Built in 1904 to house two hand-pulled chemical fire engines, one engine now resides at the Wilkin County Museum in Breckenridge, Minnesota, and the other resides in Arizona with a private owner. The former small wood frame building with a bell tower and flag mast also housed the city jail in the back of the structure.

When the Tenney Town Hall needed a new cook stove, local women designed the Tenney Quilt, a signature quilt from 1928. In all, 570 people paid ten cents each to embroider their name on the quilt. Heidi Haagenson owns the quilt, which was purchased by her great aunt, LaVanche Prolifka Gill, at the auction. Heidi wrote a book about the women who made the quilt, an object literally stitched with the history of the village of Tenney.

Disaster struck on July 3, 1912, when a fire started
in the drug store and destroyed the entire business
district, sparing only the blacksmith shop.

TOP: Roy Johnson Memorial Park

Tintah

A Train Full of Orphans

WHEN THE MINNESOTA ORPHAN TRAIN RIDERS of New York stopped in Tintah on June 14, 1914, two-year old Carmella Caputo stepped off the train onto the platform with a number pinned on her dress. Prior to her arrival, a priest from the New York Foundling Hospital had visited St. Gall's Catholic Church in Tintah to determine if families were interested in adopting homeless children. One couple, Peter and Mary Schend, who had lost a baby shortly after their marriage, happily agreed to take a homeless child from New York. The entire town came out to welcome Carmella to their community, an event marred only by the fact that the little girl was very sick with pneumonia, which she contracted on the train. Born April 16, 1912, in Manhat-

tan, New York, to Annunciata Nunzio Caputo, a thirty-year old Italian immigrant, Carmella later learned that both her mother and sister had died in an apartment fire. Following graduation from Teacher's College in St. Cloud, Minnesota, in 1933, Carmella married Ray Keaveny, and together they raised their ten children on a farm near Tintah. Carmella was not the only orphan rider; between 1854 and 1929, over 250,000 children from the East Coast, mainly New York, were transported by train for adoption or indentured service to homes across the country.

Forty-two years before Carmella's arrival on James Hill's Great Northern Railway, the village of Tintah organized around the railway station in 1872, and incorporated in 1889. Surrounded by a vast virgin prairie left by Lake Agassiz, Father Hennepin inspired the name Tintah when he described the Dakota as "the nation of the prairies, who are called Tintonha." The promise of rich farmland lured James E. Henry from New Hampshire, who purchased 7,000 acres from the railroad in 1880. Mr. Henry hired eighty men to work on the Big Tintah Farm, until his daughter, Ida, and her husband, Parker A. Putnam, took ownership in 1888. The five sections of farmland included three sets of farm buildings, a boarding house for employees, a granary, and two barns to house 150 cattle, 450 sheep and 50 horses.

By 1905, Tintah boasted a progressive Main Street including Flynn's Hall on the second floor of the Flynn Brothers Furniture and Hardware Store. Owner John Flynn purchased a new piano from Stone's Music House in Fargo for school programs, vaudeville shows and rollerskating. When a wrestling exhibition arrived in town, women were excluded from watching local men who were invited to challenge the professional wrestlers.

Unheard of in a small town, Tintah boasted three resident physicians. One doctor, J. T. Leland, arrived during a flu epidemic, made enough money to buy a team of horses, and sold out to Dr. Nathan Doleman in 1904. A graduate of Boston Medical School, Dr. Doleman also worked for the telephone company, and occasionally had to be retrieved from a telephone pole for an emergency. The good doctor worked in Tintah until his death in 1945.

Disaster struck on July 3, 1912, when a fire started in the drug store and destroyed the entire business district, sparing only the blacksmith shop. Mrs. Roleke, owner of the drug store, slid down a pole from upstairs to escape the fire.

The early settlers immediately set out to establish a church. Catholic mass was first celebrated in Peter Flynn's home in the section house of the Great Northern Railway, but a new church became a reality when James Hill donated four acres of land in 1892 to the parish. Named St. Gall in honor of Bishop Otto Zardetti, who hailed from St. Gall, Switzerland, the church hosted 45 families. In 1913, the Catholic grade school opened its doors to 100 eager students, and the following year the Catholic high school opened with 33 students. Despite attempts to keep the schools open, the high school closed in 1921, and the grade school closed in 1932.

One U.S. Senator and Two Lovely Churches

In 1909, citizens voted to build a new four-room brick school on two acres of land purchased from the Catholic Church for $500. When Eugene McCarthy graduated from St. John's University in 1935, he found his first teaching job in Tintah. One of our country's most influential politicians in the last century, Senator McCarthy served five terms in the House of Representatives, two terms in the U.S. Senate, and in 1968 he lost the Democratic nomination for President to Lyndon Johnson. In 1959, Senator McCarthy spoke at the graduation ceremony in Tintah.

St. Gall's Catholic Church celebrated its centennial in 1981 under the leadership of Father Robert Schmainda. An original 1893 structure, First Congregational Church is quite striking in its simplicity. Beautiful stained glass adorns the altar, and two handcrafted quilts grace the back wall of the church. Signed by the Ladies Aid women from 1956, in one quilt each family's name is showcased in an individual square along with a symbol of the church. The church celebrated its centennial in 1991.

Tintah Today

Today, Tintah is home to John's Bar on Main Street, Roy Johnson Memorial Park, American Legion J.F.B. Post 610, and the Tintah Fire Department, with an original 1903 fire engine. A former elevator, now the Tintah Grain Company, sold in 1978 to local farmers, and is used for grain storage. Sister Julia Denery recalled the day President Theodore Roosevelt stepped off the train in Tintah in 1908, and commented, "It is nice to see so many men, women, and children here."

Disaster struck in 1926 when Father Lauer of St. Gall Catholic Church deposited the church bazaar funds in the bank (after hours) only to learn that the bank failed the next day. Thankfully, the church survived. By 1962, the old church made way for a new, modern building under the leadership of Father William Wey.

Population: 46   Incorporated: 1950

INSETS L to R: Former school, restored as apartments •
Main street • USPO • Welcome area

Looking for a great place to learn to ballroom
dance? Look no further than the Trail's End Bar,
in Trail, Minnesota.

TOP: Buggy ride during Trail Polka Octoberfest

Trail

A Ballroom Dancing Destination

LOOKING FOR A GREAT PLACE to learn to ballroom dance? Look no further than the Trail's End Bar, in Trail, Minnesota. Every Sunday owner Leasha Clark serves up great food, and music, like the three-piece Kathy Erickson Band from Middle River, and the local duo, H & V Melodies, also known as Harold and Vonnie. An Octoberfest visit left standing room only, as seasoned dancers alternately waltzed and schottisched around the former pool hall, built in 1939 by Andrew Weber.

When the federal government issued a proclamation declaring a portion of the Red Lake Indian Reservation open to settlement on May, 15, 1896, settlers arrived to stake their claim. Norwegian immigrants Iver and Beret Strand were ready when L. J. O'Neil fired the gun,

beginning the race for land. Traveling by train from North Dakota to McIntosh, and then by lumber wagon to their homestead in Trail, Iver named his land the River View Farm and kept the farm in the family until 1974, a total of 78 years.

In 1906, Joney Wichterman opened a creamery and general store to support the local farmers and Indians traveling west to the prairies to hunt buffalo. He named the busy area Trail because of the Indian trail close by, which was used by the Ojibwe Indians from Lower Red Lake, Cass Lake and Bemidji. When the Soo Railroad bought eighty acres of land to plot a village in 1910, several more businesses opened, including a post office, an elevator, a livery barn, a feed mill, a hotel, a bank, two more general stores, a blacksmith shop, a barber shop, a hardware store, and a telephone office. Community leaders in Trail, like Albert Aaknes, were hardworking, resourceful folks. When his grandfather, Ole Aaknes, was paralyzed by a mad bull in 1922, twelve-year old Albert took care of his grandfather and the farm. To earn extra cash, Albert started the fire in the wood stove at school, trapped game, and helped build barns around the area. If this young entrepreneur wasn't working, he was playing with his eight-piece band, Al Aikens and his Cowboys. The Hruby sisters, Adeline, Vi and Delores, provided vocals for the band while dressed in shirts and leather vests that Albert sewed for the group. A mechanic, blacksmith and businessman for thirty-nine years, Albert also served on the school board, as trustee at Mt. Olive church, and as the town's mayor. On Al and his wife Rose's fortieth wedding anniversary, a grandchild asked what he would do for his fiftieth anniversary. He replied, "Just like when we got married, have a wedding dance in Carl Anderson's barn and serve free sack lunches and coffee."

The first school to serve the Trail area was built in 1897 on a corner of Thomas Olson's farm with teacher E. A. Schneider holding classes in both Gully and Trail. Children carried their lunches, used slates instead of paper, and wrote on blackboards that were plain boards painted black. A beautiful brick two-story school complete with a bell tower was built in 1913 and remains intact today. Following the school's closure in 1970, Wally Groberg had a sewing plant in the building for a number of years. Luckily, the city council had the foresight to preserve this lovely historic building, and opened the doors for the city centennial in 2010.

Two Norwegian churches remain a vital part of the community. Mt. Olive Lutheran Church formed in 1919 and moved a church building from Gully to Trail in 1953. The Ladies Aid paid the bulk of expenses for the move acquiring the money through countless bake and fancywork sales. A block away stands Sand Valley Lutheran Church, built in 1917. The church bell, altar chairs, and pews were purchased from Trinity Church in Hayfield, Minnesota in 1921, and once again the Ladies Aid carried the day by contributing $5,191.32 to cover expenses, while the Luther League donated $1631.09.

Working Hard to Maintain a Reputation as a Party Town

Trail has always been a party town and they work hard to maintain their reputation. For the last fifty years on the 4th of July, the city draws hundreds of folks for the best fireworks display in little Minnesota. There is fun for the kids too. Pilot Cory Carlson drops ping pong balls while flying over the city, each containing a prize for the lucky child. Two nights of dancing and a terrific roast pork dinner complete the celebration.

The community pulls out all the stops for the annual Trail Polka Octoberfest with great food and music. Along with solid restaurant fare, the local cooks put together a great picnic supper with barbecues, potato salad, beans, and delicious homemade pies, each for a dollar. All afternoon two local farmers offer antique buggy rides.

The Trail Community Club organized in February 1960 to plan the 50th Anniversary celebration of the completion of the Soo Line Railroad, which was held June 24–25, 1960. The community has rallied support for a 75th celebration, a Minnesota Centennial celebration, and in 2010, the Trail Centennial.

Trail Today

Today, Trail is home to the Trail's End Bar, VFW Post 6426, Northern Sand and Gravel, and the post office, housed in the former 1912 bank building. Entrepreneur Cindy Erickson recently open Stitch 'n Trails, an embroidery studio, located in the former Joyce's Café.

The old schoolhouse is also a sight to see. Freshly painted with red trim, the Trail Schoolhouse is meticulously maintained and picture-postcard perfect. Walk up the high steps, and imagine attending school there in 1915 as a young child.

TOP: Former Turtle River Depot, now a private residence

Population: 77   Incorporated: 1901

INSETS L to R: Old school • 71 Bar •
remaining insets from Salem Lutheran

Every July in Turtle River women packed up their
children and pails to pick blueberries on the Red
Lake Indian Trail. Settlers typically canned up to
400 quarts of berries for the long winters.

Turtle River

A Sportsman's Paradise

JUST TEN MILES NORTH OF BEMIDJI on Highway 71, Turtle
River sits on the north edge of beautiful Turtle River Lake. Touted in
a 1908 promotional brochure as "the sportsmen's Eden," tourists were
invited to the area for the best fishing and hunting in the state. The first
European pioneers, Simon Bright and his son George, traveled in 1898
by stagecoach from Bemidji, winding through beautiful Norway pines
with tops that seemed "to reach clear up to the clouds." From their
one-room homestead on the Indian Trail between Leech Lake and Red
Lake, the pair witnessed continuous travel by the Indians between the
two reservations. Long before European settlement, Indians journeyed
over the ancient trail, which had been widened and improved under the

Old Crossing Indian Treaty of 1863. Initially Turtle River developed
on the south arm of Turtle River Lake, but moved to the north end to
accommodate the arrival of the Minnesota & International Railway
in spring of 1901. Incorporation followed on May 18, 1901. The Kelso
Lumber Company opened a sawmill on the lake, building houses for the
employees and barns for the horses. Typical of boom lumber towns, the
population jumped to 228 in 1905, as lumberjacks moved in for jobs as
scalers, planers and loggers. The railroad ran a spur off the main line
down to the planing mill, where two hoists lifted logs out of the lake onto
the rail cars. Main Street originated with the railroad track and depot
on the west end, and ended with the sawmill on the lakeshore.

The log post office opened in 1899, and the local newspaper, *The*

Turtle River Pine Tree, operated from 1901–1904. It included business ads for the A. O. Johnson Store, Hyatt's International Hotel, Mrs. Gerald's Millinery and Dressmaking Store, Trudell's Hotel, Larkin and Dale Livery and Feed Barn, and the Larkin and Dale Saloon. On warm summer afternoons, lumberjacks sat on empty beer kegs in the shade of the saloon to keep cool, with their horses hitched to the post in front of the saloon. Stories are told of pranksters switching horses in the late evening and the settlers waking up the next morning to find a strange horse in their barn. When liquor sales were banned in 1914 as a result of the Indian Territory Act, all the saloons closed.

Every July, women packed up their children and pails to pick blue-berries on the Red Lake Indian Trail. Up to twenty-five Indian families picked alongside the white settlers to sell to the A. O. Johnson Store, who then shipped the berries to an outside market. Indian mothers would tuck their infants in tikinogans and hang them from the limbs of trees where the wind would gently swing the contented babies back and forth. Settlers typically canned up to 400 quarts of berries for the long winters.

As in all small towns, the school built in 1898 was the center of activity. Set in a grove of Norway and white pine, the two-room building employed one teacher for grades 1–5, and another teacher for grades 6–8. Children walked to school until 1910, when a horse-drawn school bus consisting of a small house with a wood stove, built on a sleigh or wagon, transported the children to school.

The first church in town was the Congregational Church built in 1904 on the north side of Main Street. The ladies of the church spent countless hours preparing for the Christmas program, an eagerly anticipated event complete with a beautiful candle-lit tree, bags of candy and popcorn, and the appearance of Santa bearing gifts. One very cold Christmas Eve, George Knutson, a clerk in A. O. Johnson's store, pad-ded up with pillows to play the part of Santa. He was obliged to stand outside until the program ended, and the younger men offered George a few drinks to keep him warm. By the time he got in the church, he could hardly stand up to hand out gifts. The incident increased tension in an already strained relationship between the church people and saloon keepers. By 1910, two fires had wiped out most of the buildings on Main Street, including the church.

A small group of determined Norwegian immigrants met in 1920 to form Salem Lutheran Church, the only church in town today. The church now has a new home, built in 2004, which holds regular services.

A Destination for Language Learning

Turtle River is also home to the world-renowned Concordia Language Village. Located on the south arm of Turtle River Lake, children from all over the world visit to learn a foreign language for a week to a month in the summer.

Turtle River Today

Main Street ends on the shores of beautiful Turtle River Lake. The spacious public landing where the sawmill once ran twenty-four hours a day is now the starting point for navigation through a dozen lakes connected by short channels. The spring-fed lake is home to delicious Minnesota walleye.

The *Taste of Turtle River*, held the third Saturday in August at Salem Lutheran Church, draws a large crowd for live music, family games, and terrific barbecued chicken and pork. Continue the celebration with *Turtle River Days*, the last Saturday in August. The community hosts a pancake breakfast, craft and food vendors, and a parade beginning at the 71 Bar and ending at the Turtle Creek Saloon.

The deep wagon ruts of the nineteenth-century Ojibwe trail between Leech Lake and Red Lake are still visible in Turtle River. This historic trail, home to oxcarts and foot travel, is in the process of partial restoration.

TOP: Sacred Heart Catholic Church

Population: 54   **Incorporated:** 1947

INSETS L to R: Inspiration Peak • Sacred Heart churchyard • Urbank Ag Service and grocery • Community Park

Just west of Urbank lies one of the best kept secrets in Minnesota—Inspiration Peak, which stands at 1,750 feet, about 400 feet above the surrounding rolling hills.

Urbank

"There's to be seen a glorious 20-mile circle of some 50 lakes scattered among fields and pasture, like sequins fallen on an old paisley shawl. —Sinclair Lewis

Inspiration Peak and Other "Haunts of Beauty"

JUST WEST OF URBANK LIES one of the best kept secrets in Minnesota—Inspiration Peak. Among the collection of glacial features known as the Leaf Hills, Inspiration Peak stands at 1,750 feet, about 400 feet above the surrounding rolling hills. Well known to local folks, it was a favorite spot of author Sinclair Lewis, who scolded Minnesotans for ignoring the "haunts of beauty" in their own backyard.

Located in the southwest corner of Effington Township, surrounded by rolling farmland and hills, Urbank is anchored by the Sacred Heart Catholic Church and the Urbank Baseball Field. The village of

Urbank formed in 1903 around the newly opened church. Prior to the settlement of Urbank, thousands of young men from Prussia and Bavaria fled the compulsory three years of military service, when Otto von Bismarck, known as the "Iron Chancellor," annexed Germany to Prussia in 1868. Peter Seih, the eldest of six children and recognized as the first settler in Effington Township, left northern Germany against the wishes of his parents to hire on as a cabin boy to a sea captain. An avid reader of English and German literature, Peter traded his sea adventures for a farmer's life in rural Otter Tail County. His hopes and dreams of the railroad passing near his growing colony were destroyed when the railroad skipped Effington Township and traveled from Alexandria through Parkers Prairie, bypassing the future Urbank.

Focused on clearing land for farming and building homes, German Catholic settlers had little time to think of building a church until 1902. Missionary priests, Fathers Ignatius Tomazin, Joseph Buh, and Francis de Vivaldi used Our Lady of Seven Dolors Parish in nearby Millerville as a center of operation for outlying settlements, providing mass in homes, schools or hotel lobbies. Early pioneers trekked eight miles to Millerville to deliver produce and buy supplies, and many marriages and baptisms took place at the church. Eventually, the families chose to divert their tithes from the Millerville church to build Sacred Heart Parish and a new village, Urbank. Due to a shortage of priests, Bishop Trobec tried to dissuade the congregation from building a new church, but in the end recognized their perseverance and financial stability. Three men donated choice land on top of a swell—the highest elevation in the new village. Bishop Ireland, too, had insisted that the St. Paul Cathedral sit on a hill as high as the state capitol building, as a symbol of the importance the church held in the community.

Once the parish formed, the city of Urbank took shape. German immigrant John Terfehr sold off sections of his land for development. The first general store and post office opened in 1903. At age 68, Prussian immigrant Mike Wacholz opened a blacksmith shop and hardware store, followed by George Kraemer's implement store, Matt Cichy's furniture store, Clement Arken's shoe repair, a bank, J. J. Lodermeier's insurance company, and a feed mill. Peter Lenarz operated the creamery, and entrepreneur Hubert Koep started a café, dance hall, and moving pictures emporium. Peter Revering and Joseph Suchy opened a garage, but Suchy left the partnership to build a bowling alley and tavern.

Although German-Americans outnumbered all the other nationalities in Minnesota, the First World War spread anti-German sentiment throughout the state. German-born Otter Tail County boys over age 13 without naturalization papers were required to register at the post office as resident enemies, and carry photo identification with their signature and fingerprint. Priests offered homilies in English along with their native tongue, and by the time World War II arrived, the Catholic schools had stopped teaching in German. No less patriotic than other Americans, the German-Americans had to prove their loyalty. Despite worries for family in Germany, they enlisted or were drafted at the same rate as others.

Sacred Heart Catholic Church

Flanked by stately pines, the Sacred Heart Catholic Church celebrated its centennial in 2002. The old stained glass windows, each donated by members of the church, and the arched Italianate ceiling add elegance to a simple structure. A well-tended cemetery and grotto surround the church.

Urbank Today

Today Urbank lives on in the Sacred Heart Catholic Church, the Urbank Co-op Grocery Store and Feed Service Center, Norlund Car Service, the baseball field, and 54 dedicated citizens.

Named by Sinclair Lewis, Inspiration Peak offers a panoramic view of nine lakes and three counties. The second-highest peak in northern Minnesota, it became a State Wayside Park in 1926 along with Lake Carlos State Park, which manages the site. Former hunting grounds for the first European settlers in Otter Tail County, sightseers have replaced the hunters. Benches line the quarter-mile trail to the top, and the view is well worth the moderate workout. A recreation area at the base of the hill provides picnic tables and restrooms, a popular stop for families in the summer. Next to the park entrance off County Road 38, Peak Supper Club Wine & Grill serves hikers in summer and snowmobilers in winter.

The Urbank Co-op Grocery Store and Feed Service Center is a rare commodity in a small city. They carry everything from peanuts to bolts, and you are welcome to join the coffee group for free coffee in the back.

An absolute treasure of Minnesota rural history, the Peters Museum owned by Jerome and Cheryl Peters, houses a 1928 Model "A" Ford, vintage John Deere tractors, and other farm and household collectibles.

TOP: Viking Diner & Antiques, Jerome Peters and Ardelle Anderson

Viking

The Bachelor Capital of Minnesota

WHAT SMALL TOWN IN NORTHERN MINNESOTA was designated "Bachelor Capital of Minnesota?" Look no further than Viking, a remote Scandinavian farming community that caught the attention of *Minneapolis Tribune* writer Evelyn Burke back in 1948. Her column on February 29 titled, "Leap Year Lure: Single Men of Viking, Minn. Outnumber Women 100 to 1," cited a very unusual population breakdown: Of the 180 people living in town and outlying farms, 100 were bachelors. Perhaps this factor explains the population decline of this proud and tidy community.

Like most small towns in Minnesota, Viking developed with the arrival of the Soo Line Railroad in 1905 and incorporated as a village April 12, 1921. Named by Reverend Hans P. Hansen, a Norwegian Lutheran pastor, the trainmen dubbed the town "the Lord's City" due to a complete lack of liquor sales. Meanwhile the depot functioned as the social center where the young folks congregated to wait for the evening passenger train. After the train departed, the party and romances began.

Multiple businesses opened including the Farmers Co-op Store, now the Viking Café. Farmers brought in cream, eggs, butter, and hay for shipping out on the new railroad. The Stryland Brothers Store, the Franson Building which housed Hans Olson's telephone exchange, Nordgard's Store, Ed Sorenson's Hotel, and Hegg's Blacksmith Shop served the local citizenry well. Traveling "Medicine Shows" sold liniments promising a cure for all and provided music for dancing.

Viking's two active churches remain vital forces in the community. Typical of many Scandinavian communities at the turn of the century, the Swedes and the Norwegians would form their own churches to preserve their native customs. The Swedish Viking Covenant Church, erected in 1898 and moved to town in 1913, hosted many celebrations, including the 36th wedding anniversary of Claus and Hilma Johnson. In the church parlor decorated in coral and sapphire, a lengthy musical and literary program listed a piano solo, trio selections, and poetry readings. Pastor Bowman jocularly wondered how Claus dared to take a bride with a maiden name Svard, which means "sword" in Swedish. Claus replied that a "sword pierced his heart and it was still there."

The Norwegian Zion Lutheran Church organized in 1906, and ten years later, Reverend Skogerboe broke tradition by preaching in Norwegian in the morning and English in the evening. On November 28, 1948, parishioners seated in the elegant curved pews witnessed the dedication of a beautiful altar, pulpit and baptismal font, hand-carved by an artist from Wisconsin.

The Peters Museum, a Treasury of Rural America

An absolute treasure of Minnesota rural history, the Peters Museum owned by Jerome and Cheryl Peters, houses a 1928 Model "A" Ford, vintage John Deere tractors, and other farm and household collectibles. The museum also displays unusual "trench art," vases shaped from cannon shells while soldiers whittled away the hours in wartime trenches.

Pastor C. T. Thompson formed the Bachelor's Club in 1948 for the guys, who outnumbered the gals by a ratio of one hundred to one. After hearing about the abundance of bachelors, Ruth Peterson, a single woman living in Minneapolis wrote to Pastor Thompson, who handpicked a few young men as possible suitors. Ruth didn't hear back from the shy country boys but did receive a letter from Tillie Sustad, the mother of Leroy Sustad, who was sick with scarlet fever and unable to correspond. Leroy and Ruth celebrated fifty-four years of marriage before Leroy died in 2004.

Viking Today

Even though the depot now resides in Pioneer Village in Thief River Falls, and the Village Hall is gone, Viking still claims the Viking Diner, a post office, a community center, the Peters Museum, and a well-tended park with an ice rink and tennis courts. A new business, Cold Country Scrapbooking, recently hosted a scrapbooking party on the eve of Prince William and Katherine's wedding. The pride of the community, the Viking Elementary School, houses kindergarten through third grade. Local organizations, including the Town and Country Garden Club, the Viking Volcanoes 4-H Club and an active fire department, work hard to maintain the attractive outdoor park and facilities. The Great Plains Railroad still sails through Viking from Thief River Falls to western North Dakota. Next to the tracks, the newly renovated 1953 brick creamery anticipates a new business. Due to the existence of an early temperance organization, the International Order of Good Templars, and two strong churches, Viking has always been a dry city. Carpenter's Corner, a small roadhouse four miles away, is the local watering hole.

The Viking Diner & Antiques on Main Street serves breakfast and lunch in a sparkling new facility with quality antiques for sale. A joint partnership between the city and owner Jerome Peters, the diner donates the proceeds from one dinner a month to the city for maintenance of the building.

The annual Vikings Good Old Days Celebration in August delights the locals and former residents with a movie and bonfire at the skating rink, a parade, music in City Park, threshing demos, and lefse-making at the museum.

Following the death of his wife, Maria, in 1886, Mathias Tostrup donated a portion of his farm for the Viking Cemetery. His only stipulation was that no one would ever be charged for a plot. One grave remains unknown. A man traveling through Viking fell off the train at night, and could only speak English, no Swedish. The Tostrups put him in their buggy, but he died on the way to their home.

TOP: U.S. Post Office

Population: 78   **Incorporated:** 1908

INSETS L to R: Life-sized elephant in Nyberg Park •
Vining Lutheran • Vining Palace Liquors •
Giant pliers in Nyberg Park

Vining is famous for Nyberg Park, a magnificent display of scrap metal sculptures. Some of the sculptures include a gigantic cup of coffee suspended in the air, a life-sized elephant constructed of lawn-mower blades, and a northern pike with a spear.

Vining

An Astronaut, Scrap Sculptures and a Family Dynasty

YOU CAN'T TALK ABOUT VINING without mentioning the Nybergs. Home to Ken Nyberg's enormous scrap steel sculptures and the birthplace of his daughter, astronaut Karen Nyberg, Vining carries a lot of clout among Minnesota's smallest cities. The Nyberg dynasty goes way back to one of the earliest pioneers, Mathias Nyberg from Norway, who homesteaded with his wife and son Sam in a sod hut with hand-hewn log furniture and a barn dug into the hillside. The sod hut is gone, and the astronaut now lives elsewhere, but Ken Nyberg's delightful sculptures pop up everywhere around the city.

The city was initially named Lund after Andrew Lund, who convinced the railroad to furnish ties and steel for a siding. The name changed to Vining in honor of Mark Lyman Vining, the stationmaster at Wadena for the Northern Pacific Railroad. When the first locomotive arrived on December 21, 1881, the depot followed within the next year. Ten months later the town was officially surveyed, platted, and designated as Town of Vining. Andrew Lund was appointed Postmaster, Jens Olson built the first house in the new village, and John Gysler, a Civil War veteran with the front half of both feet missing from frostbite, launched the first general store. A spinning wheel factory opened to supply a wheel for every Norwegian woman, who without a minute to spare in a day, would knit while she walked to town.

Three elevators quickly opened for business on the Northern Pacific Railroad, including the Andrews Grain Company managed by

Mr. Lund, the Thorvald Froslee Elevator, and the Farmer's Elevator, a cooperative formed by the Famer's Alliance. With Vining providing the nearest railroad connection, farmers from Urbank and the surrounding area hauled their wheat to Vining with oxen, and later, horses. Half a million bushels of wheat shipped out of tiny Vining in a year. One Halloween prank involved the placement of a buggy on top of the Farmer's Elevator. No one could figure out how to get the buggy down, and it remained there for a long time. The good natured culprits eventually took the buggy down the same way they put it up: piece by piece.

When the town incorporated in 1909, city leaders Mr. Froslee and Mr. Lund led the city council. That same year, the Vining Co-operative Creamery organized to manufacture cheese and butter.

The village school, built in 1939 after fire destroyed the former brick building, closed in 1968, when decreasing enrollment forced consolidation with Henning. Only two students possess diplomas from Vining High School: Pearl Berge Norum, who became a teacher, and Albert Larsen, a farmer in the area.

Fantastic Sculptures and Some Fairly Famous Folks

Dr. Karen Nyberg, a NASA astronaut and mission specialist, grew up in Vining where her parents, Kenneth and Phyllis Nyberg, still reside. Her father, Kenneth Nyberg, is perhaps as famous as his space-faring daughter, at least locally; his Nyberg Park, a magnificent display of scrap metal sculptures located next to Bigfoot Gas and Grocery, is unequalled in Minnesota. Some of the sculptures include a gigantic cup of coffee suspended in the air, a life-sized elephant constructed of lawnmower blades, a northern pike with a spear, and a pair of pliers prepared to flatten a three-foot cockroach. An Apollo astronaut planting a flag is a tribute to his daughter. On the west side of town a 1,200-pound steel foot with a gigantic big toe makes for a perfect photo opportunity. Look for the magnificent sculpture of an Indian on horseback in front of the fire department.

Vining is also home to an award-winning journalist. Kevin Wallevand, reporter for WDAY-TV in Fargo and winner of an Emmy for his documentary, *The Quilt: Hope from the Heartland*, is a native of Vining. He was also awarded the National Edward R. Murrow Award in New York City.

Vining Today

Today the well-maintained school functions as a community center for senior citizens, a history center, and home to the Leif Erickson Sons of Norway Lodge. A life-sized statue of Leif Erickson symbolizes the strong Norwegian roots in Vining.

A picnic shelter and playground offer outdoor play and socializing on warm days. Bigfoot Gas and Grocery, Blue Heron Antiques, the Old Sweet Song, and the Vining Purple Palace provide essentials and entertainment for the residents of the area. The former Lund State Bank in 1913, a brick structure finished in marble and mahogany, now serves as the Vining post office.

Vining Lutheran Church, built by the first Norwegian settlers in 1882, calls members to worship with the original bronze bell cast at the McShane Bell Foundry in Baltimore, Maryland, in 1897. Vining Lutheran Church celebrated its centennial in 1972 with 350 members and friends enjoying a Scandinavian meatball dinner. The next day, the church service was held in Norwegian, and another 400 folks enjoyed a ham dinner buffet. Although the church has been renovated throughout the years, the building is the original structure completed in 1896. The church's six stained glass windows on each side of the church, the beautifully carved pews, altar, and railing, and the original painting of Jesus with Moses in the parting of the Red Sea are simply stunning.

Vining welcomes three to four thousand people for their annual Watermelon Days, celebrated on the third Saturday of each August since 1972. Participants enjoy good food, music, games, and lots of free watermelon. The winner of the watermelon seed spitting contest is the hero of the day.

TOP: Speltz Elevator

Population: 73   Incorporated: 1903

INSETS L to R: Walters Jail • City Park •
Rathai's Roadhouse • City Hall

Originally named Foster, early residents attempted to name the town after a local family. Proposed names included Greenville, Yostown, Kliebenstein-burgh, Meyerapolis and Ludtkefast.

Walters

A Bicentennial Destination

DURING THE SUMMER OF 1976, the resourceful citizens of Walters advertised their upcoming Bicentennial Celebration with a float pulled by a team of mules in all the local parades. The city mascot, a beautiful St. Bernard dog, attracted considerable attention. Their marketing plan worked, as over 5,000 visitors celebrated our nation's bicentennial in Walters on the weekend of September 5, 1976. Designated a Bicentennial City earlier that year, the city chose the title "Walters Wunderbarfest." The celebration opened in Walters Park with music by the Kiester-Walters High School Band, the Community Choir and the Heritage Choir, who sang in German and Norwegian. The solo, "Beautiful Savior," was sung by Karlene Gormley, and signed by Delrene Peterson,

Miss Deaf Minnesota. A potluck dinner, lengthy parade, and softball games were followed by a dance that completed the perfect day.

Originally named Foster, the only hamlet in Foster Township was renamed Walters by officials of the Chicago, Rock Island and Pacific Railroad in 1900. In an attempt to name the town after a local family, residents proposed a variety of names for the new town including Greenville, Yostown, Kliebensteinburgh, Meyerapolis, and Ludtkefast, without any luck. Soon the town began to grow. The post office opened January 19, 1901. Entrepreneur F. W. Yost immediately built a store to supply the needs of the emerging city, and the city incorporated in 1903. Even the Hamm's Brewing Company of St. Paul saw a future in Walters. The company erected a large building on Main Street, and hired Fred

Peterson to operate the saloon. An ounce of whiskey cost 15 cents, and a large glass of beer was 5 cents, either of which bought you a seat at the bar. Free sausage and crackers were served all day. In 1915, the liquor license fee rose to $1,850, a tidy sum for the times. A newspaper, *The News*, opened briefly in 1904, and street lamps were installed in 1908. By 1920, the city boasted electric street lights and a population of 116.

On July 4, 1904, the city celebrated with a rousing speech by Reverend Daugs, an exciting horse race, and a hotly contested baseball game. The pride and joy of the city, the Walters Band performed crowd favorites for the all-day party. The highly regarded Walters Band played all over the surrounding area for their neighbors' county fairs, Fourth of July festivities, and other community celebrations.

Over the years, the city of Walters has had its share of excitement, but nothing as dramatic as the tornado of 1905. Former pupils attending the one-room school tell the story of the day a tornado lifted the school, children and all, carried them over a fence, and deposited everyone, unharmed, in a pasture. Citizens moved the school into town until a new two-story school complete with a bell tower opened September 17, 1906. Another new school was built in 1957, closed in 1975, and now houses grain for drying and storage.

Proud patrons of the community held an all-day picnic on August 29, 1935, to celebrate a new creamery. Crops were good that year, rural electricity was reaching area farms, and the country saw the Depression on the wane. The brainchild of O. H. Koetke, the Merchant's Egg Association formed in a new building near the elevator to store eggs, egg cases, and supplies for the produce market. A truck delivered 1.5 million eggs annually from surrounding small stores to Walters for shipment by railroad to Chicago, New York or Philadelphia, wherever the market was most profitable. Then 1939 ushered in World War II, and on October 16, 1940, every male citizen in the country between the age 18 and 65 was required to register for the draft. Walters registered seventeen men, out of a total of 67 for the township.

A Bicentennial City and a State Representative

Under the leadership of Richard Michaelis, Chairmen of the Walters Bicentennial Commission, Walters was designated a Bicentennial City on February 7, 1976, with a program at United Lutheran Church. The crowd outnumbered both the Minneapolis and the St. Paul Bicentennial presentations.

Former Minnesota State Representative Henry Kalis, a farmer from Walters, served in the House of Representatives from 1974 to 2002. A conservative Democrat, Representative Kalis earned a reputation as a champion for agriculture and transportation. One of the first representatives to report for the opening session each year, Kalis stated, "I enjoy this job and I think when you like something you should show people you like it."

Walters Today

Today, grain trucks rumble through town on their way to the elevator and its six grain storage bins, located next to the railroad tracks on the northern edge of town. In the late 60s St. John's Lutheran and Faith Lutheran Church merged to form the United Lutheran Church, the center of community activity. Walters supports the Walters Fire Department and Town Hall, the Walters First Responders, the Speltz Elevator, Rathai's Roadhouse Bar & Grill, and Krohnberg Garage.

Constructed in 1909 at a cost of $685, the Walters Jail housed renegade bootleggers and petty criminals until the jail closed in 1924. According to former Mayor Marvel Prafke, the first female mayor in Faribault County, "Walters was once known as a place where people came to have a good time. There were bootleggers there, and sometimes people got out of hand." When the jail stood empty, the eight by ten foot brick facility with grilles covering the windows served as occasional lodging for railroad workers.

For the bicentennial celebration in 1976, the Walters Community Care Club meticulously restored the jail, and in 1980 the historic jail received the honor of placement on the National Register of Historic Places.

Population: 84   Incorporated: 1901

INSETS L to R: Pohlen Chapel • St. Mathias Church • Exterior of
USPO • Inside of USPO with Carol Jenniges and Mary Olson

Dismayed at the thought that any of their four
sons would fight against their relatives in Germany
during World War I, German immigrants Joseph
and Margaret Pohlen pledged to build a chapel in
thanksgiving if none of their sons were drafted
into the service.

TOP: Wanda Legion Post #385 "To All Wanda Area Veterans"

Wanda

A Prospering Bank in a Town of 84

AUTHOR STEVE HOFFBECK, who teaches at Minnesota State
University Moorhead and continues to bank in Wanda, states that the
Wanda State Bank is the best bank in the world, where the employees
are exceptionally friendly and all the services are free. How does a
100-million-dollar bank in a town of 84 continue to grow and prosper?
According to Mary Olson, a former teacher, families in Wanda had
many children, and although only one of the sixteen stayed, the other
fifteen continued to bank in Wanda.

Platted in 1899 by the Chicago and Northwestern Railway and
incorporated in 1901, the name Wanda derives from the Ojibway word,
wanenda, meaning "to forget" or forgetfulness. Both the State Bank of

Wanda and the *Wanda Pioneer Press*, published by Paul Dehnel, opened
their doors in 1902 to serve the city of 178 residents. A German Evangelical Lutheran Church formed in town, and St. Mathias Catholic Church
followed in 1906. After a fire destroyed the Catholic Church in 1907,
the parishioners erected a beautiful brick structure in 1910. They started
a Catholic School in 1953 under the direction of Father Bertrand, who
also drove the school bus the first year, picking up children by 6:45 a.m.
so he could return for eight o'clock mass.

Residents built a stately, three-story public school building in 1913,
staging class plays and community events on the third floor of the brick
building. An exceptional janitor and teacher, Max Darkow retired after
teaching woodworking classes for forty-four years. Numerous awards

won by his students at the county fair were a testament to Mr. Darkow's outstanding leadership. In 1967, the high school consolidated with Wabasso, and the school closed completely in 1976. Former city Mayor and bank President Don Schumacher retains bricks from the former school, which was demolished in 2005.

Life is not always quiet in sleepy Wanda. On February 2, 1979, bank employee Dan Weber left the bank for lunch and was approached by a man wearing a blue ski mask. Armed with a pistol, the man ordered Dan back into the bank and collected $6,000 in cash before locking Dan and three other employees into a walk-in vault. Just a block away from the bank, the robber lost control of Weber's car on the icy roads and got stuck in a snow bank. On foot, the thief stopped local farmer Jim Arlbeck and took his pickup at gunpoint. By May, four men were arrested for the robbery.

A Beautiful Church and a Concertina Legend

Originally named St. John the Baptist because of the Irish contingency, the Germans won out when the new church was built in 1910 under the reign of Father Joe Jagerman. In 1983, St. Mathias Catholic Church celebrated their centennial under the leadership of a woman, Pastoral Administrator Sister Kay Fernholz, one sign of many changes in the church over the years. Good music and an excellent choir leading the congregation have always been important parts of mass. When Father Bertrand appealed to the parishioners for funds to purchase a new organ and saw the amount collected, he said, "I told you I wanted to buy an organ, not a piccolo!"

Born December 25, 1922, in Wanda, Christian "Christy" Hengel is one of the city's claims to fame. A legend of the concertina world, he bought his first concertina at age 16 with money from trapping "skunk weasels." In 1952 he traveled to Chicago to buy the remaining concertina manufacturing inventory from the old Otto Schlicht factory. Known for their perfect pitch and clear, crisp sound, Christy's instruments are considered the industry standard around the world. National Geographic magazine featured his work in 1991, and he was inducted into the Minnesota Music Hall of Fame in 1999. One of his concertinas is on display at the Minnesota Historical Society museum.

Wanda Today

Today Wanda is home to Wanda City Hall and Fire Department, American Legion Post 385, Wanda State Bank, St. Mathias Church, and Riley's Tavern. An annual city-wide mowing bee keeps the city tidy. An excellent example of Art Deco architecture, the post office remains solvent due to the volume of mail they handle from the bank. The Lutheran Church closed in 1970, followed by St. Mathias School in 1975, which consolidated with St. Anne's in Wabasso, and is now a used clothing center for Groundswell. The Wanda Commercial Club and the American Legion joined forces in 1978 to provide fencing and lighting for the city park, named for Phil Schoo, a longtime softball enthusiast. Four camping spots with water and electrical hookups complete the well-used park. On the other side of town sits another Legion Field surrounded by cornfields, right out of the movie *Field of Dreams*.

Dismayed at the thought that any of their four sons would fight against their relatives in Germany during World War I, German immigrants Joseph and Margaret Pohlen pledged to build a chapel in thanksgiving if none of their sons were drafted into the service. In 1918, son John was drafted, but the Armistice was signed before he left for induction. True to his word, Joseph built *The Pohlen Chapel* in Wanda on the grounds of St. Mathias Church. The octagon-shaped chapel, symbolic of their eight children, displays a lushly painted ceiling and hand-built altar for scripture and communion.

Farmer Michael Beranek and his wife Krista Daniels grow two acres of grapes just south of Wanda. A local winery, Fieldstone Vineyards, purchases their LaCrescent and Frontenac Gris for white wine and Marquette grapes for red wine.

Mail delivery by train was interesting. While the train barreled through town at 60 miles an hour, a man in the mail car would snatch a mailbag hung on an arm rail by the depot. Another man in the mail car tossed the mailbag for West Union out the door towards the depot platform.

TOP: City view, St. Alexius Catholic Church

West Union

Lake Wobegon Country

THE 46-MILE-LONG LAKE WOBEGON TRAIL meanders through West Union on the way to Osakis. In August 2007 Garrison Keillor and friends biked from West Union to meet another 2,000 bikers in Osakis for the *Wobegon Central Bike In to the Pretty Good Trail Connection*. The party celebrated the completion of the "Forgotten Four" miles between the Lake Wobegon Trail and the Central Lakes Trail. Keillor reflected on what railroad magnate James J. Hill would think of his former railroad track, now that it is a bike trail. He also told the crowd, "The people along the Lake Wobegon Trail are hardworking people that aren't really brought up to have fun. What we call workaholics today, they call dedication."

One of the oldest cities in Todd County, West Union lies in the richest farmland and among the hardest-working people in Minnesota. Ten brave souls arrived by oxcart in 1857 and decided to stay in spite of the remote location, fears of an Indian conflict, and the impending Civil War. On September 2, 1863, settler John C. Hoffman was shot in the back by a suspected Dakota Indian while out searching for a stolen horse, and this brought growth to a standstill. In 1881, settlement began in earnest, when German families bought farmland in West Union. That same year, Abbot Alexius Edelbrok from St. John's Abbey in Collegeville, Minnesota, purchased over 1,000 acres of prime farmland. He opened Brotherhood Farm and St. Alexius Priory to secure food for the college, and to enable boys to attend a college prep school. A frame church erected on the farm in 1888 moved one year later to West Union, the site of St. Alexius Catholic Church today. A money-losing proposition, the farm sold in 1901, and in 1967 Larry and Rita Marthaler bought Brotherhood Farm.

The combination of rich soil and the arrival of the Great Northern Railway in 1872 predicted excellent growth for this agricultural community. Until 1962, freight trains passed through town to pick up grain from the West Union Grain Elevator and livestock from the cattle corrals, and dropped off farm machinery, lumber, and household goods along the route from the Twin Cities to Seattle. The depot also acted as a finely tuned pickup spot for the mail. While the train barreled through town at 60 miles an hour, a man in the mail car would snatch a mailbag hung on an arm rail by the depot. Another man in the mail car tossed the mailbag for West Union out the door towards the depot platform. Depending on the accuracy of the throw, Postmaster Leo Schlicht often picked up the mail three blocks away, when the mailbag finally stopped bouncing. Shortly after the city incorporated in 1900, Main Street bustled with a town hall, the Union Hotel, Bentfield's General Store, the elevator, Joe Marthaler's hardware store with a barber shop, West Union State Bank, a lumberyard, blacksmith shop, and West Union Co-op Creamery. Thursday night the farmers gathered at Ben Servatius' Pool Hall for pool and ice cream. A new school, District #4, built in 1912 for $4,000, held 72 students, and closed in 1970.

By 1910 the population peaked at 250, but proximity to the larger cities of Long Prairie, Osakis and Sauk Centre stymied any future growth. A city landmark, West Union Feeds, recently closed after a century of service. A small menagerie of scrap metal farm animals is left to mourn the closing.

A Mission Style Church and a Leader in Fighting Cancer

Following a destructive fire on February 22, 1917, St. Alexius Catholic Church dedicated a new church on November 18, 1917. The Mission Style interior, with an arched ceiling and beautiful stained glass windows, has recently restored a carving of the Last Supper set in the base of the altar. A painting of their patron saint, St. Alexius, shows him lying on the floor under the stairwell of his parents' home where he lived and died, unrecognized by his family. A Christmas nativity set, carved by the Brotherhood Farm and rescued from the 1917 fire, graces the altar during Advent.

After the death of her two-year-old son, Isaac, from cancer in 2008, Linda Lieser created the Isaac Foundation, a fund to raise money for childhood cancer research. Team Isaac raised $45,000 from their annual Chili Feed and Hope Run, all donated to the University of Minnesota for pediatric cancer research. On July 16, 2010, Linda was crowned Mrs. Worldwide Queen of Hope in Tempe, Arizona, for her work with childhood cancer.

West Union Today

West Union continues to use original buildings from the turn of the twentieth century. The Sidewalk Bar & Grill (the former bank and general store), West Union Garage (the old creamery) and West Union General Antiques (the former grocery store and post office) provide an ongoing sense of permanence in the historic city. Although the railroad tracks are gone, the West Union Depot remains carefully preserved in Pat and Don Miller's backyard.

St. Alexius Catholic Church serves smoked sausage, sauerkraut, spare ribs, head cheese, and all the trimmings at their annual October Sausage Supper, a venue for great German food. Enjoy live music, the refreshment stand, and games for everyone. You can place your order early to take home a holiday supply of headcheese, sauerkraut, and sausage.

Sidewalk Bar and Grill has been serving beer since the twenties, even during Prohibition. Bartender Micki Friedrich tells us that the beer would arrive in armored trunks and head right for the speakeasy in the basement. The original Sidewalks sign still hangs, a reminder of 1934, when Joe Direnberger called his new business "The Sidewalks of New York."

TOP: City view

Population: 57   **Incorporated:** 1926

INSETS L to R: Minnewaska Go-Kart Racing • 10 Mile Tavern • Gjerke Farms • Westport Lake

Early Westport settler Tom Pennie recalled the Grasshopper Plague of 1876 as a dark cloud descending from the northwest, almost obscuring the sun.

Westport

The Grasshopper Plague of 1876

EARLY SETTLER TOM PENNIE recalled the Grasshopper Plague of 1876 as a dark cloud descending from the northwest, almost obscuring the sun. As the cloud drew near, millions of grasshoppers covered the grain fields, meadows, animals, and gardens, eating everything, even the onions. With grasshoppers four inches thick everywhere, Tom's father was forced to stop building his barn. The farmers tried to end the plague by plowing furrows in the fields and pouring kerosene on the grasshoppers. Even fire could not kill the larvae in the soil, and the eggs hatched again in the spring. Once again they devoured everything in sight before leaving for greener pastures. But nothing nature has thrown at this community has stopped this hardy city.

The city of Westport lies just east of Westport Lake, a small, undeveloped lake known for good fishing and as a prime waterfowl habitat. When D. M. Durkee opened a log hotel in 1866 on the northeast side of the lake, he built next to the Wadsworth Trail, a part of the Red River Trail. General Sibley created the trail in 1863 to supply wheat and goods for Fort Wadsworth, South Dakota. That name was later changed to Fort Sisseton in honor of the Sisseton Indians. Used by wagon trains and stagecoaches until 1882, the Wadsworth Trail eventually disappeared when the Little Falls and Dakota Railroad (later the Northern Pacific) arrived in 1882 to transport wheat and the mail.

After the train arrived, the post office opened in 1883, followed by three elevators, two hotels, a blacksmith shop, a creamery, and the train depot. A fire in the Westport Barbershop in December 1927 threatened to burn Main Street, but the quick work of firemen saved the day. The owner of the building, Mr. Flannery, bought everyone lunch and cigars at the M. C. Frederick Hotel. A Methodist church, the only church in Westport, opened in 1879, and closed in 1953 to join the Villard congregation. Mr. Heil West published *The Westport World* from 1920 to 1923. He also owned Thor's Resort on Westport Lake until 1943, when he sold the business to Pearl and Charles Gordon. When Westport incorporated on March 13, 1926, 41 citizens voted yes to incorporate, 20 voted no and the population count soared to 102.

Musical fame arrived in 1927, when Mrs. Al Hermanson from Westport whistled several numbers over WCCO radio, accompanied by a talented quartet. Merrill later won a contest at the McCauley Opera House, and was awarded 40 private lessons at the McPhail School of Music. Folks in town loved to dance, and faithfully drove to Glenwood in the '40s for the annual Roosevelt Birthday Ball on January 30th at the Lakeside Ballroom. All proceeds were donated to polio research. In January 1941 Joseph McArdell of Westport was among the first to be drafted from Pope County, and was inducted at Fort Snelling.

In 1883, the school district built a two-room school, which served until the WPA erected a modern concrete structure in 1940. Principal Leroy Foote and teacher Willa Hogan taught grades one through eight in the newer four-room school. Forerunners to the present PTA, the Westport Mother's Club organized in 1920 to support School District 15. Lunch, served at 10 cents a plate, raised enough money to purchase school playground equipment. The Mother's Club celebrated Minnesota's Centennial in 1958 and the club's 50th anniversary in 1970, when charter members Bertha Frederick, Selma Thompson and Cynthia Bodeker were honored for their dedication to the school. When the club celebrated its 60th anniversary, May Stalker received her 50-year pin. All the parties were held in the Westport School.

On April Fool's Day, 1954, a fire raged through main street Westport, destroying Hamilton's Grocery, the post office, and Adolph Dziengel's Garage and home. Eleven years later, April again was cruel to the residents, as thawing snow and rain created a flood, forcing many residents to leave their homes. The post office remained open until 1970. The depot closed in 1957, the last train rolled through three years later, and the tracks were removed in 1982.

Have a Beer in the Old Schoolhouse

The Ten Mile Tavern, the former WPA school building, is a good example of a concrete school built in the forties. Well known for the Wednesday night Taco Bar and the Friday All-You-Can-Eat-Shrimp and Fish Special, the bar also draws patrons for the outdoor sand volleyball league. The bright purple door is a stark contrast to the irrigators and farmland surrounding Westport. The brick interior décor is new, but the maple flooring and restroom stalls are original and part of the old school.

In 2003 Gjerke Farms opened a diversified swine and beef farming business with 31 employees. The company expanded to include Glacial Lakes Ag Management, a bookkeeping and service training division. The owners received the Good Neighbor Farm Award from the Minnesota Department of Agriculture in 2010.

Westport Today

Westport is now home to Gierke Farms & Glacial Lakes Ag Management, Dustin Engle's Custom Sandblasting and Painting, and two independent welding shops owned by Al Koppen and Tom Kirkoff. The Westport School closed in 1967, and the building is now the Ten Mile Tavern. The Minnewaska Go-Kart Track (MAGKRA) fills the city up on weekends.

Race fans relocated the Minnewaska Go-Kart Race Track to Westport in 2007 to promote racing and family fun. The one-eighth mile, oval track hosts an average of fifty families on Sunday afternoons from Memorial Day through Labor Day.

Nestled along the Root River State Bicycle Trail,
Whalan is home to the best pie shop in the state.

TOP: Ernie's Station, Ernie and Joan Johnson

Whalan

The Best Pie Shop in the State

NESTLED ALONG the Root River State Bicycle Trail, Whalan is home to the best pie shop in the state. Owner Maggie Gergen and her sisters, Pat Davis and Kathy Boudreau, know the way to a pedaler's heart. Bicycles line the outside of the Aroma Pie Shop, and the owners are lined up inside, choosing from a terrific selection of pies baked fresh each morning. After pie and coffee, Whalan offers an unconventional history to savor and enjoy.

In 1962, a Minneapolis newspaper dubbed Whalan "The Tobacco Capital of Minnesota." Whalan was home to Spanish Leaf tobacco, which was locally manufactured into the Daisy cigar. According to local sources, the Daisy would put any Cuban cigar to shame. For one hundred years, from the 1880s until 1980, everyone in Whalan grew a little tobacco, a cash crop far more profitable than wheat. Five acres of tobacco would yield about the same profit as twenty-five acres of wheat. Drying tobacco leaves still hang from the rafters of the old Tydol gas station, restored by Ernie Johnson. His grandfather, John Bostrack, owned the original cigar factory in downtown Whalan.

Whalan incorporated as a city in 1876 on land donated by Irishman John Whaalahan. He insisted the town site should be formed in the shape of a Greek cross, that every 20th lot remain his, and that a train depot be built to service the arrival of the Southern Minnesota Railroad. The mainly Norwegian community acceded to his every wish. In the early 1970s, the train no longer stopped in Whalan, and the depot now sits on a former tobacco field on the other side of the tracks. Surrounded by limestone bluffs and rolling hills, the old railroad track, now the Root River State Bicycle Trail, meanders through the town. According to locals, the trail has breathed new life into the picturesque community. A fresh flower bed in memory of teacher and avid bicyclist Mary Berube, a gazebo built in 1999 in memory of John Whaalahan, and a miniature golf course along the trail showcase the spark of renewal in Whalan. The crown jewel is the Aroma Pie Shop, with its delectable selection of homemade pies that entice the steady stream of pedal pushers to return again and again.

The Stand Still Parade

Every third Saturday in May, Whalan hosts the Stand Still Parade, where the parade stays put and the viewers do the walking. Co-chairmen Ernie and Joan Johnson, along with an incredible committee, bake fresh lefse and cook *rømmegrøt* all day for the hungry crowd. Aging members of the local American Legion Post are happy to stand still rather than march in step. After walking in endless parades, local politicians like the idea of standing still and handing out buttons. Without a corn or soybean queen of their own, area royalty, including the Lanesboro Beef Queen, are invited to sit in the parade. Bill Geist and the CBS crew once showed up to film this national phenomena of floats, marching bands, queens and their courts, all waving gaily from their parked vehicles.

Whalan Today

Local citizens are committed to preserving the buildings and history. The old bank is now an antique shop, the Bank of Treasures, while the 1888 Town Hall, now the Whalan Museum, holds artifacts from the past and present. Other businesses include Gator Greens Mini Golf and Kayak Rental, Whalan Lutheran Church and Parish House, Doc's Auto Body, and American Legion Erickson-Rose Post 637. The Cedar Valley Resort, a former mink farm, now owned by Larry and Sheryl Johnson, hosts

family gatherings in their comfortable log sided cabins overlooking the Root River State Bicycle Trail. Although the post office closed in 1993, the lettering remains on the face of the building, now a private home.

The Whalan Museum displays the theater curtain used for stage productions back when the town hall hosted vaudeville acts, concerts and school plays. In 2010, the museum resurrected outdoor movies by screening the film *Second Hand Lions* on the outside wall of the building. Well over 200 film buffs attended the event, with plans to continue the tradition in summers to come.

Antique car clubs travel from all over the state to visit Ernie's Station, a gas station built by Carl Svertson in 1917 and later owned by Norman and Adeline Larson from 1954 to 1991. Norman took Ernie Johnson under his wing when Ernie lost his father at age eight, and allowed him to help out at the gas station through his teen years. When Norman died and the garage contents were auctioned off, Ernie bought the empty station. Lovingly restored to the original state by Ernie and his wife, Joan, the station is now a museum of antique pumps, signs and cars. One wall displays photos and drawings of Ernie's Station sent by antique car owners in appreciation of Ernie and Joan's effort to preserve the past. While you can't buy gas there anymore the trip down memory lane is priceless.

For the past thirty-five years, the Whalan Fastpitch Baseball Team has also hosted an annual baseball invitational tournament at the Gene Johnson Memorial Field, a well-kept park with picnic tables and playground equipment. Team managers Everett Johnson and Dean Hungerholt led the 1990 Whalan team to a second-place finish, bowing to the powerful Snapper-Ostrander team.

Every February, many folks trek to Whalan to ski by candlelight for the annual February Whalan Candle Light Ski. The Root River Trail transforms into a ski trail, lined with candles and ending with a bonfire. A delicious soup supper awaits skiers at the village hall.

Wilder's former Breck School was named after missionary James L. Breck, who worked with Bishop Whipple (also known as *"Straight Tongue"* by the Ojibwe and Dakota tribes), to win the trust of the Native Americans and advocate for their rights.

TOP: Original site of the Breck School

Wilder

The Breck School and Wilder

IN 1871, RAILROAD MAGNATE AUGUST WILDER chose excellent farmland near Timber Lake for the future site of Wilder as a station along the new line of the Chicago, St. Paul-Minneapolis and Omaha Railroad. In order to spur growth on this stretch of track from St. Paul to Sioux City, Iowa, Mr. Wilder offered 110 acres and a few town lots to Bishop Whipple for a new home and farm school. The Bishop believed the school would attract Episcopal families to Wilder, and that dream spurred the creation of the Breck Mission and Farm School. An early catalog of the progressive school states the school was to "provide a place where young men and women, too old for the district and graded school, may take up just the studies they need, in classes composed of students their own age, and be allowed to advance as rapidly as they are able. No matter how backward a pupil is he will find classes to suit him, and no matter how old he is he will not feel out of place." And the price was right— $110 for room, board, tuition, steam heat, and bed laundry.

Young men and women aged 10 to 30 flocked to Wilder from the Midwest and the Breck school also lured students from overseas. Native American children were educated at the school, also. By its second year, a total of 506 students enrolled to obtain their high school education, take courses in business and the sciences, and acquire their rural teacher's certificate. An innovative school ahead of its time, Breck School discarded all theoretical classes in bookkeeping and banking, and instead set up a mock First National Bank where students learned hands-on while working. Except for sports, girls had equal opportunities. The school's catalog stated that, "The young ladies are permitted to enjoy equal rights and privileges as the young gentlemen. God made the family and we do not presume to improve on his plan." Liquor was forbidden as well as tobacco, bullying and card playing.

By 1895, downtown Wilder was home to several businesses, including a new creamery, where butter maker Sam Rank churned the farmers' milk into butter. Later, he sold the creamery to a farmer's cooperative and opened a general merchandise store. However, Sam Rank's real claim to fame is that he owned the first automobile in town, a Holiday.

When Wilder incorporated in 1899, the census tallied 195 citizens. Prosperity blossomed in 1906 when the Malchow Brothers built an implement and hardware store from lumber shipped from the 1903 World's Fair & Louisiana Exposition. Local farmer Charles Johnson bought several train cars full of the recycled lumber to build a granary, a chicken barn and oak floors for his dining room. Tragedy hit the village when a tornado passed through on July 1, 1903, killing Daniel Gallagher and his wife and daughters on their family farm.

Two early grain elevators along the tracks were purchased by Warren Lecy in 1954, who added 15 round bins and two corn dryers. The only private owner of the elevators in Wilder's history, Mr. Lecy sold them to Lakefield Farmer's Coop Elevator Co. In 1973 they added another bin to build storage capacity to 300,000 bushels.

Wilder's last public school, built in 1921, expanded from two years to four years of high school to allow Kermit Runke, Violet Malchow, Tillie Egge, and Gladys Engbritson Anderson to graduate in 1925. During World War II, the acute shortage of teachers closed many smaller schools, and the class of 1943 signaled the end of high school in Wilder. An all-school reunion took place in the summer of 1958, and one oft-repeated memory was the "still" set up in the tunnel of the school by an early janitor, who constantly worried that the apparatus would blow up and damage the school. In 1960, the elementary school consolidated with Windom, and the building took on a new life as a furniture store until 1979.

A worship alternative to the Episcopal Breck Chapel, the Methodist church opened in 1896. When the rock foundation needed repair in 1939, the Union Ladies Aid helped raise money for repairs. Several ministers offered their services to the church, including Vice President Walter Mondale's father, the Reverend Theodore Sigvaard Mondale, from Heron Lake. When the Ladies Aid dissolved in 1965, the city remodeled the church for a town hall.

The Breck School, Candy Bars, and the Freedom Train

Breck School is named after missionary James L. Breck, who worked with Bishop Whipple (also known as *Straight Tongue* by the Ojibwe and Dakota tribes), to win the trust of the American Indians and advocate for their rights. After Reverend Breck's death, his colleagues honored his work by naming the school for him.

Once a busy railroad town with eight passenger trains passing through daily, the last passenger train sailed through the city October 24, 1959. In 1976, the local residents were treated once again to the sounds of the familiar steam engine and whistle, when the Freedom Train passed through Wilder just before dawn on a summer's morning. The Freedom Train carried documents and relics of America's history in commemoration of our country's bicentennial.

Wilder Today

Breck School closed its doors in 1909 after 21 years and moved to Golden Valley, Minnesota, and Wilder's dream of prosperity slowed to a standstill. Today, the one-mile square city is home to the vacant Methodist Church, a new City Hall, and the Wilder elevator. A weathered sign marks the land where the Breck School once stood.

A gifted student at Wilder's Breck School, Frank Mars founded the company Mars Incorporated, where he created the Mars candy bar, followed by Milky Way, Snickers, Three Musketeers, and M&Ms, in that order.

Finland and Minnesota meet in Wolf Lake.
Thousands of Finns migrated to northern
Minnesota in the nineteenth century.

TOP: Wolf Pack Amateur Baseball

Wolf Lake

The Histories of Three Countries Meet in One Town in Minnesota

THE HISTORIES OF RUSSIA, Finland and Minnesota meet in
Wolf Lake. Thousands of Finns migrated to northern Minnesota in the
nineteenth century to flee Russian rule, the Czar's military draft, and a
declining standard of living in Finland. In 1703, Peter the Great chose
Finnish land belonging to Sweden as the site for his new capital, St.
Petersburg. Caught in the crossfire between Russia and Sweden, peaceful
Finland was eventually ceded to Russia in 1809. While Swedish rule over
Finland was benign, Russian domination was ruthless, especially with
the ascension of Nicholas II to the throne in 1894. Finns were drafted un-
willingly into the tsarist army and strict censorship was placed on artists
and intellectuals, including the young composer Jean Sibelius, who wrote

the great patriotic composition *Finlandia*. A few hardy souls found their
way to Menahga and New York Mills, and the hardiest continued on to
Wolf Lake to claim 160 acres of homestead land in Minnesota.

This proud Finnish community borders Wolf Lake, which measures
1,400 acres and has 11 miles of lakeshore. Early pioneers named the lake
and town for the large population of wolves in the area. Abundant farming, fishing, hunting, and logging attracted settlers to the area. With an
entirely Finnish population in 1881, the Wolf Lake community became
an organized township on February 14, 1896. In 1888 one of the earliest
settlers, John and Minnie Wirkkanen and their two sons, arrived in New
York Mills by rail, where they purchased a team of oxen, and traveled
thirty-five miles through brush and woods to Wolf Lake. The family

cleared the roadway by hand in six weeks, averaging five miles per week. More families followed the Wirkkanens, and other settlers, including Jacob Aho, just wanted to go so far "that they wouldn't be in anyone's way." Born in Alaharma, Finland, he arrived in 1894 with a 50-pound sack of flour, a gun, and a sharp ax, ready to claim the 70 acre plot of shoreland he purchased on Wolf Lake. The winding footpath along Wolf Lake that he followed to his claim is still there today. Jacob Aho eventually built a large home measuring sixty by forty feet, three stories high with twenty-three rooms to house his wife, seven sons, four daughters, three daughters-in-law, two adopted children, twelve grandchildren, and one hired man.

The first post office opened in 1898 at the William Isola farm and then moved to the village in 1947. Turn-of-the-century stores included the Wolf Lake Young People's Association Hall, a cooperative creamery formed in 1911, Kinnunen Store, J. Rajanen's Garage, two taverns, a bakery, Jampsa Blacksmithing, Kangas Implement, Wiitanen Well Drilling, Han's Barbershop and Watch Repair, and Dahlquist's Sawmill. The city waited to incorporate until May 12, 1949.

The Harvest Festival and the Wolf Lake Laestadian Church

Since 1983, Wolf Lake has hosted an August Harvest Festival beginning with the Miss and Little Miss Wolf Lake Pageant, the winners reigning over the weekend festivities. Following the coronation, a parade, pie social, arm wrestling contest, a horseshoe tournament, and a softball tournament keep the crowd moving. And if that isn't enough activity, join in the 5K Walk/Run before stopping at the Klondike Café for a free blood pressure check. After that, reward yourself with a great home-cooked meal at the annual Lions Club dinner at the Lions Hall.

The Wolf Lake Laestadian Church, formerly the Apostolic Lutheran Church, was built in 1898 to minister to the early settlers in the community. Their famous pastor, Johan Hjort, was the son-in-law of Lars Laestadius, a well known Lutheran minister who led a pietistic revival in the Scandinavian countries in the mid-nineteenth century. Laestadians flourished in rural areas where they led a spartan, family-centered life emphasizing faith and hard work.

Wolf Lake Today

Wolf Lake today is home to Ray's Repair, Farmer's Coop Sampo, Wolf Lake Body Repair, Wolf Lake Liquors, VFW Post 8165, the Lion's Club Community Hall, Klondike Café, and the former Kinnunen Store, now Jepson's Auto Body and Used Car lot. The Wolf Lake VFW Post 8165 boasts sixty-four members under Post Commander Clarence Paurus. The city council meets in the former freezer of Dick and Evelyn Pollock's Locker Plant, now the Wolf Lake Rescue building. Three churches, Spruce Grove Lutheran, Laestadian Lutheran, and Christ Lutheran, all remain vital forces in the community. All business and church services were conducted in Finnish until the '30s and both the Laestadian and Spruce Grove churches conduct occasional services in Finnish. The Minnesota Finnish-American Historical Society Chapter 29 meets monthly in Wolf Lake to preserve the Finnish heritage.

The Wolf Lake Wolf Pack baseball team has advanced to the Class C State Baseball Tournament more than any other smallest city in Minnesota. The team won runner-up honors in 2004. Baseball great Virgil Nordby was inducted into the Minnesota Amateur Baseball Hall of Fame in 1992.

A hand-hewn millstone by John Wirkkanen, the first township settler, stands proudly in the center of town in dedication to the first Finnish settlers.

Since 1983, Wolf Lake has hosted an August Harvest Festival beginning with the Miss and Little Miss Wolf Lake Pageant, the winners reigning over the weekend festivities. Following the coronation, there is a parade, a pie social, an arm wrestling contest, a horseshoe tournament, and a softball tournament. If that isn't enough, take part in the 5K Walk/Run.

Al Zoerb opened a creamery in 1923 and made "Red Clover" brand sweet cream butter. The creamery made 182,271 pounds of butter in 1928.

TOP: Bethlehem Lutheran Church

Wright

Wrong Days in Wright

ON THE THIRD WEEKEND IN JULY, the city celebrates "Wrong Days in Wright," an annual funfest since 1965. Following the coronation of the King and Queen (the kids who sell the most Wrong Days buttons), the Volunteer Fire Department holds a steak fry, and fireworks light up the city after dark. Saturday starts with a softball tournament where the ballplayers run the bases backwards and ends with a dance in the pavilion. By Sunday, the First Responders are reviving the crowd with a pancake feed, and the softball tournament continues for those who still have a sense of equilibrium. To quote former city clerk Lynne Black, "It's just general mayhem, and we all look forward to it." The citizens of this city have known how to survive and how to have a good time,

through all the changes of the last century.

Wright proudly bears the name of two men, both influential railroad employees, and both born on the East Coast. Surrounded by beautiful lakes on all sides and 400-year-old pines up to 250 feet tall, it is easy to understand how the area attracted the attention of George Burdick Wright, a land developer from Vermont. An employee of the Northern Pacific Railroad and the founder of Fergus Falls in 1871, he organized a railroad branch from Wadena to Fergus Falls and Breckenridge that same year. Earlier in 1870, the railway ran through Wright from Superior to Staples with Mr. Wright in charge of Wright's Station. The name also honors Charles Barstow Wright, director and president of the Northern Pacific during the Depression of 1873. Born and raised in Philadelphia, he was instrumental in developing the line between St. Paul and Brainerd in 1877.

By 1912, Wright had three sawmills, all busy logging the rich mixture of spruce, tamarack and pine trees surrounding the community. Typical of logging in that era, all the finest pine, some measuring up to six feet in diameter, were harvested, leaving only crooked trees and stumps. One clever pioneer businessman, Fred Groth, saw money in the cut-over forests and began harvesting the leftover timber for lumber, pulp, ties, lath, poles and posts. After opening a lumberyard in Wright, he expanded his business with a line of farm implements and created another lumberyard in Deer River, both successful today.

Along with logging, Wright reigned as one of the largest farm centers in the area. Potatoes, hay, horses and, later, dairy provided a solid living for small farmers. All the farms housed horses for pulling logs in the winter logging camps. When the farmers realized the potential for profit in dairy production, the Farmer's Cooperative Company formed to ship their dairy products east. After years of declining revenue resulting in bankruptcy, Ellen Peterson was hired as cooperative manager and helped the business to become solvent. After 50 years of her capable leadership, the Co-op remains a viable business today. Following the formation of the Red Clover Guernsey Breeding Association, Al Zoerb opened another creamery in 1923, and made "Red Clover" brand sweet cream butter, a step up from the sour cream butter everyone else made. The creamery made 182,271 pounds of butter in 1928, before the business sold to the Farmer's Cooperative two years later. Now the post office sits on the land where Mr. Zoerb once made his delicious butter.

The original 1908 brick school closed and was used as a hospital during the Influenza Epidemic of 1918. It remained closed after the epidemic ran its course. Named the Wright Lincoln School, the brick school was replaced with a new brick two-level school in 1940, and the old school was converted into a gym. The school consolidated with Cromwell in 1993, and the building is now owned by a private party. An original Art Deco marquee sign, *WRIGHT*, graces the entrance to the school.

A Great Place for a Picnic

Travelers along Highway 210 make a point of stopping at the Wright City Park to picnic under the log shelter and to use the playground and restroom facilities. Local residents enjoy the horseshoe court, the baseball diamonds, and the *Big Top Pavilion, Home of Wrong Days in Wright,* for dances and parties. The park also houses the Veteran's Memorial, a simple black marble slab anchored by a flagpole and lighting to honor their veterans. The Soo Line South Recreational Trail traverses the park on its way from Royalton, MN, to Superior, WI.

Wright Today

Wright maintains a healthy mix of business on Main Street and a beautiful park on Highway 210. Businesses in town include the post office, Kalli's Place, The Black Jack Grill, Steve's Auto Body, BJs Highway Express, the Groth Lumber Company, the Farmer's Cooperative and Feed Mill, a Senior Citizen's Center, and the Volunteer Fire Department. The city's admiration for their fire department is reflected in city clerk Lynne Black's comment, "They are the heart and soul of every fundraiser in this little city. Everyone has been touched by the guys in some way at some time, and when they need something, we all give to the max." Three churches call the citizens to worship: the Evangelical Free Church, Bethlehem Lutheran Church, and St. John's Lutheran Church, the oldest church in town, originating in 1906.

Located in the original brick building, the Farmers Co-op has anchored the community for over 80 years. The co-op sells everything from clothing to birdseed, and if they don't have it, you don't need it.

TOP: City view towards Deer River School

A huge part of the business district in Zemple disappeared when the veneer mill burned to the ground in June 1919.

Zemple

Where the Blacktop Ends

ZEMPLE HAS BEEN CALLED "Deer River's industrial suburb," much to the dismay of residents living in Zemple. "You can call us anything, even late for supper, but don't call us a suburb of Deer River," stated Bazil Mayo, a late resident of Zemple. In order to arrive at the quiet residential community, you drive through the south end of Deer River past the athletic field, until you reach the point where the blacktop ends.

During the early 1900s Zemple buzzed with activity. Millions of logs floated down the Mississippi River to White Oak Point, where the Rathburn, Hair & Ridgeway Co. box mill, the Bahr Bros. veneer mill, and a sawmill run by Itasca Lumber Company processed the logs. The Minneapolis & Rainy River Railway operated a roundhouse with twelve

engines, all hauling logs from multiple logging camps back to the mills in Zemple. On May 6, 1911, *The Itasca News* reported: "A village Wanted at the Deer River Mill. Supt. Wallace presented a petition asking for an election to make a village of that part of Otenagon Township lying south of the village of Deer River." The village incorporated May 29, 1911. One year later on March 16, 1912, the newspaper announced an election in which 24 votes were cast in this "milling suburb to the south of Deer River." R. T. Zempel, who owned a farm on the south edge of the village and most of the village land, was elected the first mayor and put his name on the burgeoning village. For reasons unknown, in 1926, the spelling was changed to Zemple. Harriet Zempel Crabtree writes, "As usual, the name Zempel is misspelled, even on a map of Minnesota. My dad, R. T. Zempel, was bookkeeper for the mills. We sometimes called the town 'Mill Town' since it was surrounded by mills. Sometimes we called the town 'Dog Town' because there were so many dogs there!"

Life revolved around the mills, the forest and the train. For several years the mills operated a general store for the employees, where they could purchase food, work clothing, tobacco and snuff. The hardworking sawmill workers and loggers were well fed in a boarding house in a beautiful wooded area, run by cook Jim Martindale. Harriet Zempel Crabtree remembers eating at the boarding house with its long tables and tin cups. Following lunch, a favorite trail took her across a "corduroy" road, with the logs laid side by side, crosswise, to prevent sinking into swamps. Another frequent walk led from Zemple to Deer River on a road made of sawdust from the mills. The comfortable "soft" walk filled your shoes with sawdust. Norma Newkirk Grife's father, Bill Newkirk, held the post of night watchman at the train roundhouse. She recalls riding with her father on the engines as he filled the cars with coal, and then backed the engine onto the turntable in the roundhouse.

Children attended the one-room Zemple School for their first three years. By fourth grade, they walked to Deer River for school, often walking home for lunch and back to Deer River to finish the school day. The Zemple School closed in 1928. A church opened, but no saloons, as Deer River had the night life covered. A huge part of the business district disappeared when the veneer mill burned to the ground in June 1919. According to Dorothy Mayo, "It was such terrific heat the lumber would go up into the sky. The whole village was so lit up the birds came out and started flying around."

By the late 1920s, the lumber industry had faded and boathouses began to line the shores of White Oak Lake.

A Site Replete with History

Listed on the National Register of Historic Places since 1972, the White Oak Point Site offers a look at the archaeological history of Minnesota. The point reaches through an extensive marsh, on high ground directly accessible from the lake and the Mississippi River beyond. In 1949 and 1954, University of Minnesota professor Lloyd A. Wilford excavated a large village site and two of six burial mounds on the shores of White Oak Lake. The pottery excavated in the village site, preserved in well-stratified layers which reflect the history of several different eras of occupation, dates back over 2,500 years. Archeologists believe the area had been used for thousands of years before that. These excavations and later studies gave archeologists valuable insight into the Woodland Indian culture of the Northern Headwaters area.

Henry Rowe Schoolcraft, Zebulon Pike, and other Mississippi explorers camped on or near the area. Schoolcraft reported that his Native American guides helped them, "to avoid numerous curves, which would have consumed much time in coursing around, and led the way through extensive fields of reeds and grass, assuming the character of semi-lakes."

Zemple Today

Zemple no longer has a commercial business district. A new sign, which welcomes you to *City of Zemple, Where the Blacktop Ends*, proudly proclaims the existence of a city that contributed much to the history and settlement of northeastern Minnesota. Now a purely residential neighborhood, only City Hall and the foundation of the Itasca Lumber Company mills at White Oak Lake remain of this once-flourishing logging community.

The White Oak Learning Center & Fur Post, located one mile north of Deer River on MN 6, sponsors the White Oak Rendezvous each August to commemorate the history of the White Oak Trading Post, which operated in the late eighteenth century. Dressed in period costumes, the volunteers and guests participate in activities geared to the times of the trading post era.

Men Who Died In War From Little Minnesota

Men and women from Little Minnesota have honorably served our country in the military, and the men listed below died in wars, from World War I to the present. Please forgive any omissions as most of the men registered under their counties, and not from their hometown.

ALDRICH
World War I: Private Harry Myrin, 360th Infantry 90th Division, died November 2, 1918, and is buried in Meuse-Argonne American Cemetery, France.

ARCO
World War I: Private Arthur J. Daly died of disease October 1, 1918, while stationed in France.

World War II: Private Glen Jorgensen died July 27, 1943, in the South Pacific, and is buried in Manila American Cemetery, Philippines.

BARRY
World War I: Private Daniel Connelly was reported killed in action overseas on November 5, 1918.

World War II: Staff Sergeant Gerald T. Reinart died May 6, 1945, and is buried in Manila American Cemetery in the Philippines.

BEJOU
World War II: U.S. Army Corporal (Tech. 5) Ben Santjer, Company C, 48th Engineer Combat Battalion, died defending his comrades during the assault on Mount Porcia, Italy, January 7, 1944. President Franklin D. Roosevelt awarded Corporal (Tech. 5) Santjer the Distinguished Service Cross posthumously.

BELTRAMI
World War I: Beltrami men died in war. Private Alva Leslie Law died of pneumonia October 5, 1918, at Camp Grant, Rockford Illinois, and is buried in Beltrami Fairview Cemetery.

World War II: Sigwald Anderson American Legion Post 626, is named in honor of Private First Class Sigwald M. Anderson, who died on March 28, 1945, in Luzon, Philippines, and is buried in Fort Snelling National Cemetery.

BENA
World War I: Wagoner Frank D. Michaud with the American Expeditionary Forces died on October 20, 1918, in France.

World War II: Machinist's Mate First Class Russell James Cummings died January 12, 1945, in Bermuda from an electrical accident, and is buried in Pine Grove Cemetery, Cass Lake, Minnesota.

The Vietnam War: Army Specialist (SP4) Dale Clarence Schummer, son of Clarence and Mildred Schummer, died January 17, 1967, in South Vietnam at age 21.

BORUP
World War I: Private John Peter Ambuehl died October 15, 1918, and is buried in Ada Cemetery, Ada, Minnesota.

Private George M. Benthagen was killed October 8, 1918, in France, and is buried in Jevnaker Cemetery in Borup, Minnesota.

World War II: Private Joseph R. Hogetvedt was killed in action September 17, 1944, and is buried in Winchester Lutheran Cemetery, Borup.

USNR Ensign Sigurd Harold Lindseth died January 19, 1945, in Guam, and is buried in Trysil-Bethesda Cemetery, Douglas County, Minnesota.

The Korean War: Marine Corps Major Marvin Leland Berg, a veteran of World War II, died November 30, 1950, during an air strike near Kudam-ni, North Korea. Pilot of an F4U-5N Corsair night fighter with the Marine Night Fighter Squadron 513, he developed engine trouble during the air strike and crashed near the Chosin Reservoir. Presumed dead on December 3, 1953, his name is inscribed on the Tablets of the Missing at the Honolulu Memorial, Hawaii.

BOY RIVER
World War I: American Legion William H. Robbins Post 458 is named for World War I casualty William H. Robbins, Wagoner for the 17th Field Artillery 2nd Division, who died January 23, 1920. He is buried in Fairview Cemetery, in Federal Dam, Minnesota.

World War II: Private Harold Snell survived the Bataan Death March April 1942, but died a prisoner of war at Camp O'Donnell in the Philippines May 22, 1942. On the day that he was officially declared dead, all business was suspended, and flags were flown half-mast in Boy River to honor his memory. He is buried at Zion Lutheran Island, Boy River.

The 1946 school annual was dedicated to two former students at Boy River High School: Private Otto W. Peterson who died fighting on November 8, 1944, and Aviation Machinist's Mate Third Class Bruce Christian Johnson who died on July 31, 1945.

BROOKSTON
World War II: American Legion Tester-Niemi Post 562 is named for Army Air Force Private Rodney Lee Tester and Private Mathews J. Niemi. Private Tester died on April 29, 1942, when his B-18A aircraft caught in a downdraft and crashed, while trying to clear the ridge of Sheratin Mountain, Kodiak Island, Alaska. Seven crew members were killed on the aerial photography mission, and amazingly, one crew member, Sergeant Orville Blake, survived the crash. Private Niemi died May 1, 1943, in the North African Campaign, and is buried in North Africa American Cemetery, Carthage, Tunisia. Another World War II casualty, Merchant Marine Oiler Wallace Dean Colson died on January 9, 1945, when his ship, the *Jonas Lie*, was torpedoed and sunk by U-Boat 1055 at the entrance to the Bristol Channel, United Kingdom. Two men were killed and sixty-seven survivors escaped by lifeboat.

CEDAR MILLS
World War I: Private James F. Standish was killed in action on July 20, 1918, in France, and is buried in Oise-Aisne American Cemetery, France. Staff Sergeant Walter O. Kurth died September 27, 1944. His parents received his pocket bible with a hole from the gunshot. Private First Class Arthur A. Hackbarth died December 15, 1944, and Corporal (Tech. 5) Milton O. Stoll died March 16, 1945. All men are buried in St. John's Lutheran Cemetery, Cedar Mills.

COMSTOCK
World War II: Fireman Third Class Ernest George Haarstad died November 12, 1942, when his transport ship was sunk off the coast of Africa by a German U-boat, and is memorialized in North Africa America Cemetery, Tunisia. Sergeant Kenneth Swanson died when his B-29 was shot down over Nagoya, Japan, on December 18,

1944, and he is memorialized on the Honolulu Memorial, Hawaii. Aviation Machinist's Mate Second Class Allen Duane Nelson was killed in action July 22, 1945, and is memorialized at Manila American Cemetery, Philippines

CORRELL
World War I: Private Fritz Arnold Hanson died September 28, 1918, in France.

DANVERS
World War II: Army 2nd Lieutenant Paul G. Bliven died July 15, 1944, in Normandy, France, near the Ay River. Army Private Vincent J. Dolan was killed in the Battle of the Bulge, Belgium, on January 1, 1945. He served in General George Patton's Third Army, the unit credited with securing Bastogne from the German army. In 1945 Private Daniel J. Hughes died while doing demolition work at Marquestein, Germany. All three men are buried at Church of the Visitation Cemetery, Danvers. 1st Lieutenant Donald J. Doyle, 422nd Night Fighter Squadron, died October 12, 1944, and is memorialized at Henri-Chapelle American Cemetery, Belgium, and Church of the Visitation Cemetery, Danvers.

The Vietnam War: Army Sergeant David Julien Barduson died in South Vietnam on March 24, 1968, and is honored on the Vietnam Veterans Memorial, Washington, D.C.

DELHI
World War I: In August, 1930, Mrs. August (Greta) Fredericksen left for Europe on a government-sponsored pilgrimage for mothers and widows who lost a son or husband overseas in World War I. Her son, Private August C. Fredericksen died September 26, 1918 and is buried in the Saint Mihiel American Cemetery in Thiaucort, France.

World War II: Lieutenant Clarence H. Housman, serving in the Army Air Corps, died in a training accident in Florida July 24, 1943. Army Lieutenant Victor H. Malmrose died of wounds in Europe December 26, 1944, and is buried in Fort Snelling National Cemetery. Marine Private John Gray Stevenson was killed in action in Okinawa April 14, 1945. AOM/3 Homer B. Hanson, serving in the Naval Air Corp, was killed in action in the Pacific on June 22, 1945, and is memorialized on the Tablets of the Missing, Manila American Cemetery, Philippines.

DENHAM
World War I: Private Hilmer E. Anderson died of influenza on October 2, 1918, in Hershey, England, and is buried in Magdalena Hill, Winchester, England. On June 5, 1920, Private Anderson was reburied at Swede Park Cemetery in Denham.

World War II: Staff Sergeant Ray S. Lound was killed in action July 2, 1944, and is buried in Florence American Cemetery, Toscana, Italy.

DONALDSON
World War I: Private George F. Eisenrich died October 8, 1918, from the Spanish Influenza in training camp at Fort Barren, Texas. He is buried in Greenwood Cemetery, Hallock, Minnesota.

World War II: Navy Ensign William Murray Jr. was declared MIA in the Pacific in 1944.

The Korean War: Airman 1st Class Orville A. Ryden died in a car accident on March 1, 1955, while training at Offutt Airbase during the Korean War, and is buried at Hillcrest Cemetery in Donaldson.

DORAN
World War I: Private Thomas Haroldson died August 9, 1918, and is buried in

Stiklestad Cemetery in Doran, Minnesota. Corp. Robert Michael Woytcke died October 1, 1918, and Private Emil Huagen died November 11, 1918. Both are buried in Meuse-Argonne American Cemetery, France. On October 14, 1918, Private Ole S. Karlgaard died of pneumonia while stationed overseas. Private Harry H. Hansen died of influenza on November 23, 1918, at Fort Bliss, Texas, and is buried in Riverside Cemetery, Campbell, Minnesota.

World War II: Staff Sergeant Henry Martin Hunkins died in 1945, and is buried in St. Mary's Cemetery in Breckenridge, Minnesota.

DOVRAY
World War I: Private Julius Johnson, 23rd Co. 161st Depot Brigade, died in 1918, and is buried in Our Savior's Cemetery, Dovray.

World War II: US Navy Radioman Second Class Halge Hojem Smestad, son of Halge Smestad Sr., died during the attack on Pearl Harbor, December 7, 1941. His name is etched on the *USS Arizona* Memorial, Honolulu, Hawaii. US Navy Shipfitter Third Class Aaron Luverne Johnson, son of John R. Johnson, died February 4, 1943, in the Battle of the Flores Sea in Indonesia. His ship, the *U.S.S. Houston CA-30*, came under intense air attack by Japanese aircraft, and he was one of fifty-seven men killed in battle.

DUNDEE
World War I: The Joseph Suding American Legion Post 386 and Auxiliary is named for Dundee barber Private Joseph Suding, who died November 1, 1918, in the Argonne Forest, France. Private Peter J. LaMaack died September 24, 1918, and is buried in Meuse-Argonne American Cemetery, France.

World War II: On April 8, 1944, Staff Sergeant Donald A. Krogman died in a plane crash in England, and is buried in the Dundee Cemetery.

The Korean War: Private Leo Kirchner was killed in action July 6, 1953, in North Korea.

EFFIE
World War I: American Legion Waldron-Flaat Post #182 honors Private John B. Waldron, who died of wounds October 21, 1918, in France, and Private First Class Thomas Flaat, who died October 8, 1918, and is buried at Meuse-Argonne American Cemetery, France. Private Harry Trafton died of pneumonia on November 3, 1918, at Camp Forest, Georgia.

World War II: Army Corporal (Tech. 5) Cecil R. Stevenson died October 12, 1942. USNR Fireman Second Class Robert Dean Kanne died March 12, 1944, in Guadalcanal, and USN Warren Grover Moore died in a plane crash on November 4, 1944. Both are buried in Bigfork Cemetery, Bigfork, Minnesota. Previously wounded at Pearl Harbor on December 7, 1941, Staff Sergeant Elwyn O. Rahier died December 7, 1945, while on board the Boeing B-17 *Chief Seattle* en route to Rabaul Harbour, New Guinea. No contact was ever made with the *Chief Seattle* and her ten man crew again. 2nd Lieutenant James Todd Knight died February 18, 1945, in Italy, and is buried in the Florence American Cemetery, Italy. 1st Sergeant Howard C. White, who died May 20, 1945, at the Battle of Okinawa, Japan, had mailed a letter to his wife, Grace, stating that "he helped put the flag up." He is buried in the Lakeview Cemetery, Bigfork, Minnesota.

The Vietnam War: On June 9, 1966, Major Theodore James Shorack Jr. died in a midair collision in North Vietnam.

EVAN

World War II: Private First Class Waldo L. Engholm died March 16, 1944, and is buried at Sicily-Rome American Cemetery in Italy.

Pvt. James Howard Anderson, died September, 14th, 1957, in an accident riding in the back of a transport truck with a group of soldiers in Italy. He is buried in Home Cemetery, Sleepy Eye, Minnesota.

The Vietnam War: Specialist Gary Lester Barnes died June 9, 1969, in Thura Thien-Hue Province, Vietnam.

FARWELL

World War I: OGMAR American Legion Post #268 was organized in 1919 by several World War I vets including Tom Thronson, who worked nights at the Depot. The name OGMAR stood for five men from Pope County killed in World War I: Edward Olmein, Magnus Grondahl, Carl Moe, Alfred Anderson and Arthur Rosenberg. During the fifties the post was moved to Kensington. Private Arthur C. Rosenberg was killed in action on September 28, 1918, and is buried in Meuse-Argonne American Cemetery, France. Sergeant Axel R. Molander died in an accident on July 20, 1918, and is buried in Oise-Aisne American Cemetery, France. Private Arthur A. Thompson died October 13, 1918, and is buried in Somme American Cemetery, France.

World War II: On October 13, 1944, Corporal (Tech. 5) Donald O. Bollum died fighting in France, and is interred at Epinal American Cemetery, France. USAAF Private Edward H. Dahl died with three other crew members October 21, 1945, and is buried in Fort Richardson National Cemetery, Alaska.

The Korean War: On November 13, 1950, Marine Corps Corporal John Franklin McDowell was killed in action in Korea.

FEDERAL DAM

World War II: Federal Dam soldier Seaman Second Class Almon L. Armbrust died December 18, 1944, in a typhoon, and is memorialized on Tablets of the Missing, Manila American Cemetery, Philippines.

FLORENCE

World War I: Army Private Martin Ofstad died October 6, 1918, and is buried in the Meuse-Argonne American Cemetery, Romagne, France.

The Korean War: Army Private First Class Richard Whalen, member of Company 71st Medium Tank Battalion, 1st Calvary Division, died August 6, 1950, in the Korean War, and is buried in Kumchon, Korea.

FORT RIPLEY

World War I: Corporal William H. Patton died in France on August 6, 1918, and is buried in Immaculate Conception Cemetery, Watertown Minnesota. Private John F. L. Larson died August 26, 1918, and is buried in Oise-American Cemetery, France. Private Matte Eisel died September 20, 1918, and Private Louis J. Gravell died September 29, 1918. Both are buried in Meuse-Argonne American Cemetery, France.

World War II: Navy Aviation Radioman First Class Malcolm James Gordon died October 26, 1945, and is memorialized on the Tablets of the Missing, Manila American Cemetery in the Philippines.

GOODRIDGE

World War I: Private Henry Svare died October 10, 1918, from influenza at Camp Grant, Illinois, and is buried in Rosendahl Cemetery, Goodridge. Both Private Carl G.

Vake, who died October 24, 1918, and Private Elmer Alvin Dahlen, who died November 8, 1918, were killed in action in France, and are buried in Ekelund Cemetery, Goodridge.

World War II: Sergeant Lloyd H. Iverson, 95th AAF Bomb GP, died July 12, 1944, and is buried in Goodridge Cemetery.

The Korean War: Private First Class Roy L. Sunsdahl died December 5, 1950, in Korea and is buried in Ekelund Cemetery. Corporal James Norman Sund was captured February 12, 1951, and died while a prisoner of war on April 4, 1951, in South Korea. Corporal Robert Edward Cullen died July 27, 1951, in Korea, and is interred in Poplar Grove Cemetery, Espelie, Minnesota.

The Vietnam War: Private First Class Frank Walter Asp was killed in action in South Vietnam on January 29, 1968, and is buried in Greenwood Cemetery, Thief River Falls, Minnesota.

GULLY

World War II: Corporal (Tech. 5) Palmer C. Ringstad, member of the tank division under General Patton, died March 5, 1945, at Trier, Germany, and Private Henry L. Kroll, 337 Infantry, 85 Division, died of wounds April 22, 1945. Both are buried in Lund Lutheran Cemetery, Gully.

HADLEY

World War II: US Marine Corps 1st Lieutenant Duane A. Dahlquist, son of Oscar and Edith Dahlquist, died August 19, 1944, on a flying mission in the Pacific. He had joined flying ace Major Joseph Foss as a member of the 4th Air Wing 22nd Squadron.

HALMA

World War I: Halma-Lake Bronson Olaf Locken American Legion Post #315, named after the first serviceman killed in action from the community, obtained their official charter in March 1927. Private Olaf Locken died October 3, 1918, while fighting in the Argonne Forest in France, and is memorialized on the Tablets of the Missing at Meuse-Argonne American Cemetery in France. Private Locken is one of the American boys memorialized in the movie *The Lost Battalion*, the story of 500 men surrounded by the enemy in the Argonne Forest during the closing weeks of World War I. Another local boy, Private Henry M. Spilde, died earlier that year on April 10, 1918, from scarlet fever at Camp Dodge, Iowa, and is buried in the Eidsvold Cemetery, Halma.

World War II: World War II claimed the life of Private Arthur I. Kolberg in Luzon, Philippines, on January 10, 1945. He is interred in Bethania Cemetery, Greenbush, Minnesota.

The Korean War: Private Phillip O. Peterson died in North Korea on December 2, 1950, and is memorialized on the Tablets of the Missing, Honolulu Memorial in Hawaii.

The Vietnam War: Twenty years later, Phillip's brother, Private First Class Marlin Trent Peterson, was killed in action in South Vietnam on February 11, 1970. His grave lies in Pine Hill Cemetery, Williams, Minnesota.

HAZEL RUN

World War I: During World War I Private John B. Johnson died from wounds on November 3, 1918, and is buried in Clarkfield Cemetery, Clarkfield, Minnesota. On November 30, 1918, Private Ole M. Anderson was killed in action, and is buried in Meuse-Argonne American Cemetery, France.

World War II: The old schoolhouse from District 82 is now home to the American Legion Anderson-Tongen Post No. 559 and Auxiliary. Chartered in 1946, the Post honors two local servicemen who died during World War II. 1st Lieutenant Leon Anderson died July 31, 1944, while serving in General Patton's Third Army during the invasion of France. Staff Sergeant Jerald I. Tongen, 185th Infantry, was killed in 1945 on Negros Island in the Philippines. Both are buried in Hazel Run Lutheran Cemetery. Jerald I. Tongens from Hazel Run died April 9, 1945.

HEIDELBERG
World War II: Seaman 1st Class Harry James Ambroz died March 24, 1943, and is buried in St. Scholastica Cemetery, Heidelberg.

HENRIETTE
World War II: Private Wilfred Strom, the local school janitor, died October 10, 1942, during World War II. Ensign USNR Orville Thorson died February 18, 1945, in a plane crash on the East Coast. Both are buried in the Henriette Cemetery.

HILLMAN
World War I: Private Delaney Stanley Giles, died November 15, 1918, and is buried at Riverview Cemetery, Elmore, Minnesota;

World War II: American Legion Wojciak-Talberg Post 602 is named in honor of Private John A. Wojciak, who died June 9, 1942, in basic training at Camp Wallace, Texas, and Corporal William J. Talberg, who died September 27, 1944, following a land mine accident in Italy. Private Wojciak in buried in Brennyville, Minnesota, and Corporal Talberg is interred in Florence American Cemetery, Italy. Private First Class Lawrence N. Mikel died November 20, 1943, memorialized on the Courts of the Missing, Honolulu Memorial, Hawaii; Corporal (Tech. 5) Alvin G. Probasco died February 29, 1944, burial Sicily-Rome American Cemetery; Private Andrew R. Brummer died January 7, 1945, at Battle of the Bulge, Belgium, burial Henry-Chapelle American Cemetery, Belgium;

The Vietnam War: Army Specialist (SP4) Alvin Edward Kurtz died December 11, 1966, in Vietnam, burial Holy Family Cemetery, Hillman; and Army Corporal Larry Lee Nieken died July 8, 1970, in South Vietnam, burial Lakeview Community Church Cemetery, Hillman.

HOLT
World War I: On Memorial Day, 1920, six elm trees were planted on the school grounds in memory of six local servicemen who died in World War I: Private Gustav Adolph Sollom died September 29, 1918, burial in St. Mihiel American Cemetery, France; Private Richard A. Swenson, died October 3, 1918, burial in Arlington National Cemetery; Private George Svendeson died Oct 7, 1918, burial in Meuse-Argonne American Cemetery, France; Private John Reierson died November 10, 1918, burial in Holt Cemetery; Private Alfred C. Olson died November 11, 1918, burial at Rock Island National Cemetery, Illinois; Private Peter Kolden died November 28, 1919, of tuberculosis at the Naval Hospital in Fort Lyon, Colorado. A bottle containing a record of each man's service, a United States flag, a picture of President Wilson, and other war documents were buried with each tree.

World War II: On February 25, 1945, Private First Class Rubin L. Ness was killed in action in the Philippines, and is buried in Fort Snelling National Cemetery.

The Korean War: Army Master Sergeant Norman Ellsworth Olson was captured by the enemy on January 1, 1951, while defending his position, and died a prisoner of war on June 23, 1951, in Korea. His name is inscribed on the Courts of the Missing at the Honolulu Memorial, Hawaii.

HUMBOLDT
World War I: Private Fred Jorgenson died from the Spanish Flu on October 9, 1918, at Camp Grant, Illinois, and is interred in the Humboldt-Clow Cemetery. Private First Class George R. Easter, Jr. died 15 days later from the flu on October 24, 1918, and is buried in St. Mihiel American Cemetery, France.

World War II: On July 28, 1943, World War II US Navy Ensign Anthony Merck Jr. died in a naval aviation crash in Jacksonville, Florida, and is buried in Greenwood Cemetery, Hallock, Minnesota.

IHLEN
World War II: Private First Class Truman A. Meling died of wounds on January 1, 1945, in the Battle of the Bulge, Belgium, and is buried in the Ihlen Cemetery.

The Korean War: Marine Corps Private First Class Thomas Henry Johnson was killed in action on September 17, 1951, while fighting in Korea. He is buried in City Cemetery, Jasper, Minnesota.

IRON JUNCTION
The Korean War: Iron Junction Private Rodney D. Thompson, 9th Infantry Regiment, 2 Infantry Division, was killed in action October 11, 1951, in North Korea.

JOHNSON
World War I: Private John J. Minners died overseas in 1918 and listed Johnson as his home town.

KERRICK
World War II: Army Private First Class William J. Clewitt (also spelled Cluett), died December 10, 1942, in the South Pacific. Sergeant Rolland "Red" Rowe died January 6, 1944, and is buried in Fort Snelling National Cemetery. Exactly one year later, on January 6, 1945, Flight Officer Donovan J. Hogan died in an airplane crash near Carson City Nevada, and is interred in St. Michael's Cemetery in Kerrick. Private First Class Jack E. Berger was killed in action August 5, 1944, in Ille-et-Vilaine, France, and is buried in Brittany American Cemetery, France. On March 6, 1945, Marine Corps Private First Class John W. Parker died of wounds while fighting in Iwo Jima.

The Korean War: On February 14, 1951, Private First Class George Daniel Klein was killed in action in South Korea, and is buried in Fort Snelling National Cemetery.

The Iraq War: Army Chief Warrant Officer Matthew Scott Lourey, son of Gene and Becky Lourey, died in a helicopter crash on May 27, 2005, in Buhriz, Iraq, while fighting in the Iraq War. He is buried in Arlington National Cemetery, Arlington, Virginia.

KINBRAE
World War I: World War I Army Private Emil Kopping died October 3, 1918, in Dartford, England.

World War II: Army 2nd Lieutenant Leighton Keith Zeiner lost his life during an air raid against Germany December 30, 1943. The aircraft navigator for the 510th Bomber Squadron, his plane was hit by enemy fire and crash landed. The plane was too close to the ground when his turn came to jump, and the parachute failed to open. Lieutenant Zeiner is buried in Cambridge American Cemetery, England. On January 30, 1945, Private Wilbur C. Wright died fighting in Battle of the Belgian Bulge.

A paratrooper with the 82nd Airborne Division, he first saw action in Holland and later in Belgium. Private Wright is buried in Worthington Cemetery, Worthington, Minnesota. USNR Sargeant First Class Herman A. Thelander was reported missing December 15, 1945, while training in the Bermuda Triangle. Called one of the most baffling mysteries of naval aviation, the total disappearance of five TBM Avenger Bombers on Flight 19 has never been solved.

LA SALLE
World War I: Private Joseph Bottem, son of Mr. and Mrs. T. Bottem, died of wounds October 5, 1918, in the Meuse-Argonne offensive in France. He is buried in Tincourt New British Cemetery, France.

LASTRUP
World War II: Sergeant Earl L. Gross was one of nine crew members killed when their B-24 bomber crashed near the Army Air Field in Walla Walla, Washington, on June 15, 1945. He is buried in St. John's Cemetery, Lastrup.

LENGBY
The Korean War: Army Private First Class, Bill Harold Berry was killed in action on May 8, 1951, in South Korea while attempting to escape from his tank that had been hit by enemy mortar fire. Private First Class Berry is buried in Fridhem Lutheran Cemetery, Lengby.

The Vietnam War: Private First Class Leo Vernon Beaulieu, born September 2, 1944, in Lengby, died May 16, 1966, in Vietnam. Though wounded twice defending his Marine battalion during a surprise ambush, he continued manning his machine gun until the third and fatal wound. Private First Class Beaulieu was awarded the Navy Cross for his extraordinary heroism.

LEONARD
World War I: Two Leonard men died in World War I: Private Emery Leranzo Frame died September 16, 1918, and is buried in St. Mihiel American Cemetery, France. Private Carl G. Johansson died October 2, 1918, and is buried in Meuse-Argonne American Cemetery, France.

LOUISBURG
World War I: Private Alfred Moen was reported killed in action in France, September 30, 1918. Private Alvin L. Mattson died October 14, 1918, in France, and is buried in Louisburg Cemetery, Louisburg. On November 4, 1918, Private Anton Kleven died of pneumonia at Camp Forest, Georgia. Private Stefanus Sorenson died November 5, 1918, and is buried in St. Mihiel American Cemetery, France.

World War II: On August 1, 1943, Staff Sergeant Arnold M. Holen was declared missing in action in France, and a memorial stone lies in Louisburg Cemetery.

MANCHESTER
World War I: Manchester Private Theodore R. Myran, husband of Mary Myran, and son of Ole and Torgan Myran, died of illness on December 4, 1918, in Machine Gun Training Camp at Camp Hancock, Georgia. He is interred in West Freeborn Cemetery, Manchester.

MCGRATH
World War II: Private Edwin Joel Iverson died on the island of Saipan in the central south pacific on July 9, 1944. His interrment is in Holden Cemetery, Aitkin. Both Private First Class Frank L. Leitner and Private First Class Robert E. Horne were killed in action on March 23, 1945. Private First Class Leitner is buried in Lorraine American Cemetery, France, and Private First Class Horne is interred in Fort Snelling National Cemetery.

MCKINLEY/ELCOR
World War I: Marine Sigurd Peter Moe died in the Battle of Belleau Wood near the Marne River, France on June 12, 1918. While fighting the German army, he and fellow Marine Willis Showmaker left a shelter trench during heavy bombardment to rescue a wounded comrade. Moe died in the attempt. For his bravery, the French government honored him the Croix de Guerre, the cross of war awarded to soldiers for acts of heroism during combat with enemy forces. Two other McKinley men died in World War I: Private Matt Smuk died of wounds on August 21, 1918, while fighting in the Belgium France campaign. Private Peter Stark died November 7, 1918, only four days before hostilities ceased, and is buried in France.

World War II: World War II took the lives of four classmates from nearby Elcor: Sergeant Rudolph J. Indihar died during the Normandy invasion June 22, 1944, and received the Army Silver Star for conspicuous gallantry in action. Private Leroy Thomas Veralrud, who served in General Patton's 3rd Army Corps, died September 2, 1944, in France, and is buried in St. Louis County. On February 17, 1944, USNR Lieutenant Lloyd Nicholas, a pilot with the Torpedo Bomber Flying Unit, disappeared on a night flying attack on Truk Lagoon, and is memorialized at Fort Snelling National Cemetery. Staff Sergeant Robert H. Brady died December 3, 1944, and is buried in Lorraine American Cemetery, France.

MINNEISKA
World War I: Henry Nickelson died November 1, 1918, during the flu epidemic, and is buried in Winona County.

The Vietnam War: Army Major Richard John Schell died July 5, 1977, in South Vietnam while in the service of his country. He remains missing in action.

MIZPAH
World War II: The Mizpah American Legion and Auxiliary Curb-Lusk Post #541 is named for two local men: Technical Sergeant Cyril E. Curb, a radioman and gunner for the 8th air force, died February 4, 1943, and is memorialized on the Tablets of the Missing at the Cambridge American Cemetery, England. Staff Sergeant Eugene Lusk, who was killed in action January 14, 1944, is interred at Fort Snelling National Cemetery. Navy Machine Mate Second Class Edward Howard Engholm died January 29, 1943, while a prisoner of war, and is buried in the Oakwood Cemetery, Mora, Minnesota. Navy Hospital Apprentice 1st Class Kenneth Roy Davis died June 4, 1945, in the Pacific, and is memorialized at the Honolulu Memorial, Hawaii. When the Legion chapter closed in 1963, members transferred to the Larry McKenzie Post # 3869 Northome, named for Army Sergeant Larry Dean McKenzie, who died fighting in South Vietnam on June 3, 1969.

MYRTLE
World War I: Private William F. Golnick died of pneumonia on October 6, 1918, in France, and is interred in Pilgrim's Rest Cemetery, Myrtle. On October 19, 1918, Seaman Second Class Frederick W. Winkelman died on the hospital ship the *USS Solace* of complications from pneumonia.

World War II: Private Fernly E. Bush died June 16, 1944, and is buried in Normandy American Cemetery, France.

NASHUA

The Vietnam War: Air Force Captain Milo George Maahs died in a plane crash on January 21, 1969, in Bien Hoa Province, South Vietnam. He is buried in Fort Snelling Cemetery.

NASSAU

World War I: Private Martin Kanthak died October 15, 1918, and is buried in Meuse-Argonne American Cemetery, France.

World War II: Sergeant Harold M. Meyer, only son of Ernest and Tillie Meyer, died February 4, 1944, in the first days of the Battle of Monte Cassino (the Battle for Rome) in Italy, and is buried in Fort Snelling National Cemetery. Navy Seaman Second Class Harold Donald Kaufman was declared missing in action on December 18, 1944, and is memorialized on Tablets of the Missing, Manila American Cemetery, Philippines. Sergeant Clifford J. Thompson, 777th Tank Battalion, died April 16, 1945, in Germany, and is interred in Netherlands American Cemetery, Netherlands.

World War II: Specialist 5 Frank M. Kaiser died in a helicopter accident in Vietnam on February 6, 1968, and is buried in St. James Cemetery, Nassau.

NIELSVILLE

World War: I Private Gilbert John Kittleson, brother of Henry Kittleson, died of pneumonia at Jefferson Barracks in Lemay, Missouri, on May 4, 1918, and is buried in Becker County.

The Vietnam War: Marine Corporal Alan Morris Hanson, son of Alfred and Betty Hanson, was wounded near Quang Tri, Vietnam and died July 2, 1967. He is buried in the St. Petri Cemetery, Nielsville.

NIMROD

World War II: After flying 25 missions, 1st Lieutenant James J. Graba was killed in action on August 26, 1944, and is buried in Cambridge American Cemetery, England. Private Wallace A. Skaar died January 9, 1945, in Arden, Belgium, and is buried in Bethlehem Cemetery, Pine River, Minnesota. Private Clarence R. Lehner died in France on March 7, 1945, and is buried at Fort Snelling National Cemetery.

NORCROSS

World War I: Private Oscar Hillestad, Private Arthur F. Pelo, and Private Albert H. Felix died in World War I.

World War II: Navy Fireman 1st Class Warren Irvin Hakenson, and Seaman 1st Class Lloyd Otto Lundgren were both killed in action December 18, 1944, and Fireman 1st Class Victor Nathaniel Borgeson died August 10, 1945. All three are buried in Manila American Cemetery, Philippines.

ODESSA

World War I: Private August F. Ehlert died May 16, 1918, at Camp Custer, Michigan, and is buried in Odessa Trinity Lutheran Cemetery.

PERLEY

World War I: Private Helmer O. Hovland was killed by a sniper on September 14, 1918, and is buried in St. Mihiel American Cemetery, France. Private Helmer Ellenson died September 30, 1918, and is buried in Meuse-Argonne Cemetery, France. Both Private Alfred Hoff and Private Oscar Clay Hovland succumbed to influenza at Camp Custer, Michigan: Private Hoff died October 10, 1918, and Private Hovland died November 3, 1918.

World War II: Petty Office Third Class John Marvin Emery died December 7, 1941, at Pearl Harbor, and is listed on Tablets of the Missing, Hawaii. Private First Class Roy M. Lee was killed in action November 17, 1944, overseas. Private First Class Stanton J. Shefveland died of wounds in Moffin, New Guinea, July 5, 1944. First Lieutenant Herman J. Sundstad, who fought with Merrill's Marauders in the Northern Burma Campaign, died June 5, 1944, and is buried in Manila American Cemetery, Philippines. Private First Class Carl Robert Emery died while fighting in the English Channel during the invasion of France on June 7, 1944. Staff Sergeant Gerard Burton Petersen died August 8, 1944, in a tank explosion, and is buried in Brittany American Cemetery, France. Sergeant Vernon J. Hoff, commander 737th bank battalion, died August 10, 1944, and is buried at Brittany American Cemetery, France. 2nd Lieutenant Donald J. Swenson, navigator on a B-24 Liberator, died February 7, 1945, after his ship was struck by an anti-aircraft shell in Italy. Private First Class William W. Kroshus died February 12, 1949, from a stab wound inflicted by an unknown assailant in Yon Village, Guam.

REGAL

World War II: Seaman 1st Class Othmar Peter Braun, son of John and Susan Braun of Regal, died when his ship, the *U.S.S. Luce*, was sunk by a Japanese kamikaze airplane near Okinawa on May 4, 1945. His brother, Virgil, now a priest, still remembers the car coming up the driveway to the farm to deliver the telegram. Two of Othmar's brothers also served in the military during World War II: Walter in the Army in Europe, including the Normandy invasion and the Battle of the Bulge, and Al, who served stateside in Missouri. Othmar's memory lives on at the Othmar Braun American Legion Post #612 in Lake Henry, Minnesota.

REVERE

World War I: The Francis Harnack Post #582 is named for Francis Harnack, who died October 8, 1918, at Camp Grant, Illinois, a casualty of the Spanish Influenza epidemic. Private Nate Hollingsworth died in World War I, and listed Revere as his hometown.

World War II: Private First Class Herman Hoffrogge, who served in World War II with the U.S. Army's 137th Infantry Regiment, 35th Infantry Division, died in Normandy, France on July 14, 1944. Private First Class Hoffrogge is buried in Normandy American Cemetery, France. Sergeant Leroy E. Johnson died August 29, 1944, over the Czech Republic. The B-17G on which he served as waist gunner was one of nine bombers shot down when German fighters attacked his 20th Squadron and two other bombers over the White Carpathian mountains. Forty were killed on that day, and of his crew only the navigator survived. Sergeant Johnson is buried in a mass grave with six others of the 20th at Jefferson Barracks National Cemetery, St. Louis, Missouri.

RICHVILLE

World War I: Both Private Clarence Lamphere, who died October 4, 1918, and Private Grover Cyles Aldrich, who died October 8, 1918, were killed in France, and are buried in the Richville Cemetery. Corporal (Tech. 5) Edward S. Stoering died September 18, 1944, and is memorialized on the Tablets of the Missing, Hawaii. Corporal Glen A. Bixby, 5th Marine Division, died February 26, 1945, on Iwo Jima, and is buried in Fort Snelling National Cemetery.

The Korean War: Private First Class Walter Lee Ellis died May 8, 1951, in Korea.

The Vietnam War: On December 29, 1966, Private First Class Richard Ned Lillis died in Vietnam.

SARGEANT

World War I: Sergeant Edwin Oscar Estby died on October 1, 1918, at Camp Custer, Michigan from the Spanish flu. On October 2, 1918, Private Adrian Isaac Lee died of pneumonia at a base hospital in France.

World War II: Private Verlyn D. Hegna was killed in action on July 16, 1944. All three men are buried in Evanger Lutheran Church Cemetery in Sargeant.

SEAFORTH

World War I: In 1925 the American Legion Ralph Lamb Post 275 purchased a 15-foot-tall memorial monument, a replica of the Washington Monument in Washington, D.C., to commemorate local servicemen. Forty veterans from Seaforth served in World War I, including three who gave their lives: Private First Class Ralph F. Lamb died August 14, 1918, and Marine Private Francis B. Goudy died September 24, 1918. Both were killed fighting in the trenches in France and are buried in Oise-Aisne American Cemetery, France. Seaman Second Class Edward Richard Katzenberger drowned when the liberty boat returning from Key West, Florida, to his ship capsized on September 29, 1918. He is memorialized in Key West Cemetery, Key West, Florida.

World War II: Three Seaforth soldiers were killed in action in World War II: Army Air Corp Staff Sergeant Gordon R. Maxa died September 25, 1944, in Germany, and is buried in Fort Snelling National Cemetery. Staff Sergeant Ernest R. King died November 10, 1944, in the Philippines, and Lieutenant Robert L. Goudy, 135th Infantry, died May 24, 1944, in Italy.

The Korean War: Corporal Alfred J. Bernardy died November 29, 1950, in Korea, and is memorialized on the Tablets of the Missing, Honolulu Memorial in Hawaii. The monument is next to the legion building.

SEDAN

World War I: Private Ole C. Peterson and Private Harry O. Vestrud died in World War I.

World War II: Seaman Apprentice Omar Julian Kolstad died August 10, 1943, and is listed on the Tablets of the Missing at the Manila American Cemetery, Philippines. Private First Class Kenneth V. Nelson died April 27, 1945 and is buried in Manila American Cemetery, Philippines

The Korean War: Private First Class Herbert L. Erickson died December 6, 1950, near Hagaru, North Korea. He is buried in Fort Snelling National Cemetery.

SOLWAY

World War I: Three men from Solway died in World War I. Private William Henry Heath died in England on October 4, 1918, and is buried in Jones Township Cemetery, Beltrami County, Minnesota. On November 1, 1918, Private Harold Anderson died in France, and is buried at the Meuse-Argonne American Cemetery in Romagne, France. Private Arthur C. Thoren died November 12, 1918, in France, and is buried at Arlington National Cemetery in Arlington, Virginia.

The Vietnam War: The Vietnam War took the life of Army Sergeant Lloyd Loren Willard in South Vietnam on May, 25, 1968.

SPRING HILL

World War I: Private George H. Stalboerger, son of Mr. and Mrs. Carl Stalboerger, died in action in France on September 3, 1918, at age 23. He is buried in St. Michael's Cemetery.

SQUAW LAKE

World War II: USAF 1st Lieutenant Einar H. Suomi, missing in action since May 1, 1943, was last sighted in his aircraft south of Belle Isle, off the coast of central France. He is memorialized at Cambridge American Cemetery, England. Navy seaman Eino August Miettinen died November 4, 1943. Army Staff Sergeant Harold V. Terho, a flying gunner, flew sixteen missions before he was shot down over Cheiti, Italy on December 2, 1943. Private Arnold Wilsing, Coast Artillery Corps, died in Normandy on June 7, 1944, the day after D-Day, and is buried in Fort Snelling. Private First Class Larry A. McNew, army paratrooper, died December 16, 1944, during the Battle of Leyte and is memorialized in Manila American Cemetery, Philippines. Staff Sergeant Emmett T. Loucks died of wounds February 4, 1945, at the Battle of the Bulge, and is buried in Luxembourg American Cemetery. Seaman Second Class Morris John Olson died February 28, 1945, and is memorialized in Cambridge American Cemetery, England. Private Carl Richard Horton was killed in action in Germany and is buried stateside.

ST. ROSA

World War II: Two sons of Mr. and Mrs. Lambert Bruns died during World War II in the service of their country. Private Alfred P. Bruns died on October 24, 1944, from wounds during action in the Italian campaign, and is buried in Florence American Cemetery, Italy. Two months later, Corporal Norbert W. Bruns died in action in Luxembourg December 26, 1944. He is buried in the Luxembourg American Cemetery.

The Iraq War: Staff Sergeant Brian R. Hellerman, 82nd Airborne Division, died in Iraq on August 6, 2003, when an Iraqi vehicle opened fire on his unit.

ST. VINCENT

World War II: Two brothers from St. Vincent died in World War II: Private Jerome Gooselaw was killed in action July 27, 1943, on New Georgia Island, and Private Arthur Gooselaw, died November 15, 1944, in Metz, Germany. Their graves lie side by side in St. Vincent Cemetery.

STRANDQUIST

World War I: Chartered June 1, 1920, Sam R. Hougard American Legion Post #466 is named in honor of Private Sam R. Hougard, age 19, who died October 10, 1918, and is buried in American Cemetery Fleury sur Aire in France. Fellow World War I soldier Roy Talvid Quarnstrom died October 1, 1918, and is interred in Salem Cemetery, Stephen, Minnesota.

World War II: Both Private Ellsworth Onger and Private First Class Walter T. Kostrzewski died June 6, 1944, and are buried in Normandy American Cemetery, France. Private Herman I. Holmstrom, who died July 12, 1944, and Sergeant Elmer Kittelson, who died March 25, 1945, were both killed in France and are buried in Mamreland Cemetery, Strandquist. Staff Sergeant Gordon O. Nelson died June 22, 1945, and is listed on the Tablets of the Missing, Honolulu Memorial, Hawaii. Captured as a prisoner of war April ,1942, Corporal Ferdinand V. Kuznia, survived the Bataan Death March to Cabanatuan Prison in the Philippines. On October 24, 1944, en route from Formosa to the Japanese mainland aboard the ship *Arisan Maru*, he and 1,800 other POWs were killed when a U.S. Navy submarine torpedoed the ship.

In 1943 Hazel E. Thompson Anderson made Minnesota history by enlisting as the first woman in the Army Air Corps during World War II. She commented, "I had to eat four bananas and drink so many glasses of water to bring my weight up."

The Vietnam War: Despite death threats from fellow soldiers, Strandquist son Private

First Class Robert M. Storeby reported the rape and murder of a young Vietnamese woman on November 17, 1966, by four men in his platoon. His persistence in reporting the crime to higher authorities resulted in the conviction of four men to prison terms from life to four years. This story is the basis for the motion picture *Casualties of War*, starring Michael J. Fox as Private First Class Storeby.

STRATHCONA

World War I: Army Private Stephen Gust died September 19, 1918, and is buried in Gust National Cemetery near Strathcona. Private Carl C. Johnson died November 6, 1918, at Camp Forrest, Georgia, and Private Olof Julius Oberg died October 6, 1918. Both are buried in Greenwood Cemetery, Strathcona.

World War II: Missing in action on July 12, 1944, Technical Sergeant Harold E. Winjum was officially declared dead July 13, 1945. He is memorialized in Sicily-Rome American Cemetery, Italy. Army Private First Class

The Vietnam War: Sheldon Lee Gulseth died in South Vietnam on March 1, 1971, and is buried in Klondike Cemetery, Roseau County, Minnesota. Army Spc.4 Ervind Strandberg died in South Vietnam on January 3, 1967, and is buried in Greenwood Cemetery, Strathcona.

SUNBURG

World War I: Private Christian Evenson died October 5, 1918, of influenza at Camp MacArthur, Waco, Texas.

World War II: During World War II, Private First Class George Alton Boe died on January 8, 1945, in France, and is buried in Epinal American Cemetery, France. On March 25, 1945, Staff Sergeant Vernon R. Peterson was killed in action, and is buried in West Norway Lake Lutheran Cemetery, Sunburg.

TAMARACK

World War II: Private First Class August Oja was killed in action June 15, 1944. His name is etched on the eight courts of the missing, Honolulu Memorial, Hawaii. USMCR Private Robert G. Anderson died January 15, 1943, and is memorialized on the Honolulu Memorial, Hawaii.

TAOPI

World War I: Army Private George Arnold Johnson died of wounds at base hospital #34 on August 26, 1918, and is interred at Oise-Aisne American Cemetery, France. Private Alfred Knudson died November 5, 1918, of disease at Camp Forest, Georgia.

World War II: World War 2 took the life of U.S. Army Private Howard V. Hanson, a Taopi businessman, who died January 22, 1945. He is buried in the Luxembourg American Cemetery in Luxembourg. He left behind his wife and two young children.

TENNEY

World War I: Private Frank R. Weisser died September 19, 1918, and is buried in St. Mihiel American Cemetery, France. Private Louis F. T. Kath died November 4, 1918, and is buried in Meuse-Argonne American Cemetery, France.

TINTAH

World War I: Tintah World War I casualties include Private Nels L. Anderson, who died September 26, 1918, and is buried in Meuse-Argonne American Cemetery, France, and Private James F. Keane, who died October 6, 1918, and is buried in St. Gall's Cemetery, Tintah.

World War II: American Legion Post J.F.B. Post 610 is named in honor of three Tintah men who died in World War II: MM2 Clayton Ordin Johnson died November 11, 1943, and is memorialized on the Tablets of the Missing, Manila American Cemetery, Philippines. PhM3 Robert L. Forsberg died June 16, 1944, and is memorialized on the Honolulu Memorial in Hawaii. On January 21, 1945, Private First Class Sylvester "Jess" M. Beckman was killed in action, and is memorialized in Manila American Cemetery.

TRAIL

World War I: Private Paul Myhre died September 29, 1918, after thirty days in the front line trenches in Argonne, France; Private Halvor Bjugson died in Europe October 24, 1918, and is buried in the Valley Lutheran Cemetery in Trail; Private Ole Tvedten died September 14, 1918, and is listed on Tablets of the Missing, St. Mihiel American Cemetery, France.

World War II: Army Captain Oscar T. Hanson died November 30, 1944, and Private Hilbert G. Haugan died January 1, 1945. Both are buried at Fort Snelling National Cemetery. Private First Class Archie L. Olson died February 12, 1945, and is buried in Manila American Cemetery, Philippines.

The Korean War: Corporal Alvin C. Burman died April 25, 1951, in Korea and is buried in New Sweden Cemetery, Polk County.

TURTLE RIVER

World War I: Private William A. Hunt died October 11, 1918, in France, and is buried in Glenwood Cemetery, Gelenwood, Iowa.

World War II: Seaman Second Class Earl Richard Burger was killed October 23, 1944, in the South Pacific during the Battle of Leyte Gulf, Philippines. Initially buried in the Philippines, he was brought home to rest in Greenwood Cemetery, Bemidji.

URBANK

World War I: Private John Peter Gappa died of influenza in France on October 19, 1918, and was reburied at Sacred Heart Cemetery November 15, 1920.

World War II: Private Frank Michael Bettin died May 29, 1943, in the Aleutian Islands, Alaska, and is buried in Sacred Heart Cemetery, Urbank.

VIKING

World War I: Private David A. Gustafson died October 2, 1918, and is buried in Meuse-Argonne American Cemetery, France. Army Mechanic Edward Rud died December 9, 1918, and is buried in St. Mihiel American Cemetery, France. Corporal Peter Nygren died February 10, 1919, and is buried in Oise-Aisne American Cemetery, France. On April 2, 1919, Private Elmer Lindquist died in training camp in Germany.

World War II: Private Bertil Q. Gustafson died January 3, 1945, in Belgium, and Private First Class Glenn A. Ranum died January 27, 1945, during the invasion of Iwo Jima, Luzon, Philippines. Both are buried in Fort Snelling Cemetery, Minnesota.

The Vietnam War: Spc.4 Kenneth Russell Dau died December 15, 1967, in Vietnam, and is buried in Viking Cemetery, Viking.

VINING

World War II: Tec5 Orval Henry Christianson died August 1, 1944, and is buried in Vining Lutheran Cemetery.

The Korean War: U.S. Marine Corps Sergeant George Albert Wark, Jr. died February 18, 1953, serving his country in the Korean War. He is buried in Inman Cemetery, Henning, Minnesota.

WALTERS

World War I: Frank J. Kalis, Battery D, 305th Field Artillery, son of Mr. and Mrs. John Kalis, died overseas from pneumonia on October 21, 1918. Private Henry F. Meyer died October 17, 1918, and is buried in Arlington National Cemetery.

World War II: Corporal Welver C. Vaughan died November 20, 1943, in the Battle of Tarawa, a series of coral islets 2,500 miles southwest of Hawaii. He is memorialized on the Tablets of the Missing in the Honolulu Memorial, Hawaii.

WANDA

World War I: Private Fred Gadde died of influenza at Camp Grant, Illinois, on October 3, 1918, and is buried in the German Lutheran Cemetery in Wanda.

World War II: On December 24, 1944, Private Helmer M. Eichten died during the attack on Climback, France. He is buried in Lorraine American Cemetery, France. Private First Class Lawrence A. Storch was killed in action on April 13, 1945, in Germany, and is buried in Netherlands American Cemetery, Margraten, Netherlands. Private First Class Darvin F. Lange died of wounds on May 21, 1945, in Luzon, Philippines. Army Technical Sergeant Jerome L. Gorres died in Simmern, Germany, on June 13, 1945. Staff Sergeant John M. Zitzmann died on January 13, 1943, in Japan. He left behind his wife, Jean, and seven children.

The Vietnam War: Spc. 4 Gene M. Kosel died in Vietnam on January 20, 1968. On January 3, 1970, Sergeant Ronald A. Jenniges died at Long Bien Hospital, three days after he had been wounded by a mine north of Saigon. Age 20, he had only 25 days left of Vietnam duty.

WEST UNION

World War I: Private Henry H. Kraemer died August 11, 1918, and his tombstone is inscribed, "Auf Dem Schlachtfelde in Frankreich," which translated means: On the battlefield in France.

The Korean War: On October 6, 1951, Private First Class Gordon A. Dietrich was killed in action in Korea.

The Vietnam War: Specialist 4th Class Robert Frank Marthaler died in Vietnam on May 22, 1970, and CW2 Anthony Joseph Mensen died in Vietnam on October 22, 1971. All three are buried in St. Alexius Cemetery, West Union.

WESTPORT

World War I: Westport Sergeant Albert C. Welch lost his life in World War I.

World War II: RAF pilot William D. Wendt died June 7, 1944, at the age of 28 in France. An American citizen who participated in the British air training plan, Wendt held the rank of flying officer, and served as a pilot in the No. 19 Fighter Command Squadron of the Royal Canadian Air Force. He is buried at Eturqueraye Churchyard Burial Grounds, Eturqueraye, France.

WHALAN

World War I: Private John Iverson was killed in action on November 1, 1918, and is buried in Flanders Field American Cemetery, Belgium.

World War II: Marine 2d Lieutenant Donald V. Rose died September 13, 1942, at Guadalcanal, Philippines. He is interred at Fort Snelling Cemetery.

The Vietnam War: Army Private First Class Kerry Ray Gossman died October 15, 1970, in South Vietnam at age 18.

WILDER

World War I: Private Andrew Nelson died on December 1, 1918, of pneumonia at Camp Grant, Illinois.

World War II: Two men from Wilder were killed in action during World War II: Private LaVerne W. Nelson died August 9, 1944, in France, and Technical Sergeant Myril A. Lundgren died February 25, 1945, in Germany. Sergeant Lundgren is buried in Clear Lake Swedish Lutheran Cemetery, Sibley County, Minnesota.

WOLF LAKE

World War II: Private First Class Herman W. Baumgart was killed in action in North Africa on April 5, 1943. He is buried in Spruce Grove Union Cemetery, Menahga, Minnesota. Staff Sergeant Robert L. Harju was killed in action March 3, 1944, and is buried in Sicily-Rome American Cemetery, Italy.

The Korean War: Private First Class Donald J. Mickelson died January 11, 1955, in Korea, and is buried in Bethany Lutheran Cemetery, Wolf Lake.

WRIGHT

World War II: US Merchant Marine Peter Anthony Chernich died December 2, 1943, while serving on the merchant ship *Samuel J. Tilden*, a liberty war ship built for World War II. The surprise air attack by German bombers on Allied forces in Bari, Italy, lasted just over one hour and was named "Little Pearl Harbor," due to heavy casualties. 105 German Junkers destroyed 17 ships, killing 1,000 military personnel and 1,000 civilians.

The Korean War: Three Wright men were killed in action in the Korean War: Army Private Walter J. Rassat died August 19, 1951, in North Korea, and is interred in St. Timothy Cemetery, Maple Lake, Minnesota. Within three months, Army Private Aloysius Witschen died in Korea on September 3, 1951, and Private First Class Henry J. Mattson died on November 25, 1951. Both men were members of the 17th Infantry Regiment, 7th Infantry Division.

Sources

ALDRICH

John Lindblom Diary (The History of Early Aldrich, Minnesota). Wadena Historical Society Collections, Wadena, MN.

Minnesota Place Names Online. "Aldrich," http://mnplaces.mnhs.org/upham/index.cfm (accessed 3/23/11).

Pratt, Sandi, interview with author, March 18, 2011, in Wadena, MN.

Verndale Historical Society. *Pages from History: Verndale, Minnesota 1883-1983.* Wadena: WATCO Publishers, 1983.

Waldahl, Lyle, phone interview with author, March 28, 2011.

ARCO

Arco, Minnesota 1927–2002. Bethany Lutheran Church. Red Wing, MN: Look Media Productions, 2002. Video.

Henriksen, Marie, interview by author, October 14, 2010, in Arco, MN.

Lincoln County Centennial History Committee. *Lincoln County Minnesota 1873–1973*. Lake Benton: Journal Printing Company, 1973.

Remick, Denise, and Russell Ringsak. *Minnesota's Curiosities*. Guilford: Globe Pequot Press, 2002.

BARRY

Gary, Nelia, phone interview by author, March 22, 2011.

Guenther, Frank, phone interview by author, March 22, 2001.

Shelsta, Norman. "Musings from the Museum." *The Northern Star*, 2008.

Temple, Nathan, phone interview, May 2, 2011.

Wulff, Lydia Sorensen. *The History of Big Stone County*. Ortonville: L.A. Kaercher, 1959.

BEJOU

Bejou Diamond Jubilee Committee. *History of the Bejou Area; 1905–1980*. Mahnomen: Mahnomen Pioneer, 1980.

Bejou Fourth of July Centennial Committee. *Bejou Centennial; 1905–2005*. Mahnomen: Mahnomen Pioneer, 2005.

Bendickson, Albertha, phone interview, May 2, 2011.

Kramer, Joanie, phone interview by author, May 6, 2011.

Lewis, Larry. "Lecture 83: The Implementation of Allotment Policy, 1887–1934," http://daphne.palomar.edu/llewis/AIS102/102%20Lectures/M4/Lec83.htm (accessed May 04, 2011).

Mahnomen Pioneer, "Stepping Back into Bejou's History during Cemetery Walk 2010." September 23, 2010.

Minnesota Senate. "American Indian Communities in Minnesota—White Earth Band," http://www.senate.leg.state.mn.us/departments/scr/report/bands/whiteearth.HTM (accessed July 26, 2008)

Swiers, Elaine, telephone interview by author, January 31, 2010.

White Earth Land Recovery Project & Native Harvest, http://www.welrp.org (accessed May 4, 2011).

BELTRAMI

Beltrami, Minnesota Centennial: July 2 and 3, 1983 (Beltrami: Pamphlet, 1983).

Boyer, Jerome Lawrence. *Growing up in Beltrami*. Minnesota: J.L. Boyer, 1983.

"Joseph H. Ball," *Wikipedia, the Free Encyclopedia*, http://en.wikipedia.org/wiki/Joseph_H._Ball (accessed 12/19/2010)

Wentsel, Claude Eugene. *Polk County, Minnesota, in the World War*. Ada: C.E. Wentsel, 1922.

BENA

Buck, Anita. *Behind Barbed Wire: German Prisoner of War Camps in Minnesota*. St. Cloud: North Star Press, 1998.

Geving, Renee, and Cecelia McKeig. *Centennial History of Bena*. Brainerd: Bang Publishing, 2007.

"Guide to Bena, Minnesota," http://www.lakesnwoods.com/Bena.htm#Locater (accessed September 23, 2010).

Simmons, Dean B. *Sword into Ploughshares: Minnesota's POW Camps during World War II*. St. Paul: Cathedral Hill Books, 2000.

U.S. Department of the Interior, National Park Service. The National Register of Historic Places, "Bena," http://nrhp.focus.nps.gov/natregsearchresult.do?fullresult=true&recordid=0 (accessed 5/2/11).

Wooley, Matthew, interview with author, March 2, 2011, in Bena, MN.

BORUP

Borup Centennial Committee. *Our Heritage: A History of the Borup Area*. Ulen: Ulen Union, 1988.

Kolness, John. *The Last One Hundred Years in Norman County, Minnesota, 1900–2000: a Century of Change*. Hendrum: Heritage Publications, 2000.

Myers, Carol, phone interview with author, May 1, 2011.

Norman County Historical Society. *In the Heart of the Red River Valley: History of the People of Norman County, Minnesota*. Dallas: Taylor Publishing Co., 1976.

Owen, Al and Jen, interview by author, April 27, 2011, in Borup, MN.

BOY RIVER

Fogle, Mark, interview by author, September 15, 2007, in Boy River, MN.

McKeig, Cecelia. *Battle of Sugar Point October 5, 1898*. Federal Dam: C. McKeig, 1999.

McKeig, Cecelia. *History of Boy River 1889-1998: All School Reunion Edition*. Federal Dam: C. McKeig, 1999.

McKeig, Cecelia, phone interview by author, October 7, 2007.

Proviso East High School Bataan Commemorative Research Project, "Private Harold A. Snell," http://www.proviso.k12.il.us/bataan%20web/Snell_H.htm (accessed April 28, 2010).

Russell, Carol. *In Our Own Backyard: A Look at Beltrami, Cass, and Itasca Counties at the Turn of the Century*. Bemidji: North Central Minnesota Historical Center, 1979.

BROOKSTON

Carroll, Francis M., and Franklin R. Raiter. *The Fires of Autumn: The Cloquet-Moose Lake Disaster of 1918*. St. Paul: Minnesota Historical Society Press, 1990.

Eklund, Nels, "Narrative family history of Nels Eklund" (pamphlet), 1969.

Melin, Douglas and Betty, phone interview with author, February 26, 2011.

CEDAR MILLS

Flom, Sam (Mayor), phone interview by author, March 27, 2011.

French, Verlyce, email to author, May 12, 2011.

Kurth, Linda, email to author, April 14, 2011.

Lamson, Frank. *Condensed History of Meeker County*. Litchfield: Brown Printing Company, 1939.

Markworth, David, interview by author, April 11, 2011, in Cedar Mills, MN.

Meeker County Historical Society. *Meeker County Memories*. Dallas: Taylor Publishing Company, 1987.

COBDEN

Blick, Jenny, "Stern New Owner of Iron Horse Saloon in Cobden," *Sleepy Eye Herald Dispatch*, July 6, 2000.

Caspers, Jean, "Cobden still has 'determination,'" *Sleepy Eye Herald Dispatch*, November 5, 1981.

Heiling, Jim (Mayor), phone interviews by author, September 7, 2010; April 18, 2011.

Ibberson, Anne, interview by author, October 11, 2010, Cobden, MN.

BrainyQuote.com, "Richard Cobden," http://www.brainyquote.com/quotes/authors/r/richard_cobden_2.html (accessed July 26, 2011)

Phelps, Nathan, "It's a small, small world for Cobden," *New Ulm Journal*, July 11, 1996 (accessed at Brown County Historical Society, New Ulm, MN).

COMSTOCK

Butenhoff, Peggy, phone interview with author, June 16, 2011.

Guest, Pamela, phone interview with author, June 15, 2011.

History Committee. *Comstock Centennial: 1890–1990*. Gwinner: J & M Printing, 1990.

CORRELL

Correll Centennial Committee. *The Correll Chronicle 1881–1981*. Milan: Standard-Watson Journal, 1981.

Jorgenson, H.G. *A History of the Artichoke Baptist Church: In Commemoration of its Sixtieth Anniversary 1877-1937*. Ortonville: Ortonville Independent, 1937.

Koepp, Diane (Mayor), phone interview by author, October 25, 2010.

Shelsta, Norm, "Musings from the Museum," *The Northern Star*, July 17, 2008.

Wulff, Lydia Sorensen. *History of Big Stone County*. Ortonville: L. A. Kaercher, 1959.

DANVERS

Connolly, John, email to the author, January 15, 2011.

"District 84 at Danvers Observes Centennial," *Swift County Monitor*, May 13, 1949 (accessed at Stearns County Historical Society, Benson, MN).

Gallagher, Marlys, letter to the author, January 11, 2011.

Lathrop, Alan K., Bob Firth. *Churches of Minnesota*. Minneapolis: University of Minnesota Press, 2003.

O'Malley, Chuck, interview by author, April 11, 2011, Danvers, MN.

Swift County Historical Society. *Swift County, Minnesota*. Chicago: Arcadia Publishing, 2000.

DELHI

Rasmussen, Linda. *Delhi, MN. 1884–1984*. Delhi, MN: 1984.

Webb, Wayne E. and Jasper Swedberg. *Redwood: The Story of a County*. Redwood Falls. Redwood County Board of Commissioners: 1964.

Werner, Brenda, interview by author, October 12, 2010, in Delhi, MN.

DENHAM

Anderson, Karen (City Clerk), telephone Interviews with author, September 5, 2010, and February 26, 2011.

Cordes, Jim. *Pine County…and its memories*. North Branch: Review Corporation, 1989.

Jacobson, Gordy, email to author, May 14, 2011.

Johnson, O. Bernard. *The Homesteaders*. Staples: Nordell Graphic Communications, 1973.

Ketchmark, Bob, phone interview with author, April 5, 2011.

Long, Tony, "May 19, 1910: Halley's Comet Brushes Earth With Its Tail," http://www.wired.com/thisdayintech/2009/05/dayintech_05191.

DONALDSON

Bothum, Lori, "Nordic Korner, a piece of Donaldson history, is gone," *North Star News*, January 5, 2006.

Donaldson Record. June 10, 1907.

Estlund, Charles J. *Kittson County Minnesota: The Banner County of the Red River Valley*. Hallock: County Commissioners of Kittson County, 1911.

"Fiftieth Anniversary Kittson County Enterprise 1881–1931," *Kittson County Enterprise*, September 11, 1935 (accessed at Kittson County Historical Society, Lake Bronson, MN).

Kittson County Historical Society. *Our Northwest Corner: Histories of Kittson County, Minnesota*. Dallas: Taylor Publishing, 1976.

DORAN

"Battle of Stiklestad," *Wikipedia, The Free Encyclopedia*, http://en.wikipedia.org/w/index.php?title=Battle_of_Stiklestad&oldid=437603962 (accessed July 26, 2011).

Martin, Annetta (City Clerk), phone interview, April 20, 2011.

Wilkin County Historical Society. *Wilkin County History*. Dallas, TX: Taylor Publishing Co., 1977.

DOVRAY

"Hotdish: Serving Community Spirit," http://hotdish.areavoices.com/2007/10/01/serving-community-spirit/

Iverson, Helen, telephone interview with author, November 5, 2010.

Luehmann, Maxine. *The Sun and the Moon; A History of Murray County, Minnesota*. Murray County Board of Commissioners, 1982.

Murray County Historical Society. *A History of Murray County*. Marceline, MO: Walsworth Publishing Co, 1982.

DUNDEE

Fulda Quasquicentennial Book Committee. *Fulda, Minnesota Celebrating 125 Years*. Fulda: Fulda Free Press, 2006.

Kruger, Brenda, interview by author, October 13, 2010 in Dundee, MN.

Norton, Betty, phone interview by author, October 31, 2010.

Shipper, Mary Ellen. *Dundee, Minnesota 1898–1998*. Dundee: 1998.

EFFIE

Bicentennial Committee. *Homestead Days: A Bicentennial Souvenir Booklet of Effie Minnesota*. Effie, MN: 1976.

Knight, James. *We Homesteaded*. New Brighton: Printcraft, 1975.

Powell, Kathy, interview by author, March 1, 2011, in Effie, MN.

EVAN

Alt, Dan, phone interview by author on October 22, 2010.

Hansen, Darlene Olson, phone interview by author, April 19, 2011.

Lamecker, Jerry, "Faces: Alice Radel," *The New Ulm Journal*, August 5, 1977.

Scherer, Brenda, "Evan recalls midnight tornado of 1947," *Sleepy Eye Herald Dispatch*, June 22, 1987.

Sleepy Eye Herald Dispatch, August 17, 1987.

Toda, Ann Marie, "Evan eyesore slated to be demolished," *The New Ulm Journal* April 29, 1987.

Winch, Wanda, "Evan plans to celebrate 100th year with gala party," *The New Ulm Journal*, July 29, 1987.

FARWELL

Armstrong, Hart. *A Hundred Years of Greatness: Pope County, Minnesota Centennial Memorial Book, 1866–1966*. Pope County Historical Society; Pope County, 1966.

Colvin, Jo, "Leaving it all behind," *Midwest Boomers*, October 2010.

Danielson, Brenda, phone interview by author, October 29, 2009.

Thronson, Tom, "OGMAR American Legion Post #268," Pope County Historical Society, Glenwood, MN, September 26, 1972.

Turnquist, Gladys. *History of Farwell*. Farwell: Farwell, 1986.

FEDERAL DAM

Cass County Historical Society. *Cass County Heritage*. Dallas: Taylor Publishing Company, 1999.

Cass County Historical Society. *Images of America: Cass County*. Chicago: Arcadia Publishing, 2008.

Craven, Dan, "Muskie Rampage," *Minnesota Conservation Volunteer*, July/August (2004), http://www.dnr.state.mn.us/volunteer/julaug04/muskierampage.html (accessed April 6, 2011).

Gravett, Galen "Abe," interview with author on March 2, 2011, Federal Dam, MN.

McKeig, Cecelia. *Federal Dam: The Settlement of Gould Township & the Village of Federal Dam*. Federal Dam: C. McKeig, 1996.

FLORENCE

Anderson, Torgny. *The Centennial History of Lyon County*. Marshall: Henle Publishing, 1970.

Conyers, Ellayne, "Ghost Towns in Southwestern Minnesota," *Marshall Independent*, September 28, 2009.

Rose, Arthur P. *An Illustrated History of Lyon County Minnesota*. Marshall: Northern History Publishing Company, 1912.

Schroeder, Roger, "East-West Twin Lakes Area," http://singingwings.rohair.com/ (accessed May 14, 2011).

Erb, Linda, "Southwest Minnesota Birdwatching," http://www.swmnbirding.com.

Van Nevel, David F., interview with author on October 14, 2010, Florence, MN.

FORT RIPLEY

Baker, Robert Orr. *The Muster Roll: A Biography of Fort Ripley, Minnesota*. St. Paul: H.M. Smyth Co., 1970.

Boulay, Peter. "History of Weather Observations: Fort Ripley, Minnesota 1849–1990," Minnesota State Climatology Office, St. Paul, MN, January 2006.

Erickson, Sandra Alcott. *Fort Ripley: 1930–1960*. Chicago: Arcadia Publishing, 2007.

Treuer, Anton. *The Assassination of Hole in the Day*. St. Paul: Minnesota Historical Society Press, 2011.

Zapffe, Carl. *It Happened Here; a budget of historical narratives, pertaining to central Minnesota, but especially Crow Wing County*. Brainerd: Brainerd Journal Press, 1948.

FUNKLEY

Erickson, Emil, personal interview, February 16, 2011.

Potter, Dean S. "Funkley, Minnesota: Its New York Adventure and Honor." *Mesabi Northwest Airlink*, November/December, 1988, 24–25.

The Portage County Gazette, http://www.pcgazette.com/commentary/2003/dec03/hiney12-5.htm (accessed September 23, 2010).

"Tiny Funkley Takes a Trip," *Life Magazine*, May 25, 1953, 57–60.

Vargo, Andrea, "Waverly Lions try to help save Funkley," *Howard Lake Herald*, September 1, 1997.

GENOLA

Fisher, Harold L. *The Land Called Morrison (Bicentennial Edition)*. St. Cloud: Volkmuth Publishing Company, 1972.

Fuller, Clara K. *History of Morrison and Todd Counties. (Vol. 1.)* Indianapolis: B. F. Bowen & Co., 1915.

Mans, Jim, "Genola: Population 71," *Lake Country Journal*, July/August 2003, 24.

Preimesberger, Dolores, phone interview with author, November 30, 2010.

Vardas, Lorae, "Cities of Genola and Hillman developed around Soo Line Railroad," *Morrison County Record Visitors Guide*, May 18, 2003.

GOODRIDGE

Hanson, Dale, phone interview with author, June 20, 2011.

Hanson, Norma, interview with author, June 14, 2011, Goodridge, Minnesota.

Hanson, Norma. *The Town They Painted White: 75 Years 1915–1990*. Thief River Falls: Goodridge Historical Society, 1990.

Lovly, John, phone interview with author, June 16, 2011.

Pennington County Historical Society. *Pioneer Tales: A History of Pennington County*. Dallas: Taylor Publishing Company, 1976.

GULLY

Gully Centennial Committee. *One Good Cookbook, by Gully! Gully, Minnesota Centennial 1910–2010*. Audubon: Jumbo Jack's Cookbooks, 2008.

Kolling, Cindy, email to author, May 10, 2011.

Lee, Nancy, phone interview with author, March 27, 2011.

"Pine to Prairie Birding Trail," http://www.mnbirdtrail.com (accessed March 27, 2011).

HADLEY
Busman, Caryl, and Diane Clercx, eds. *Murray County, Minnesota, 1857 to 2007; A Scrapbook of Memories*. Virginia Beach: Donning Co. Publishers, 2006.

Forrest, Robert B., "A History of Western Murray County," http://www.rootsweb.com/-usgenweb/mn/murray/history/home.htm

"Hadley, Minnesota," http://resources.rootsweb.ancestry.com/USA/MN/Murray/

Shaver, Wally, "Buttermakers Baseball: Best Buy in Sports," http://www.letsplaysoftball.com/263shaver.htm (accessed October 16, 2010)

Pavlis, Dale, interview with author, October 15, 2010, Hadley, MN.

HALMA
Eidsvold Lutheran Church. *100th Anniversary Eidsvold Lutheran Church*. Halma: 1986.

Kittson County Historical Society. *Halma: The First 100 Years 1904–2004*. Lake Bronson: Kittson County Historical Society, 1979.

Kittson County Historical Society. *Our Northwest Corner: Histories of Kittson County, Minnesota*. Dallas: Taylor Publishing Co., 1976.

McCarter, W. C. "Our Schools." *The Rotarian*, 2 (August 1912), 29.

HATFIELD
Magnuson, Chad, interview by author on October 12, 2010, Hatfield, MN.

Pipestone County Historical Society. *Pipestone County History*. Dallas: Taylor Publishing Company, 1984.

Smith, Deanna, phone interview by author, May 4, 2011.

Vanderplaats, Janet, phone interview by author, February 6, 2011.

Vosburgh, Michael R, "Windy Hatfield was named for unusual reason," *Daily Globe*.

Wachendorf, Myron. *Chuck Cecil. Myron Lee and the Caddies; Rockin' 'n Rollin' Out of the Midwest*. Brookings, SD; Enterprise Books, 2004.

Wiener, Walter. "The History of Hatfield, Minnesota," typescript, May 1983, Hatfield, MN.

"Hollyhock Ballroom 1960s slide show," *YouTube*, www.youtube.com/watch?v=QucrMZVNqGk- accessed 17 June 2010.

"Hollyhock Ballroom, Hatfield, Minnesota," *The Sensational Showmen Blog*, http://the-sensationalshowmen.blogspot.com/2009/11/hollyhock-ballroom-hatfield-minnesota.html (accessed June 17, 2010).

HAZEL RUN
Anderson, Brent, interview with author, October 14, 2010, Hazel Run, MN.

Erp, David, interview with author, October 14, 2010, Hazel Run, MN.

Martin, Doris, phone interview with author, April 25, 2011.

Narvestad, Carl, "Fiddling Gift Skips One Generation," *Sound Post* (Summer 1996), 5.

Narvestad, Carl and Amy. *A History of Yellow Medicine County, Minnesota 1872–1972*. St. Paul: Yellow Medicine County Historical Society, 1972.

Hardanger Fiddle Association, http://www.hfaa.org/ (accessed 03/11/2009).

Long, Violet, "Hazel Run is 100," Hazel Run: Centennial Booklet Committee, 1984.

Roske Odden, Karen, email correspondence, March 10, 2009, March 13, 2009.

HEIDELBERG
Heidelberg Athletic Association. *An Era of Progress: 1878–1976, Heidelberg, Minnesota*. Heidelberg: The Association, 1976.

Hinderscheit, Melvin and Theresa, phone interview with author, June 21, 2011.

Odenthal, Millie, phone interview by author, June 8, 2011.

HENRIETTE
Koenig, Janice, interview by author, June 1, 2011.

McNeil, Sue, interview by author, June 1, 2011.

Sigurdson, Alberta. *Henriette…and the way it was*. Henriette: Henriette, 1991.

Thorson, Melvin "Rasty," interview by author, June 1, 2011.

HILLMAN
Bauer, S. N, "Parish the thought," *St. Cloud Visitor*, May 18, 1995, 19.

Fisher, Harold L. *The Land Called Morrison*. St. Cloud: Volkmuth Printing Co., 1972.

Mans, Jim., "Our Town Hillman," *Lake Country Journal*, November/December 2002, 22–23.

Rinkel, Ronald, letter to the author, January 24, 2011.

Rinkel, Ronald, phone interview with author, December 4, 2010.

Immanuel Evangelical Congregation of Hillman. "60th Anniversary of Immanuel Evangelical Congregation of Hillman 1921–81," September 13, 1981.

Virnig, Doris, "Geological Survey underway in Lastrup-Hillman area," *Morrison County Record*, August 17, 1981, 5.

HOLT
Filer, Andrew, email correspondence, February, 26, 2008; March, 14 2008.

Haulsee, W.M. *Soldiers of the Great War, Vol 2*. Washington, D.C: Soldiers Record Publishing Association, 1920.

Peterson, Emilie Carlson, interview with author in April 5, 2011, Bemidji, MN.

Sannes, DelRay. *Holt Township Centennial: 1889–1989*, Thief River Falls: Thief River Falls Times, 1989.

Solum, Nancy. *Self Portrait of Marshall County*. Dallas: Taylor Publishing Company, 1976.

Swan, Mary Ann, interview with author on April 26, 2011, Holt, MN.

HUMBOLDT
Federal Writers Project, Works Progress Administration. *WPA Guide to Minnesota*. St. Paul: Minnesota Historical Society, 1985.

Lewis, Trish Short, "St. Vincent Memories" (web log), http://56755.blogspot.com/ (accessed November 14, 2010).

Kittson County Historical Society. *Our Northwest Corner: histories of Kittson County, Minnesota*. Dallas: Taylor Publishing Company, 1976.

Stewart, Wayne G. *Humboldt Centennial 1907–2007*. Grafton: Morgan Printing, 2007.

Strom, Claire, "James J. Hill Empire Builder as Farmer," *Minnesota History*, Summer 1995, 243–246.

Farley, Cal, *The Handbook of Texas Online*, http://www.tshaonline.org/handbook/online/articles/FF/ffa8.html (accessed August 9, 2010).

IHLEN

Centennial Committee. *Ihlen Memories, 1888–1988*. Ihlen, 1988.

Pipestone Historical Society. *A History of Pipestone County*. Dallas: Taylor Publishing Company, 1984.

Rodman, Joyce, phone interview by author, May 19, 2011.

Swenson, Steven, "Glass House turns 50," *Pipestone Star*, March 4, 2009.

U.S. Department of the Interior, National Park Service. The National Register of Historic Places, "Split Rock Bridge," http://www.nps.gov/history/NR/travel/pipestone/srb.htm (accessed 5/21/2010).

Vatne, Jim, phone interview with author, May 5, 2011.

IRON JUNCTION

Halunen, Rod, "Ghost Towns and Locations of the Mesabi Iron Range." M. A. Thesis. University of Minnesota, 1992.

Klabechek, Frank, interview with author on March 7, 2011, Iron Junction, MN.

Mattson, Thomas and Peggy, interview with author, March 7, 2011, Iron Junction, MN.

JOHNSON

"Andy Bear's Truck is 'Staff Favorite Choice,'" *The Northern Star*, August 20, 2009.

Johnsrud, Donald and Elaine, phone interview by author, March 22, 2011.

Johnsrud, Donald, correspondence with the author, May 7, 2011.

Shelsta, Norman, "Musings from the Museum," *The Northern Star*, 2008.

Wulff, Lydia Sorensen. *History of Big Stone County*. Ortonville: L.A. Kaercher, 1958.

KENNETH

Groen, Dave, interview with author, October 13, 2010, Kenneth, MN.

Halvorson, Nora, interview with author, October 13, 2010, Kenneth, MN.

Rose, Arthur P. *An Illustrated History of Rock and Pipestone County, Minnesota*. Luverne: Northern History Publishing, 1911.

Tweet, Sue (Clerk/Treasurer), phone interview, August 5, 2010.

Vander Ziel, Kristy, interview with author, October 13, 2010.

KERRICK

Carlson, Christine, phone interview, February 5, 2011.

Carlson, Christine. *Queen Norway and a Visual Smorgasboard*. Askov: American Printing, 1995.

Cordes, Jim. P*ine County…and its memories*. North Branch: Review Corporation, 1989.

Keyport, Shirley, phone interview by author, September 3, 2010.

Stadin, Deb, interview by author, March 8, 2011, Kerrick, MN.

KINBRAE

Bos, Sheila Gehl, phone interview, April 5, 2011.

"Five TBM Avenger Bombers Lost in the Bermuda Triangle," *Historynet.com*, http://www.historynet.com/five-tbm-avenger-bombers-lost-in-the-bermuda-triangle.htm (accessed May 3, 2010).

Fulda Quasquicentennial Book Committee. *Fulda, Minnesota Celebrating 125 Years*. Fulda: Fulda Free Press, 2006.

Goff, Al. *Nobles County History*. Worthington: Nobles County Historical Society, 1958.

"Kinbrae, Minnesota," *Wikipedia, The Free Encyclopedia*, http://en.wikipedia.org/w/index.php?title=Kinbrae,_Minnesota&oldid=437617246 (accessed May 6, 2011).

Rose Arthur P. *An Illustrated History of Nobles County*. Worthington: Northern History Publishing Company, 1908.

LAKE HENRY

Jacobson, Michael, "A passion for the game," *Paynesville Press*, August 23, 2000.

Phillips, Mary, "Baseball, community spirit keep Lake Henry folks busy," *St. Cloud Times*, August 13, 1989.

Stalboerger, Tony, interview with author on April 7, 2011, in Lake Henry, MN.

Stelling, Linda, "Lake Henry Legion celebrates 50th anniversary," *Paynesville Press*, July 30, 1997.

LA SALLE

Branstad, Gwen Sletta, interview with author, October 12, 2010.

Gross, John. *La Salle: Whistle-stop on the Prairie, 1889–1999*. Medford: J.F. Gross, 1999.

Pearson, Archie, interview with author, October 12, 2010.

"Who's Who—Alvin York," *Firstworldwar.com*, http://www.firstworldwar.com/bio/york.htm (accessed June 14, 2010).

LASTRUP

Gross, Steve, interview by author, November 28, 2010.

Mans, Jim, "Our Towns: Lastrup," *Lake Country Journal*, July/August 2004, 28.

Vardas, Lorae, "Ortman farm in Lastrup designated Century Farm," *Farm Record*, August 24, 1981.

LENGBY

Froshe, Erin Hemme, "Altar Art," *The Lutheran*, March 2001, 30.

Hilliard, Beatrice, interview by author on October 9, 2007, Lengby, MN.

Kildal, Elaine, interview by author on October 9, 2007, Lengby, MN.

McIntosh Historical Committee. *Saga of the Thirteen Towns; 75th Anniversary of the Original Thirteen Towns, 1883–1958*. McIntosh: McIntosh Historical Society, 1958.

Saterstrom, A. J., "Early History of the Village of Lengby" (pamphlet), 1976.

Stafford, Amy (City Clerk), interview by author in October 9, 2007, Lengby, MN.

LEONARD

Boorman, George and Winifred. *The History of the City of Leonard & Dudley Township*. Gonvick, MN: Richards Publishing Company, 1982.

Clearwater County Historical Society. *History of Clearwater County: Headwaters of Mississippi River*. Gonvick: Richards Publishing Company, 1984.

Gerlot, Diana, interview by author on September 25, 2007, Leonard, MN.

Lundmark, Bev, phone interview by author on September 26, 2007.

Reichert, Kelli, interview by author on September 25, 2007, Leonard, MN.

LEONIDAS
Halunen, Rod, "Ghost Towns and Locations of the Mesabi Iron Range." M.A thesis, University of Minnesota, 1992.

Hermanek, Amy Lynne. *Leonidas Merritt Days Excursion: August 8, 1992: Commemorating the 100th Anniversary of the first shipment of iron ore from Mt. Iron*. Duluth, MN: St. Louis Historical Society, 1992.

Lamppa, Marvin G., *Minnesota's Iron Country: Rich Ore, Rich Lives*. Duluth: Lake Superior Port Cities, 2004.

LOUISBURG
Dove, Paul, interview by author, January 26, 2010, Park Rapids, MN.

Gardner, Denis P. *Minnesota Treasures*. St. Paul: Minnesota Historical Society, 2004.

Letrud, Joyce, phone interview by author, May 9, 2011.

Johnson, Terry G, phone interview by author, May 9, 2011.

Willard, Jon. *Louisburg, Minnesota: An Illustrated History*. Louisburg Centennial Committee: Louisburg, 1987.

MANCHESTER
Freeborn County Heritage Book Committee. *Freeborn County Heritage*. Dallas: Taylor Publishing company, 1987.

Hannegrefs, Angie, phone interview with author, April 22, 2011.

Jensen, Paul, interview by author on October 15, 2010, Manchester, MN.

Nelson, Michael, Genealogy Trails, "Manchester Platted in '82," http://genealogy-trails.com/minn/freeborn/history_manchester.html

Solberg, Wilda, phone interview by author, May 20, 2011.

Ylvisaker, Marguerite, phone interview by author, May 20, 2011.

MANHATTAN BEACH
"2009 Manhattan Beach Comprehensive Plan Review," The City of Manhattan Beach, http://manhattanbeachmn.org/pdfs/2009%20Manhattan%20Beach%20 Comprehensive%20Plan%20Review.pdf

"About Us," Manhattan Beach Lodge, http://www.mblodge.com/aboutus.html (accessed December 30, 2010).

Brunkhorst, Kista, interview with author, January 6, 2011, Manhattan Beach, MN.

Crosslake Area Historical Society. A *Taste of History; Tales and Tastes of the Crosslake Area Past*. Crosslake: Crosslake Area Historical Society, 2004.

MCGRATH
Bailey, Carol. *McGrath, MN; 1908–2008 Centennial*. McGregor Printing: McGregor: 2008.

Clark, Dawn (City Clerk), email correspondence from June 1, 2010, June 3, 2010, and June 7, 2010.

Walters, Charles K. *The History of McGrath, Minnesota*. Minnesota: 1977.

MCKINLEY
Bergan, Kathleen. *Iron Range Beauty*. Gilbert: Iron Range Historical Society, 2009.

"Explore Minnesota: Iron Ore," Minnesota Minerals Coordinating Committee, http://www.irrrb.org/_site_components/files/2011IronOre8x11.pdf.

Glavan, Gregory, email correspondence with author, March 20, 2011.

Lamppa, Marvin G. *Minnesota's Iron Country: Rich Ore, Rich Lives*. Duluth: Lake Superior Port Cities, 2004.

Eleff, Robert M. "The 1916 Minnesota Miners' Strike Against U.S. Steel." *Minnesota History*, Summer 1988, 63–74.

MINNEISKA
Heaser, Margaret, and Father Casper Koegel. *Historical Writings on the History of Saint Mary Catholic Church and of the Village of Minneiska*. Winona: Diocese of Winona, 1989.

Langseth, M. H., interview by author on October 11, 2010, Minneiska, MN.

"The City of Minneiska," The City of Minneiska Home Page, http://minneiska-mn.com/ (accessed May 4, 2011).

"U.S. Route 61," *Wikipedia, the Free Encyclopedia*, http://en.wikipedia.org/wiki/U.S._Route_61 (accessed April 20, 2011).

MIZPAH
Siats, Roxann. *Northome, Mizpah, Gemmell, Minnesota History 1903–1907*. Northome: Northome Bicentennial Book Committee, 1977.

Soper, E. K., "The Peat Deposits of Minnesota," Bulletin No. 16., the University of Minnesota: 1919, 173–175.

MYRTLE
Curtiss-Wedge, Franklyn. *History of Freeborn County*. Chicago: H. C. Cooper, Jr. & Co., 1911.

Freeborn County Heritage Book Committee. *Freeborn County Heritage*. Dallas: Taylor Publishing Company, 1987.

"The Bohemian National Cemetery," Freeborn County Historical Museum, http://www.smig.net/fchm/bohemian.htm

Quad County Rotary Press. *Minnesota-Iowa Tornadoes of Sunday, April 30, 1967*. Waseca: Quad County Rotary Press, 1967.

NASHUA
Rittenour, Sharon, email correspondence with author, February 18, 2011.

Wilkin County Historical Society. *Wilkin County History*. Dallas, TX: Taylor Publishing Co., 1977.

NASSAU
Putzier, Verene, "Nassau Centennial Celebration July 16, 17 & 18, 1993," *The Ortonville Independent*, 1993.

Schuelke, Trish, interview by author on October 16, 2010, Nassau, MN.

NIELSVILLE

Centennial Committee. *Bicentennial History of Polk County, Minnesota*. Dallas: Taylor Publishing Company, 1976.

Holcombe, Maj. R. I., and William H. Bingham, Editors. *Compendium of History and Biography of Polk County*, Minnesota: W. H. Bingham & Co.,1916, 21–26. http://www.archive.org/stream/compendiumofhist00hol#page/20/mode/2up.

Larson, Bruce, telephone conversation on May 7, 2011.

Minnesota Department of Tourism. *Historic Highway 75*. St. Cloud: North Star Visitor Guides, 2009.

Nettum, Nancy, interview by photographer on May 6, 2011, Nielsville, MN.

Nielsville Centennial Committee. *Nielsville: Memories of Home*. Crookston: Ye Old Print Shop, 1997.

Warren, William W., *History of the Ojibway People*. Minnesota Historical Society Press (Borealis) 1984; 363–364.

NIMROD

Crandall, John M. *Silhouettes of Time: A History of Wadena County Focusing on Shell City and Nimrod*. John Crandall: 1984.

Graba, Jack, phone interview with author, March 29, 2011.

Lerude, Sue. Interview by author, 11 May 2011.

Loween, Lorraine, interview by author on April 20, 2010, Nimrod, Minnesota.

Mevissen, Jerry. *Nimrod Chronicles*. North Star Press: St. Cloud, 2003.

Zosel, Robert. "Nimrod, Minnesota Also Known as William's Landing." *Review Messenger*, May 14, 2008.

NORCROSS

Grant County Historical Society. *The Heritage of Grant County, Minnesota*. Dallas: Taylor Publishing Company, 1991.

Olson, Silas, "A Brief Description of Norcross, Minnesota," *Herman Review*, July 19, 1973.

Richards, Olivia, "Norcross Town Hall Remembered," *Herman Review*, September 25, 1997.

Richards, Olivia, "Norcross Women's Community Club," *Herman Review*, December 6, 2001.

Ripperger, Nick, "Norcross School 1938 WPA Project," *Herman Review*, August 14, 1997.

Satter, Deanna, phone interview by author on May 4, 2011.

ODESSA

Andersen, Tony. *Small Town Minnesota A–Z*. Afton: Afton Historical Society Press, 2000.

Gerber, LeVon and Virgil, phone interview by author, May 5, 2011.

Janssen, Arlo T. *Parsonage in a Pear Tree*. Xlibiris, 2009.

Koehntopp, Duane, phone interview by author, May 5, 2011.

Shelsta, Norm, "Musings from the Museum," *The Northern Star*, 2008.

Wulff, Lydia Sorensen. *History of Big Stone County*. Ortonville: L.A. Kaercher, 1959.

PERLEY

Kuball, Grace, and Maxine Workman. *Minnesota Cemeteries: Volume 4, Norman County*. Fargo: Red River Valley Genealogical Society, 1984.

Manley, Anne, phone interview by author, May 31, 2011.

Perley, Minnesota: 1883–2008. Hendrum: Heritage Publications, 2008.

Wentsel, C. E. *Norman County, Minnesota in the World War*. Ada: Pfund & Wentsel, 1922.

REGAL

Jacobson, Michael, "Cornstalk set for Regal on July 18–19," *Paynesville Press*, July 2, 2003.

Jacobson, Michael, "Lost at Sea," *Paynesville Press*, May 25, 2005.

Kandiyohi County Historical Society. The Centennial History of Kandiyohi County 1870-–1970. Wilmar: Color Press, 1970.

Wuertz Denise, interview by author on April 7, 2011, Regal, MN.

REVERE

Maker, Hazel Prokasky. *Revere Memories 1885–2001*. Revere: 2001.

Parker, Warren and Ollie, phone interview by author, March 17, 2011.

Richards, Charles W., *The Second Was First*. Bend: Maverick Publications, Inc., 1999.

RICHVILLE

Ebner, Gilbert, phone interview by author, June 15, 2011.

Halena, Susan, "Celebration planned for Richville's 75th anniversary," *Fergus Falls Daily Journal*, August 15, 1979 (accessed in Otter Tail Historical Society "Richville" file, Fergus Falls, Minnesota).

Hoover, Trean Whitney. "Richville Community History," typescript, Richville: 1933.

"Richville Celebrating its 100th," *Perham Enterprise Bulletin*, August 22, 2004 (accessed in Otter Tail Historical Society "Richville" file, Fergus Falls, Minnesota).

Widness, Sheila, phone interview with author, June 20, 2011.

SARGEANT

History Committee. *Mill on the Willow: A History of Mower County, Minnesota*. Lake Mills: Graphic Publishing Co., 1984.

History Committee. *Centennial-Bicentennial Year, July 24–25, 1976*. Sargeant, MN: 1976.

Sparks, Wendy, phone interview with author on April 22, 2011.

SEAFORTH

Curtiss-Wedge, Franklin. *The History of Redwood County Minnesota*. Chicago: H. C. Cooper & Co., 1916.

Eighmey, Rae Katherine, and Debbie Miller. *Potluck Paradise: Favorite Fare from Church and Community Cookbooks*. St. Paul: Minnesota Historical Society, 2008.

History Committee. "*Where Friends Meet: Seaforth, Minnesota 1901–2001.*" (pamphlet), Seaforth: 2001.

Sheeran, Pam, email correspondence with author, June 25, 2009.

Schneider, John Webb and Wayne E. *Redwood; the Story of a County, 1963–1987*. Redwood Falls: Prescott's Printing Service, 1988.

SEDAN

Holz, Eunice Hawn, phone interview with author, April 13, 2011.

Holz, Eunice Hawn. *The History of Sedan, Minnesota: The First One Hundred Years, 1887–1987.* Sedan: 1987.

"Memorial Day Remembrance: Honoring Pope County's War Dead," *Pope County Tribune*, May 31, 2010.

SOLWAY

Greg Booth, "Shake-up in Solway," *Ag Innovation News*, October 2001.

Vandersluis, Charles, Dr. *A Brief History of Beltrami.* Bemidji: Bemidji Historical Society, 1963.

Johnson, Jo. *Lest We Forget Lammers and Solway.* Solway: 1982.

Saltnes, Nels. *Solway 60th Anniversary Homecoming: 1898–1958.* Solway: 1958.

SPRING HILL

Decker, John. "Eine Kleine Gemeinde Auf Der Prarie." Stearns County Historical Society Newsletter, vol.7, no.1, February, 1981.

Freiler, Shawn, email correspondence, October 6, 2010.

Miller, S. Mary Gordian, OSB. *St. Michael's on the Hill.* Waite Park: Park Press, 1993.

Phillips, Mary. "Spring Hill baseball keeps town talkin'," *St. Cloud Times*, August 20, 1989.

"The Spring Hill Chargers," http://www.shchargers.com/ (accessed September 18, 2010).

Schwagel, Dorine and John, interview with author on April 7, 2011, Spring Hill, MN.

SQUAW LAKE

Bryan, Jan, interview by author on March 1, 2011, Squaw Lake, MN.

Deer River Area Centennial Committee. *Deer River Area Centennial History: 100 Years Great in 1998, 1898–1998.* Deer River: Deer River Publishing, 1998.

Greiger, Danielle, interview by author, March 1, 2011, Squaw Lake.

Hart, Judi, interview by author, March 1, 2011, Squaw Lake.

Leino, Bruce, phone interview by author, March 11, 2011.

ST. ANTHONY

Horwich, Jeff, "All you need is a church and a bar," Minnesota Public Radio, 2001, http://minnesota.publicradio.org/features/200112/10_mainstreet_ourtown-m/church (accessed January 19, 2009).

"Rich Farmland Surrounds St. Anthony," *Stearns-Morrison Enterprise*, December 12, 1978.

Wenning, Jeff, interview with author on April 7, 2011, St. Anthony, MN.

ST. LEO

Antony, Carol, phone interview with author on April 27, 2011.

Jelen, Paulette, phone interview with author on May 2, 2011.

Narvestad, Carl and Amy. *History of Yellow Medicine County, Minnesota 1872–1972.* St. Paul: Yellow Medicine Historical Society, 1972.

"St. Leo 1." *The Columbia Encyclopedia, Sixth Edition, 2008,* Encycopedia.com, http://www.encyclopedia.com (accessed April 25, 2011).

ST. ROSA

Bauer, Linda, interview by author on April 7, 2011, St. Rosa, MN.

Butkowski, George H. and A. Yzermans. *The Mill in the Woods.* St. Rosa: Millwood Township Historical Association, 1973.

Keillor, Garrison, "Lake Wobegon Country," *New York Times*, August 26, 2001.

ST. VINCENT

Lewis, Trish. "St. Vincent Memories Web Log," http://56755.blogspot.com/, December 21, 2010.

Kittson County Historical Society. *Our Northwest Corner: Histories of Kittson County, Minnesota.* Dallas: Taylor Publishing Co, 1976.

"Red River Angler's Guide," North Dakota Game and Fish Department, http://gf.nd.gov/fishing/redbro.html (accessed April 19, 2011).

STRANDQUIST

Borch, Frederic L. *Judge Advocates in Vietnam: Army Lawyers in Southeast Asia, 1959–1975.* Honolulu: University Press of the Pacific, 2004.

Janssen, Jennifer Anderson. "Strandquist Centennial Celebration 1904–2004," typescript, Strandquist, Minnesota, 2004.

Musburger, Jim, interview by author on January 30, 2008, Bemidji, MN.

Solum, Nancy. *Self Portrait of Marshall County.* Dallas: Taylor Publishing Company, 1976.

Stromgren, Gula, email correspondence with author, February 21, 2011.

STRATHCONA

Hanson, Harvey, interview by author on April 26, 2011, Strathcona, MN.

Kleiman, Dena, "De Gustibus: In the Wilderness and Truly Paradise." *The New York Times*, September 19, 1990.

Roseau County Historical Society. *Roseau County Heritage.* Dallas: Taylor Publishing, 1992.

Ryden, Shirley, phone interview by author, March 23, 2011.

SUNBURG

Centennial History Committee. *The Centennial History of Kandiyohi County 1870–1970.* Wilmar: Color Press, 1970.

Pohlen, Jerome. *Oddball Minnesota.* Chicago: Chicago Review Press, 2003.

Post, Tim, "Norway in a Café," Minnesota Public Radio, http://news.minnesota.publicradio.org/features/200212/19_postt_oldnorske/ (accessed April 1, 2009).

Reigstad, Hanley. *History of Sunburg.* Plowville (Brochure), 1994.

Rudningen, DeWayne. Interview by author, September 26, 2010, Sunburg, MN.

TAMARACK

Harder, Robert O. *A Minnesota Remembrance: Lost Innocence, Lost Fortunes.* Aitkin: Aitkin County Historical Society, 1999.

Harder, Robert O. *A Minnesota Remembrance: From the Pinery Camps to the Columbus Day Holocaust.* Aitkin: Aitkin Historical Society, 1998.

Haugse, Kathy, interview by author in March 8, 2011, Tamarack, MN.

Keen, Eileen. *Tamarack, The Marcus and A.R.T.S.* Tamarack: Tamarack Printing, 1989.

"Precious metals exploration stung by economic slump," *Minnesota Mining*, http://www.miningminnesota.com/news_view.php?id=115.

TAOPI

Diedrich, Mark. "Christian Taopi, Farmer Chief of the Mdewakanton Dakota." *Minnesota Archeologist* 40, June, 1981, 65–77).

Kiefer, James, phone interview by author, May 7, 2011.

Meier, Marjorie A. *The Tall Grass Prairie Speaks*; Taopi. Adams. Night Owl Press, 1993.

Meier, Marjorie A. *Wind on the Prairie; Taopi, 1930–2000*. Adams: Night Owl Press, 2000.

"Taopi's postmark may be record for tiny community," *Austin Daily Record*, September 28, 2000.

TENNEY

Haagenson, Heidi, "The Tenney Quilt: Tenney's Moment of Fame," February 3, 2008, http://tenneyquilt.blogspot.com/2008/02/tenneys-moment-of-fame.html (accessed February 23, 2010).

Haagenson, Heidi. T*he Tenney Quilt: Celebrating the Women of Minnesota's Tiniest Town*. Minneapolis: Mill City Press, 2007.

Schwab, Kirsten, phone interview by author, May 15, 2011.

"Tenney, Minnesota," *USA Cities Online*, http://www.usacitiesonline.com/mncounty-tenney.htm.

Wilkin County Historical Society. *Wilkin Family History Book: A History of Wilkin County Minnesota*. Dallas: Taylor Publishing Company, 1977.

TINTAH

Centennial Committee. *Celebrate a Century Tintah Minnesota, 1888–1988*. Wheaton: Gazette Publishing, 1988.

"Minnesota Orphan Train Riders of New York," *Orphan Train Riders of Minnesota.com*, http://orphantrainridersofminnesota.com/rider2.html (accessed February 23, 2010).

Petermann, Marcia. Email to author, June 12, 2010.

Pugmire, Tim, "Eugene McCarthy, who galvanized a generation of war opponents, dies," December 10, 2005, http://news.minnesot.publicradio.org/featured/2005/06/15_olsond_genemccarthy/

Putnam, Jeanne, phone interview by author on April 15, 2011.

TRAIL

Flateland, Howard, phone interview by author, January 9, 2008.

Oklee Jubilee Committee. *Memories of the Past and Present Oklee, Minnesota 1910–1985*. Gonvick: Richards Publishing, 1985.

Trail History Book Committee. *Trail History Book: Centennial 2010*. Gonvick: Richards Publishing, 2010.

Weber, Tony and Virginia, interview by author, October 24, 2010, Gully MN.

TURTLE RIVER

Burger, Gary, telephone interview by author, November 11, 2007.

"The Sportsmen's Eden," (Brochure), Turtle River, MN, 1908.

Carlson, Margaret, interview by author, October 20, 2007, Turtle River, MN.

Hagg, Harold T. *The Mississippi Headwaters Region*. Bemidji: Beltrami County Historical Society, 1986.

Krause, Joanne, telephone interview by author, November 17, 2007.

Marchand, Louis. *Bemidji*. Bemidji: Beltrami Historical Society, 1998.

Ryan, J. C. *Tall Timber*. Duluth: St Louis County Historical Society, 1982.

Siems, Ladora, "Salem Lutheran Church: 75th Anniversary Celebration 1921–1996," (typescript) 1996, Turtle River, MN.

URBANK

Ethen, Fr. Jeff. "Crossroads of Faith: 100th Anniversary: Sacred Heart Catholic Church, Urbank, Minnesota 1902–2002," (Pamphlet) Otter Tail County Historical Society, Fergus Falls, Minnesota.

Paprock, John-Brian, Teresa Paprock. *Sacred Sites of Minnesota, Wisconsin*. Trails Books, 2004.

Breining, Greg, "Minnesota's Best Lookouts," *Minnesota Conservation Volunteer*, April 1997.

VIKING

Anderson, Ardelle, interview with author, April 27, 2011, Viking, MN.

Krohn, Joan, and Arne Samuelson. *History of Viking Township*. Warren: Warren Sheaf Print, 1985.

Nelson, Grant. "Rural Reflections," http://grantnelson00.tripod.com/ruralreflections2/id210.html (accessed January 16, 2008).

Peters, Jerome, interview with author, April 27, 2011, Viking, MN.

Solum, Nancy. *Self Portrait of Marshall County*. Dallas: Taylor Publishing Company, 1976.

VINING

Anniversary Booklet Committee. "*One Hundred Twenty-Five Years 1872–1997: Vining Lutheran Church*." Vining: 1997.

Book Committee. *Vining Centennial, 1882–1982*. Vining: 1982.

Mason, John. *History of Otter Tail County Minnesota*. Indianapolis: B.F. Bowen & Co., 1916.

Pohlen, Jerome. *Oddball Minnesota*. Chicago: Chicago Review Press, 2003.

WALTERS

Harada, Masaaki, "Much about Walters jail is a mystery," *Mankato Free Press* (accessed at Faribault County Historical Society, Faribault, Minnesota).

MacArthur, Kyle J, "An $11 million LEC? Turn of the century jail cost $685," *Faribault County Register*, July 23, 2007.

Tuff Publishing. *The Heritage of Faribault County*. Dallas: Curtis Media Corporation, 1987.

Walters Community Care Club. *Then & Now, 1900–1980: Walters, MN*. Walters, MN: 1980.

WANDA

Curtiss-Wedge, Franklin. *The History of Redwood County Minnesota*. Chicago: H.C. Cooper Jr. & Co., 1916.

Jenniges, Rick, email correspondence with author, October 26, 2010.

Olson, Mary, interview by author, October 15, 2010, Wanda MN.

St. Mathias Parish, 1883–1983. Tracy, MN: Tracy Publishing Company, 1983.

Schneider, John T., and Wayne E. Webb. *Redwood; the Story of a County, 1963-1987*. Redwood Falls: Prescott's Printing Services, 1988.

Schumacher, Don and Donna, phone interview by author, October 24, 2010.

WEST UNION

Bentfield, Barbara, phone interview with author, May 5, 2011.

Friedrich, Micki, interview by author on September 26, 2010, West Union, MN.

Hanson, Harry, "Depot once center of town," *Sauk Centre Herald*. April 24, 2007.

Hanson, Harry, "West Union celebrates 150 years," *Sauk Centre Herald*. July 3, 2007.

Hanson, Harry, "West Union Parade turns 20," *Sauk Centre Herald*. July 8, 2008.

"Isaac's Foundation donates $30,000 to childhood cancer research," *Sauk Centre Herald*, December 28, 2010.

Macey, Jan (City Clerk), telephone interview, August 3, 2010.

Marthaler, Sister Andre, and Joan Marthaler Pfannenstein. *Celebrate West Union*. Sauk Centre: Sauk Centre Herald Press, 1993.

Simpkins, Dawn, "Close to 2000 attend trail party," *Sauk Centre Herald*. August 8, 2007.

"Isaac's Foundation," *Isaac's Foundation.org*, www.isaacsfoundation.org

WESTPORT

Centennial Book Committee. *Villard-Westport Centennial: 100 Years of Farming, Fishing & Friendship*. Westport: 1983.

"Minnewaska Go Karting Association," http://www.minnewaskagokarting.com, (accessed October 28, 2009).

WHALAN

Dregni, Eric. *Minnesota Marvels*. Minneapolis: University of Minnesota Press, 2001.

Geist, Bill. *Way off the Road: Discovering the Peculiar Charms of Small Town America*. New York: Broadway Books, 2007.

Johnson, Ernie and Joan, interview by author on October 10, 2010, Whalan, MN.

Whalan Museum. "Welcome to Whalan Walking Tour." (pamphlet), Whalan, MN.

WILDER

Brodin, Robert M. Wilder Friendship Club. *A Story of Wilder, Minnesota*. Wilder: 1985.

El-Hai, Jack. *Telling Our Story at Breck School*. Minneapolis, MN: 2000.

"Franklin Clarence Mars," *Wikipedia, the Free Encyclopedia*, www.wikipedia.org/wiki/Franklin_Clarence_Mars, (accessed 31 July 2010),

"The Freedom Train," Freedomtrain.org, www.freedomtrain.org/html/aft_home.htm (accessed 31 July 2010),

WOLF LAKE

Holmquist, June Drenning. *They Chose Minnesota*. St. Paul: Historical Society, 1981.

Jokela, Harvey, phone interview with author, April 14, 2011.

Paurus, Clarence, phone interview with author, April 14, 2011.

Ristinen, Les. *Wolf Lake Township 1896–1996*. (Self Published), Wolf Lake, MN.

Trotter, William R. *Frozen Hell; The Russo-Finnish Winter War of 1939–1940*. New York: Algonquin Books, 1991.

Wasastjerna, Hans R. *History of the Finns in Minnesota*. New York Mills: Northwestern Publishing Company, 1957.

WRIGHT

Black, Lynne, email correspondence with author, September 29, 2009.

Carroll, Francis M. *Crossroads in Time: A History of Carlton County, Minnesota*. Cloquet: Carlton Historical Society, 1987.

Mahlberg, Roy W. *The Wright Pioneers; A Brief History of Its Settlers*. Superior: Savage Press, 1997.

ZEMPLE

Deer River Area Centennial Committee. *Deer River Area Centennial History: 100 Years Great in 1998, 1898–1998*. Deer River: Deer River Publishing, 1998.

Lugenbeal, Edward N. "Brainerd Ware Occurrence and Chronological Relationships." *Some Studies of Minnesota Prehistoric Ceramics*, A. R. Woolworth and M. A. Hall (eds.), Fort Snelling: Minnesota Archaeological Society, 1978.

Mason, Philip P. *Schoolcraft's Expedition to Lake Itasca*. Michigan State University Press, 1958.

About the Author

JILL A. JOHNSON grew up in Strandquist, population 73, and Karlstad, population 700, in remote northwestern Minnesota. In 2001, she opened Beagle Books, an independent bookstore in Park Rapids, Minnesota, and sold the business in 2007, excluding Kallie, the beagle. Jill has worked as a physical therapist since 1974, and is currently employed at the hospital in Park Rapids. She lives in the woods with her husband, Deane, and their notorious dog.

About the Photographer

DEANE L. JOHNSON has been an active photographer since acquiring his first Canon FTb in 1976. He grew up in Grand Forks, ND, and has spent most of the rest of his life living in and traveling around northern Minnesota. A retired family physician, he is a founding member of the Jackpine Writers' Bloc, plays clarinet and saxophone, and was a co-owner of Beagle Books of Park Rapids with his wife, Jill.